"A hypnotic narrative"
—*The New York Times*

"Better than any movie about the war"
—*Boston Herald*

"Maybe Vietnam is best seen through a shattered helicopter windshield. *Chickenhawk* is one bloody, painfully honest, and courageous book."
—Martin Cruz Smith

"When Mason flies, so does his book."
—Lee Lescaze, *Washington Post Book World*

"Arresting, lean, cool, grotesque, telling"
—*Village Voice*

"More than any other writer, Mason has been able to capture the feeling of what it was like to be there."
—John Del Vecchio, author of *The 13th Valley*

PENGUIN BOOKS

CHICKENHAWK

Robert Mason was born in 1942 and grew up on farms in New Jersey and Florida. His boyhood dream of becoming a pilot was finally realized when he earned his private pilot's license prior to his graduation from high school. After studying at the University of Florida from 1960 to 1962 and then working at a variety of jobs for the next two years, he enlisted in the army in 1964. He flew more than 1,000 helicopter combat missions in Vietnam before being discharged in 1968. Mr. Mason is married and the father of one son.

Chickenhawk

Robert Mason

PENGUIN BOOKS

PENGUIN BOOKS
Published by the Penguin Group
Penguin Group (USA) Inc., 375 Hudson Street, New York, New York 10014, U.S.A.
Penguin Group (Canada), 90 Eglinton Avenue East, Suite 700, Toronto,
Ontario, Canada M4P 2Y3 (a division of Pearson Penguin Canada Inc.)
Penguin Books Ltd, 80 Strand, London WC2R 0RL, England
Penguin Ireland, 25 St Stephen's Green, Dublin 2, Ireland (a division of Penguin Books Ltd)
Penguin Group (Australia), 250 Camberwell Road, Camberwell, Victoria 3124, Australia
(a division of Pearson Australia Group Pty Ltd)
Penguin Books India Pvt Ltd, 11 Community Centre, Panchsheel Park,
New Delhi – 110 017, India
Penguin Group (NZ), 67 Apollo Drive, Rosedale, North Shore 0632, New Zealand
(a division of Pearson New Zealand Ltd)
Penguin Books (South Africa) (Pty) Ltd, 24 Sturdee Avenue, Rosebank, Johannesburg 2196,
South Africa

Penguin Books Ltd, Registered Offices:
80 Strand, London WC2R 0RL, England

First published in the United States of America by Viking Penguin, Inc. 1983
Published in Penguin Books 1984
This edition published 2005

30th Printing

Grateful acknowledgement is made for permission to reprint portions of copyrighted
material that originally appeared in *Newsweek*, copyright © Newsweek, Inc., 1965; *The
New York Times Magazine*, copyright © The New York Times Company, 1966; and *U.S.
News and World Report*, copyright © 1964 and 1966 by U.S. News and World Report.

Unless indicated otherwise, photos are by Robert C. Mason

THE LIBRARY OF CONGRESS HAS CATALOGUED THE HARDCOVER EDITION AS FOLLOWS:
Mason, Robert, 1942–
Chickenhawk.
Reprint. Originally published: New York: Viking, 1983.
ISBN 978-0-14-303571-8
1. Mason, Robert, 1942–.   2. Vietnamese Conflict, 1961–1975—Personal narratives,
American.   3. Vietnamese Conflict, 1961–1975—Aerial operations, American.
4. Helicopter pilots—Biography.   5. United States Army—Warrant officers—
Biography.   I. Title.
DS559.5.M37   1984   959.704'348   84-440

Printed in the United States of America
Map by David Lindroth

For Patience and Jack

Author's Note

This is a personal narrative of what I saw in Vietnam and how it affected me. The events all happened; the chronology and geography are correct to the best of my knowledge. The names of the characters, other than the names that are famous, and unimportant characteristics of all the persons in the book have been changed so that they bear no resemblance to any of the actual people in order to preserve their privacy and anonymity.

I'd like to put in an apology to the grunts, if they resent that term, because I have nothing but respect for them and the conditions under which they served.

I hope that these recollections of my experiences will encourage other veterans to talk. I think it is impossible to know too much about the Vietnam era and its effects on individuals and society.

Instead of dwelling on the political aspects of the war, I have concentrated on the actual condition of being a helicopter pilot in Vietnam in 1965–66. The events, I hope, will speak for themselves.

I want to thank Martin Cruz Smith, Knox Burger, Gerald Howard, Constance Cincotti, Jack and Betty

8   Chickenhawk

Mason, Gerald Towler, Bruce and Susan Doyle, and Jim and Eileen Helms for their generous aid and encouragement.

I am particularly indebted to my wife, Patience, for her unflagging support in difficult times, both in the writing of the book and in the life that it's about.

Contents

Author's Note   7

Map   11

Bell HU-1 Iroquois ("Huey")   12–13

Prologue   17

I Virgins

1 Wings   21

2 An August Cruise   51

3 Setting Up Camp   70

4 Happy Valley   113

5 Ia Drang Valley   164

II Swave and Deboner

6 The Holidays   233

7 The Rifle Range   253

10   Contents

8 Bong Son Valley   280

9 Tension   321

III   Short-Timer's Blues

10 Grounded   351

11 Transfer   371

12 La Guerrilla Bonita   400

13 Tell Me You're Afraid   434

Epilogue:
And Then What Happened?   464

Afterword   477

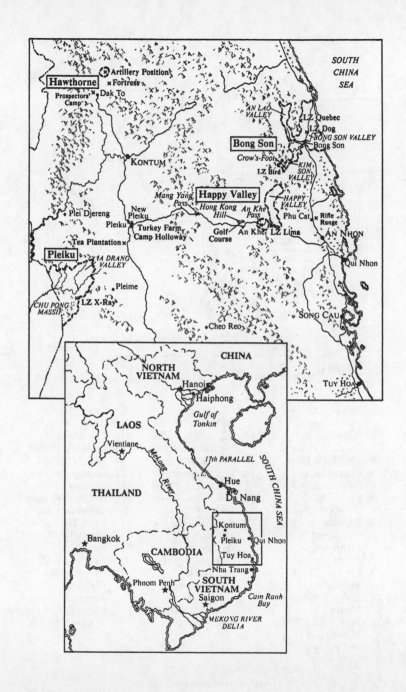

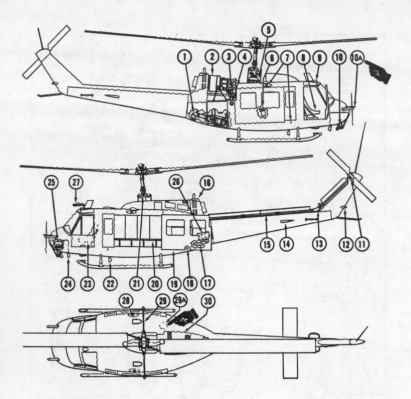

1. Heating Burner and Blower Unit
2. Engine
3. Oil Tank Filler
4. Fuel Tank Filler
5. Transmission
6. Hydraulic Reservoir (Pressure Type)
7. Forward Navigation Lights (4)
8. Pilot's Station
9. Forward Cabin Ventilator (2)
10. Cargo Suspension Mirror
10A. Pitot Tube (Nose Mount)
11. Tail Rotor (90°) Gear Box

12. Aft Navigation Light
13. Tail Rotor Intermediate (45°) Gear Box
14. Synchronized Elevator
15. Tail Rotor Drive Shaft
16. Anti-Collision Light
17. Oil Cooler
18. External Power Receptacle
19. Cargo-Passenger Door
20. Passenger Seats Installed

21. Swashplate Assembly
22. Landing Light
23. Copilot's Station
24. Search Light
25. Battery
26. Alternate Battery Location (Armor Protection Kit)
27. Pitot Tube (Roof Mount)
28. Aft Cabin Ventilators (2)
29. Stabilizer Bar
29A. Hydraulic Reservoir (Gravity-feed type)
30. Engine Cowling

General Arrangement Diagram

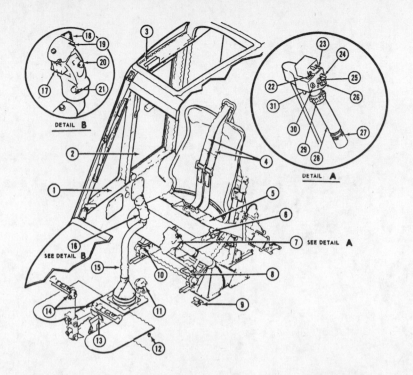

1. Pilot's Entrance Door
2. Sliding Window Panel
3. Hand Hold
4. Shoulder Harness
5. Seat Belt
6. Shoulder Harness Lock-Unlock Control
7. Collective Pitch Control Lever
8. Seat Adjustment Fore and Aft
9. Collective Pitch Down Lock
10. Seat Adjustment Vertical
11. Directional Control Pedal Adjuster
12. Microphone Foot Switch
13. External Cargo Mechanical Release
14. Directional Control Pedals
15. Cyclic Control Friction Adjuster
16. Cyclic Control Stick
17. Microphone Trigger Switch
18. Hoist Switch
19. Force Trim Switch
20. Armament Fire Control Switch
21. External Cargo Electrical Release Switch
22. Search Light ON-OFF Stow Switch
23. Landing Light ON-OFF Switch
24. Landing Light EXTEND-RETRACT Switch
25. Search Light EXTEND-RETRACT LEFT-RIGHT Control Switch
26. Engine Idle Release Switch
27. Collective Pitch Control Friction Adjuster
28. Power Control (Throttle)
29. Power Control Friction Adjuster
30. Governor RPM INCREASE-DECREASE Switch
31. Starter Ignition Trigger Switch

Pilot's station—typical

Chickenhawk

Prologue

I joined the army in 1964 to be a helicopter pilot. I knew at the time that I could theoretically be sent to a war, but I was ignorant enough to trust it would be a national emergency if I did go.

I knew nothing of Vietnam or its history. I did not know that the French had taken Vietnam, after twenty years of trying, in 1887. I did not know that our country had once supported Ho Chi Minh against the Japanese during the Second World War. I did not know that after the war the country that thought it was finally free of colonialism was handed back to the French by occupying British forces with the consent of the Americans. I did not know that Ho Chi Minh then began fighting to drive the French out again, an effort that lasted from 1946 until the fall of the French at Dien Bien Phu, in 1954. I did not know that free elections scheduled by the Geneva Conference for 1956 were blocked because it was known that Ho Chi Minh would win. I did not know that our government backed an oppressive and corrupt leader, Ngo Dinh Diem, and later participated in his overthrow and his death, in 1963.

I did not know any of these facts. But the people who decided to have the war did.

I did know that I wanted to fly. And there was nothing I wanted to fly more than helicopters.

I

Virgins

1.
Wings

The experimental division authorized to try out [the air assault] concept is stirring up the biggest inter-service controversy in years. There are some doubts about how practical such a helicopter-borne force would be in a real war.

—*U.S. News & World Report,* April 20, 1964

June 1964–July 1965
As a child I had dreams of levitation. In these dreams I could float off the ground only when no one watched. The ability would leave me just when someone looked.

I was a farm kid. My father had operated his own and other farms, and a market, in Pennsylvania, New Jersey, and West Virginia. When I was nine he started a large poultry farm west of Delray Beach, Florida. Here, in between chores, I daydreamed about flying to the extent that I actually built tall towers to get off the ground.

By the time I started high school my father had switched from farming to real estate, and we moved to town. In my junior year a friend, a fledgling pilot, taught me the basics of handling a small plane. The airplane was

21

a vast improvement over my dreamy mechanisms. It worked every time. By the time I graduated, I had a private pilot's license.

In 1962, after two years of sketchy attendance at the University of Florida, I dropped out to travel around the country.

A year later, in Philadelphia, two very important things happened to me. I met Patience, my wife-to-be, and I applied to be a pilot candidate in the army.

I thought I had finally achieved my goal of goals when I arrived at the U.S. Army Primary Helicopter School at Fort Wolters, Texas, in June 1964. I drove through the main gate. Helicopters flitted over the nearby mesas; helicopters crisscrossed overhead; helicopters swarmed everywhere. My companion, Ray Ward, craned his head out the window and grinned. He had also joined the army to fly helicopters.

We drove up to a group of concrete buildings that looked like dormitories. A sign out front said WARRANT OFFICER CANDIDATES REPORT HERE. We were impressed. Having gone through basic training at Fort Dix and a month of advanced infantry training at Fort Polk, we thought that all buildings in the army were World War II vintage, wooden and green. I stopped the car.

"Hey, this is nice." Ray smiled. "Ask that guy where we should put our baggage."

The guy he was referring to was walking quietly toward us, a sergeant wearing a white helmet and bright armbands. But we were no longer trainees and had no need to be afraid.

"Say, Sergeant," I asked amiably, "where should we put our luggage?"

"Luggage?" He flinched at the civilian word. Neither Ray nor I had on uniforms.

"Uh, yeah. We have to check in before five, and we need a place to change into our uniforms."

"You're candidates?" he asked calmly, quietly, with the ill-hidden contempt I had witnessed so many times before in basic training.

"Uh-huh." I nodded, bracing myself.

"What the *fuck* are you doing driving around here in civvies? You think you're *tourists*?"

"No—"

"You get that car over there in that lot. Now! You will *carry* your *luggage* back here, double time! Now, git!"

"Yes, Sergeant," I said automatically. As I backed away, the sergeant watched, glaring, fists on hips.

"Turn the car around," said Ray.

"Not enough time." I backed all the way to the parking lot.

"Oh, shit," said Ray. "This is not gonna be a picnic."

Neither of us had suspected that the army taught people how to fly helicopters the same way they taught them to march and shoot. But they did.

The 120 candidates in our class were known as WOCs—for "warrant-officer candidates." A warrant officer is appointed, not commissioned, and specializes in a particular skill. There are electronic-technician warrants, supply warrants, and warrant-officer pilots, among many other specialties. The warrant ranks—WO-1, CW-2, CW-3, and CW-4—correspond to second lieutenant, first lieutenant, captain, and major, and warrant officers receive the same privileges and nearly the same pay as commissioned officers.

When I first heard of the warrant-officer-aviator program, I was a civilian and cared little what the rank meant. All I knew was that they flew.

The flight program was nine months long. It began with one month of preflight training and four months of primary flight training at Fort Wolters, followed by four more months of advanced flight training at Fort Rucker, Alabama. Preflight training was a harassment period designed to weed out candidates who lacked leadership potential. If you made it through that initiation, you got to the flight line and actually began to learn to fly. Then they tried to wash you out for mistakes or slowness in flight training, on top of the regular hassles in the warrant officer program.

Preflighters ran wherever they went, sat on the front edge of their chairs at the mess hall, and had to spit-shine the floors and keep precisely arranged clothing in their closets. We were allowed to leave the base only for two hours on Sunday, to go to church. It was the same kind of bullshit I had gone through in basic training, except worse.

The TAC sergeants assigned us to various slots in a student company: squad leaders, platoon leaders, first sergeant, platoon sergeants, and so on. One of us would be the student company commander. We would hold these positions for a week while the instructors tried to drive us crazy and graded our reactions. Unfortunately I was assigned to be the first student company commander.

Some seasoned army veterans had volunteered to be flight candidates. Others, like Ray and me, were just out of basic. To be fair, God should have put one of the experienced guys in the company-commander slot. But God, personified in the form of TAC Sergeant Wayne Malone, was seldom fair.

My first official act as the student CO was to get the company to the mess hall, four blocks away. Pretty simple stuff. Attention. Left face. Forward, march. Stop. Eat.

But Sergeant Malone, his fellows, and the senior classmen created obstacles. They stood directly in front of me, yelling in my face, while I tried to tell the company to come to attention.

"Well, candidate. Are you going to the mess hall or not?" screamed a senior classman whose nose almost touched mine.

"Yes, sir. If you'd get out of my way, I'll—"

"What?" Shock and disbelief. "Get out of *your* way!" Immediately my antagonist was joined by others.

"Candidate, you can't talk to your superiors like that!" ... "Get this mob to the mess hall before they close the place!"

"Yes, sir!" I could barely hear my own voice. "Company, attention!" I yelled. No one heard me over the screaming TAC sergeants and seniors.

"They can't hear you," yelled a senior, his breath blasting into my face.

I tried again. Still, no one could hear. I raised my arm straight up and back down and heard a student platoon leader yell, "Attention!" Command hand signals?

As soon as my classmates came to attention, some seniors leapt among the ranks, yelling, "Did you hear him call attention, candidate? Then why did you come to attention, candidate? There are no arm signals for attention, candidate!" And so on. Eventually, because the mess hall *would* close, they allowed my commands to get through.

Then it was double time to the mess hall, and chin-ups and push-ups outside. Inside, we sat on the edge of our chairs and ate with our forks rising vertically from the plate and making a right angle to the mouth. Harassment is common to all officer-candidate schools, but what did it have to do with flying? The answer is that everybody in the army is a soldier first, his specialty second. It was going to be a long nine months.

During that first week, I had to get us to classes on

time, see that our rooms were perfect, and God forbid anyone had a dirty belt buckle. I never broke down and cried during the hazing, as some did, but my reaction was still unsatisfactory. I returned the glaring screams of the hazers with glaring screams of my own. Resistance plus obvious inexperience got me a poor grade for my turn at command. Sergeant Malone, who kept a plaque in his office inscribed *Woccus Eliminatus*, would often whisper in my ear while I stood in formation, "You'll never make it, candidate." And when the four weeks of preflight ended, Malone had indeed put me on the list of twenty-eight candidates who would go before the elimination board.

I remember feeling sick in a dim hallway the night before I was to see the board. I had failed before I had even gotten a chance to *sit* in a helicopter. If they washed me out of flight school, I would have to serve my remaining three years of enlistment as an infantryman. The embarrassment was intolerable. Ray Ward and I had come through basic and advanced infantry training to get to flight school, and I had failed in the first month. Ray had encouraged me before the list was posted, telling me that I had really done well, that they weren't going to eliminate me. I remembered Malone's whispered threats. Also, a TAC officer announced that I was definitely not pilot material, based on his analysis of my handwriting. I knew I'd be on that list. I was.

Patience and I had decided that she and our one-month-old son, Jack, would live with my parents in Florida until I had made it past preflight. Then they would come out to Texas and live near the base. I almost called to tell her I had blown it. I couldn't. I decided to wait until after the elimination board.

The next day, the board called in the twenty-eight doomed candidates one by one. By the time my name was called, after lunch, I was numb. I remember walking into the board room tingling with fear and energy. I sat on the edge of a chair in the middle of the room. A major looked at me for a few moments and then at the report in front of him. Seven other members of the board watched me closely. A stenographer's fingers moved at a machine when the major spoke.

"It says here that you failed to show any sort of enthusiasm in the leadership drills. Your instructors say you weren't interested in participating seriously when you were selected to be the student company commander."

And then I talked. I can't remember exactly what I said, but I said it calmly and rationally, opposite from the way I felt. I told them I was just out of basic and inexperienced. I was very serious about getting through this school, but I might not have shown it. I had been flying since I was seventeen. "I want to be a helicopter pilot," I said. "I've studied for that, and I think my grades from ground school prove it. When I'm out there someday flying soldiers around, I expect to be one of the best pilots that ever came out of this school. Won't you give me that chance?" I went on for five minutes.

The stenographer nodded that the words were down. The major made a mark in my folder. "Wait in the company area until you hear from us."

I waited with packed duffel bags, watching my classmates avoid me and the other washouts. When a runner from the office called my name, I jumped out of my skin. I burst through the door at the student company headquarters, came to attention, and screamed, "Candidate Mason reporting as ordered, Sergeant!"

Malone only looked at my feet and screamed, "You missed the white line, candidate! Go out and try again."

I about-faced, went outside, and tried again to hit the painted white line in front of Malone's desk with just the tips of my boots, without looking down. After two more attempts, I succeeded. Malone swaggered menacingly up to me, coming in from the side. My eyes were glued to the wall in front of me. Malone talked into my ear.

"It pains me to tell you, candidate, that the elimination board, in its infinite wisdom, has decided to reinstate your ass."

I turned, grinning at the news.

"Eyes front, candidate!" My head snapped to the front. "Yes, they have decided to reinstate you, over my violent objections, I might add. So get your lucky ass out of here and go join your classmates. Git!"

I turned and ran out the door, laughing all the way back to the barracks. I called Patience and told her to come.

The next morning, I was called back to the office. The board's decision to reinstate me had ruined the student-instructor ratio at the flight line. Malone grinned. "So, Candidate Mason, you will be starting preflight all over again with the next class. Maybe this time I'll see you eliminated."

The second time through preflight was much easier. I had already taken all the classes, so I scored terrific grades on every test. I had learned to play the leadership game with great zeal. I became the almost perfect pre-flight candidate, but Malone said, "You've had plenty of practice, Candidate Mason."

Two months after I had driven through the main gates, I finally got to the flight line. We were issued flight suits, flight helmets, flight gloves, sunglasses, Jeppson course plotters, wind-face computers, and new textbooks. We were told to wear our hats backward on the flight line, the traditional mark of the unsoloed pilot candidate. We still ran everywhere else, but we were driven to the flight line. We were starting the real business of this school.

We marched into a low building adjacent to the main heliport and sat at gray tables, four candidates to a table. The flight leader gave us a brief talk and then the IPs (instructor pilots) came into the room. IPs were mythical beings whom we held in the highest respect. They were civilians. We had heard a hundred stories about their training methods, their short tempers, and how they liked to get rid of students so they would have a lighter load. They strode through the door wearing the same gray flight suits we wore, a kind of mechanic's coverall with a crotch-to-neck zipper and a dozen pockets all over it. The IPs had something sticking out of each pocket. We knew they were privileged by how sloppy they were.

The IP who came to our table would take the four of us on our orientation flight, the only "free ride" in the course. We had been preparing for this day by studying helicopter controls and basic flight maneuvers. Many of us felt we could fly in an hour or so.

I had spent many evenings in my room reviewing the flight controls, what they did, and how I would have to move my hands and feet. I could hear the ground school's aerodynamics instructor in my head. "The names of the controls in a helicopter refer to their effect on the rotating wings and the tail rotor," the voice would say. "The disk formed by the rotor blades is what really flies. The rest of the fuselage simply follows along suspended from the disk by the mast." In my chair I formed a strong mental image of this disk spinning over my head. Then I would start to review the controls. "The collective control stick is located on the left side of the pilot's seat. Pulling it up increases the pitch angle of both main rotor blades at the same time, collectively, causing the disk, and the helicopter, to rise. Lowering the collective reduces the pitch, and the disk descends. The throttle twist grip on the end of the collective stick has to be coordinated with the up and down movements. You must twist in more throttle as you raise the collective, and roll it off as you lower it." I raised and lowered my left hand by my side, twisting it from side to side as I did.

"The cyclic control stick rises vertically from the cockpit floor between the pilot's legs. Moving the cyclic stick in any horizontal direction causes the rotating wings to increase their pitch and move higher on one half of their cycle while feathering on the other half. This cyclic change of pitch causes the disk they form to tilt and move in the same direction as the cyclic stick is pushed." Now, along with my left hand moving up and down and twisting, my right hand moved in small circles above my knees as, in my mind, I flew.

"The force that rotates the main rotor system clockwise as seen from the cockpit also tries to rotate the fuselage under it in the opposite direction. This effect is known as torque. The way it is controlled is with the antitorque rotor, the tail rotor located at the end of the tail boom. When it is spinning, it pushes the tail sideways against the torque. The amount of push, and therefore the direction the nose points, is controlled by pushing the foot pedals. Pushing the left pedal increases the tail rotor pitch, which pushes the tail to the right, against the torque, moving the nose to the left. The right pedal reduces the pitch and allows the torque to move the nose to the right. Because this left-and-right turning requires more and less power, you will have to adjust the throttle accordingly to maintain the proper engine and rotor rpm. Got that?"

I thought I did. I moved my left hand up and down, twisting it, to control the imaginary collective and throttle; my right hand moved in small circles, pretending to control a cyclic; my feet controlled the tail rotor by pumping back and forth. Eventually I could do all these movements simultaneously. These exercises and the fact that I already had a fixed-wing pilot's license gave rise to the fantasy that I would be able to fly a helicopter on the first try.

"Okay. See that tree out there?" The orientation instructor's gravelly voice hissed in my earphones. I was finally getting my chance. The instructor held the H-23 Hiller trainer in a hover in the middle of a ten-acre field.

"Yes, sir," I said, squeezing the intercom switch on the cyclic stick.

"Well, I'm gonna take care of the rest of the controls, and all I want you to do is to keep this bird pointed in the direction of that tree." He jutted his chin forward. I nodded. "You got that?"

"Yes, sir." My senses were overwhelmed by the clamor and bouncing and vibrations of the H-23. The blades whirled crazily overhead; parts studied in ground school in static drawings now spun relentlessly and vibrated, powered by the roaring, growling engine behind my back. All the parts wanted to go their own way, but somehow the instructor was controlling them, averaging their various motions into a position three feet above the grass. We floated above the ground, gently rising and falling on an invisible sea.

"Okay, you've got it," my instructor said. I pushed first one and then the other of the spongy pedals, trying to turn the machine while the instructor controlled the cyclic and collective. All I had to do was point the helicopter at the tree. The tree swung wildly one way and then the other.

"You see the tree I'm talking about?"

"Yes, sir."

"Well, try to keep us pointed that way, if you don't mind." This instructor, like all the IPs in the primary phase of instruction, was a civilian who'd been in the military. The fact that they were now civilians did not cramp their cynical teaching style.

I concentrated even harder. What could be wrong with me? I already knew how to fly airplanes. I thoroughly understood the theory of controlling helicopters. I knew what the controls did. Why couldn't I keep that goddamn tree in front of us? Swinging back and forth in narrowing arcs, learning to anticipate the mushy response in the pedals, I finally succeeded in keeping the tree in front of us most of the time, plus or minus twenty degrees anyway.

"Not bad."

"Thank you, sir."

"Now that you have got the pedals down nice and good like you do, maybe we ought to show you how this collective-pitch stick works."

"Okay, sir."

"What I'm going to do is to take all the controls again"—the IP put his feet back on the pedals, and the tree immediately popped to a stable position dead ahead of us—"and then let you try your luck with the collective. Just the collective. Try to keep us about this high off the ground. Okay?"

"Yes, sir."

"You got it." This phrase always preceded the transfer of control.

"I've got it." The moment I grabbed the collective stick in my left hand, the helicopter, the same helicopter that had been sitting placidly at three feet, lurched to five feet. It seemed to push itself up. I pushed down too hard to correct. We strained up against the harnesses as the ship dropped. I panicked and overcontrolled again as the ground rushed up. I pulled up too hard, causing us to pop back up to six or seven feet.

"About three feet would be fine."

"Yes, sir." Sweat dripped off me as I fought to achieve a stable altitude above the ground. It wasn't a matter of just putting the collective in one position and leaving it there; constant corrections had to be made. After a few minutes of yo-yo-ing up and down I was able to keep the machine about where the IP wanted it.

"That's real good. You're a natural, kid."

"Thank you, sir."

"I've got it." The IP took control of the collective. "One small thing you're going to have to know is that when you pull up with the collective, that takes more power, which causes more torque, which means you have to push a little left pedal to compensate. You have to push a little right pedal as you reduce the collective."

"Yes, sir."

"The next control we're going to try is this here cyclic stick. You don't move this one much, see." I looked at the IP's right hand as it held the cyclic-control grip. It was moving plenty. The top of the cyclic vibrated in agitated harmony with the shaking machine.

"It looks like it's moving a lot to me, sir."

"I didn't say it wasn't moving; I said you don't move it much. There's a difference. The H-23 is famous for the excessive motion of its cyclic. That's the feedback from all that unbalanced crap spinning around up there. Try it for a while. You got it."

"I got it." I put my hand on the wavering cyclic grip between my knees. I could feel strong mechanical tremors vibrating in many directions within my white-knuckled grasp. The IP had the rest of the controls. The H-23 held its position for a few seconds and then began drifting off to the left. I pushed the tugging grip to the right to correct. Nothing seemed to happen. We still drifted left. I moved the grip farther to the right. The ship then stopped its leftward drift, but instead of staying stable, like I thought it would, it leaned over to the right and drifted in that direction. It felt like there was no direct control of the machine. I pulled the cyclic back to the left quickly, to correct, but the machine continued to the right. The helicopter was taking on a personality, a stubborn personality. Whoa, I thought to the machine-turned-beast. Whoa, goddamn it. I increased pressure away from its drifting, and once again it halted, seemingly under control, and then drifted off in another direction.

"I would like it better if you kept the helicopter over one spot or another that we both know about, if you don't mind."

"Yes, sir." After a series of hesitating lurches in many different directions, I finally caught on to the control delay in the cyclic. After five minutes of sweaty concentration I was able to keep it within a ten-foot square.

"Well, you got it now, ace."

"Thank you, sir."

"Next thing to do, now that you've got the cyclic down, is to let you try *all* the controls at once. Think you're up to that, kid?"

"Yes, sir."

"Okay, you got it."

"I got it." The cyclic tugged, the collective pushed, and the pedals slapped my feet, but for a brief moment I was in complete control. I was three feet off the ground hovering in a real helicopter. A grin was forming on my sweaty face. Whoops. The illusion of control ended abruptly. As I concentrated on keeping us over one spot with the cyclic, we climbed. When I pushed the collective back down to correct, I noticed we were drifting backward, fast. I corrected by pushing forward. Now I noticed we were facing ninety degrees away from where we started. I corrected with the pedals. Each control fought me independently. I forgot about having to push the left pedal when I raised the collective. I forgot the cyclic-control lag. We whirled and grumbled in a variety of confusing directions, attitudes and altitudes all at once. There were absolutely too many things to control. The IP, brave man that he was, let the ship lurch and roar and spin all over that field while I pushed the pedals, pumped the collective, and swept the cyclic around, with little effect. I felt like I had a handful of severed reins and a runaway team of horses heading for a cliff. I could not keep the machine anywhere near where I wanted it.

"I got it." The IP took over the controls. The engine and rotor rpm went back to the green. We drifted down from fifteen feet to three, pointed away from the sun and back to the tree, and moved back to the spot where we had started. I felt totally defeated.

"Well, it's true what they say about you all right, ace."

"What's that, sir?"

"You're a natural."

"A natural? Sir, I was all over the field."

"Don't worry about it, kid. We'll just keep practicing in smaller and smaller fields."

Our actual flight training with our regular instructors began the following day at a stage field, one of many scattered over the central Texas prairies. The stage fields provided each flight with a private airfield, thereby separating advanced and beginning students. The first challenge was to solo. To this end, the IP concentrated on basic maneuvers like hovering, takeoffs, landings, and simulated forced landings, which are called "autorotations."

The army taught us to fly the machine as if the engine would quit at any moment. Throughout training, whether you were trying to hover, take off, land, or just cruise, the IP would cut the power, to see how you'd react. When he decided you might survive a real emergency alone, then you would solo.

My IP, Tom Anderson, would wait to cut the power until we were crabbing sideways or bucking in somebody's rotor wash or ballooning too high in a hover. He wanted to see how we would react when everything else was going wrong. There was no way you could be ready for it. We learned to react automatically when the power quit.

There were two ways to autorotate. In a hover, you held the collective where it was when the power was cut until the skids were six inches from the ground; then you pulled it up to cushion the landing. In flight, you immediately pushed the collective fully down to neutralize the pitch angle. With the pitch flat, the rotors would continue spinning, providing lift, as the helicopter descended. If you held the collective in flying position, the rotor blades would slow and stop. Because the rotor blades were rigid only by virtue of the centrifugal force of their spinning, the stopped blades would simply fold up and the helicopter would fall like a streamlined anvil. It was fatal not to push the collective down. Autorotations were quick. A Hiller in autorotation descends at 1700 feet per minute. From 500 feet we had twenty seconds to react to the power failure, bottom the pitch, find a spot, and land. In this short glide you maneuvered the machine to any clearing in range. At roughly fifty feet from the ground you pulled the cyclic back, making the ship flare, trying to slow it from 45 knots to zero. With the nose high in the flare, you waited until the tail rotor was close to the ground, pulled a little pitch, and leveled the ship. You saved the rest of the pitch to cushion the landing. That was how it was supposed to go.

At first I hit the ground too hard, or pulled the pitch too soon, or landed crooked. After bouncing around awhile, practicing hovering autorotations in the parking area and down the lane at the stage field, we'd get to the takeoff mark at the end of one of six lanes. There I would attempt to hover the machine, talk to the tower, and be ready for a hovering autorotation at any moment.

"Zero-seven-nine lane three for takeoff." After saying this, I would turn ninety degrees, wait for clearance, and make the takeoff.

For takeoff from a hover, you pushed the cyclic slightly forward and added a little power by pulling up on the collective, twisting the throttle appropriately to maintain rpm. The helicopter would accelerate across the ground, pretty much at hover altitude, until it reached the point of translational lift. Translational lift was that speed—in the H-23 trainer it was about 20 miles an hour—at which the rotor system moved into undisturbed air and suddenly became more efficient. At that point you could feel it jump into the climb. (That is how overloaded helicopters, unable to hover, can still fly if they make running takeoffs.) From translational lift you attempted to hold a constant airspeed and climb rate until you reached the altitude where you turned to follow the traffic pattern. Because there were six lanes at the stage fields, staying accurately in the traffic pattern was crucial. Midair collisions were not uncommon between students.

Once airborne, we were subject to autorotations on each leg of the rectangular pattern. After we took a few turns around the pattern, practicing landings and takeoffs, the IPs usually took us out to the surrounding countryside and had us work on cruising flight and autorotations.

We spent an hour each day in the cockpit and three or four hours in the bleachers watching our classmates. We read the flight-school syllabus of maneuvers. We attended ground-school classes in aerodynamics, weather, and maintenance. We lived and breathed flying. We waited expectantly for the first of our classmates to solo.

After two weeks, one did. We threw him into a pond, the traditional honor after the first solo. He could also wear his hat forward. By the end of the third week, nearly half the class had been thrown into the pond and were wearing their hats forward, and I was one of them. At the end of the fourth week, those who hadn't been able to solo were eliminated from flight training.

The next challenge was to learn all the primary maneuvers well enough to pass a check ride in four more weeks. We flew more often. Each day, I flew an hour of dual with Anderson. Additionally, he assigned us another hour-and-a-half solo in which to eliminate whatever errors he had pointed out. When next we flew dual, we would be expected to demonstrate improvement. Pleasing the IP meant becoming a pilot and a warrant officer instead of a pfc infantryman. Getting the maneuvers right in the air, and worrying about them on the ground, became a total occupation.

The IPs believed that student errors were premeditated attempts on their lives, and reacted accordingly. (When later I became an IP at the same school, I shared this feeling.) The IPs had several different ways of showing their displeasure. Most of them shouted over the intercom at every repeated mistake. At least one of them hit his students with a stick. All of them used bad grades to underline bad performance. Tom Anderson, however, used extreme disappointment to point out our mistakes.

A week before I was to take my primary check ride, Anderson cut the power as I cruised toward the stage field. I bottomed the pitch immediately, turned into the wind (everything that flies lands into the wind—it reduces ground speed at touchdown), and glided down in autorotation, just like an automaton. I was very proud of the fact that I had remembered to bottom the pitch satisfactorily, and was intent on landing straight ahead, into the wind. But Anderson had picked a place where to turn into the wind was also to turn toward some huge power lines. Being a dumb candidate, I was concentrating on doing the maneuver by the numbers. I noticed Anderson shaking his head forlornly, out of the corner of my eye. My feeling of pride and competence turned to stark terror. I saw the power lines. I turned abruptly away from them, but I was now very low, heading for a stand of trees. Anderson kept shaking his head sadly.

"I've got it," said Anderson. A hopeless tone in his voice completed the rest of the sentence wordlessly. "I've got it, *asshole*." I nodded my head in agreement. How could I have not seen all those wires? Anderson restored the helicopter to intelligent control, brought back the power, and nursed us gently away from the trees. He looked like he was attending a funeral.

"Bob, if you land in the wires, you will get killed." At that moment, I would have preferred death to his disappointment. Back at cruising altitude, he gave me the controls again. "Let's just go to the stage field. Maybe you can land without hurting us?" He sighed.

I nodded eagerly. I would definitely get us back okay. "I've got it," I said.

Anderson nodded and sat back with his arms folded. When I turned to look for the stage field, he cut the power again—at the same place, with the same power lines. This time I looked for a clear spot first, then maneuvered to approach it into the wind. Anderson just sat there. When we were fifty feet from the clearing I had picked and he hadn't taken over the controls, I knew he was going to let me go all the way. I hit the ground and skidded twenty feet into a shallow ditch I hadn't seen and came to a halt.

"That's more like it," he said, smiling.

I knew then that I would pass my primary check ride.

After the check ride we concentrated on advanced maneuvers: takeoffs and landings in confined areas and pinnacles, cross-country navigation, night flying, night autorotations.

Anderson very carefully demonstrated the flight school's procedure for getting into and out of confined areas. It was a method designed to minimize damage. A student helicopter pilot wallowing around in a hover in a tight clearing is an accident waiting to happen. You circled the clearing you picked until you had determined the best approach path over the lowest obstacles, into the wind. You would then pick a spot in the clearing and make your landing. On the ground, you would lock the collective down and the throttle at idle position and get out of the helicopter, leaving it running. You put a rock or a stick under the chin bubble so you could see it from inside. Then you went to the downwind side of the clearing, paced a distance equal to the length of the helicopter plus five paces safety margin back from the nearest obstacle, and deposited another marker. Then you paced it out to see if you were able to turn around in a hover over the first marker without hitting the trees at the upwind side of the clearing. If you could, you were finished analyzing the area and could get back into the machine. If you couldn't turn it and were going to have to hover backward from the upwind marker to the downwind marker, you had to install a line of markers between the two points as a guide for your rearward flight.

Each clearing was different. Some required much pacing and marking to get out of. Others were so big and free of obstacles that the drill of placing markers seemed pointless. Months later, in Vietnam, I realized that I automatically analyzed each clearing before I landed. The drill worked.

Anderson sometimes took two of his students on a demonstration ride, to save time. One day we landed in a very small, confined area marked with a red tire, signifying that it was to be used only with an IP. Hovering at the front of the clearing, the tail rotor was only a few feet from the rear. Anderson backed the helicopter a few feet and tried to take off. Several factors were against us. One, it was a very hot day, making the density altitude very high, giving us less than normal lift. (Air density is corrected for altitude, temperature, and humidity. Hot, humid air raises the density altitude; cold, dry air lowers it.) Two, the machine was overloaded for this density altitude. (This was a common flying condition in Vietnam.) Anderson made one attempt to get over the trees in front of us and had to abort the takeoff midway, sliding backward into the clearing. The ship would not go. I offered to get out and walk to a nearby field.

"Not necessary," said Anderson. He picked up to a hover and began to circle around in the tiny clearing, just missing the trees with the rotors. My classmate and I thought he had gone nuts. But after two tight turns we could see what he was trying to do. He was accelerating in a circle to translational-lift speed. When the ship lurched into translational lift, Anderson aimed for the gap between two trees and went. He made it. It was a much tighter fit than a student would be allowed to try, but he made it. I never forgot that takeoff. There is always a way.

A few days later I ended my five months at Fort Wolters with an hour-long, sweaty check ride in which I successfully demonstrated my abilities to the army inspector. Our class was to continue the course at Fort Rucker.

We arrived with eighty-five hours of flight time from Wolters. We logged eighty-eight more in the H-19 Sikorsky, learning to do confined areas without markers, landing on pinnacles, and doing lots of cross-country and tactical flying. During the last month we would log twenty-seven hours in the ship everybody lusted to fly:

the Bell HU-1 Iroquois, known as the Huey. Huey time was divided between ten hours of orientation and seventeen hours of instrument flying.

Though the flight training progressed noticeably, our status did not. We had become senior candidates at Wolters, only to begin over again as junior classmen at Rucker. It wasn't a complete regression, though. Married students were allowed to live off base with their wives.

The two trainers we flew at Rucker occupied two poles in the technological developent of helicopters. The H-19 Sikorsky, which looked like a giant tadpole with four wheels, was so tall there were built-in steps leading from the ground to the cockpit. The monster was powered by a heavy, thirteen-cylinder radial engine that took up a large percentage of its potential cargo capacity. The ten seats in its hold, filled with passengers, rendered the machine unhoverable on most days. It had to make running take-offs even with moderate loads.

The Huey, on the other hand, with its powerful, light-weight engine, had power to spare. It could hover and take off with ten passengers and a crew of two. It was also quiet, started easily on cold mornings, and was simpler to maintain. Flying the two ships was a telescoped course in the development of helicopters.

For all its drawbacks, the H-19 was still a good trainer. The H-23 had had direct mechanical linkages to control the rotor system and required heavy-handed operation. The H-19 had hydraulic controls which required a light touch. Its sensitive controls, coupled with its under-powered bulk, made it fly like an overloaded Huey.

We expected to jump into the new trainer and show our new IPs we were pilots. On my first try, as happened to everybody else, the H-19 just sank to the ground when the IP let me have the controls.

"The reason you're sinking is because you're moving the cyclic too much. That dumps the air cushion from under the disk. Use pressure. If you can see the controls move, that's too much. If nothing else, flying this machine will teach you subtlety on the controls."

And so it did. In a few hours I didn't think about the control response at all. I even enjoyed flying the monster.

The last twenty hours or so in the H-19 were spent in the field, simulating air assaults in student aviation companies. We flew reconnaissance missions, day and night cross-country, and were given turns at planning and leading air assaults composed of many ships flying in loose formation.

Near the end of our training with the H-19 we began to see more and more of the Huey in our ground-school classes.

"The Huey is the army's latest utility helicopter," said the narrator of a training film. A Huey flying low level filled the screen. The camera zoomed in to the main rotor hub spinning above the engine nacelle. "The T53-L-11 gas-turbine engine develops eleven hundred horsepower yet weighs only five hundred pounds. The turbine is basically a jet engine with a fan placed in the exhaust." An animation showed an engine cutaway. A twelve-inch-diameter turbine fan spun in the gases behind a jet engine. "This single turbine fan is connected by a shaft running back through the engine to the transmission. The pressure of the gases pushing through this fan generates sufficient force to turn the forty-eight-foot rotor system and the eight-foot tail-rotor assembly and lift the 5000-pound machine plus a maximum load of 4500 pounds into the air." The animation dissolved to a Huey banking away to swoop down to a jungle. "The Huey's streamlined design allows a maximum cruise speed of 120 knots." We laughed at this point, because our H-19s flew at 80 knots. The film showed a Huey sitting in a clearing. As the announcer spoke, the craft began to rise vertically. "Though not recommended, the Huey is capable of hovering vertically up to an altitude of 10,000 feet on a standard day." The film went on to show how it was variously configured as an air ambulance (Medevac) carrying six litters; as a gunship (Guns) carrying pilot-directed machine guns, rockets, or grenade launchers; and as a troop carrier (Slick) with room for ten soldiers and two crew-operated door guns.

My first impression of the machine was that it was pure silk. When the IP squeezed the starter trigger on the collective, the response was a shrill whine as the high-speed starter motor began slowly to move the blades, not the clacking cough and roar I was used to. At operating speed there was no roaring, vibrating, or shaking, just a smooth whine from the turbine. The IP signaled me to pull up the collective. The big rotors thudded a little as they increased their pitch, and the machine left the ground like it was falling up.

I overcontrolled the pedals, making the tail wag back and forth. This was a common reaction to the sensitive controls and was called the "Huey shuffle."

The heavy, thudding noise of the main rotors—the characteristic wop-wop-wop sound—was caused by their huge size, 48 feet from tip to tip, and a 21-inch chord (width). With ballast weights at each blade tip, the whirling rotor system had tremendous inertia. The IP demonstrated this inertia with a trick that only a Huey could do. On the ground at normal rotor speed (330 rpm) he cut the power, picked the machine up to a four-foot hover, turned completely around, and set it back on the ground. Incredible! Any other helicopter would just sit there, not rising an inch, while the rotors slowed down. These big metal blades with the weights in the tips would serve me well in Vietnam. Their strength and inertia allowed them to chop small tree branches with ease.

During this orientation period in the Huey, Patience

drilled me at home on the checklist. Her method was negative reinforcement. She kicked me in the shins at each mistake. I learned it so well that even now, when I recall the Huey cockpit check, I get a twinge in my leg.

Flying an hour each day, it took two weeks to finish the orientation in the Huey. Next was instrument flying.

We were one of the first classes to get instrument training. Helicopter pilots traditionally maintained eye contact with the ground. To the old pilots, VFR (visual flight rules) and IFR (instrument flight rules) were one and the same: "visually follow roads" and "I follow roads." If a storm got bad, you just flew slower and lower. If it got real bad, you stopped in a field. That innocent philosophy was coming to an end. The helicopter was going to war; in war you can't fly slower and lower or stop just because the weather is bad.

I enjoyed the instrument training very much. You got into a Huey with an instructor, put on the hood (a device which restricted your vision to inside the cockpit), flew all over Alabama, making practice landings at airports you never saw, and returned an hour or two later, never having seen the ground or the sky or anything except the inside of the cockpit. On my final check ride I flew from Fort Rucker down to Gainesville, Florida, and back, making four approaches to strange airfields and two course intersections. The dreamlike flight lasted four hours. The only clues that I was flying were moving needles in gauges and radio conversations with various control towers. I had to use this training only a few times in Vietnam, but it saved lives when I did.

On May 11, 1965, we got our warrant-officer bars and our silver wings. My father and sister and Patience and Jack were there to see me graduate. (My mother was sick, and couldn't attend.) I was very proud. It had been the most eventful ten months of my twenty-three years.

Sixty percent of our class were sent immediately to Vietnam. I was among the forty percent who thought they had somehow lucked out by getting assignments in the States. This was an illusion. I had asked for and been assigned to the 3rd Transportation Company, Fort Belvoir, Virginia—the VIP flight. This unit flew congressmen and senators around Washington and maintained a twenty-four-hour scramble-alert status to rush certain people to underground installations in case of Bad Times. The tour was traditionally eighteen months to two years. This duty was too good for brand-new pilots. It was where you went as an old salt. The post was manicured; the local town, Washington, D.C., was fun; and the officers' club was posh, overlooking the Potomac. We were too dumb to realize that we had been sent here just to be in a holding pattern for a few weeks. Patience and I went out shopping for furniture for the first apartment since our marriage.

For a few weeks life was okay. I got up in the mornings, put on my orange flight suit, and drove ten miles to the airfield. There I spent two or three hours transitioning into the tandem-rotor Piasecki. After that I would sit around and talk flying with the other pilots.

Some of the pilots had been to Vietnam. They told us that you could get a stereo in Saigon for about a third of what it cost in the States. That's what I knew of Vietnam: It was a good place to buy stereo equipment. Many of those pilots had flown in support of the Army of the Republic of Vietnam (ARVN) in a nine-to-five war whose objective was to gain control of the South Vietnamese in the face of Ho Chi Minh's popularity. The Vietnamese Communists in the South—the Vietcong, or VC, as they were called—hadn't stopped fighting since President Diem had refused to hold the scheduled free elections in 1956. I didn't know these facts then, but I did know that these pilots talked of the ARVNs as reluctant warriors in an American operation. They had used helicopters to lift the ARVNs to battles they almost always lost. Meanwhile, the VC continued to gain strength.

Three weeks after arriving, I received orders to report to Fort Benning, Georgia. The orders were not accompanied by explanations.

"What the fuck is at Fort Benning?" I asked a friend who had received the same orders.

"I hear they're forming up a big, new division. Probably we're going to Vietnam."

"Huh?"

At Fort Benning was the 11th Air Assault Division (Test), which had been developing and testing helicopter air-assault techniques for more than two years. After several big war games in the Carolinas, in which the 11th Air Assault fought a simulated enemy played by elements of the 101st Airborne Division, it was decided that the techniques did indeed work and that an actual air-assault division should be formed and sent to the interior of Vietnam. Since there were all these helicopters and pilots already there, they simply changed the name of the test division to the 1st Cavalry Division (Airmobile) and acquired more pilots and aircraft to bring it up to full strength.

Hundreds of pilots arrived at Benning in the middle of June, but until July 28 we were told that there was no special reason for this buildup. "There's no truth to the rumors that we're going to Vietnam, but don't sign a lease" was how they put it.

We were given a rush course in some of the combat techniques the old salts from the test division had devised. Their specialty was low-level flying, called "contour flying." This technique was supposed to keep exposure to ground fire to a minimum. They had a special low-level route called a "confidence course" where we were taught tricks like flying under power lines and making low-level turns so steep the rotor tips nearly touched the ground. These guys were cowboys.

On one flight with an old salt named Bill James, I experienced the lowest and fastest helicopter ride I had ever seen. With three air-force pilots along for the ride, James flew along a railroad track bordered by tall trees. At more than 100 knots, he squeezed the fuselage down into this channel of trees while the rotor just brushed the tops. It was blinding. The air-force pilots screamed, "He's crazy! Tell him to stop! Stop!" James accelerated when he heard them yell. At 120 knots, between two rows of trees, the world is a green blur. I had no idea how James was able to see what he was doing.

Another procedure the old salts had refined was formation flying. In flight school our formations could be defined as two or more helicopters flying within sight of each other in the same sky. We had not been taught close formation flying, because it was considered too dangerous. But to get a flight of four Hueys into a small landing zone (LZ) at the same time required that they fly, land, and take off very close together.

Closeness was measured in rotor diameters. The range for the old salts was from one to three rotor diameters. In actual practice they flew at one or less. When I first experienced this, visions of commingling, counterrotating, and splintering rotor blades danced in my head. There was also talk that these daredevils flew with their rotor blades *overlapped* by several feet, just for fun.

I saw these techniques—the low-level, the close formations—performed much more often than I did them. We had very little time. The new pilots would be getting their Huey experience and air-assault training on the job in Vietnam.

When they announced that we must turn in all our underwear to have it dyed olive green, and that we were to paint our flight helmets the same color, we knew the time was near. On July 28 I heard President Johnson announce on television, "We will stand in Vietnam," and "I have today ordered to Vietnam the Air Mobile Division." A tingle of fear mixed with excitement came over me. The games were over. Life was getting very serious for helicopter pilots.

The next day, in a moment of grim rationality, I bought a double-barrel derringer as a secret, last-ditch weapon.

My sister, Susan, was up from Florida to pick up Patience and Jack. I was feeling very cheated. I hadn't got a chance to live even one month as a normal human with my wife and son. Now I was going away for a year, or maybe forever. Patience and Jack had lived five months in a sweaty room in Texas, four months in a trailer in Alabama, a month in an empty apartment in Virginia, and now another month in another trailer in Georgia. I felt I had not provided very well for them, and now, to top it off, I was leaving.

To make it even worse, I wasn't a believer. Now that I was interested enough to read about it, I thought the Vietnamese ought to be able to decide what kind of government they wanted, just like we had. If they wanted to be Communists, then they ought to be. They probably wouldn't like Communism; but, then, everybody has to make his own mistakes. If democratic capitalism was better for them, then they'd fight for it.

Probably my feeling that the Vietnam war was a crock was spawned by my fear of dying young. It was a revelation, political or not, that came too late. I was going. I owed the army three years of service for teaching me to fly helicopters. And there you had it.

I held Jack, and together we smiled at the camera. Patience snapped the shutter. We all got in the car and drove to the fort. While soldiers piled duffel bags into buses, I held Patience, and she cried. I watched, numb, as my sister, my wife, and my son got into the car and drove away. In the parking lot, surrounded by hundreds of green-clothed men milling around Greyhound buses, I felt very lonely.

We drove from Columbus to Mobile to board the USNS *Croatan*. It took four aircraft carriers, six troop carriers, and seven cargo ships to move the entire division to the other side of the world. An advance party of a thousand men was being flown over to meet us at our highlands campsite near the village of An Khe.

We boarded. I wrestled my enormous flight bag through the turns of the dark passageways. The heavy bag tore the button off the front of my uniform as I stepped through the hatchways. The air was still and musty; the steel walls were scaly with rust. I came out onto a deck that was under the overhanging flight deck. I pulled the bag over to the hatchway, trying to figure how to get it down without breaking anything.

"Throw it down, Chief," the warrant at the bottom of the ladder yelled. He was standing on the deck where we would be quartered.

"This bag?" I said.

"Yeah, sure, throw it down to me. You can't carry it down."

"This bag weighs as much as I do."

"Look, Chief, you want to cause a traffic jam? Throw it down to me."

As I tossed the bag down the ladder well, the warrant stepped back. The bag crashed on the steel deck.

"I thought you were going to catch it."

"Did I say that?" grinned the warrant. "That's your bunk over there. Have a nice trip."

2.
An August Cruise

We do not want an expanding struggle with consequences that no one can foresee, nor will we bluster or bully or flaunt our power. But we will not surrender and we will not retreat.

—Lyndon Johnson, July 28, 1965

August 1965

On the crowded ship I finally met all the members of my company. During the month of hectic packing and training at Fort Benning, I barely knew who they were.

I was in Company B, 229th Assault Helicopter Battalion, one of two such battalions in the 1st Cav. Our company commander was Maj. John Fields, who would be replaced a couple of months after we got to Vietnam. Fields was well liked, but I would never know him well. My platoon leader was Capt. Robert Shaker, a black man, tall and skinny and very professional, which is to say a hardass. My squad leader and the man I would deal with the most was Capt. Dan Farris, a squarish, sturdy man with a built-in smile. He was military, but maintained his sanity nevertheless.

"Goddamn it, Connors, you just hit my eye with your elbow," growled Len Riker, a tall, skinny CW-2.

"Sorry, Len. This fucking Mae West almost had me then."

While we waited for Ensign Wall and Colonel Dogwell to inspect the lifeboat drill, Connors would wrestle endlessly with his preserver. If the wait lasted a half hour, that's how long he took to put it on. Besides being the company's IP, Pat Connors was our resident clown.

"There." He slipped his shoulder under the strap and straightened suddenly, only to fall against his friend Banjo Bates. "Oops. Sorry, miss."

"Watch it, Connors. I'm in no mood for your horsing around." Banjo folded his arms across the front of his Mae West, scowling, not looking at Connors. Bates almost always looked pissed off, except when Connors got to him, like he was doing now. Connors kept grinning at Banjo, not put off by stern looks.

"This is fucking crazy," Banjo said angrily. "Not only do I have to go through this stupid boat drill every other day to prove I can wear a life preserver; I have to put up with a genuine asshole like you, Connors." He turned and had to smile at Connors's grinning face.

"At ease," said Shaker. Farris and the other squad leader called at ease. "Okay, roll call." Shaker read the names.

I still didn't know most of the men in my platoon by name. In the other platoon I knew Wendall, the camera nut, and his friend Barber, along with the model-maker, Captain Morris, and his buddy, CW-2 Decker.

"Daisy."

"Here." Capt. Don Daisy loved political arguments and played a lot of chess.

"Farris." Capt. Dan Farris. I liked him from the beginning.

"Gotler." CW-2 Frank Gotler, a soft-spoken man with a slight German accent who claimed to have flown for a short time in the Luftwaffe.

"Kaiser." CW-2 Bill Kaiser. He was short, with quick, darting eyes, and very aggressive. He took no shit from anybody, gambled constantly, and won most of the time. Had he been assigned to fly gunships instead of slicks I think he would have been a real killer.

"Leese." CW-3 Ron Leese. He was the highest-ranking warrant in our platoon, the rough equivalent of a captain. Leese was frail-looking, almost elfin, and very experienced in combat flying, having flown gliders in the Pacific and fighters in Korea. He often talked quietly with Gotler. He was new to the Cav. He had taken a leave of absence from his white-collar job to fly in Vietnam. Next to Connors, he was the best pilot in our company, certainly the most experienced in combat.

"Mason." WO-1 Bob Mason. Me. Brand new to the unit, just out of flight school, with 250 hours of flying time. I was five ten, 140 pounds, and wore my brown hair daringly longer than the others. I had high cheekbones and squinty eyes. I was attempting to cope.

"Nate." Another CW-2. He smoked a pipe constantly and had a voice much deeper than his light build would lead you to expect.

"Resler." WO-1 Gary Resler. Another guy new to the Cav and to army aviation.

"Riker."

"Here." After getting his eye poked by Connors's elbow, Riker's normally ruddy complexion had flushed to lobster. He was a serious man, almost humorless.

"Okay." Captain Shaker folded the roster sheet and put it under his arm and awaited inspection. Unlike the rest of us, he was not wearing a rumpled flight suit. He preferred to dress out in fatigues after the morning exercises, with shined boots. Being the platoon leader, he was serious about being a soldier first, a pilot second.

Ensign Wall of the navy and Col. Roger Dogwell of the army strolled around the corner from the other side of the ship as Shaker finished. Wall always seemed ready to burst into giggles. He was the only navy man on board and therefore in charge of the ship and equal in position to Dogwell. Dogwell was big and looked as if he would have liked to tie the ensign into some kind of handy knot. Shaker gave a loose salute, and the grinning ensign tapped his forehead with a finger. Dogwell scowled.

"Everybody here?" asked the ensign.

"Yes, Mr. Wall, everybody's here." Shaker's tone implied, Where do you think they are, walking in the park?

"Sir, where's Banjo?" Connors suddenly asked.

"I'm right here, you asshole." Banjo gave Connors a jab with an elbow.

"Oh, thank God, thank God."

"That's enough." Shaker turned and glared. Wall grinned. Dogwell looked positively vicious. The colonel said the only word I heard him say on the trip: "Pilots."

Leese sat next to me at breakfast.

"I've assigned you to fly a ship off the carrier when we get to Qui Nhon." He smiled.

"Really?" I smiled back weakly. I still wasn't at all confident about flying the Huey.

"Something wrong?" Leese asked. "You look kind of sick. This chow getting to you?"

"No, the chow's okay. I'm not too sure about my ability to fly a Huey off a carrier."

"It says here"—he produced a penciled note—"that you're checked out in Hueys. All four models." He looked back at me.

"Well, I *have* flown them, but it was mostly time under the hood at altitude. I had about ten hours of contact-flying instruction in them."

"How long have you been out of flight school?" I noticed smile wrinkles around his eyes as he looked at the front of his paper and then at the back.

"I graduated in the middle of May."

"So you don't feel too confident flying off the ship?"

"That's right."

"Okay." He put his notes on the plastic tablecloth next to his food tray. "I've just reassigned you to fly with me."

"Thanks. I'd rather not end my tour just getting off the boat."

"Oh, I'm sure you wouldn't have any trouble, but I need a copilot, and from what you say, you need the practice."

After breakfast I went back to my bunk to find my checklist. I was rusty on the start-up procedure. I got the checklist from my flight bag and walked back to the hangar deck to find a Huey to practice in.

The trail from our hatchway back through the interior of the ship to the mess hall was like a jungle path through piles of boxes, bags, coils, barrels, cases, and Hueys. Usually the trail was crowded, but I was alone between feeding shifts. In the middle of the deck I squeezed between two fuselages and pushed toward where a large light bulb glowed into the cockpit of a Huey. This was far enough away from the trail for privacy. I didn't want the old salts to see me. Those guys could go through the entire start-up procedure about as quickly as I used my Zippo.

I opened the left cockpit door. Everything inside looked the same except for the armored pilots' seats. The armor meant that bullets were *expected* to be whizzing through the cockpit. Why had I argued so strongly with the elimination board?

I would be flying one of these into battle, something I had never considered as a kid daydreaming about saving flood victims, rescuing beautiful girls, or floating among the treetops picking apples. Not once in any of my fantasies did I have people shooting at me.

I sat in the first pilot's seat—the right seat—and looked around. Because our Hueys had no guns except the machine guns the crew chief and gunner used, they were called slicks. Our job would be to carry troopers into the landing zones. People on the ground would be trying to blast us out of the air. Unlike the gunship pilots, we would not be able to shoot back. I could not imagine how that was going to feel.

The armor added 350 pounds to the aircraft and displaced two grunts. I knocked it with my knuckles. The ceramic and steel laminations, built up to about half an inch thick, fit around and under the seat, made of aluminum frame with red nylon mesh. A sliding armored panel on the side of the seat next to the door pulled forward, protection for the torso but not for the head. We'd be issued chest armor when we got to Vietnam. It seemed pretty complete. I could not imagine bullets going anywhere but into the armor, because in the hangar deck of the *Croatan* no one was shooting.

I put my checklist down on top of one of the radios in the console between the two pilots' seats and twisted around to look at the cargo deck behind me. It was U-shaped because of the intrusion of the hell-hole cover that enclosed the transmission and hydraulics directly under the mast. Our two door gunners would be stationed on either side of the hell-hole cover—in the pockets—firing M-60 machine guns attached to pylons. During our first two months, though, the machine guns would simply be strung from the top of the open doorways on elastic bungee cords. With the crew chief and gunner in the pockets, there was enough room for eight or ten troopers on the cargo deck.

I turned around to face front, and relaxed. While the

Croatan rolled on the sea, I reviewed the cockpit check, and remembered Patience.

"Sitting around like this all day makes a feller want to go out and strangle somebody, just for fun," said Decker. Decker was an Arkansan from the other platoon. A dusty, disheveled guy whose sandy crew cut even looked rumpled, he was always with his close friend and fellow Arkansan Captain Morris. Together they swapped Southern aphorisms like "He was happier than a dead hog in the sunshine."

Morris was close to forty, and though he kidded with Decker, he looked worried. His thinning black hair was combed back with Brylcream, and his mouth was set thoughtfully, from years of concentration. He was a model-maker. He had acquired the plans of the *Croatan* from the boatswain and was spending most of his time building a detailed model of it. He even had the rust in the right places. When I got tired of watching the bow or reading or playing chess, I would often watch Morris at work. It was fascinating. His careful hands and peaceful face told me he liked doing what he was doing. But why the *Croatan*? Morris explained that the *Croatan* was the last of its kind. I liked and respected Morris. He seemed to be coping better than I during these endless days.

If I had a favorite time of day, it was the late afternoon, as the sun was setting. One day, as I stood in the bow watching the sun drop into the sea, I spotted something far ahead on the horizon—something on the ocean besides the *Croatan*. Contact with aliens. We are not alone.

A guy came up on the bow and propped his elbows on the steel ledge to brace his large binoculars. The thing out in front of us was dark and twisting, like a sea serpent.

"Looks like a tree branch," he said. "Something on it, too. Can't tell what, though." We waited. "Those things on it are seagulls," the guy announced to the growing crowd. "They're turned away from us. I don't think they know we're coming."

The *Croatan* was on a collision course with the twenty-foot branch and its two passengers.

I turned to look up to the bridge, off to the starboard side of the flight deck. A T-shirted man stood just outside the glass, pointing ahead.

"These boys aim to run those birds down," said Decker, who had just arrived. "Anybody'd do that's just as likely to rape your dog or scatter your garbage."

By then fifty men were crammed into the bow. I was at the point. The gulls still roosted, facing away from us. They had found the one place in the middle of the Pacific Ocean where they could stop and rest.

I leaned way over the edge to watch the collision. A perfect hit. The branch shattered in half, and the gulls crouched to leap, only to be sucked under the bow waves. They disappeared. Moments later, on the starboard side of the ship, about twenty feet behind the bow, first one and then the other bird scrambled out through the foam of the waves, shaking its head as its wings slapped the water.

Leese and I leaned against the starboard railing as we passed Bataan. Blue-gray mounds rose above the sea on the horizon. It was the only land we saw between California and Vietnam. Leese stared silently at the distant islands. He had landed a glider there.

"What was it like?" I asked.

"Real hot." He turned to me, smiling. "It was the worst feeling I've ever had. Those fucking gliders didn't land; they crashed. I thought that I was in control of those things during training, but when they were loaded up with men, they flew like fucking anvils." He swore only when he talked about gliders.

"You crashed?"

"Well, I walked away from it, so you could call it a landing. Some people got hurt on mine, killed on others. It was a terrible idea, gliders. . . . These Hueys at least will be able to fly back after we drop off the troops."

"So what did you do after the landing?"

"You were on your own. That was the job. You made the landing, and then you found your way to friendly lines if you could. Some didn't."

"Damn! So how'd you get into gliders?"

"My whole flight-school class was suddenly redesignated as glider-pilot candidates and shipped out. No reason. One day we were flying powered trainers and the next we were on our way to glider school."

"You flew in Korea, too?"

"Yeah. Tactical air squadron."

"Did you like that?"

"It was okay. As long as it has an engine, I like to fly it."

"Why did you quit your job to come into the Cav?"

"I dunno, exactly. I guess I just like to fly too much. In combat. Combat flying is . . . a challenge. It scares the shit out of me every time I do it, but I think about it a lot. Getting into the Cav was good for me, I think. That desk looked more and more like a coffin every day. You know what I mean?"

I nodded, but I wasn't sure.

"Yeah. At least in combat, it's quick." He grinned.

"Are you betting on the anchor drop?" I asked Kaiser.

"Fuck no. That's strictly amateur crap," he replied as he puffed into some dice in the break room. "Anyone who'd waste a bet to guess the exact time we drop anchor is an asshole," he added.

"I put a buck on 9:37," said Connors.

"You're an asshole."

"No wonder my mother was so disappointed."

I had put in a buck, but I didn't tell Kaiser.

Within a day of landing, the ship became a hive of activity. We received unofficial encouragement to "find usable surplus equipment" from the boat for our new camp. Ensign Wall agreed that certain "musty old mattresses" could be removed from the ship, and he went on a tour with Colonel Dogwell to discuss what specifically we could remove to our Hueys.

While hundreds of men scavenged stuff from every compartment of the ship, others were in the process of getting the Hueys ready. The vinyl coating on the flight-deck Hueys was peeled off and thrown overboard. A few days of sea air would not hurt them. Boxes of rotor blades were brought up to the deck to be sorted out and attached to their original mountings, so the Hueys on the flight deck would be ready to fly almost immediately upon arrival at Qui Nhon. The rest, including the one Leese and I would fly, would be brought up on the hangar-deck elevator when the deck was clear. It was supposed to take three days to get the Hueys assembled, checked, loaded, and off the ship.

Gear from the scavenger hunt was stashed on the helicopters. Work crews of enlisted men, warrant officers, and lieutenants carried stacks of mattresses, coils of rope, wire, yards of canvas, tools, and even lumber to the hangar deck and concealed the stuff in the Hueys. This wasn't junk we were taking. The mattresses were new, and so were the ropes and tools. Obviously we were cleaning up.

The ship was going back to the States after it dropped us off, and they could get more gear there. We were going to live in the middle of the jungle somewhere and felt that we needed all the help we could get. I more or less agreed with this attitude, but I did have some pangs when I saw just how much we were packing into the helicopters.

Before we landed, I got the boatswain's mate to make me a holster for my derringer. He wanted me to get him a couple dozen folding P-38 can openers from our C rations. During the confusion of this last day at sea, he came to our quarters and handed me the finished holster. A leather ring fitted over each shoulder, with an elastic band stretched between them across my back. The leather ring on my left shoulder had the holster sewn on near the bottom. I slipped the heavy derringer into the holster while the mate watched proudly. With the weight of the gun, the holster slid comfortably and invisibly under my arm. Maybe it would save my life; maybe I would use it to kill myself if I was captured. I really didn't know why I wanted it.

When I climbed out of the hatch and looked beyond the rail, there was something to see, distant and gray, but unmistakably land. Two hours later we were in Lang Mai Bay, south of Qui Nhon, ready to drop anchor. The marine helicopter carrier *Iwo Jima* was on our right, and ten military-contracted freighters from the Lykes line were on our left. The anchor hit the water at a little after 11 a.m. on the thirteenth of September. It had taken us thirty-one days to get here from Mobile. The rest of our division had left a week after we had and arrived a week before.

While our helicopters were being readied for flight, the pilots hung around above decks, watching the doings of the other carrier.

Marine pilots flew their big H-34s off the rolling deck of their carrier to the hazy coastline and then returned. The marines' concept of using helicopters was not the same as ours. We would live with our troops in the field. They returned to the safety and comfort of their ship each day. Knowing that made us feel tough.

The *Iwo Jima* was one of the ships that supported the recent battle of Chu Lai, which had occurred while we were en route. It was reported as the first regimental-size battle since Korea, involving more than five thousand American ground troops, ARVNs, and navy artillery. The final score was seven hundred VC killed and fifty U.S. Marines. No one seemed to care how many ARVNs were killed.

"By mid-afternoon of the second day, all Viet Cong resistance had ceased. Boots, equipment and weapons were scattered haphazardly across the fields, and great black scars in the earth still smoked from napalm. The bodies of the enemy hung in pieces from trees and hedgerows or lay charred in their tunnels and caves. . . ." The battle, according to *Time*, had "proved that by combining accurate intelligence reports, fast planning, and careful selection of where and when to fight, the U.S. [could] more than hold its own in Vietnam."

The combination of U.S. Marine and ARVN ground troops and heavy fighter and artillery support had produced big numbers of dead Vietnamese. *Time* reported more than 2000 VC killed, but there was a controversy as to how many of those killed were actually innocent villagers trapped in the crossfire.

"As far as I can see," said Decker, "anybody'd be dumb enough to hang around during them battles deserves what happens to him."

"Decker, they're saying that they found ten-year-old kids shot in those villages. Do you think they're VC?" objected Wendall.

"Maybe," answered Decker, "and maybe not. But this is war. Everybody gets hurt in a war. Hell, we can't go crying about the innocents that get killed. Innocents have

been getting knocked off in wars since the beginning of
time. If we want to win this thing for the Vietnamese we
got to be ready to see it as it is: war, plain and simple and
nasty."

"That's right," said Connors, "either we're fighting
this war or we aren't. The Cav is here now, and those
gooks are going to shit when they see us in action. We're
beyond a *reason* to be here. We're *here*."

Captain Sherman and John Hall, a warrant from our advance party, had brought bags of mail that had accumulated while we were en route. I spent a long time reading
the dozen or so letters Patience sent. Of those, I record
this:

[August 25]
I miss you so much my darling dear husband. I took a
nap on Suzi's bed today and kept imagining that you
were there next to me trying to comfort me (as if we'd
had one of our dumb fights). I'm going to write Lois
today to see if Jayne can come down here to Naples. I
wish you could come. I bet it's pretty dull on the ship.
I'M MORE EXCITING! COME TO THE CASBAH WITH
ME!!

Bobby, I miss you so much. I've been trying to be
busy. Your dad stopped by and we got your film back
from the Panama Canal—shall I send you the pictures
or keep them? Only one was a little blurry. I like the
one of you. You look more tanned already. After Dad
left I pushed the stroller (AND JACK!) up to the Sunshine for some Coppertone and then down to the beach
for a short swim. Now it's two in the afternoon—thun-
derstorming outside and nothing to do except remember how we used to take showers together, and play
Monopoly and kiss and make love and hold each other.
I miss you so much I could die, but I won't, as long as

you come back. And PLEASE HURRY! I wish it were next August.

Jack still misses you, I can tell—he is very attracted to men and he says "Da-da" when he's very excited and happy. I love you! VERY MUCH!

It is so insane to me that such a short while ago we were living together, fooling around, laughing over Jack and the kitty. It's inconceivable that you're gone, but you obviously are. Please write me a lot. You know those old war flicks where the guy's sitting in a foxhole up to his ankles in water while the mortars fall all around, writing a letter to his girl on toilet paper—well that's what I expect!

Jack just said "Down" when he wanted to get out of his high chair! Last night at supper the kitty was meowing under his chair and he looked down at her and said "Meow!"

I love to write you. It makes me feel more secure as well as giving me something to do. But I better end this.

I LOVE YOU MADLY &
THE MOST,
Patience

"Well, we're going right into the middle of it, men," Major Fields announced. We were gathered in the break room for a briefing, and Fields pointed to the map he had taped on the bulkhead. "Our camp is just two miles north of this village." He pointed. "It's the village of An Khe, about halfway between Qui Nhon and Pleiku on this hundred-mile east-west stretch of road called Route 19. This whole area"—he gestured at the map—"is considered VC territory. The highway was just opened by the ARVNs in July. The Cav will be the first unit to locate right in the middle of VC-land, and the idea is to be right there in the middle of 'em, to clean 'em out of here, pronto." He smiled as his fingers tapped some papers on the table. "So when you fly in, your route will be the road. And stay high. All these little villages you'll see on your way through the south end of the valley are VC-controlled, and some ships have reported sniper fire up at a thousand feet. About forty miles inland you'll come to this pass, the An Khe pass, which marks the end of the valley and the beginning of the highlands. The division's base camp is here, about ten miles beyond the pass in the high ground. They say we'll have cool sleeping weather there. Our division takes up a big piece of real estate. It's still being cleared. The heliport is 3000 by 4000 feet, and nearly twenty thousand men are camped all around that." Fields took a sip of coffee. "When you get out there, you'll be briefed in detail about the camp, our company area, and like that. I haven't seen the place myself yet.

"Our company's radio call sign will be 'Preacher.'" Fields picked up a sheet of paper from his stack that had FM, UHF, and VHF written on it, with the appropriate frequencies printed carefully next to them. "Copy these numbers down. They'll change when you get there, but this is what you should have on your radios for the flight in." We hunched over our pocket notebooks and recorded the information.

"Now, about all this crap that's being stuffed on the aircraft." Fields paused as the men laughed knowingly. "I don't know what exactly you've put in them, and I don't want to know, either." He smiled, shaking his head. "But I'm here to tell you that the navy—Ensign Wall—has complained that some supplies, unauthorized supplies, are missing. Now, I don't think anyone in *our* company would be so greedy as to *steal* from this ship, but I do have to pass the complaint along." The major beamed at his mischievous boys. "So, I don't have much more to say except that we'll be leaving at twenty-minute intervals starting today. The last Huey should be off the *Croatan* in two days. You've got your ship assignments, your maps, and your radio frequencies. Are there any questions?"

"Yessir," Banjo called out. "Does the advance party have our tents set up yet?" Laughter.

"Yeah, I'm sure they do, Banjo. Complete with floors, featherbeds, and private baths."

By eleven the next morning, Leese and I and the crew chief, SP-5 Don Reacher, were ready to go. Reacher had worked on the assembly team to get our Huey ready. Leese and I had done a very careful preflight. Underneath some shabby canvas tarps on the cargo deck were stacked a dozen bulky mattresses and twenty thick pine boards. Leese had decided to make the takeoff, which pleased me.

Connors and Banjo were running up their ship about seventy-five feet away. It was at full rpm, and I could see the disk tilt back and forth as Connors checked the controls. I stood at the nose of our Huey and watched. The first breeze came to me as Connors pulled in the collective. The disk coned as it began to pull the ship off the deck. He waited a few moments in a five-foot hover, and the full blast of the rotor wash hit me with the sweet, kerosene smell of warm turbine exhaust. He nosed over and left the carrier on his way to the airfield at Qui Nhon, to top off his tank. After thirty-two days of waiting, we were finally getting off the ship. Leese and I were next. I felt the breast pocket of my fatigues for my notebook and cigarettes. My army .45 was secure in its black leather holster over my concealed derringer. I gave myself the now automatic check down the front of my uniform. My belt buckle was covered with green tape. My fatigue pants were so baggy they almost concealed my combat boots. It felt strange to be dressed this way for flying. We'd always worn flight suits before.

Leese had been talking to someone at the edge of the flight deck while Connors took off. He walked toward the Huey. "Let's go."

I opened the left door, put my foot on the skid, and leaned over to grab the far edge of the armored chair. Leese was getting in on the other side, and my cyclic stick moved as he bumped his with his leg. I slid my leg between the cyclic and the front of the seat and lowered myself onto the nylon mesh. Reacher stood outside next to me and handed me the shoulder straps and radio cord from behind the high-backed seat. I clicked the lever over to anchor the shoulder straps to the wide lap belt. Another crew chief from the ship behind us helped Leese with his straps. Strapped in, Leese released the inertial reel lock so that he could lean forward to do the cockpit check. Starting at the bottom of the center console beside his left foot, he moved his hand over the many switches and circuit breakers, checking their positions. His hand moved over the top of the console between us and checked that the radios were off. I followed him and clicked in the proper frequencies. I pulled on my brand-new leather flying gloves. They would last two weeks in this climate. Leese pushed in the igniter circuit breaker on the overhead console and announced, "Okay, we're ready to crank."

We slipped our flight helmets on. I grabbed the base of mine on both sides to spread it slightly and pulled it over my head. I forgot to pull the earphones back with the outside strings, so one of them lodged crookedly against my left ear. I pulled the string loop on that side to pull the rubber cup away and reseat it. The phones were dead until Leese flipped the master switch. He squeezed the radio trigger switch on his cyclic to the first click and said through my phones, "Ready?" I did a thumbs-up. He turned to look out his door window, to make sure someone was posted there with a fire extinguisher. Someone was. He nodded, and the man raised the red bottle to the ready. Leese rolled the throttle open to the indent starting position and squeezed the trigger switch on his collective. The electric starter motor whined shrilly. The rotors accelerated slowly. I was always amazed that any electric motor could turn the engine, transmission, and those big rotor blades. The rotor blades blinked. A loud hissing noise, audible over the moan of the starter, meant that the fire had caught in the turbine. Leese watched the exhaust-gas temperature gauge (EGT) carefully. The needle rushed past the red line, and the rotors spun to a blur. The EGT stayed pegged in the danger zone as usual for a couple of seconds before it moved back into the green, operating range. Leese did a thumbs-up to the watching fireman. The danger of a hot start had passed. The Huey had snapped into smooth operation after more than a month of storage.

I tapped all the gauges on my side of the instrument panel. Everything was in the green. "Everything okay back there?" Leese called to Reacher on the intercom.

"Yes, sir, everything is secure." We carried no gunner on this trip.

The deck rolled while the *Croatan* lay at anchor. Leese opened the throttle to the operating position and briefly checked the blurry edge of the rotor disk to see that it moved correctly as he pushed the cyclic around. As he slowly pulled the collective up, the nose of the Huey characteristically rose first, and he corrected for drift inclinations. When the helicopter was stable, he raised the collective and pulled us above the moving deck.

I looked out at the circle of spectators and saw their clothes flapping in our gale. Leese hovered for a few seconds at six feet, checking the gauges one last time before he nosed the ship forward with an imperceptible push of the cyclic. I watched the edge of the flight deck move under us through the chin bubble at my feet. The sea churned below us. We were on our way.

3.
Setting Up Camp

In the final analysis the final outcome of the war will be decided by the sustained fighting of the ground forces, by the fighting at close quarters on battlefields, by the political consciousness of the men, by their courage and spirit of sacrifice.

—Lin Piao, September 1965

September 1965
We landed at Qui Nhon to have our tank topped off to its 1200-pound, 200-gallon capacity before the flight to An Khe. Beneath the overcast sky the air was hot and moist. The smell of human waste drifted from the sand dunes beyond the concertina wire that bordered the runway, apparently part of the city's latrine. I saw people squatting among the dunes and shreds of paper drifting in the breeze. We stared like tourists at the people we had come to save. A young boy wiped himself with a bare hand and then licked same.

"Gawd." Leese shook his head and turned away.

Leese flew. I followed the map, keeping track of our position so I could radio in our coordinates if we went down. The VC-controlled valley between Qui Nhon and the An Khe pass was a vast swamp of rice paddies. The road we were following was considered partially safe. Leese climbed up to the cloud ceiling at 3000 feet.

The map was dotted with names like An Dinh, Luat Chanh, Dai Tio, My Ngoc, and a hundred more, crowded around the outskirts of Qui Nhon. The valley stretched twenty miles north to Bong Son and stopped just a kilometer (or "klick") south of us at the foothills. Fingers of high ground pushed nearer from the south along the road. These ridges were about 1500 feet high and completely covered with lush jungle. Occasionally I saw clearings on the sides of the hills where banana trees grew. While Leese flew, I conjured up grinning VC who sighted along the barrels of their guns as they stood concealed under the green canopy. It suddenly became obvious to me that I was completely exposed to any fire that came from the front. Chest protectors would be nice. Total armor with a slit to see through would be better. Flying back to the ship would be even smarter. I looked over at Leese. He smiled. The pass loomed ahead.

"Here, you take it for a while."

"I got it."

Below us the narrow road twisted upon itself as it began to climb up through the steep foothills. As the ground rose toward us, I could not resist pulling a little pitch. Two hundred feet higher and we flew through occasional wisps of cloud. The world disappeared for a few seconds each time.

At the top of the pass the ground rose to within 800 feet of us. The empty road ran through thick jungle. A tall hill called Hong Kong Hill, ten miles ahead, marked our camp.

"A lot of nice places to hide down there," I said.

"I'll say," Leese said quietly as he watched the ground. From our vantage point Vietnam looked very big and very green with its thick covering of jungle. It looked like a great place to have a guerrilla war, if you were going to be the guerrilla. "I'll say," Leese repeated.

The overcast was breaking up ahead, and the jungle glowed green between dark shadows formed on the ground. Leese reached over to click the radio to our company frequency. I felt the cyclic move slightly as he squeezed the radio trigger. "Preacher base, Preacher eight-seven-niner." Our ship's tail number.

"Roger, Preacher eight-seven-niner. Go ahead."

"Preacher eight-seven-niner at the pass. Where do we park?"

"Preacher eight-seven-niner, call Golf Course control and they'll clear you to land at our parking area. We're located at the south end of the field on row three. We'll send someone to pick you up. You copy?"

"Roger, Preacher base. Eight-seven-niner out."

As the land sank toward An Khe, I reduced the collective and let the ship descend slowly. Dead ahead of us, just north of the road, was Hong Kong Hill, the western border of Camp Radcliff. The Golf Course, the heliport cleared of all its trees, stood out against the green.

"Golf Course control, Preacher eight-seven-niner, five miles east for landing instructions."

"Roger, Preacher eight-seven-niner. You are cleared for a straight-in approach to the south on row three. Follow your ground guides."

The skinny Song Ba River ran beside the eastern perimeter of the camp. Two miles to the south it grew to a hundred yards wide near the village of An Khe. Near the river, between the village and the camp, was a small airstrip built by the French. The Cav's fixed-wing aircraft were using it now.

Leese rogered the instructions from Golf Course control, and I swung off to the right so I could loop around and come back toward the field on a southerly heading, for a straight-in approach.

"Keep it high until we get closer," said Leese

"Okay."

The sun shone brightly as we cruised over the jungle north of camp and turned south to line up on row three. I started my descent about a mile away and a thousand feet high. Our advance party had done a big job. The Golf Course was dotted with thousands of stumps. Around it the trees stood thickly.

"Preacher eight-seven-niner, short final."

"Eight-seven-niner, cleared to land."

I reduced the pitch and pulled back on the cyclic to set up my approach flare. The top of Hong Kong Hill rose above the horizon on our right as I descended below it. As we got closer, the Golf Course looked very rough.

"Man, look at all the stumps," I said.

"Incredible."

Six straight, parallel rows of helicopters were divided by vehicle tracks that jogged through the mud among ravines and stumps. Olive-drab tents, trucks, water trailers, Jeeps, and people littered the cleared area past the south end of the Golf Course, where we would be living.

At 500 feet I crossed a swath cut through the trees that formed the northern perimeter of the camp. The edge of the Golf Course was still 500 feet ahead. Among the trees below I saw hundreds of pup tents. Thousands of our troopers were camped along the meandering perimeter, guarding the rest of us.

I flared steeply at 200 feet to slow the Huey for the landing. Just above the top of my instrument panel, at the south end of the Golf Course, I saw a man waving his arms as he stood on a Jeep.

"See him?"

"Got 'im," I said.

I came to a high hover in the center of the rough dirt row. I was nervous about hitting the tail rotor on the rough ground. The man who had waved us in now motioned us over to a parking slot between two other ships. My inexperience was showing. I overcontrolled the sensitive tail-rotor pedals and waggled toward the slot.

"Takes a while to get used to the tail-rotor control in a Huey," said Leese.

Six weeks ago I had had no trouble with the tail-rotor pedals. Now I was handling them like a student.

"Why am I having trouble now?" I complained.

"It's common, Bob. You just need some flying time to get the feel of the ship. There's no substitute for experience, you know." Leese used his floor switch to talk to me so he wouldn't have to touch the cyclic while I hovered.

I floated over a very large stump and nosed into the slot. A reverse slope rose toward the tail. As I pulled the cyclic back to stop, I could imagine the spinning tail rotor smashing into the dirt. The Huey hovers tail low anyway. I was too cautious. I let the ship down so gently that a gust picked us back up. I overcompensated and we dropped rapidly. I overcompensated for that and we rose abruptly.

"Relax," said Leese. "You're doing fine."

That's what an instructor says to a nervous student. I felt the heat of embarrassment rise in my cheeks.

First the heel of the left skid touched ground lightly, followed by the heel of the right skid, not lightly, and then the ship plopped forward ungracefully and settled flat on the skids.

"A little work on your last three feet is all you need," said Leese. "Your air work and the approach were top notch."

The ground guide drew his hand across his throat, signaling me to shut down the ship.

And so I made my first landing on Vietnamese soil.

———

We threw our flight bags in the back of the Jeep. Reacher stayed behind to supervise the unloading of the booty from the *Croatan*. As Leese and I rode 500 yards along the waffle-tracked ruts to our company's area, I saw the five sky cranes I had heard so much about. Even by helicopter standards they were ungainly-looking. They were skeleton-framed helicopters designed to lift 20,000 pounds. Removable, pre-loaded, mobile-home-size pods fitted neatly under them, including a completely equipped emergency-surgery room. And they could sling-load big artillery pieces, as well as any aircraft the army owned, including the twin-rotor Chinook, which usually retrieved the downed Hueys.

"Welcome to Camp Radcliff," said Captain Owens, the operations officer. He had come out of the operations tent, one of our two general-purpose (GP) tents (these tents measured 20 by 40 feet). He and CW-3 White, the other OPS officer, lived in the back.

"Where'd they get the name Radcliff?" asked Leese.

"A major in the advance party who got killed at the Mang Yang pass," Owens said.

"Where's that?" I asked.

"Up the road about twenty more miles," said Owens. His olive-drab T-shirt was dark from sweat. "On the way to Pleiku," he added. He pulled his dark-stained cap off and pulled the bottom of his shirt up to his face. Sweat dripped out of his hair and beaded across his beard stubble. "His ship got shot down from three thousand feet over the pass by a fifty-caliber machine gun. Tracers picked him out and followed him all the way to the ground."

"So, how is it around here?" asked Leese, as he struggled with his flight bag, pulling it out of the back of the Jeep. It weighed as much as he did.

"Very confused." Owens leaned up against the front

fender, hat in hand. "Every night there's a bunch of firefights on our perimeter. A lot of it's our own troops
shooting at our patrols coming back to the line." He
turned around to face north. "Up there last night"—he
pointed—"five guys in a patrol were killed trying to get
back in. My advice to you is not to walk around the camp
at night. You're liable to get blown away by nervous
grunts. I don't blame them, though; some of the action is
VC, too. There's no physical perimeter line around a lot
of the camp, so the boundaries aren't clear to everybody.
The guards get confused and shoot at anything that
moves or makes a noise." Owens laughed suddenly as he
replaced his cap. "Couple of nights ago, they must've put
a hundred rounds into a water buffalo."

"Where do we sleep?" asked Leese.

"You have to set up a pup tent for the time being. Our
platoon tents aren't here yet. Probably still on some boat
somewhere in a Conex container. The major said to set
up on this side of that GP there." Owens pointed to the
other GP tent, a hundred feet past his. "Good luck," he
said.

That night while rain tapped on my tent I wrote Patience
a letter by candlelight. I told her how painful it was to be
so far away, how I missed her and Jack, how much I
loved her. Small-arms fire popped and crackled in the
darkness. I had talked to a guy at Belvoir who had told
me how great his Vietnam tour had been. He had a villa
overlooking the ocean, willing hooch maids, casinos, and
great buys at the PX. He had been stationed with a group
of advisers somewhere along the coast, where he flew of-
ficials around from one Special Forces camp to another. I
thought of him and cursed my luck.

Everybody was busy working in the company area the
next morning. I was leaning against a stack of mattresses

that I was about to lay out in the sun when a Jeep bounced out of the slop of the perimeter road. A colonel got out. After a brief word with Major Fields, he turned to us.

"We have heard reports that some mattresses and other supplies were taken off the *Croatan*." He walked closer to me and the mattresses. "Now, I know that no one from the 229th would do this, but you know how the navy is. Complain, complain, complain. So I've got to officially ask you men if you have seen any of these missing mattresses and ropes and lumber and stuff from that ship."

I pushed myself away from the stack of hot merchandise. He looked at us and smiled warmly. His eyes did not so much as glance at the stack. He pinned his look on Connors.

"No, sir," said Connors. "I sure haven't seen anything like that. I'd sure like to have one of those mattresses, too."

"I'm sure you would, son," said the colonel, nodding kindly. "Anybody else know anything about this missing gear from the *Croatan*?" the colonel said as he walked toward the GP tent. Nate, standing next to the canvas doorway, said, "No, sir. Haven't seen anything like you're talking about around here." A huge pile of ropes lay nearby.

"Not a thing, sir," said Riker, leaning against a stack of lumber.

"Nothing, sir," said Kaiser.

Twenty pairs of eyes sincerely, innocently denied that all this stuff lying in full view existed.

"Well, thank you, men, for your time and your cooperation." The colonel smiled and turned to Fields, who walked him back to his Jeep.

While the sun dried our gear, Fields called us together for a briefing. The map tripod was set up in front of the operations tent. Fields was wearing a set of the new jungle fatigues and boots that the advance party had picked up for him. The rest of us were waiting for them to be issued. Jungle fatigues fitted loosely. The top wasn't tucked in; it was more like a safari jacket. The boots were canvas-topped and vented to keep your feet dry.

"Okay, men, now that you are all here, this is what's happening." Fields held his folding pointer collapsed in front of him. "All that activity you saw out on the Golf Course yesterday was the 227th"—our sister assault-helicopter battalion—"going out to help the 101st." He unfolded the pointer and then snapped it shut again. "They got the Airborne out of a bind and lost some ships and people doing it. I don't have accurate figures yet." (Four ships shot down, one crew lost, it turned out.) He opened his pointer and turned to the tripod. "The reason for this briefing is to give you the lay of the camp and what we're going to be doing for the next couple of weeks." He pointed to a drawing of the camp on the first page of the big pad. "Our four companies are grouped here, below the southeast corner of the Golf Course." He described the camp layout and then stopped and tore off the page, revealing another drawing. "This is a plan for Bravo Company's area." He pointed. "Now, notice that this road here on the map is not on the ground over there." He pointed toward the medical tent that marked the division between us and Charlie Company, nicknamed the Snakes. "Nor is this ditch, or this bunker, nor any of these tents. Putting these things in place on the ground will be our job. The only flying will be admin flights and courier missions. We must finish setting up camp before we start work. Everyone will work. That means all officers and warrant officers as well as NCOs and enlisted. There will be police call every morning and plenty of work details every day. Furthermore, some of you will have to go out on the Golf Course and chop out the stumps." Fields paused as some of us turned around to look at the 275-acre heliport and the thousands of stumps.

"You mean, the engineers aren't going to push them things out?" said Decker.

"That's right." We turned around as Fields spoke. "The engineers aren't being used, because we don't want to expose the dirt. When we get into the dry season, the dust will be fierce around here." We looked back around to the muddy trails and ravines. It didn't look as though it could be much worse than it was.

"What do we do with the stumps after we dig them out?" Decker was very interested in the stump operation.

"When we get enough of them loose, the plan is to haul them away with the Hueys. That's down the road. In the meantime, I need a detail to fill sandbags for the bunkers, a detail to cut the road, a detail to dig the ditches, and a detail to put in phone lines."

Somehow the glamour of being an army aviator eluded me. I dug ditches along the company road. Resler, Banjo, Connors, Nate, Riker, and Kaiser dug, too.

We were worrying out a small stump in the middle of the road when a little green snake wriggled out of the roots.

"Hey! A snake," yelled Banjo.

"Hey yeah," said Connors, "let's catch it."

The snake was trying to get back into the protection of the roots. Armed with a variety of sticks, shovels, axes, and other probing instruments, we rolled the stump away and surrounded the snake.

"Is it poisonous?" asked Nate.

"Naw," said Connors. "It's a green snake. I've seen them a hundred times back home." Connors jumped abruptly as the snake, which he was trying to pin with his stick, struck fiercely. "Damn. I've never seen them do that before."

"Shit, Connors. You going to let a green snake scare you?" laughed Banjo. He squatted down with a stick to try his luck.

Captain Farris came to see what the commotion was all about. "Hey, don't touch that snake," he yelled. "That's a bamboo viper. Deadly poisonous!"

The circle of snake hunters widened quickly.

"Poisonous?" Banjo turned and glared at Connors. "Shit, Connors, I was just about to grab that little fucker. Green snake, my ass!"

"It's green, ain't it?" yelled Connors.

"Yeah," said Farris. "It's a green bamboo viper." Farris took a shovel from Resler and quickly pushed the blade through the snake and firmly into the ground. The two halves twitched and wriggled in the dirt. Its mouth yawned wide in its death throes.

"Just remember," said Farris, "of the thirty-three kinds of snakes over here, thirty-one are poisonous."

"How do we tell them apart?" asked Resler.

"I think that with those ratios, you could afford to come to a prejudicial, sweeping generalization—like, kill them all." Farris turned and left.

The dirt from the ditches was shoveled into sandbags. Our squad was divided. Five of us filled the bags while the other half carried the sixty-pound sacks a hundred feet to the site of our first bunker.

We laid a foundation of sandbags measuring fifteen feet square with one opening for the door, deciding after much debate that the walls only needed to be one bag thick. Once the foundation was laid, more guys from the platoon joined us to speed up the work. By late afternoon we had the walls six feet high.

Another work detail had been given the task of getting large trees to serve as the rafters for the roof. These were smoothed and trimmed to size with axes. Just before evening chow, we had them set in place across the top of the sandbags.

"Look at the shit in this dip water." Captain Morris, the mess officer, scowled at the garbage can of steaming water. Kerosene immersion heaters were supposed to keep the water boiling to sterilize our mess gear. As the first few men walked past and dipped their gear, the water began to cool and collect a thin film of grease and assorted debris. Morris stomped angrily into the mess tent, presumably to confront the mess sergeant.

Decker eyed the water disdainfully. "This damn water is rank enough to bury," he said loudly.

"Yeah," said Connors from behind me in the chow line, "they should bury it in the same pit they throw whatever else died in there." He nodded toward the mess tent.

"That's our chow you smell," said Banjo.

"I'm gonna puke." Connors made a face and grabbed his stomach. "What is that shit? Why can't we eat C rations?"

"Gainesburgers," said Banjo. We had named the army's canned ground-beef patties, served in gravy, after the dog food. The preserving process had converted real meat into an unidentifiable, chewy, dry substance soaked in grease.

The line moved past the front of the mess tent. Into the two halves of my mess kit the servers poured, placed and plopped a variety of foods: "Gainesburgers," instant potatoes, boiled cabbage, stewed corn, and circles of sliced canned bread. I walked back to the bunker to join my comrades as they ate sitting on a pile of sandbags.

"Is there going to be beer tonight?" Connors asked.

"Tomorrow. I'm going to Qui Nhon to pick up a ship-load," said Nate.

"How come you get the fun details?" Connors complained.

"Luck, skill, experience, ass-kissing. You know," quipped Nate. He had finished eating and was now beginning the ritual of the pipe.

"Think that bunker will take a direct hit?" Resler asked me.

"I don't think so. But I guess that depends on how thick we made the roof."

"How thick are we gonna make it, Captain Farris?" Resler turned to our squad leader.

"I think Captain Shaker wants us to make the roof two bags thick," Farris answered as he balanced the two halves of his mess kit on his knees.

"Will that take a direct hit?"

"Naw," said Farris.

Before noon the next day we had laid sheets of perforated steel planking (PSP), normally used for roads and runways, across the tree rafters, and laid a roof two bags thick across them. It sagged a little in the middle, but you could walk around inside it if you bent your head down. From outside it looked massive and sturdy indeed, a pattern for the other three.

After lunch we worked for three hours filling more sandbags when PFC Berne, a runner from operations, ran up to us. He looked concerned.

"Mr. Connors, you and Banjo are supposed to get in the air right away!"

"What's up?" Connors threw his shovel down.

"Nate got shot down on the beer run."

"C'mon, Banjo." Connors ran toward the operations tent. Resler and Riker and Leese and I watched them go.

In the midst of the digging and building, I had forgotten that there were people outside who did not want us here.

In the pale moonlight that night, we celebrated the beer run. Four pilots, each holding an unopened can of beer, marched around the bunker. With flourishes and chants of "Oh noble leader," they approached Fields, who sat laughing in a lawn chair. They put the beer on the bunker and backed away, having delivered the fruits of the mission. Those four lonely cans were all that survived of the 100 cases that Nate and Kaiser had picked up in Qui Nhon.

The Snakes loaned us enough beer for the party. We sat on and around the bunker while Nate and Connors told the story.

"I was flying at two thousand feet with Kaiser when they got us," said Nate. "I didn't see where it came from, but we heard them hit. Two rounds severed the fuel line near the engine, and a few seconds later it got real quiet."

"Quiet's not the word for it," Kaiser interrupted. "I could hear my heart beating."

"This was my first real autorotation. I bottomed the pitch and looked for a place to land. The ton of beer in the back made the trip down real fast, but I made it okay."

"Yeah," said Kaiser, "he landed okay. He put the skids two feet into the fucking ground. Landed okay, my ass."

"So, I hit a little hard. I didn't bend anything," said Nate.

"I don't care if you bent anything; I'm glad you're all still alive," said Fields, smiling. "What happened then?"

"Well, we're on the ground in grass up to our ass looking at the tree lines. Kaiser called for help on the emergency channel when we were hit. The crew chief and gunner stayed at their guns and covered us." Nate held his lighted pipe in one hand while his other hand held his elbow. His back arched as he talked, and he periodically used the pipe as a pointer to emphasize a fact. "We musta landed beyond the VC, because there was no more shooting. About two minutes after we landed, a slick from the Snakes came over, checked us on the radio to make sure it was clear, and came in to get us. We stripped the radios and brought them and the machine gun with us. Kaiser wanted to bring some beer out, but the Snake ship wouldn't wait. As soon as our asses touched the deck, they were gone." Nate's pipe pointed up. "So while we were being picked up by the Snakes, Major Fields and Connors and Banjo came out to join us along with a gunship. We met them on the way in and circled back out. From the time we left our ship to the time we got back it was about a half hour." Nate gestured toward Connors.

"My turn?" Conors grinned. "Well, when we got to the scene, the gooks had been busy. I could see them scrambling off into the woods as we came up. The gunship dove down after them, but it was too late. When the gunship said it was clear, we came in." Connors stopped to laugh with Nate over a private joke. "Look, I want you to realize that the grass in that clearing was real deep." Connors took a drink of beer. "Like I said, the gooks had been busy. They had tried to sabotage the ship, I guess, because they had spent the time slashing the seats to ribbons, smearing shit on the instruments, piling dirt into the cockpit, and cramming sticks down the hell hole. Bright guys, these Vietnamese. They did get one thing right, though. They had taken every single one of those cases of beer off with them. Now, that's terrorism."

"But—" Nate added, with raised eyebrows.

"But they missed one case. One case had dropped into the grass, and nobody knew where it was until I landed that six-thousand-pound machine right on top of it." Fields was practically crying, he was laughing so hard.

"But," Connors continued, "I did manage to spare some of those cans." Connors pointed to the four Budweisers on the bunker. We cheered. Connors raised one of the cans up high and proclaimed, "To the Preachers. May we have more beer and less action."

The party broke up early when the sky darkened and the first drops of rain fell. As the storm clouds erased the moon, I remembered that I had yet to improve the drainage trench around my tent.

"Man, if a snake got in here with me tonight, I don't know whether I would just lie here and let him bite me or jump out into this fucking rain." Resler's voice was muffled through his tent and mine.

"Snake?" I heard Leese call out. He was on the other side of Resler. The rain pounded so hard it sounded like tearing fabric. My flaps were tightly closed, and I watched the rivulets of water run along the bottom edge of the canvas at the back of the tent. Where the water dripped onto my dirt floor, I scraped a trench with my pocket knife to let it drain out.

I wrote my nightly letter to Patience. I told her about my tent, not flying, the constant racket from the perimeter, and a sergeant who had been bitten by a snake. He had not checked his bedroll before he got in. Luckily we had antivenom, which was rumored to be as painful as the bite.

Above the roar of the rain I could hear the *whump* of mortars and artillery from nearby positions. Small-arms fire crackled from all directions. I could imagine what it would be like to be on perimeter guard duty on a night like this.

Something moved under the covers. I froze. I felt something cold squirm against my calf. Snake? What should I do? If I yelled or moved, he would bite. While the rain pounded the canvas, I sweated in the stifling air.

When it crawled onto my knee, I realized what it was. I pulled the covers back, and a giant brown insect flew into the side of the tent.

"Snake! Snake!" Connors's voice was muffled but loud in the storm. I pushed my head outside and pointed my flashlight toward his tent. It was gone. He and his tent spent the rest of the night in the GP.

I sat with my ass inside the tent to put my boots on. The storm had stopped during the night. The morning was bright, even pretty. Morris and Decker were shaving behind the GP, using their steel helmets as basins. I laced my pant legs into my boots and got up shirtless to walk to the piss tube. The rain had even washed some of the ammonia smell away from the area around the empty rocket case stuck into the ground. These piss tubes were strategically located around the company area. They worked pretty well until they filled up. The soil would absorb only so much. When they were full, the bad smell helped us find them at night without a flashlight.

I was thinking about going back to my tent to shave before breakfast when I noticed the crowd around the bunker.

"I cannot fucking believe it." Shaker walked back and forth in the middle of the crowd. "I asked you to build a goddamn bunker. A bunker. Look at what I get. I get a fucking burlap-covered mud pile. That's what I get!"

The bunker had collapsed. Trees and PSP lay at odd angles, with sodden sandbags drooping among them. Nothing rose more than two feet high in the jumbled wreckage.

"Goddamn it." Shaker stalked away.

"Maybe we should've made the walls thicker," Resler said.

Almost everyone in the company sweated in heavy physical labor every day. New tents were set up. Their guy wires blocked our makeshift trails. The company road was finished. We were trenching around tents and hacking and digging the stumps on the Golf Course. The company's bunker project had been abandoned. I still lived in the pup tent, but I had reduced the chance of snakes crawling into my bed roll by squeezing a cot into the tent and sleeping at the peak. It worked. Police call continued every morning, even though there was nothing to pick up except twigs. Fresh gray dirt was scattered everywhere as evidence of our work.

A select few of our company flew administration flights to neighboring units in Pleiku, 50 miles west; Qui Nhon; and even Saigon, 260 miles south. Our commanders and their friends got a chance to secure important information about building bunkers and such, to do a little scouting, to go on beer runs, and to get laid.

When the rest of us finished working at the end of the day, we sponged ourselves clean with water from the water trailer, using our combat helmets as washbasins. The administrators took showers at the Special Forces camps they visited.

Feeling that I had been sold into slavery, I was honored when Shaker told me to come with him on an admin flight to Pleiku. I packed a clean set of clothes and my dop kit. The Special Forces adviser compound in Pleiku had showers. I would also get a chance to fly for the first time in almost two weeks.

Being alone with Shaker was more like being alone. During the entire flight over and back, he said not a word to me. I guessed that he was checking me out, but if so, he was doing it in silence.

The adviser compound was great. I walked on sidewalks, took a shower, put some change through a slot machine, and bought some junk, including a small camera, at the PX.

"You should've waited and bought yourself a good camera," Wendall examined my 16mm Minolta back at our company area. "A good camera, like a Nikon F."

"Yeah, maybe," I said, feeling bad that I had bought the thing. "I'll just keep it around for quick shots. I'm going to get a good camera as soon as we get some at the PX—when we get a PX."

"Let me go with you when you do," said Wendall. "I know everything about every camera ever made."

The day after the flight to Pleiku, I got my first chance to meet some Vietnamese. Hundreds of them.

"We're clearing a field here"—Shaker pointed to a spot outside the northern perimeter on the map in the operations tent—"for a refueling depot. Vietnamese labor. They started a couple of days ago, and it's our turn to supply a overseer. That's you, Mason."

"What am I supposed to do?"

"Just watch 'em. They've got a Vietnamese boss who knows the details. You're there to make sure they're working and to watch for tricks."

"Tricks?"

"Yeah. They've been finding trimmed poles pointing right at our mortar and machine-gun positions. Obviously some of the people in the work crew are VC."

Truckloads of Vietnamese had already arrived at the clearing when I got there. I rode in a Jeep driven by Sergeant Meyers. Four large deuce-and-a-half trucks were crammed with 150 men, women, and children—refugees, I was told, who were glad to have the opportunity to earn money. The men were paid a hundred piasters a day and the women and children seventy-five. (A piaster was worth roughly a penny.) When Meyers and I pulled up, the truck drivers allowed the workers to get out.

I had no idea what to do next, but their boss did. Black pajamas and conical hats piled out of the trucks and hurried purposefully off in all directions while the boss yelled orders. A group of adolescents lingered near one truck, and the boss ran over and kicked one of them in the ass. The boss was of sergeant quality. In less than five minutes I was standing in the center of a circle of Vietnamese peasants armed with slashing machetes and flashing axes, watching the edge of the clearing dissolve as they hacked away like large, maddened termites.

The boss surveyed his charges, and when they all seemed busy, he walked toward me with a big grin.

"You like, Da wi?" That was the word for captain. Neither of us knew the word for warrant officer.

"Yeah. Looks like you've got everything under control."

"You like?"

"Yes."

"Ah."

"What's your name?"

"Nguyen, Da wi."

I saw a group of teenage boys talking in a group, facing camp.

"What are those guys doing over there?" I pointed.

Nguyen followed my gesture and immediately rattled off some harsh words that sent the boys back to work. Were they VC? Was Nguyen VC? Was anybody VC? So far, VC were rumors to me, noises on the perimeter at night.

The chopping continued in the blazing sun. Children dragged the debris back toward the center of the circle and piled it up for burning. Everyone sweated profusely. I sweated just sitting on a felled tree trunk. The air sweated.

Sergeant Meyers sweated as he came over from the Jeep.

"What should I be doing, sir?"

Do? I thought to myself. Do? How the fuck would I know what to do? Do you see a sign on me that says Jungle Clearing Specialist? I'm the pilot, you're the sergeant. Sergeants are supposed to know what to *do* with work details. Everyone knows that.

"Ah," I finally said, "just wander around the circle of workers, Sergeant, and watch the people. Uh, watch for signs, too."

"Signs, sir?"

"Yeah, these people might put markers on the ground to point out our defense positions."

"Oh, I got it." He turned and walked away. I decided to give him the advice always given to me. "Be careful, Sergeant." He turned and nodded gravely.

I had wandered away from the tree I was using for a seat while I talked to Meyers. When I turned to go back, Nguyen was attending to a wounded young girl as she sat on the tree. When I walked up to them, the girl jumped up, but Nguyen barked and she sat back down.

She had a two-inch cut on her ankle. Nguyen wiped at it with the filthy rag that had been his headband. I called to Meyers—who was leering at one of the women fifty feet away—to get the first-aid kit out of the Jeep. The girl watched me carefully, curious and scared.

Meyers got back with the kit, and Nguyen stepped aside, visibly miffed at the intrusion. The girl's dark eyes looked even more frightened in the clutches of an American. Was that whàt she was thinking? "I'll do it, sir," said Meyers. He rolled her black silk pant leg up past her knee and began to clean the wound with cotton swabs and hydrogen peroxide. The wound foamed with pink bubbles and the girl whimpered. I guess she'd never seen hydrogen peroxide work before. I told Nguyen to tell her it was good medicine.

"Good?" He looked surprised.

"Yes, good." I nodded. "Tell her."

He did, and the girl smiled.

As the girl limped off to have lunch with her family, I decided I would have her teach me some Vietnamese. I told Nguyen. After a lunch of C rations for Meyers and me and rice and unidentifiables for the Vietnamese, the girl sat on the tree trunk with me.

She told me her real name but insisted that I call her by an American name. This beautiful and innocent girl on the other side of the world insisted that I call her Sally. It was depressing.

I learned words by pointing at objects and writing what she said in my notebook—phonetically, of course. Before the day ended, I had recorded many words: among others, clock (*damn ho*), knife (*kai zowa*), tooth (*zing*). We spent an absorbing hour making up sentences that worked with the words I was learning. In the process of teaching me, she became more relaxed, and smiled.

I heard Nguyen yelling, and looked up. He was scolding a group of people at the south side of the clearing. I noticed that Meyers was sleeping in the Jeep with his hat on his face. I stood up and looked around the circle. At the north side I saw a man sitting in the field, in the midst of busy machetes. I was wondering why he would sit down there when Sally tapped my shoulder.

As she taught me the Vietnamese word for a thing, she would ask me the English word. She tapped my shoulder because I was looking around now instead of teaching her more English. "Tree," I said as she patted our bench. That was not what she meant. I got up and walked toward the Jeep. On the way, I looked back at the man who had been sitting. He was now lying down. That was enough. Give 'em an inch and they take a mile. I called Nguyen over. "Go tell that guy to get to work." I pointed to the malingerer, about a hundred yards away. Nguyen ran off.

"Get up, Sergeant," I said as I got to the Jeep. Meyers lurched forward, dropping his hat. "Sorry, sir. I was on guard duty all night." That was possible. "Okay, but try to stay awake for the hour or so we have left."

"Yes, sir."

As Meyers walked off, I looked to see how Nguyen was doing. He was on his way back. Behind him, the man still slept.

"What's going on, Nguyen?"

"He not work more, Da wi. He dead."

"Dead?" I blinked. "Did you say dead?"

"Yes, Da wi," Nguyen nodded matter-of-factly.

There must be some mistake. This dumb gook doesn't know what I'm saying. The guy's asleep, and Nguyen is trying to protect him. If the guy was dead or dying, all those people around him would have said something. Was it a trick? Nguyen's a VC and he wants me to go over there and be hacked to pieces? Certainly Meyers would never notice.

I walked toward the sleeping man. Nguyen ran up beside me. The guy's probably his brother-in-law.

"Nguyen, I know this guy's sleeping, so don't try to stop me."

Nguyen didn't answer. I felt a tightening in my throat, but I didn't know why.

The man did not get up when I stood next to him. He lay comfortably on his side in the grass while flies and gnats swarmed around the sores on his legs. (All of the Vietnamese had sores on their legs.) He did not breathe. Meyers came up from somewhere, knelt, and checked the man's pulse at his throat. "He's dead, sir."

Nguyen showed me what killed him. Six feet from his body was a beheaded snake. Somewhere among the mass of sores and cuts on his leg was a snakebite. He had been bitten, killed the snake, and then sat down to die. His friends working around him did not stop their work to help. They knew, and he knew, that when that snake bit you, you died. So he did.

At quitting time the refugees lined up fifty feet away from the waiting trucks. The pay officer arrived just as a Jeep was taking the body to an aid station inside the camp. He carried a black vinyl briefcase that looked very out of place in the jungle and from which he produced Vietnamese cash to pay the workers.

While he paid the people, I looked for Sally. I had not seen her since the snakebite incident. She was the only person I knew outside the army. She seemed bright and sensitive. I harbored fantasies of somehow saving her from a grueling existence. I could not find her.

While I looked, I noticed a boy near the front of one of the lines step back onto the toes of the man behind him. The man immediately smashed him on top of the head with his closed fist. The kid sank weakly, almost to the ground, grimacing, but did not say a word.

The trucks drove off. Meyers and I made one last check before we left. We found three distinct arrows pointed at sandbag positions on our distant perimeter. Hash marks on the stems presumably indicated the range. We scattered them.

Late that afternoon I drove into the village of An Khe with Shaker, Farris, and Resler. It was an official trip to buy stuff for the men—candles, kerosene lamps, rice mats, and plastic lawn chairs. Resler and I were along to do the carrying.

The village was small and dusty. A few other Jeeps were parked here and there. One bar seemed pretty lively, but Shaker wouldn't let us go in.

When I looked down the streets, I wondered where the refugees who had worked on the refueling depot lived. I didn't see anybody I recognized.

"Mason, they found a couple of platoon tents this morning," Resler announced through the canvas. I wasn't up yet. He usually beat me to breakfast. "They want us to move out of the pup tents but keep them pitched for now."

"Why?" I said groggily.

"They're going to use them for storage. There's still going to be twenty men in the GPs, so there won't be much room for your golf clubs and polo gear."

Hello, big time. The platoon tents, or GPs, were made of heavy olive-drab canvas stretched over a huge ridge pole. The sides were kept rolled up during the day because the tent's dark color absorbed so much heat that you could feel the outrush of air, like a hot, stale breath, as you walked in the doors. The combination of heat and moisture generated great quantities of mildew and fungus. The tents were mostly uninhabited during the day because of the heat, and because we were supposed to be outside working anyway.

That night the pup-tent colony moved into the cozy new GP. My bed and eight others lined one side of the tent. Ten more ran down the other side. Six inches of space separated my cot from Nate's, on my right. John Hall, from the advance party, was six inches away on my left. Wendall and Barber were across the aisle from me. Still, we could stand up in the tent.

During our first night in the GP we talked about our deposed leader, Major Fields. A lingering ear infection got him grounded. At a surprise meeting before evening chow, he announced his retirement to Saigon and introduced his replacement, Major Williams. For more than two years Fields had been basically one of the boys, with gold braid. Williams gave us a sample of what was to come, with all the charm of an army textbook.

"I've got the highest respect for Major Fields and what he has done with Bravo Company. I can see how much you have done here." He did not smile as he looked over our very loose formation near the mess hall. "But, starting tomorrow, the pace quickens. We have more work to do on the company area, missions coming up, and a lot of training flights. Training is the key to survival. And survival is what it's all about, gentlemen." Heavy eyebrows slanted toward his nose. The wrinkles around his mouth pulled down sternly as he talked about the upcoming missions. His face suited the job perfectly.

"Damn, I'd like to stay around and get tough working on the Golf Course," said Connors as he walked in the crowded warrants' tent. "But our new old man is sending me out tomorrow morning with good old Mason."

"Great." I looked up as I cleaned my new Smith & Wesson .38. "Who else is going?" I slid the flashy, long-barreled, wooden-gripped revolver back into the black hip holster. They had issued these cowboy weapons after we turned in our .45 automatics the day before. Great new toys for the pilots.

"It's a joint effort. Our company's sending four ships. Me and you, Nate and Resler, Wendall and Barber, Hall and Marston." Everybody looked up from tending to his .38. Connors ambled over to Hall. "Damn. It looks like you guys are getting ready for the O.K. Corral."

"You got it wrong, partner," Hall said as he twirled the cylinder of his pistol. He snapped it shut and took aim with both hands at the tent pole. "This isn't the O.K. Corral. It's the Gee Whiz Jungle. Gunfight at the Gee Whiz Jungle." Hall winked and took a healthy swig from his canteen cup.

The mission we had been assigned to was simple: an early-morning flight over the An Khe pass toward Qui Nhon; a left turn up between two skinny ridges into Vinh Thanh Valley, known to us as Happy Valley; drop off the patrols and then go back to an LZ near the pass and laager (stand by). The grunts would call for a pickup. The Cav had been sending out patrols like this since we'd been here. This just happened to be the first one that we were part of.

The troopers assembled on row three of the Golf Course. Each group of ten men had been assigned to an aircraft number. The troopers watched us as though we might sneak away while we did our preflight inspections.

For the occasion of my first mission, I had on my cleanest fatigues, a flak vest, my new .38 in its hip holster, and a pair of real flying gloves. We didn't have chest protectors because they hadn't arrived yet. I reached inside the cockpit of the Huey and connected my helmet to the radio cord, hung it on the overhead hook, and stepped back to follow Connors's preflight.

"Too many dumb bastards have killed themselves by not knowing or caring about preflight. Everything I show you today, I want you to do every day you fly." I nodded. We stood next to the cargo deck on the left side of the helicopter. "First, check the green book." He did. "Plenty of people have missed a big red X that the crew chief put on the first page. You might miss what he's logged. Remember this is the crew chief's ship, and he's the mechanic. You're just checking his work, so first check what he thinks is the status of the ship." Connors flipped the book shut and stashed it in its pocket at the rear of the center console. Then he squatted down next to the ship. "Everybody knows you're supposed to drain some fuel before the first flight, to get the water condensation out." He pointed under the belly of the Huey. "But I bet half these bastards around here never do." I got down on hands and knees and reached the fuel-drain valve and pushed it to let a few ounces of fuel pour out onto the ground. I didn't see any water drops.

Connors continued the preflight, showing me what he considered important and felt was often overlooked. He understood the machine thoroughly and had the perfect disposition for an IP. We checked the tail rotor. I undid the rotor tie-down strap and removed it. We came to the right side after the walk-around, and Connors crawled up the side of the aircraft using the concealed foot holes between the pilot's door and the cargo door. I joined him. The roof deck of the Huey is flat, so you can walk around to check the rotor hub, the mast, the transmission mounts, and the control rods. He pointed out safety wires on parts of the swash plate, the push-pull tubes, the stabilizer bars, and the control dampers. We carefully inspected the Jesus nut at the top of the mast, which held the whole works in the air. "Everybody checks the Jesus nut, but nobody looks for hairline cracks in these blade-root laminations," said Connors. "What difference does it make if the Jesus nut holds when the blade splits and breaks off?" I nodded.

We climbed into the cockpit to face the morning sun. Stress patterns spiderwebbed brightly in the plastic canopy. A boy called Red, the crew chief for this ship, helped me strap in on the right side. The sun poured in, heating us up quickly. Dark stains grew up from my waist, and I could feel sweat dripping around my concealed derringer. That idea was not going to last long. I put my sunglasses on. Connors watched from the left seat in the classical disinterested-instructor-pilot-who-is-really-watching-like-a-hawk pose. His arms were folded across his flak vest, his head pointed to the front, but his eyes darted over to see what I was doing. I ran through the cockpit check from memory and looked outside to the lead ship, parked two ships over on our right. After a couple more minutes of sweating, I saw the flight leader, in a ship from the Snakes, whirl his hand as the crank-up signal. The starter whined, the rotors moved slowly, then the turbine caught. The rotors blurred overhead, and we were ready to go. I clicked in the intercom and asked the crew chief and the gunner if they were ready. Answering clicks said they were. "Don't forget to have them check the doors," Connors said. I nodded and asked the two men to check if the pins that held the two sliding doors fully open were in place. They were. Without the pins, the doors could jump out of their tracks and blow off in the wind.

Soon sixteen slicks and four gunships were ready on row three. The troopers waited nearby for us to hover out of our parking slots.

The flight leader assigned each group of four ships—each squad—a color as a call sign, always in the same color order: Yellow, White, Orange, Red. Within the squad we got a number that referred to our position in the formation. Connors and I were Orange Four. Each ship called out its color and number in turn. When the sequence got to our squad, I heard "Orange One." Marston.

"Orange Two." Wendall.

"Orange Three." Nate.

I called, "Orange Four." The Red flight called in after us. We picked up to a hover, moved out, and parked in a long string down the middle of row three.

The troopers—or, as I had been corrected by Connors, the grunts—jumped on board. They wore jungle fatigues and bristled with bandoliers of ammunition, M-16 rifles, M-79 grenade launchers, hand grenades, and canteens. They carried little else, because they were Cav troopers and would be resupplied constantly by us. Three of them squeezed between the crew chief and the gunner on the long bench across the cargo deck, three more on the deck in front of them, and four more in the two pockets. Ten grunts.

"How did they get the name 'grunt'?" I asked while they scrambled aboard.

"That's the IQ of a trooper," Connors said.

"I hope they can't hear that."

"Don't worry, Mason. We're all grunts in the Cav. Didn't you join the army voluntarily?"

"Yes."

"I rest my case."

Red Four called the flight leader and told him the sixteen slicks were loaded. Yellow One rogered and moments later made a sluggish takeoff. The ships followed in close sequence. When Orange One, Marston and Hall, nosed over on takeoff, I began to ease in the power to get the Huey light on the skids. The nose came up lightly and she shifted a little. I corrected the drift and waited, still light. When Nate and Resler got off, I was right behind them, feeling sluggish with the weight of the grunts. Yellow One climbed slowly over the trees north of the camp, holding his speed down to 60 knots while we closed up in the familiar V formation. As we closed, he made a slow turn to the right toward the An Khe pass. As fourth ship, I joined the left wing of the V formed by the other three ships, making it a heavy-left formation.

As I closed on Orange Three's left, she seemed to fall back, so I decelerated. Then she seemed to lurch too far ahead, and I had to nose over hard to catch her. My lack of formation training was showing. I kept oscillating from too far forward to too far back. Connors let me do it a few times, then said, "I got it."

"You got it."

We fell into position forming a straight line with Orange One and Orange Three after he took the controls. We moved in so close to Orange Three that I could hear the buzzing of their tail rotor.

"Let me show you the tricks to this formation jazz," Connors said. His grin was partially concealed by his microphone. "First you gotta find two spots on the Huey you're flying on that line up and put you at a 45-degree angle away from their tail. I'll use where the cross tube connects at the rear of Orange Three's left skid as one point and line it up with the front of their right skid, where the cross tube connects. See?" I saw that those two points were lined up, moving slowly relative to each other as the ships surged gently through the air. As he showed me, we were climbing at 80 knots along the highway, toward the pass.

"Now, those are the right reference points if you're flying about level with the other ship. You also have to find two points that work when you have to go higher than them, like when they turn toward you or you have to miss a tree or something. If you make sure you have those reference points lined up, you'll be at the right angle." Connors suddenly raised us above the rest of the flight. "Look across Orange Three's roof deck." The rotors blinked over the air-vent bulges and antennas scattered on top. "I use the air vent on this side lined up with the forward corner of the roof deck." With those two points lined up we were at the correct angle to Orange Three. As we drifted back down to the same level as the rest of the flight, Connors said, "When you fly formation, try to find your own reference points for every possible position. That way, you'll never get disoriented when the going gets rough. And if you think this is bad, wait till we start doing this shit at night."

"Night formation?"

"Yeah. The trick to that is staying close enough to see their instrument lights. You can practice by flying about this far away, one rotor diameter between the disks. Later you'll learn to move in even closer." He made it look easy. I was determined to be as good. I was so involved with what he was showing me that I barely noticed that we were crossing the pass. "You got it," he said.

"I got it." The reference points gave me something to aim for. I was soon holding us at the correct angle, without hesitating and surging as much.

"While you're holding us on that imaginary 45-degree

line, practice letting us drift farther away along that line and then back close again. No matter what the distance between us is, you should be on that line."

As I drifted back, I wondered what Red flight thought about our yo-yo-ing around. Orange Three and Orange One were still lined up. As long as I stayed on that line, I would not interfere with Red flight. When I was a hundred yards from Orange Three, I accelerated gently to maintain the position. When I was sure I was holding it where I wanted it, I nosed forward to move back up the line. I was doing fine, but this wasn't a training flight. As I got close to the flight, they turned left in front of us to follow Yellow One. I had to decelerate fast to keep away.

"Try to anticipate the turns," said Connors. "As soon as you see Orange Three begin to bank for a turn toward you, you've got to bank even harder and slow down because you're on the inside of the turn. If you're on the outside of the turn, you must be ready to accelerate as they bank to keep in position. It's kinda like cracking the whip."

I slowed correctly and held my position, but when they leveled out on a north heading up Happy Valley, I didn't anticipate soon enough and fell back. I moved back up feeling very much like a student again.

"Closer," said Connors.

I thought I had been at about the right distance, but I moved closer.

"Closer." Jesus, it looked as though we were overlapped already. I moved in toward Orange Three until I could see Resler clearly through the left door. He turned and waved. I heard the tail rotor buzz again. Way too close.

"That's about right," said Connors. I strained to keep from leaning away. I could see that it was going to take some time before I got used to flying this tight. "When we land in the LZs, we've got to stay tight so everybody can get in. And if we stay tight in the formation, we'll all arrive at the same time, land at the same time, and get the fuck out at the same time. We can cover each other, too."

As Connors spoke, I barely noticed our trip up the valley. Yellow One's call brought me back to reality.

"Okay, Dukes, start your run."

The slicks slowed from 100 knots to about 80 to let the gunships fly ahead. They were B-model Hueys and slower than ours. They were also very heavily loaded with ammunition. They eased ahead of us, dropping at the same time. Our flight continued to decelerate to about 70 knots. We were on a long approach to the LZ, about five miles ahead.

The valley was scrubby here: elephant grass, occasional tall trees, and dry rice paddies. No villages.

I saw white smoke streaming behind the gunships, about a mile ahead of us. They were in position and prepping the LZ with their flex guns and rockets. As we closed the distance and dropped lower, I could see the rockets blasting earth into the air. At 300 feet up and a quarter mile away, Yellow One radioed, clearing us to use our door guns.

"No shooting until I say so," said Connors. Red and the gunner clicked their intercom switches twice. As Yellow flight moved toward the near end of the clearing, I could hear the faint crackling of their door gunners' firing into the tall grass and bushes. Moments later, when our flight was within a hundred yards of landing, and the other ships had started firing, Connors said, "Fire at will." The guns chattered out either side of our Huey. Our guns were so close behind our seats that it felt as though someone were slapping my ears with open palms at each shot. The grunts joined in with their rifles. My adrenaline kicked in and the world got quieter. I felt strangely detached from the scene. I concentrated on the cross tubes of Orange Three. Tracers from our own guns flowed in my peripheral vision. I felt Connors get on the controls with me. It was a rule. Just in case.

The sixteen slicks flared in unison with Yellow One and settled into the tall grass. My landing was almost automatic; I just mirrored everything Orange Three did. As the heels of the skids hit the ground, the grunts jumped out and bounded off toward the edge of the clearing, firing as they went. I saw no opposition, no incoming fire to remind me that I had no chest armor. None of us did.

Yellow Three waited fifteen seconds, then made his takeoff. We all watched for his tail to move and lifted when he did, staying tight so we wouldn't straggle and delay someone on the ground.

As we climbed over the forward tree line, I heard more machine-gun fire from our flight. "See anything, Red?" Connors said as I banked hard to the left to keep up with the flight. Out his side window the trees passed directly under us. "No, sir." The gunners were just having fun.

"Take a break. I got it."

"You got it."

"You did real good, Bob. I tell you, if that's the way the assaults are going to be, we'll all live through this."

"Yeah. I didn't see any return fire at all," I nodded. "Now what?"

"We go back to the pass and wait."

"Piece of cake," said Nate.

"Nothing to it," Resler replied.

"Heard the rumor? The VC are giving up," said Wendall.

We gathered around a paddy dike and exchanged greetings and impressions. The slicks were parked at Lima, a laager area we would come to know well in the next few months. It was a giant field of dry rice paddies about two miles east of the An Khe pass and next to Route 19. The gunships were still out supporting the grunts.

The dry ground ended a hundred feet from where we were parked, and wet rice paddies ran all the way to a distant village in the east. A group of water buffalo approached from the village. Some kids rode on the buffalo as they splashed through the mud of the paddies. At the head of the line was an old man carrying a staff. As they got closer the old man veered toward us while the others continued on.

"*Bon jour*," he said.

"What'd he say?"

"He said 'good day' in French," said Nate.

"You speak French?" asked Connors.

"RSVP," said Nate. He turned and talked to the old man.

The man grinned broadly when he heard Nate. His hands were gnarled, and his legs were covered with sores. He wore a loincloth and a black shirt. He talked excitedly with Nate.

"What's he saying?" I asked.

Nate shook his head and laughed as he turned to us. The old man watched. "He says that he is glad we came back."

"What's that supposed to mean?" asked Connors.

"He thinks we're French," said Nate.

"Dumb fuck," said Connors.

"Not so dumb," said Wendall. "The French fought a lot of battles around this road. As a matter of fact, they lost a big one right over there at An Khe pass eleven years ago." We followed his hand. "And a lot of the locals around here must have been in their units. Maybe this guy was."

"How do you know that?" asked Connors.

"I read."

Nate told the man that the French had not come back and that we were Americans. Then he had to tell him what Americans were and that we had come from even farther away than the French to help him fight the Communists from the north.

"Ho Chi Minh." The old man grinned broadly.

"He likes Ho Chi Minh?" Resler was shocked.

"He says that Ho is a great man and that someday he'll unite the country."

Resler's eyes narrowed with suspicion. "Doesn't that make him a VC?"

"I don't know," said Nate. "He seems like a nice guy."

We had C rations for lunch, coffee and cigarettes afterwards. We spent the time trying to stay out of the sun. But even in the shade the muggy air let no one escape the heat.

I talked to Wendall about photography, and about the French. He had read *Street Without Joy*, by Bernard Fall. His descriptions of how the French were destroyed around here by the same people we were going against got me depressed. The major reason our leaders felt we could win where the French hadn't was our helicopters. We were the official test, he said.

Connors kidded Nate about speaking French. "Only pansies speak French, you faggot."

Resler lay in the shade beside his Huey with his head propped against the skid so that his chin almost touched his chest. He was reading a paperback. A guy from the other platoon came by to show us a mongoose he'd bought from the kids. It was young and tame, and he named it Mo'fuck.

We waited. This was much worse than the assault. Worse than the assault? God, I could see how it was going to be. I would get so bored I would look forward to the battles. Waiting. I remembered a guy saying that if he knew he would be killed during his year here, he hoped it would be immediately so he wouldn't have to put up with the bullshit and the heat and the waiting. What *are* they doing?

I heard someone whistle through two fingers and looked up front toward the flight leader. Someone waved a hand in a circle over his head.

"Crank up!" I yelled, feeling suddenly refreshed. Orange flight scrambled into their ships and lit the fires. By sundown we had picked up the grunts without incident and had them back at row three. They had spotted nothing on their patrol. Wendall said that the VC wanted to see how we operated before they engaged us.

Leese found me in the chow line the next morning and told me that he and I and Resler were scheduled to go on a training flight that night. "Resler will sit behind us while you fly for a while, and then the two of you will trade places. The old man wants me to check you two out on night approaches and a short cross-country."

So, after a day of shovel work on the Golf Course, the three of us flew night training until midnight. We stayed very high, 5000 feet, but even then we got shot at over Cheo Reo.

"Fifty calibers," Leese said calmly as the big red balls drifted up in front of us. "And they're not even close." Even so, they were close enough for me.

The perimeter around our camp was visible from the air, a hundred-yard-wide swath with barbed wire, concertina wire, land mines, and claymores. We had two weak sections, one near Hong Kong Hill and another near the river. Both areas were constantly probed by the VC at night.

If we were seriously attacked, all the ships would be flown off somewhere. I didn't know exactly where, because I wasn't in the evacuation plan. For some stupid reason, a few of us were supposed to stay behind and defend the camp. We could hide in our assholes, as they say. Resler was also part of this team of gung-ho devils.

"Do you know we have shotguns?" he asked me one day. He was actually surveying our weapons, the ones we would use for this defense.

"They're illegal," I said.

"I know, but we have about two dozen of them. You and I and the rest of the *expendables* are supposed to know about them. You know, to use when they're surging relentlessly over the ditches, screaming '*Tien-len*!' "

"What's '*tien-len*'?"

"Wendall says that's what they yell as they make their final charge. You know, the human-sea tactics."

"Fuck Wendall."

So each night was full of expectations as I lay on my cot. Listening.

At about this time I read the first article about us in a worn copy of a news magazine being passed around. The tone of the article made us seem heroic because it sounded like an old newsreel. We were referred to by a tag we never used, the First Team. Pretty heroic-sounding, not as tough as "Leatherneck," but better than "Dogface." Beginning with our secret advance team, we had chopped out our 3000- by 4000-foot heliport near An Khe with machetes to make room for our more than 400 helicopters. It mentioned that our lineage went back through Korea and the Philippines and to General Custer.

The article went on to describe why we were there. The American garrisons established in the coastal enclaves had been the first step in helping the South Vietnamese hold on to the territory they already had. The First Team was extending deep into the middle of Viet Cong territory. From there our choppers would allow us to wander freely throughout Vietnam, hunting down the Viet Cong, undaunted by obstacles such as jungles, mountains, and blown-out bridges.

The piece ended dramatically with the accurate prediction that the First Team was not going to be the last such unit to punch its way into enemy territory. More air mobile units were on the way. Music, helicopters fly into the sunset, fade.

Connors was so high after one mission that he tried to snag the rotor with the tie-down strap while it was still slowly turning. A truck came down the line picking us up and slogged to a stop in front of his ship. Calls of "Get the lead out, Connors" came from the packed deuce-and-a-half. He was the last stop. As one of the blades swooped by eight feet off the ground, Connors held the chock and tossed the loose ends of the straps over it. They wrapped around the blade, tightened, and snatched Connors completely off the ground.

"Haw, Connors, you asshole, where'd you learn that trick?" Nate yelled, delighted.

Connors stood up and tried to dust the mud off the front of his fatigues. He turned to give us a snappy reply, but the whole truckload was laughing so hard that he just looked embarrassed and grinned sheepishly. It was great. Hooray, the company IP makes a mistake. And right in front of all of us, too.

"I would never do that," said Resler, sitting next to me at the back edge of the truck. "Would you do that?"

"Not me," I said. "Would you do that, Riker?"

"Not me," said Riker very loudly. "Only an Instructor Pilot asshole would try to lasso moving rotor blades."

Leese sat smiling next to me. He and I had flown the last mission together, my first hot mission. I felt pleasantly tired, calm, and strangely satisfied.

On our last few missions we had taken patrols out to Happy Valley, dropped them off, and waited at the laager area. On this last one, grunts had made light contact and reported several skirmishes where we had dropped them. We had taken three loads to the LZ; that was three trips in, so we would have to make three trips to get them out.

As we came in for the second pickup, Leese said that Shaker was making a bad mistake flying the same path over the trees each time.

"As soon as the VC get the idea that we repeat our flight path, they'll set up machine guns along it."

We were Orange Four. I was on the controls. I was actually having fun because I was getting pretty good at formation flying. Leese's complaint reminded me that there were people down there who did not give a hoot that I flew formation well. All they wanted was to shoot me down.

"What should we be doing instead?"

"Take a different path in every time. Keep 'em confused."

We landed the second time without incident. Half the grunts jumped onto the sixteen ships, leaving the rest to wait for the last flight. After a thirty-second pause to let us load up, Shaker took off over the forward tree line. We followed his path. The ship I was flying seemed much stronger than usual. I stayed with the flight with no trouble at all, not falling back, as some of the dogships did. When everything was working right, it was exhilarating, this air-assault stuff.

"See, he took off right over the same place he did last time," Leese said through my earphones. "No good," he mumbled. I thought Leese was being too cautious. I thought we were doing fine.

It took thirty minutes to get the grunts back to the Golf Course and return. Shaker led us back to the valley at 1500 feet and 100 knots. About five miles out from the LZ, he dove down to treetop level for the approach. This was the exciting part, the low-level flying. Leese had taken the controls on the way out, and I was getting a great demonstration of low-level flying. He stayed right in the trees while at the same time keeping us close to the number-three ship. Occasionally a treetop would flash between us and them. Leese would let the fuselage pass between two trees, tilting the rotor just in time to pop over the rushing branches. A hundred knots is not all that fast until you're as close to the ground as we were, where the effect of speed is confusing.

"Same flight path," grumbled Leese as the trees streaked by. Shaker was leading us back along the textbook approach, over the lowest obstacles, up a valley of trees toward the LZ—our third trip along the same path.

"Yellow Two taking hits!" Decker's voice shot through me.

"Muzzle blasts from three o'clock." A totally useless call. No call sign; therefore, no position.

As Shaker crossed the forward tree line, he called "Flare" over the radio to warn us to slow for the landing.

"White Two, receiving fire off our right side!" Connors's voice sounded above the crackle of his own machine-gun fire.

We would be at the hot spot any second now. I had already checked the sliding armor panel on the seat. It was all the way forward, but I still felt naked. I was light on the controls, feeling Leese's quick correction. Why the fuck didn't we have chest armor?

As our right door gunner opened up with the machine gun, I tried not to flinch. I watched the passing trees and clearings to see if I could see the enemy. If I could spot them first, I could direct the gunner. Maybe. I'm gonna transfer to guns the second I get back, I thought. At least they can shoot back.

Someone ahead had slowed too much on the flare, and we had to slow even more to keep from colliding. I felt like a fly in molasses, with the swatter coming down. A gunship raced by on our right side, smoke pouring back from his flex guns. The grunts in the LZ were yelling on the radio about taking fire. I glanced across at Leese, but I could not see his face. The LZ was just ahead. For some reason Leese was now wagging the tail as we crossed the last hundred yards before the clearing.

"I saw one!" The door gunner on my side exclaimed. His gun chattered loudly.

"I got him!" His voice was very shrill. "I got him!"

"Orange Four, Charlie at three o'clock," Leese called out for the benefit of the Red flight behind us.

"Sir, I got him!"

"Keep looking," I yelled. "Keep fucking looking!"

The slicks squatted into the LZ, and the grunts raced from their cover at the tree line and jumped on board. Red Four, the last ship, called out that all the grunts were on board. Shaker acknowledged by taking off immediately. He turned slightly left, following the same path out as the last two times. Before Leese and I crossed the forward tree line, a ship in Shaker's flight called that he was taking fire. Leese turned harder left and cut the corner of the turn that Shaker had taken, wagging the tail again. He stayed lower than anybody else, too. *In* the trees. As each group of four ships passed over the tree line, I heard calls about taking hits or receiving fire. ("Taking hits" meant, obviously, bullets hitting your ship. Visible muzzle blasts, puffs of smoke, or Charlie taking a bead constituted "receiving fire.")

We darted low-level among the trees for a mile or so before climbing to a safe altitude. It was quiet now. My shoulders drooped.

"Anybody hurt?" Shaker called.

No answer. Our ships had taken only a few minor hits. Decker had one bullet hole through a rotor blade. Nate had one come through his canopy. Another of our pilots, Captain Sherman, had one stopped by his seat armor. It had knocked the breath out of him when it hit. I saw the crater it formed on the bottom of his seat when we got back. That armor really worked. Now, if only we had something in front of us. A bullet-proof helmet would be nice, too.

"How about a plane ticket back home?" said Resler as we joked in the back of the truck. "That'll keep the bullets away."

Connors crawled into the truck after he tied the rotors down. "Anyone here tells anyone back at the company about my fight with the rotors gets a bad grade on their next check ride."

4.
Happy Valley

Americans are big boys. You can talk them into almost anything. All you have to do is sit with them for half an hour over a bottle of whiskey and be a nice guy.

—Nguyen Cao Ky, July 1965

October 1965

It had been raining steadily for almost half an hour when Connors decided to take the plunge. I saw his hairy ass bouncing out the back door of the warrants' tent. He was carrying his combat helmet and a bar of soap.

"Oh, this is the life!" Connors yelled from outside. "Oh, yes. Clean, clean, clean. I wish some of you smelly bastards would take the goddamn hint!" He broke into unintelligible song.

Banjo bounded outside, naked.

"The first of the smelly bastards arrives," Connors announced. "Welcome, miss. Set your helmet down here."

"Oh, thank you," Banjo said in falsetto.

Kaiser ran out, then Riker, then Nate and some officers from the next tent. Soon most of the company was outside, showering in the rain.

Even me. Against my better judgment. Last time we tried this, the rain stopped when I was fully lathered. Several of us had got caught. We had waited around, standing in the mud, soap suds tightening on our skin as it dried, for the rain to start again. It never did.

Thirty of us played around in the mud near the long washstand we'd made. A bunch of steel helmets stood on the frame as washbasins, collecting water in case the rain did stop.

"It's my dick, and I can wash it as often and as fast as I want," somebody yelled.

"Well, I never!" Banjo minced. "Don't you know that's bad for you?"

"Well, what the hell, I've been shaving my palms since I was fourteen."

There was the usual horseplay: cover-your-asshole-when-you-bend-over jokes, soap-bar wars, falling in the mud and rinsing off. It was the first good time we'd had in a month. And we got clean.

We found some more of our missing Conex containers. Most of our tents turned up. The warrant tent was divided: nine warrant officers in one GP. Luxury at last. Five of us—Leese, Kaiser, Riker, Resler, and I—each got an eight-foot section along one side. Nate, Gotler, Connors, and Banjo each got a ten-foot space along the other side. This was to be our permanent tent.

We decided to install a wooden floor and electric lights. Four of us went to town to buy the wood for the floor and the stuff for the lights. I was in charge of getting the wire and fluorescent fixtures because I lied about knowing how to wire the place. I wanted to go to town.

As our truck passed through the division's southern perimeter, the guard pointed to a man hanging dead from the flagpole. We'd heard about this the day before.

"The local authorities caught him with some American supplies. The Cav had them hang him up there as a lesson," he said.

The man's head was bent over to one side as the noose cinched into the skin of his neck. As we drove by, the angle changed, and I watched him turn slowly and then grow smaller as we continued on.

"Some lesson, huh, Gary?" I said to Resler, who sat across from me in the back of the deuce-and-a-half.

"Yep," he said. "Guess *he'll* never steal again."

We rolled into town. Resler and I jumped out while Leese and Nate went to park the truck. They were supposed to shop for wood while Gary and I looked for the electrical supplies. First, we decided to have a look around. We hadn't been here for a couple of weeks, and the place sure had changed.

Dusty old An Khe was now a jumping army town. New bars were packed to overflowing with hundreds of GIs. The streets were crowded with busy vendors from miles around.

We walked by a girl with a baby on her back, papoose style. I had seen her approaching some GIs from a distance, but I didn't realize what she was doing until we passed her. She was asking for money, then pushing the baby toward the shopper, making it clear that she wanted to sell the kid. My head twisted around to watch her as I walked. I finally figured it out and turned to follow her. Gary said, "What's wrong?"

"I can't believe it. She's trying to sell that baby!"

"Who?" Gary hadn't noticed, but when he saw where I was going, he said, "Oh," and followed me.

The girl was all of twelve or thirteen years old. I had started to tell her that it was wrong to do what she was doing when I noticed something peculiar about the baby. Gnats were crawling all over the slits of its eyes. It wasn't blinking. I reached out to touch its pale cheek. When my fingers touched cold skin, I knew I had discovered something I didn't want to know.

"Why does she want to sell a *dead* baby?" asked Gary.

"I don't know." My voice was calm, but inside I cringed away from her. She saw the fear in my eyes. I stared at her for a moment while I thought, How could you do this? Her weary eyes flicked away from mine to find another customer.

We walked across the street, which was strewn with gum wrappers and cigarette butts. I stopped to look for a hardware store.

Gary went on ahead. There weren't any stores around here, just bars. I saw Gary duck into one of the doorways. I followed him.

I stepped through the beaded curtain. The bar was crowded with GIs and bar girls. It seemed to me there were more bar girls there than there had been people in town two weeks before.

"Buy me a drink?" a girl said as I walked farther into the mob. She pushed me to a seat at a little table. Three more bar girls argued with my captor about who was to be my girl friend. As flies and gnats swirled around us and played in the beer puddles on the table, one of the girls got out of her lawn chair to sit in my lap.

"You numma-one jai," she chopped out in a monotone as she wriggled her buttocks against me. "You numma-one jai," she repeated and moved her face closer to mine, nervous eyes darting in a smiling mask.

I think she was just as embarrassed as I was. She was new at her job. So was I. I sat there wide-eyed but trying to look nonchalant, like a warrior out to get laid.

"You numma-one jai," she said again and pushed her little, flat nose against mine and breathed fish breath into my face. That breath and her limited vocabulary were snapping me out of grinning aw-shucks-ness. I wanted to leave.

She saw my expression change, and realizing that I was getting ready to make a break for it, she pulled out the reserves.

"You numma-*one* jai!" At last, some emotional inflection. Her eyes flirted. Her free hand reached down through her lap to grab a sincere handful of my crotch.

I jumped with surprise. I was embarrassed, also a little titillated, but I stood up and put the little masher back in her chair. Once I was standing, I used the opportunity to make it obvious I was looking for Resler. So I stood there for a minute searching through the mob, slapping little, sneaky hands away, but I couldn't find him.

"Shouldn't even think about it," I muttered as I walked outside to resume my search for a hardware store. I liked that girl; at least, my hormones liked that girl. Warnings about the dreaded Vietnamese cock-rot came to mind. "Sometimes amputation is the only cure" was one description of its severity. Another was "There are guys who have been *quarantined* in 'Nam since '61 trying to be cured." Or "I heard of a guy who woke up one morning and found his pecker had fallen *off*. Son of a bitch has to squat to piss. Damn."

"Hey, Bob, where you going?" I turned and saw Resler coming up the street toward me.

"To find some light fixtures, remember? Where were you?"

"Me? I was looking for you. Did you *get* any?" We both walked down the dusty street. If there had been horses instead of Jeeps, it would have looked like an Old West town. Most of the doors we passed were entrances to small bars. Small boys ran up to every soldier, yelling, "Hey, numma one, you. Want boom-boom? You come with me. Two dollar."

" 'Get any'? Not me, Resler. I don't need the clap," I said smugly. We turned off the main street into a narrow, shaded alley. There were shops here with everyday goods behind glass windows.

"You can't get the clap, Mason. You're immune." We stopped in front of a store window featuring cheap tools, wire, small electric motors, and light fixtures. This was the place.

"What do you mean, 'immune'?"

"It's one of the advantages of being an officer. We get 'nonspecific urethritis.' Enlisted men get the clap."

The shopkeeper spoke no English, but with the objects we wanted in plain sight, we had only to point. I bought nine fluorescent light fixtures—bulbs, ballast, and wire. Now if I only knew what to do with them.

The old salts had been through the development of air-assault techniques in the 11th Air Assault, plus the full-scale test of Air Assault II in the Carolinas; but the bullets had been fake, the enemy was really on the same side, and judges told you when you were dead. Now that we were flying in the real world, the old salts were unhappy about how their commanders forgot their training.

"I cannot fucking believe it," said Connors. "You'd think that we never even *heard* of air assaults, much less done it." We sat around a picnic table in the new mess tent after our first big assault in Happy Valley.

"Captain Farris, who decided to fly low level across the rice paddies like that?" Connors pleaded as he leaned toward Farris.

"Wasn't right, was it?" Farris answered.

"How the hell can they ignore all that fucking time we spent trying out every conceivable way there is to approach hot areas. Rice paddies don't offer any cover. You only fly low level when there's cover—trees, riverbeds, valleys—something." Connors looked deflated; Farris didn't answer. There was no answer.

I was depressed. I was supposed to be learning how to be an aircraft commander in an air-assault company. I wondered if I would live through the training program.

The day before, at six o'clock in the afternoon, sixty-four ships forming an entire air-assault battalion gathered on the Golf Course, loaded troopers, and flew to Lima, the laager area just on the other side of the An Khe pass.

At that point the old salts were already pissed off. We were to spend the night at Lima, only ten miles (seven minutes) closer to our objective, Happy Valley, than if we had stayed at the secure Golf Course.

After we landed, some of our ships went back to the division to fetch hot chow for us and for the five hundred grunts. Wendall, Connors, Nate—all the old salts—complained about being there. Wendall kept pointing out that the VC were famous for their surprise ambushes against the French right around where we were camped. It was not a good night. We slept in the Hueys. Everyone was jumpy, and the mosquitoes were intense. At 0400 hours we were awake, and at 0545 we cranked up and flew the troops to an already secured LZ north of Lima to group with another Cav unit for the big push.

Instead of flying at 1500 feet, this flight leader flew low level all the way. There were no shots fired, but it was a curious move. The gaggle landed and dropped the troops only to find out it was the wrong LZ. We reloaded the grunts, and on the second attempt we made it to the correct LZ. There we waited.

During the half-hour wait, the old salts really went wild.

"Why the fuck did we come up here low level?" Connors shouted, cornering Shaker. Shaker just shrugged and looked unhappy. Apparently someone new was leading this assault, but Shaker was a platoon leader and wouldn't comment about what his brethren in the braid were up to.

I was flying with Leese, but he didn't say anything either, just looked pissed off. The second stage of the assault was ready to commence. The word came back that we should expect to receive opposition on the flight route.

"I sure wish we had chest protectors," said Resler. "You know, if they know we're going to get shot at and they still fly low level, they ought to give us some armor, don't you think?" I nodded, distracted. Seeing the regulars bitch like this wasn't good for my morale.

The other unit stayed behind to form a second wave. Our gaggle loaded up.

From there to the real LZ were ten miles of rice paddies, spotted with villages ringed with trees and an occasional lonely coconut palm or clump of bushes—the kind of place you're supposed to stay away from, especially if you know it is controlled by the VC.

If it was going to be low level, then Leese was going to make it low level. He actually tried to fly the contours of the paddy dikes at 100 knots. I sat in the right seat with my hands and feet near the controls, waiting, tense, scared. We were Orange Three. On our right front, Nate and Farris flew Orange One; on our left rear, Sherman and Captain Daisy flew Orange Four. Across the V, Resler and Connors flew Orange Two. The distance between us varied as each ship dodged occasional coconut trees and tall bushes. Over the radios I could hear the prestrike commentary going on in my earphones. From 5000 feet above us I heard our battalion commander, the Colonel, telling us to maintain a neater formation as we spread out over the flat plain.

Up ahead, from the trees around a village, I could actually see muzzle flashes. Then I heard ships in the Yellow flight calling, taking hits. Then from small brush clusters I hadn't noticed before came more bullets. Soon the radios were jammed with hit reports. Above the din I heard "Do not fire into the villages; do not fire into the villages," from the Colonel. On our left, Sherman and Daisy kept lagging back and then lurching forward, sometimes beside and sometimes behind us. I heard them call "Orange Four, we're hit!" Then they dropped back out of sight. They had taken a burst through the cockpit, and the debris from the shot had temporarily blinded Sherman. Leese tried to stay away from the villages, but there was no way to do that; they were on the flight path. Tricky flying was to no avail here. I could stare at muzzle flashes for long moments as we flew straight at them, and the VC had the same amount of time to fire at us. Low-level flying was supposed to minimize exposure time, but it wasn't working here.

The flight up the valley was lower, faster, and much hotter than anything I had yet seen. By the time we got to the LZ, my brain was numb. I don't know what I would have done if Leese had got hit.

The LZ was no different from the rest of the valley except that there were more bushes. Despite an artillery prep and rockets from our gunships, it was hot. Bullets came from the bushes, from behind paddy dikes, from hidden trenches. The grunts leapt out as soon as we touched down, increasing the confusion. Up ahead a VC jumped out of a hidden hole and charged Connors's ship. Nobody on Connors's ship saw him, but his wing man's door gunner did. He shot him in the back.

The flight leader, noticing that we had indeed "received opposition," led us back to the first LZ at 2000 feet, proving that the concept that helicopters can fly higher than four feet was known to him.

Although most of the ships had been hit, only two pilots were seriously wounded and had to be evacuated. Ten more, including Wendall, Barber, and Sherman, got minor face cuts from flying Plexiglas. Leese and I were untouched.

A few days later Farris assigned me to fly a mission with Captain Daisy—another troop lift into Happy Valley. Half the ships were from the Snakes, half from the Preachers. The LZs were getting hotter by the day. No one ever figured how the VC always knew which clearing we would use for an LZ. There were thousands of possibilities, but Charlie would almost always be waiting for us in the one we picked.

Daisy thought of himself as a war historian. He was always the most vocal in the late-night discussions about how the war should be fought. As a matter of fact, I agreed with his premise that we should be taking real estate instead of bouncing all over the place in hit-and-run exercises. But except for the bullshit of our late-night strategy sessions, we had little in common.

I was in the right seat, first pilot's position, a courtesy extended by Daisy. Later I almost always flew from the left seat, even when I was the first pilot, because the left side of the Huey's instrument panel was chopped and I could see straight down to the ground between my feet.

We flew east to Happy Valley at 3000 feet. I was always happy to be flying high. Even higher would have been fine with me. Very few pilots were killed by staying away from the ground. We had eight grunts in the back. A crew chief and gunner in the pockets behind them manned the two machine guns on the new pylon mounts. About five miles from our intended LZ, the flight leader, Major Williams, radioed the sixteen ships to descend to treetop level for the final run. As we began our dive, smoke drifted up from the jungle ahead of us. There had been a thorough prestrike by the air force and by our own gunships.

Up to this point in the mission, Daisy had been flying. As we leveled out for the low-level run, Daisy said over the intercom, "You got it." I took the controls. I remember feeling complimented that he would let me take control at the most critical part of the flight.

The flight was really moving. Using the speed gained in the dive, the whole gaggle flashed through the treetops at more than 110 knots. I concentrated on the reference points and on keeping one or two rotor diameters away from the other ship. At the same time, I let us down into the trees as close as possible for cover. I had to read the ship to my right constantly to avoid it when it swerved left and right to miss the smaller trees.

We were about a minute away from touchdown when the gunships started firing. Some of the guys were now reporting taking rounds. The rule was that on the actual approach into the LZ, and in any circumstances where the crew was under fire, both pilots were supposed to be on the controls. This procedure was to ensure control of the aircraft if the one who was flying got zapped. Daisy didn't do this. As we got within thirty seconds of our landing and the lead ships were reporting taking hits, Daisy started to hunch down in the armored seat.

I had my hands full, but other than hitting one frond on a coconut tree, I was doing okay. From the corner of my eye, I saw Daisy moving. I risked a quick glance. He gave me a weak smile and hiked his chest protector up to his nose. He had one of the few pieces of chest armor in the company. He had worked his body down in the seat so that his ass rested on the front edge. This brought his head down almost low enough for his chest armor to hide his face. He could not fly from this position. Seeing my aircraft commander ducking for cover brought me to a new level of fear.

"Preacher flight, flare!" crackled in my phones. I pulled back on the cyclic and reduced collective to flare, and looked frantically ahead, trying to see over the nose of the Huey to get my first glimpse of the still-unseen LZ. My tail rotor spun just a few feet from the ground. I saw some bushes ahead, and I pushed the right pedal to swing the rotor away. Steeply, noses high, the whole flight rapidly decelerated for the landing.

Luckily for us, the fire at the back of the LZ was lighter. A couple of pilots up front had already been wounded. The grunts jumped out even before the skids touched the ground. I looked over, and Daisy was still under cover. I was going nuts. The LZ was riddled with sniper fire. Sand kicked up in front of me. Daisy stayed low even while I cleared the last trees on the way out. As I climbed higher, hit reports decreased, and by the time we had climbed to about 1500 feet, they stopped.

As the flight leveled off, Daisy said, "I·got it," and took control of the helicopter, just as though nothing had happened. I felt like punching my head to make sure I was still there.

I sat limply in my sweat-drenched fatigues and tried to figure out what to do. Call Williams and tell him I have a chickenshit on board? I leaned forward a little and turned to look at Daisy. Actually, I stared. He glanced over for a second, calmly. Who was crazy here? He outranked me; he was the aircraft commander, with years of experience. He had been flying daily with the other guys, and now he looked as calm as a clam. Yet I knew he had done what he had done.

Finally I said, "What happens if I get hit while you're in that position?"

"I'll have time." When I turned to look at him, he wouldn't look back.

I flew two more sorties with Daisy, back to the same area. Each time, he went through the same routine of passing the ship to me and ducking for cover behind his chest protector.

"How can that jerk be an aircraft commander?" I glared at Farris.

"Hey, Bob, jerk is a strong word." Farris looked un-comfortable as we talked in his tent after the mission.

"He endangered everybody in our ship and in the rest of the formation. Even I can tell a coward when I see one." Farris could see I was agitated. Maybe I was so an-gry because I had been just as afraid as Daisy.

"Yes, well, he's better than no pilot at all," said Farris.

After a long discussion with Farris, it became clear that Daisy was just one of the circumstances of war that I would have to accept. As a new warrant, though, I ended the discussion pretty firmly.

"I will never fly with him again," I said.

"Okay," said Farris, "you never will."

And that was that. No action was taken against Daisy.

"What did you expect, a firing squad?" Connors re-marked as we stood in the chow line that night.

"No," I said. "But maybe they could ground him and put it on his record."

"Look Bob, everybody in the company knows he's a coward. Even he knows he's a coward. The only people who will fly with him are the new guys like you, who don't know any better," said Connors.

"Well, I'm not flying with him anymore."

"Now, that," another voice interrupted, "is going to shake him up, Mason." It was John Hall. He had been standing behind Connors, listening to our conversation. "What you have to do," he continued, "is teach him a lesson."

"What do you mean?"

"You'll have to kill him," said Hall.

"Why are you making fun of me?" I looked at him seriously. "I really think something should be done, like grounding him, or putting him in the operations tent with his own kind."

John looked at me quizzically. "My, my," he said. "Are you accusing the operation twins of being," he paused to look around and continued in a whisper, "of being chickenshit cowards, too?"

Connors started laughing. Owens and White, from the operations tent, never flew in the assaults. The rumor was that they were logging combat time, though, for medals.

Hall continued, "If that's the case, Mason, it's going to be messy."

"What do you mean?"

"Well, how do you expect to eliminate all three of them without making a mess?" Hall grinned madly for a second and took a giant swig from his canteen full of Scotch—his trademark.

We laagered at Lima in the drizzling rain. Most of the crews in the twenty-four ships sat in their seats, though Nate had left his, beside mine, to visit around. The village looked distorted through the raindrops on the Plexiglas. The air was hot and still and humid. The rain brought no relief. Behind me the crew chief cleaned his weapon and the gunner slept. The ship beside me was the lead ship, and the Colonel had walked up beside it to talk to our CO, Williams. We had been here two hours. Waiting.

"Sir, I bet you never saw a .45 like this before." The crew chief, Sergeant LaRoe, leaned up between the seats and thrust his gun toward me.

"Looks pretty much like a .45 to me," I said. LaRoe was not a regular crew chief; he was a maintenance supervisor getting some flying time.

"That's what it looks like, sir, but it's my private weapon, not an army issue. I've made some modifications to it."

Great. A gun hobbyist. "Really?"

"Yep. For one thing, I've filed the trigger sear so that it only takes a feather to release the trigger."

"Why?"

"Well, if you have to squeeze too hard to pull the trigger, it throws off your aim."

"Oh. Great." LaRoe had the gun wavering a foot from my face, waiting, I suppose, for me to take it to admire. I didn't. He moved back suddenly and I heard a *click-clack*. I turned and saw him pulling the magazine out of the handle.

"Try it, sir. You won't believe how light it is. I filed away a lot of the metal."

"That's okay, LaRoe, I believe you. I'm sure it's a great little weapon, all right."

"C'mon, sir. Just dry-shoot it once." LaRoe pushed the gun my way, holding up the magazine as he did. "Here, I just cleared it."

I was thinking about how much LaRoe probably liked it here with all the real guns and bullets around. I should've thought more about how he had given me the gun.

It was cocked, so I held it gingerly, though I knew it was empty. I pointed it up and looked for a target. I had never been good with pistols, rifles being my forte. The sights wavered. A Huey lined up, fragmented by the water drops. I moved the aim away from the ship, an automatic precaution. The Colonel's back filled my sights. It was really crowded out there. So I continued to sight, holding the gun now with two hands, moving it around to find a clear, though dry, shot. I settled on one of the gauges on the instrument panel in front of me. I thought about pulling the trigger, and the gun exploded, slapping back against my hand. The gauge shattered and disappeared. I went deaf and into shock at the same time. Holding the gun in front of me, watching the smoke curl lazily out of the barrel, I considered turning around and killing LaRoe. However, the gun really was empty now.

I calmly passed the gun back to him. His face was white. "Nice trigger pull, Sergeant. No doubt about it."

A small crowd had gathered around the front of my Huey to examine the exit wound in the ship and the small crater in the mud where it finally stopped. The Colonel watched with his arms folded as I climbed out. The thought balloon next to his head read, "Dumb shit." Williams just sat in his seat behind him, glaring.

Up to that point I was just beginning to feel accepted by the old salts. Shit.

Williams did not say a word until we got back to the company after the mission. Before evening chow he sent Owens, the operations officer, to fetch me.

"Major Williams wants to see you in his tent." Hee, hee.

"That was the dumbest, stupidest, most moronic move I have ever seen in my life," Williams said. But he did not say I was an asshole.

"But—"

"There is absolutely no excuse for a supposedly intelligent pilot to play with a gun like you did."

"But—" I was trying to blame it on LaRoe.

"If you ever shoot up one of *my* helicopters again, I'll have your hide. You got that, mister?" He was a little tense, so I decided to go along with him.

"Yes, sir." I saluted on the way out.

Just to rub it in, they hung the remains of the omni-gauge—a radio-navigation instrument—in the operations tent. A little note was attached to one of the uncoiled springs explaining that it was the victim of the first shot fired at the Cav from inside one of its own helicopters.

The airfield south of the Cav was built by the French, and the Cav considered it part of their property. We occupied the airfield and the land around it, including an area on the nearby riverbank that was the site for our new shower station. The Cav engineers had set up a group of special water-processing trucks next to the river. They pumped the water through self-contained devices that chemically treated, filtered, and heated the water before pumping it inside adjoining GP tents equipped with wooden-slat floors and a dozen shower heads. About six of these trucks and tents made up the bathing area.

The first time I heard somebody yell "Shower call" I thought I was hearing things. Showers were something the advisers took in their established compounds and Special Forces camps. Sure, people in Saigon, Qui Nhon, Nha Trang, and Pleiku took showers, but weren't they tourists? Until now, the Cav's brass seemed to feel that the dirtier we got, the more depressed we became, which made us madder, which made us chop stumps harder, or something like that. Anyway, we were generally filthy, so the words themselves were a touch of comfort.

The day after I shot out the omni-gauge, twenty-five of us were packed into the back of a deuce-and-a-half, smelling ripe, on the way to the shower station.

Connors had actually taken a liking to me after the incident with the gun. For him, liking someone meant including that someone in a cynical observation.

"So, Bob, did the omni-gauge make a move toward you first, or did you just ambush it?" I was on the floor with my back to the cab. Connors and Banjo sat jammed together on the bench beside me. Resler sat next to me. He started to laugh at Connors's remark.

"Yeah, Bob," said my supposed friend Gary, "did it give you any warning before it attacked? Like moving its pointer or something?"

"Look, Gary," Connors inexplicably jumped to my defense, "anyone can make a mistake." I smiled at his generosity. "I mean," he continued warmly, "how was

Mason to know that the gauge was going to come after him like that!"

The truck pulled up. We jumped out, carrying towels and fresh clothes, and ran to the shower tents.

It was luxurious. Hot water filled the tent with steam. I stayed in as long as I could, rinsing away the accumulated grime and rejuvenating my spirits.

"We have got to build one of these back at tent city!" said Marston.

"Can we do that?" I asked.

"Sure. All we have to do is figure out how to get the water," said Marston. "And the only way I figure we can get to it now is to dig a well by hand. And we're on high ground, so the well would have to be deep, maybe a hundred feet."

It sounded impossible to me at the time. We did it a few months later.

After washing, we wandered around outside the tents drying in the sun and getting dressed. I sat in the sun for a few minutes, naked. The hot water had soothed my muscles. The sun seemed to radiate energy into my body. I was completely relaxed.

I was idly watching two guys from another company as they walked near a shower tent about a hundred feet from me when they disappeared in a shattering explosion.

With the noise, I reflexively looked out to the perimeter. Who? What? Are we being attacked? My throat tightened with fear.

Not VC. Not a stray mortar round. Nothing we were prepared for. The two cleanly scrubbed grunts had made a final discovery: land mines last and last. At least eleven years, anyway. The French had heavily mined the airfield before they were driven from An Khe, in 1954.

They put the showers off limits for a few days while men from demolition burned the weeds and grass away with flame throwers and swept the area with mine detectors. Mines were found and blown up, and the spot was declared safe again.

Flying out to Happy Valley became a daily routine. It didn't seem to make much difference, unless you happened to be one of the Americans killed during these few weeks. Or one of the supposedly three hundred VC. Then it made a lot of difference. To the rest of us, the ones alive, the result of our daily grind was fatigue and irritability.

Wendall said that the VC were bending with the force to learn more about how the Cav operated. He may have been right. They seemed to control the situation. We wanted them to stand and fight and they wouldn't—very frustrating for the "First Team."

To prove they controlled the valley, they not only would know which LZ we were going to use and greet us there but would also wait until we were in the middle of an extraction to shoot again. In between it was snipers from shadows.

I was getting plenty of practice. I got very good at low-level and formation flying. I learned how to function, even though I was scared shitless, by doing it over and over again. I had become efficient, numb, or stupid. I learned that everyone adapts and becomes concerned with the details of the job at hand, no matter how bizarre.

Although I flew with several different pilots as I trained for aircraft commander, I flew the bulk of my time with Leese. He taught me things that saved my life several times.

We were on an extraction mission up Happy Valley to pull out some troops we'd dropped off the day before. We heard the ships ahead calling in hits on the way into the supposedly secure LZ. Leese put the gunners on alert.

"Tell me if you see a target," he said to me. Putting my hands and feet lightly on the controls was a completely automatic response by this time.

Our company of sixteen ships was the last flight on this extraction, so all the troopers pulled away from the tree lines and jumped on ships in groups of eight. Eight was the load for today. (How much the ship could carry depended on the density altitude, which varied with the temperature and humidity and altitude. The hotter or higher—and therefore thinner—the air was, the less we could carry. The limit was calculated daily.) But there was a fuck-up. After everybody had eight grunts on board, there were four men left over, running around being turned away. Leese saw this and immediately called for them to run back to us. Confused, they ran to the ships that were trying to tell them to come back to us. Everybody was nervous. The four grunts didn't want to be left behind. Reacher jumped out the back and waved. They finally got the message and came back. I didn't understand Leese's decision. We already had eight troopers on board. I'd been in a ship that had dragged the trees trying to get out of an LZ with eight on a day like today. Twelve was impossible. Finesse, luck, experience—none of that would get twelve grunts off the ground today.

As soon as they squeezed inside, Leese brought in the power. I could feel the air pressure build up under the rotors as they struggled, pulling the overloaded ship slowly off the ground. Then he radioed Williams that he could make it. Leese stayed in a hover as the company took off. I glanced at the power gauge. It must have been broken. It indicated that we were using 105 percent of available power. As the company lumbered over the tree line, I heard them firing down into the jungle, then a few calls of hits, then we were alone. Leese nosed the stuffed Huey gently over, letting it accelerate across the ground to gain lift. He kept it just over the grass even as the trees approached. The gauges showed he was pulling maximum power, and we were running out of room. Then, somehow, he pulled in power beyond maximum. The ship groaned up and over the trees. I felt a tug when the skids hit treetops. The company had flown to the left at take-off, but Leese turned right. I scanned the clearings and bushes below, looking for muzzle flashes or smoke, but I saw nothing. The ship climbed much slower than normal. It took us a long while to get up to the safety of altitude, but we got there.

"How did you know this ship would be able to do that?" I asked.

"Simple. This is Reacher's ship," Leese answered.

"I don't understand."

"This is the only ship in our company that can haul a load this big. Right, Reacher?"

"That's right, sir, and more." Reacher's voice hissed in my earphones.

Reacher had made certain fine, illegal adjustments of the turbine. I had never flown the ship before—Leese kept it to himself—so it was news to me. An army training film I saw would prove that it shouldn't have worked, but it did. The ship muscled through an important career for the next two months, saving a lot of lives, until I destroyed it.

The ship may have been stronger than usual, but it still took a lot of experience to know just what the limit was, and how to milk it all out. Leese was good at knowing the absolute limits of aircraft. He made that a part of his bag of survival tricks. It was Leese who taught me that our fixed position in the assault formation was really fixed only as far as our horizontal movement was concerned. You could—as he demonstrated on several occasions—move the ship up and down relative to the formation without throwing the flight off. He would do this rapidly while the flight was being shot at. On final approaches to hot LZs he kicked the tail back and forth, making us waggle into the clearings. His theory was that any movement of the target made it more difficult to hit by confusing the enemy gunners. I adopted this style of flying. Whether it really made a difference didn't matter; I thought it did. It kept me occupied in otherwise hopeless situations.

We joined our company after the long climb up with the twelve grunts. Miles ahead of us the lead company in the battalion was reporting machine-gun fire near the pass at 3000 feet. Fifty caliber. We had never encountered these heavyweight calibers before. Our company veered off to avoid the fire. We could hear the commotion on the radios as voices in the static told us what was happening.

"Big as baseballs!" A reaction to the fifty-caliber tracers.

"Jesus, Yellow Two is going down!"

"Yellow flight, break formation!" They were spreading out.

I could see those tracers, in their lazy-looking flight upward, from five miles away. In between each tracer were four more bullets. A fifty-caliber machine gun spits out bullets a half inch in diameter and an inch long. When you held one of those slugs in your hand, it had a hefty throwing weight. When blasted out of a gun at 3000 feet per second, it had incredible power and range.

The battalion veered away from the ambush, leaving the gunships behind to harass the VC. I also heard the Colonel call for artillery. Five ships got shot out of the sky; two pilots were killed; the other crews were saved. A gunship was hit sixty-six times and still flew, a record one might boast about except that the pilot was killed. The copilot flew the sieve back to the Golf Course.

Our company flew back to division, dropped off the

grunts who had been out for two days, and picked up a fresh batch. We took these to Lima, and for the rest of the day we flew more troops and equipment out to this bivouac. By late afternoon we had logged eight hours of flying time. I was tired and looking forward to getting back to division. Home, these days, was where the hot food was.

This was not to be. It was decided by someone or other that we would stay out at Lima with the grunts.

It was the second time we had done this. As with the last time, there was no warning. No one had sleeping gear, or even a decent selection of C rations.

Half a battalion, thirty-two helicopters, landed at Lima. We brought a load of grunts with us, and they jumped off to join their fellows as soon as we landed. They formed a perimeter around this now valuable patch of Vietnam. Thirty-two hated helicopters and their crews sat in the middle of VC-land waiting for the mortars to come in. Why did we do this? Why park here, seven minutes from the safety of the Golf Course?

"Well, Bob, if we had to get here early tomorrow morning, which we do, what would we do if the pass was socked in?" Farris answered. He stood next to his cargo deck sorting through his C-ration case, looking for something.

"Fly over the pass and circle back," I said.

"Well, see, that's a maybe." Farris's square jaw was set for a thoughtful reply. "If the weather isn't too bad, we could; but if it was bad, we couldn't. If we couldn't, we couldn't be here until the fog burned off." His brow wrinkled as he paused, pulling his graying crewcut forward. "That would delay the mission, and some people might die because of it."

He stopped talking. He had found a box of C rations that hadn't been robbed of the coffee packet. He smiled like he was seeing an old friend. We were always short of coffee packets because we stole them from the boxes when we had to laager for any length of time. He looked at me. "So, do you understand now?"

"Yes, I can understand that." I shook my head as Farris offered me a can of cookies. "What I can't understand, though, is why we don't plan ahead. Why is it always a surprise that we're going to have to stay out overnight?" Farris listened while he levered the folding P-38 can opener supplied with each meal around the can of cookies. He pried up the olive drab can lid to expose three big shortening cookies, which he again offered to me. I waved them away.

"Well," he answered. "That's pretty complicated, why we don't plan ahead." He dumped the cookies out of the can, back into the C-ration case, and blew out the crumbs inside the tin. Then he bent down and scraped the can across the ground to collect some sand. When it was half full, he tapped the can on the cargo deck to level it. "Sometimes we know we're going to stay overnight, and sometimes we don't." He bent down to the ground and stretched out his arm, can of sand in hand, underneath the belly of the Huey. For a few seconds all I could see of him was his legs as he pushed the can up to the fuel-drain valve. Soaking the sand with jet fuel, he pulled himself back up, carrying his fueled stove. "When we do know that we will be staying out like this before we leave for a mission, we plan for it." He sat the stove on the ground. "When we don't know we will be staying out like this, we don't." He reached back into the C-ration case and found another can of cookies. He opened the can with a few deft twists of the P-38. "This"—his brown eyes scanned the busy scene around him as if for the first time—"this is an example of one of those times we didn't plan ahead."

"Isn't it true that we could get mortared out here and lose most of our aircraft?" I was determined to get a logical explanation.

He had punched some triangular holes just beneath the top edge of the tin-can stove. This would let the flame burn when he placed the can of water on top. When he judged that all was in order, he placed the stove and tin of water on the ground about ten feet from the Huey and lighted the fire. A dark-orange flame swirled out of the can, cooling to sooty smoke. He looked up from his hunkered-down position next to his creation and said, "Yes." Grabbing the tin of water by the folded-back lid, he gently lowered it to the stove. He kept it slightly off-set, to let the flame rush up one side of the tin. Small bubbles formed almost immediately on the side where the flame danced.

"So how can they possibly justify our sitting out here like this?" I asked. "If we lost the ships out here, it would set us back for weeks or months. Being a little late in the morning, if it came to that, seems a lot less risky."

The water boiled. He picked the can off the flame, using a small piece of cardboard to protect his fingers from the hot lid. Placing the can carefully on the ground, he tore the top inch off the foil packet of instant coffee and dumped the granules into the water. The brown granules dissolved, and the smell wafted past my nose. "You're right," he said.

"So, why are we here?" I asked, perplexed.

Farris stirred in sugar and coffee creamer from their packets. Standing up, he held a piping-hot cup of coffee in his hands. He took a careful sip, breathing in sharply as he did. "I don't know." He smiled at me. Noticing the surprised look on my face, he said, "Here"—he held the coffee toward me—"Want a sip?"

The sun was setting behind the pass. I left Farris sipping his coffee and went looking for Resler.

I stopped back by my ship, where Leese was busy heating up his meal. Our case of C's was nearly empty except for some single cans of scrambled eggs, utensil packs, two or three minipacks of cigarettes, and about fifteen P-38 can openers. No complete meals. Leese was hunkered down talking WWII next to the Huey with his buddy, the ex–Luftwaffe pilot, Gotler. I told him I'd see him later, and left.

Gary had a much better selection of food—half a case of unopened, individual meals—so I had dinner with him.

"Let's see. We've got beef with noodles, beef stew, spaghetti with meatballs, boned chicken, or scrambled eggs," Gary said as he sorted through the box on the cargo deck.

"Boned chicken," I said.

"Right."

We sat eating as the last glow of light faded behind the pass. Mosquitoes began to gather, and Gary and I rolled our sleeves down to protect our arms. It was hot and muggy in the valley and it looked like rain.

We talked of war. I told him about how Leese had got out of the LZ with twelve grunts on board. He told me about taking a round through his canopy. "One minute, I'm flying along okay, and then the next split second a hole appears in the Plexiglas, right in front of my face." He stopped to point at his palm, as though it were the windshield. "No sound; it just suddenly appeared. For a second I didn't know if this was the last thing I was seeing or what. I felt like an asshole, but I asked Nate to tell me if he saw any blood coming from my face or anything. When he said no, I knew I was still alive. I know one thing now, for sure: If I do get hit in the head, I'll never know it. It's very quick."

Nate's face suddenly flashed into existence as he lit his pipe. He had walked up to us from somewhere out of the darkness. He squatted beside us and puffed loudly on his pipe. It smelled good. I made another mental note to quit smoking cigarettes and take up pipes. Without realizing it, I was smoking three and four packs a day.

His pipe bowl hissed. His sharp, triangular face with its small, serious mouth glowed periodically as he puffed. When the glow died down, his features disappeared and only the top of his hat and shoulders showed in the cloudy moonlight.

He continued to puff, not speaking. His presence had quieted Gary and me. His greater experience as a helicopter pilot somewhat intimidated us. An original member of the old 11th Air Assault, he had been shot down once.

"Gary tell you about the round we took today?" he finally said.

"Yeah, that was close," I said.

"Yes, it was. And they say things are going to get worse."

"They" again. "How do they know that?" I asked.

"Wendall read it in a book. *Street Without Joy*." Fucking Wendall again. "The guy who wrote it knows how the VC worked against the French. He says the Cav'll get it good when we move farther north." He puffed again, but the glow had burned down below the top crust of tobacco and there was only a hissing sound in the darkness.

"How does he say we'll get it?" Gary asked. I could hear him crumpling the trash from the dinner he had just finished. He snapped each plastic utensil.

"He says that when we get farther north, the landing zones are only big enough for one or two ships at a time. The Cong dig a hole in the LZ and cover it with brush. Then they leave one or two men hiding there during our prestrikes. They stay concealed in the hole during the strikes and get us as we come, with machine-gun fire up through the cockpit," Nate said calmly.

He seemed to have received special training somewhere

that allowed him to live with such possibilities without a trace of fear. He even had a book to back his theories. He offered no solution to this trap, so I pushed for one.

"So, what can we do about it? How can we avoid the trap?"

"Nothing, except to keep your eyes out for a suspicious pile of brush in the LZ," he said, as if it were just one more critical maneuver we rank amateurs had yet to learn, as though the old salts already watched for those suspicious piles of brush.

I thought about the LZs, trying to remember the bushes. I remembered the confusion, the crackling door guns, the smell of gunpowder, the yells of the grunts, the radios going crazy. But bushes? Bushes were the furthest thing from my mind. How was I ever going to learn all this? What lesson would I miss that would cause my death?

"There's a lot to look for," I said, hoping someone would tell me not to worry about the bushes, that there was a trick to it.

"Yep," agreed Resler, "remember that giant bow and arrow, Bob?"

"Yes." I lit a cigarette from my third pack. "Tell Nate about it."

"Bob was in another ship, but we both saw it. We were about ready to land when a gunship pilot said he saw something suspicious."

"Was this last month?" Nate interrupted.

"Yes. When you told me about the bushes, I remembered that I didn't see what this gunship pilot was talking about. He finally made it clear when he asked us if we saw a wire or string going across the LZ. When he said that, I saw something, too." I could see Gary grinning as the moon shone briefly between some clouds. "The guy said, 'Watch this,' and dove toward the clearing while we circled. He fired a rocket into the middle of the clearing, and the blast broke the string. Suddenly a big pole, a sapling, shot across the clearing like a giant arrow. Whoosh! I couldn't believe it!" Gary and I laughed, but Nate just puffed away on his pipe.

He stood up suddenly, tapped the pipe on the heel of his hand, and stuffed it into his breast pocket, letting the bowl hang over the top. "Well, you guys are going to have to develop your observational abilities to match those of that gunship pilot if you want to make it through this war." With this gem of friendly advice, calculated to increase our feelings of inadequacy, he turned to leave. "Good night." He dissolved into the night to visit other friends.

I was getting the trash from my meal together when Gary said, "You know, there's something about that guy that makes me nervous. Do you think it's the pipe? My father never trusted anyone who smoked a pipe."

It rained all night. Four of us lay crammed into the Huey trying to sleep. The sliding doors were open to give us ventilation. I lay on my stomach on the deck, using my rolled-up fatigue shirt as a pillow, facing out the open door. Leese lay on his back on the other side with his fatigue jacket covering his chest and face. Reacher tossed and turned on the nylon sling bench at our feet. The gunner was half sitting, half lying against the aft bulkhead in the pocket behind his machine gun. His head was bent hard forward, forcing his chin into his chest. One would think that Reacher had the best bed. Not so. The bench was designed to hold four sets of buttocks, not a reclining body. Aluminum bars that would normally pass between sitting people forced themselves against the bones of anyone unlucky enough to have to sleep there. There was no alternative. The rain kept us inside because we had no tents.

I couldn't sleep. The air was heavy and dank. It rained

only enough to keep the air saturated, not cool. Occasionally a drop would splash against the deck next to my face and spawn smaller drops that landed on my nose. I moved closer to the open doorway, hoping that the rain would scare away the mosquitoes. The GI bug repellant I had borrowed from Reacher worked well for a few minutes, but faded quickly.

"Hey, Reacher," I whispered, "you awake?"

"Uh-huh." His dreary voice barely contained the anguish of the battle he was losing with the bench.

"Let me have some more of your mosquito repellant."

"Uh-huh." He sat up in the moonlight and handed me the plastic bottle from his breast pocket and lay back down with a sigh.

There was barely enough for one application. I put a few drops on my palms and rubbed my hands together. I wiped my face. If I could keep them away from my face, I could get to sleep. I rubbed the excess on my hair and arms and looked over at Leese. He was lying under his shirt, asleep. In the partly cloudy moonlight, I checked my watch: 0200. I held the bottle near Reacher and said, "Here." Silently he reached up and took it.

When I put my head back down, I heard gunfire in the distance. It lasted only a minute and stopped. Probably a nervous grunt. Of course, it could be the beginning of an attack. I imagined how our position looked from above. The thirty-two dark shapes of our helicopters sat on the lighter-colored ground. On our perimeter, some grunts hid in their pup tents trying to sleep while others stared into the gray foliage watching. From my imaginary viewpoint, I couldn't decide which would be worse, a wave of VC swarming in on us or a mortar attack.

A mosquito bit me on the neck and brought me back to my damp aluminum deck and the drizzle. Goddamn their vicious little bug brains. I decided to think about hating mosquitoes. I hoped my thoughts would broadcast hatred and loathing enough to scare them away. I thought of torturing mosquitoes for a while, pulling out wings, squeezing heads, ripping off legs, and they stopped biting! They actually flew away. Had I made a great discovery? Would this stop our having to take malaria pills? Just hating mosquitoes intensely kept them away? But what would happen when I fell asleep? Would they come back? They would. Probably with reinforcements, too. The thing to do, I reasoned, was to call a meeting, a rally, and concentrate on hating mosquitoes, en masse, all at once. We could corral them into one big mass of frightened bugs. I saw myself reaching into that mass and grabbing a big handful and squeezing. Their screams of horror and cries for mercy only brought a smile to my face. I reached for another handful.

I smelled coffee. Leese was up. I sat up to see where he was. Reacher was gone too. My watch said 0530. I blinked for a minute while my brain tried to join me in getting awake. My face itched. My hands itched. The mosquitoes had won.

Leese squatted on the ground on his side of the Huey, boiling water. Beyond him, I could see the camp coming alive. Little orange fires flickered, and gray shapes moved among the dull-green helicopters in the morning haze.

I rolled out on my side, walked around to join Leese, and in a few minutes I had my own coffee brewing. By 0700 we had all eaten, had coffee and cigarettes, preflighted the helicopters, and were ready to get the hell out of there. Three hours later, the crews were still hanging around their Hueys, sacking out if they could, or staring bleary-eyed at nothing, like me.

Farris and Shaker called us together for a briefing.

The action in Happy Valley had disappeared. The VC had slipped away in the night. The fifty-calibers had stopped firing, too. If they had been destroyed, there was no evidence on the ground according to the grunts. Action was postponed until another day.

Leese and I, along with seven other ships, were to spend the day flying ass-and-trash (people and equipment) around the division. The rest of the gaggle were going home to dig more ditches and haul more stumps.

It was all good news to me. I hoped the VC kept right on going to wherever they were going. And I would rather do anything than chop at stumps that were bigger across than a small crowd.

It was almost dark enough to use the landing light when we finished resupplying the patrols. I hovered over the uneven ground of row three looking for an empty pad to park. I passed some spots marked for another company. They had begun painting unit numbers on pieces of PSP at the head of each slot. When I found an empty spot belonging to us, it was half a mile from our company area.

Leese had called operations on the way in, and they sent a small truck to pick us up. We were the last ship in the company to get back, according to the driver.

It was well past sunset, but a soft glow still drifted in the west. The cool light glistened off the mud-slick road. The four of us sat under the canvas covering in the back of the truck, watching the Hueys pass by as the truck labored through the mud.

When the truck stopped in front of operations, we got out and said good-bye to Reacher and the gunner as they took the two machine guns from our ship back to the armory tent. Leese and I went to the operations tent to drop off the dash-twelve page from the log book. Operations used that page to record the hours flown by the pilots, crew, and aircraft.

"Welcome back, late ones," said Captain Owens snidely.

"We're not late," said Leese. "It took this long to finish."

"Just kidding, Ron," Owens said without a smile.

Leese handed the operations officer our dash-twelve. "I guess I'm just tired."

"We'll both feel a lot better after some hot chow," I said.

"Ah," Owens said. "The mess tent closed an hour ago." He looked uneasy.

"Did the cook save us something?" Leese asked.

"Have to check with him," said Owens lamely. He had forgotten to tell the cook to save some food for us, but he did not offer an apology. We glared. If only he would admit that he'd made a mistake, but he was learning to be defensive. In a unit of assault pilots, he and his partner, Mr. White, were the only two pilots not flying combat missions.

The next morning, we got a particularly depressing sample of how poorly our intelligence-gathering system worked. Leese and I flew the last ship in a formation of sixteen slicks. The whole battalion was in the air, loaded with troops to surround a company of VC who, according to our intelligence branch, were on their way across Happy Valley to Bong Son Valley, on the coast.

Once over the pass, we turned north up the valley. After twenty miles, the three slick-ship companies separated, to land at different places around the target. Our gunship company split up in three groups to cover us.

While the formation let down for the approach, I looked ahead to find the LZ. No trees or foothills this time; it was all cleared land, dry rice paddies, and sandy, weed-patched fields. It was difficult to believe that a company of VC could be hidden there.

The lead ships got closer, and their door gunners started firing. Their tracers plunged to the earth at nothing I could see.

About a mile from a solitary tree and a hundred feet off the ground, I saw two figures tearing across the sandy field toward the tree. More than thirty machine guns were trying to hit them.

When I was close enough to see the sand puffing up at their heels, one of them dropped his rifle and turned around to get it. He looked up frantically. The sky was filled with tracers, all coming at him. As he reached for his rifle, the sand boiled at his feet and he continued down, falling through the turmoil of bullets. He must have been dead before he hit the ground.

His terrified companion was still running for his life. As we closed in, there were even more machine guns following him, chattering. I watched amazed as the bullets churned all around the running man. "Give up!" I yelled. "Give up, you dumb motherfucker!" Realizing that he would not make it to the tree, he dove for the only cover available, a shallow depression in the sand. Door gunners all around us were pulverizing the ground around him, but Leese had not given our gunners permission to fire. That dumb fucking gook, the bravest man I had ever seen, rolled over with his rifle aimed high to take on our entire air-assault battalion, machine guns blazing. He might have got off one or two shots before he was torn to pieces.

The final score for that mission? Those two VC. The intelligence branch must have read their maps upside down. Connors suggested that the intelligence branch was getting its information from smuggled Chinese fortune cookies.

In a letter I wrote to Patience on October 15, I told about Nate getting shot down for his second time. He and Kaiser were on an ass-and-trash mission along Route 19 when a lucky shot into the engine brought them down. Riker and Gotler immediately followed them down to the road and picked them up. Before they took off, they stripped the downed Huey of its radios and guns to keep them out of the VC's growing collection of American supplies. Nate looked proud, puffing on his pipe as he told us about his adventure. Once again, he had walked away from near disaster. Everybody agreed that it might have been a different story if the other ship hadn't been with him. I resolved to fly higher in the secure area.

I also mentioned—or rather complained bitterly—that I had been bumped from a planned one-day rest and recuperation (R&R) to Saigon. The plan was that everybody would get a chance to visit Saigon at least once when a ship needed work that the Cav couldn't handle. By rotating the job of flying these ships to the big depot at Ton Son Nhut air base in Saigon, everyone could make a trip sometime during his tour. These trips lasted anywhere from one to three days.

My name had come up for the next trip. A one-day R&R. I was overjoyed and spent a couple of hours gathering my stuff together, getting Marston to trim my hair, and compiling a shopping list of requests from my tent. I felt great about getting away from the Cav, even if for only one day.

The plan changed. The trip was extended to three days. It was felt by somebody that it was a waste to give a three-day trip to a brand-new warrant officer, so the ship was taken instead by two captains. Farris was angry about the sudden change in crews. Williams, the man I had impressed by shooting out the omni-gauge, probably made the decision.

While the two captains took off, I grabbed an ax and joined the work crew on the Golf Course. My opinion of our company commander was deteriorating.

———

On October 17 I was declared right-seat qualified by Williams. Right-seat qualified meant that I was now considered skilled enough in the Huey and air-assault operations to be an aircraft commander. A regular old salt, almost. For the rest of the day I didn't even notice the mud as I slogged around the company area.

Another maintenance R&R trip to Saigon came up, and this time Riker and I were scheduled to go. A three-day trip.

Rather than fly directly to Saigon, over 250 miles of VC territory in a sick Huey, we first flew to Qui Nhon and turned south to fly down the coast to Vung Tau. From there it was only twenty miles to the big city.

We flew at 5000 feet, where the air was cool and the bullets couldn't reach, a beautiful two-and-a-half-hour flight. We were both pretty excited about visiting Saigon, country boys coming in to see the big time. The crew chief and gunner were also happy. We all cracked jokes over the intercom and talked about what we were going to do. At times like this, even the Cav seemed okay.

As we cruised low level over the city toward Ton Son Nhut, Saigon was a sea of tin roofs that stretched for miles. People below us waved as we soared only a hundred feet above their huts and gardens.

"See that?" I said. "See those people waving?"

"What about it?" said Riker.

"They are obviously happy to see us. No doubt they've heard all about us working and fighting our asses off in the highlands. No doubt they'll have a reception of happy, grateful people waiting for us when we arrive."

"No doubt," Riker said, shaking his head.

We left the Huey at the maintenance depot, jumped into a cab, and ogled the scenery on the way into town. The driver was obviously an ex–kamikaze pilot. His technique for passing cars was to lay on the horn, swing out into the other lane, and persevere. Etiquette demanded that under no circumstances would he change his mind.

We got a hotel room that featured peeling paint, no windows, and a john in the shower stall. This was fine compared to the moldy tents and dirt floors at tent city.

We rushed through quick showers and changed into wrinkled civilian clothes. No uniforms off duty. I had a pair of tan cotton pants and a green checkered shirt. A loose-fitting, wrinkled white shirt emphasized Len's scrawny build and freckled complexion. It was the first time we had worn anything but fatigues for two months. We looked it, too.

"Shall we go see what we can see?" I said.

"We shall," said Len.

I opened the door as a young second lieutenant walked by. He stopped, and without saying anything, he leaned against the door jamb and looked around inside.

"Pretty bad room," he said.

"You don't like the hotel?" I asked.

"No, it's not that." He smiled. "I live here. I've just never seen this room before. Really tacky."

"Seems fine to me," Riker defended.

"Well, maybe for a one-nighter, or for the enlisted. But it's not the kind of place I would normally buy."

"Buy?" I asked.

"Yeah. I buy and lease hotels and apartment buildings for the army. I'm a real-estate officer."

"Real-estate officer?" I was amazed.

"Sure," he said. "Somebody has to do it. . . . You guys from the Cav?"

I wondered if he noticed the horse patches on our fatigues inside.

"Yeah, how did you know?" asked Riker.

"I checked the register." He grinned. "I bet you guys

are really seeing some action up there in the highlands. We hear all about the Cav down here. It's really boring here. Never any action."

He was dressed in starched jungle fatigues and polished jungle boots. We didn't have either of these, because there was a shortage. My regular boots were rotting off my feet, so I was looking for a new pair.

"Can you buy fatigues and boots in Saigon?" I asked.

"Buy?" He looked at me, puzzled. "I guess so, but my stuff is issue. Don't you all have jungle gear? The Cav?" He paused. "Come downstairs to my room and I'll show you something. You're on the way out, aren't you?"

Down in his room, we saw twelve sets of jungle fatigues carefully spaced on his clothes rod, as neat as a closet in officer's candidate school. Two pairs of jungle boots sat on the floor beneath them.

"You were *issued* all this stuff?" My feelings were obvious.

"Sure. As far as I know, we have more than we need. I don't understand why you don't have this stuff at the Cav. I'm sure you'll get it soon." He smiled, but neither of us smiled back. "Anyway, don't you think this room is nicer than the one you got? Does yours have a john or a squat hole?"

"It's got a john in the shower stall," I said.

"Well, that's something. I hate to use those damn squat holes. Don't you?" he asked. I hadn't used one yet, so I didn't know.

"Well," I said, "we're used to using outside latrines."

"Yeah," Riker interrupted, "we shit in sawed-off 55-gallon oil drums. When they're full, we burn the shit with jet fuel. Smells bad."

"Damn." He was impressed. "You guys are really roughing it. I can't tell you how much I envy you. Action. Really getting out there and doing it." He paused.

"Well," he continued, "somebody has to be down here doing the bullshit."

"Assholes better not send any more of us to Saigon!" Len exclaimed outside the hotel. "If they do, the word about this fake fucking shortage is going to get back to the suckers!"

"That's right!" I said. "They'll have division-wide riots, and everybody will quit." I started laughing. "I know I'll quit. Hell, I'll quit right now just to save the trouble of going back and starting the riots."

"Me too!" yelled Riker. "I quit!" We were both laughing. Vietnamese passed by us on the sidewalk, smiling nervously at what I'm sure they thought were two drunken, possibly berserk Americans. Exhilaration overcame us, and as we hurried to the street corner where the pedicabs waited, we sang, "We quit because we quit, because we quit, because we quit . . ." until we sat down in the back of one of the bicycle-powered cabs.

Len gave the driver a piece of paper with the name of the hotel where we could find an officers' club. I think it was the International Hotel. The young pedicab operator looked at the paper and nodded.

He pedaled tirelessly, his ass never once touching the bicycle seat. "Must be in great shape," I said. "Probably a VC by night." A blue U.S. Air Force bus plowed by. It had heavy wire screens installed over each window.

"So you can't toss a grenade inside," said Riker.

Suddenly I realized how easy it would be for someone to run up beside us and toss one in the cab seat. It gave me a case of nerves. Too many people to guard against. I was about ready to bail out of this Oriental express when the VC up front turned around, smiling. We had stopped. Obviously he had read my mind.

"*Da wa no hai,*" he said, or something like that. I

translated it as "Ah so, jai, you die now!" Actually, it meant that we had arrived. Len and I got out and paid him. He took our money and pedaled off, to buy some ammo, no doubt.

We passed ARVN MPs at the front door. After a leisurely elevator ride we found ourselves under the darkening sky on the penthouse patio at the top of the hotel. Parts of the hotel served as billets for American officers stationed here, and this roof garden was part of their club. The beautiful Saigon night spread out beyond the low parapet.

The bar served any drink you could name, made with American booze, for a quarter. Civilians and soldiers mixed with round-eyed ladies from somewhere. They drank heavily and talked loudly. Their voices made me nervous. Weren't they worried that they might draw fire with their boisterousness?

As the bourbon flowed into my bloodstream, I began to warm to the occasion. Drunk enough to relax and be hungry, Riker and I got a table overlooking the city. We had rare sirloin and baked potatoes with sour cream served with a huge tossed salad of crispy fresh lettuce and juicy tomatoes that might have been grown on a farm near my hometown in Florida.

The events of the rest of the night are lost to me. I know that both of us drank too much. Actually, it must have been me who drank too much, because Riker at least knew how to get back to the room.

Starting very late the next morning, we went to the navy BX to pick up stuff for the guys back at camp. The Saigon warriors had a complete department store. The stuff for sale here was actually better and cheaper than the merchandise sold at PXs in America—Nikon cameras for $150. A Roberts tape recorder cost $120. There were clothes, tools, canned food, books, even cases of Kotex.

Riker suggested that evening that we go back to the restaurant I had enjoyed so much last night.

"Last night?" I didn't know what he was talking about.

"Sure. Don't you remember the snails you had?"

"I have *never* eaten snails," I announced. But I was beginning to have a vague recollection.

"Well, you had about three dozen last night. Besides, there's a girl there who loves you."

"A girl? Hey, listen, Len, I'm a married man."

"So am I." He grinned. "But I still get horny away from home. Besides, you don't have to fuck 'em, you know. It's nice to just sit and talk to a girl for a change."

After dinner that evening, I began to feel very sick. By midnight I was doubled over. Len took me to the navy hospital, where they treated me for dysentery. I spent the remaining twenty-four hours of the vacation sick in bed.

The following morning I sat in our Huey with a case of the blahs. I rode as a front-seat passenger while Len flew and I watched with growing apprehension the tin roofs thinning into rice paddies and jungles as we headed back to the highlands and the Cav.

On October 22 a news magazine ran a boldly optimistic cover story about how things were coming along in Vietnam. The magazine came out while Len and I were in Saigon. Everybody read it. The article summarized for us and the folks back home just how well things in Vietnam were going. Three months before, the Viet Cong had been ready to move in for the kill, and South Vietnam was ready to quit.

But now, South Vietnam was brimming over with confidence, nearly giddy with pride and power, an incredible change from the summer before. The reason for this remarkable turnabout was one of the fastest and largest military expansions in the history of warfare. Once again

I read about how we had chopped the brush and stumps with machetes so that our choppers would not cause dust storms on the heliport. So that we wouldn't get the feeling that we were training for jobs with the South Vietnam Parks Department, they mentioned that 2500 of us were fighting in Happy Valley.

The article closed with the reproval that it was the Communists who picked South Vietnam as the first domino in the string that was Southeast Asia. Now, it claimed, they were having second thoughts. The United States had met the challenge, and not just South Vietnam but all of Southeast Asia would eventually be strengthened by the remarkable and still-growing presence of American know-how, hardware, and lives. Even the mundane act of troops unloading at Qui Nhon was transformed in the article into waves of tough, scrappy GIs pouring ashore from fleets of troopships.

The article did not say a word about our effectiveness. With all our mobility, the VC still called the shots. We fought on their terms.

The slant of the article created an impression, and the impression was hard to forget. Even I believed that it must be only the Cav that was having problems, that things in general were looking up.

At about the same time the article was published, Pleime, a tiny fort sixty miles to the west of us, in Ia Drang valley, was under a siege that had begun on October 19. Although the attack seemed relatively insignificant at the time, it would be the event that would soon bring the Cav and the North Vietnamese regulars together for the biggest battle yet.

John Hall spent most of his evenings getting drunk with Jim Storter. But, unlike Jim, John was never found sleeping it off in a wall locker or a cardboard box in the supply tent. They drank for different reasons. Storter took solace in sauce because his wife was screwing around in the States while the VC were trying to kill him here. John's problems were all in Vietnam. He believed that the Cav was taking unnecessary chances with his life to prove that air-assault techniques really worked. He had decided after the first few missions that if the VC didn't kill him, the Cav would.

"We shouldn't be landing in hot LZs, Mason." John sat against the tent pole one night at my end of the tent. "In the Eleventh Air Assault, we were taught to move troops and supplies from one secured LZ to the next. We're landing in places so hot now that you'd think we were flying armored fortresses or something. Hell, we don't even have chest protectors."

"How do we avoid the hot LZs?" I asked.

"By landing the troops near the fight, not in the middle of it. It's no better for them to land in the thick of it than it is for us."

"They already seem to know where we will land," I said. "Did you see the size of those stakes in the last LZ?" We had landed in an LZ that had hundreds of ten-foot stakes in it. The same clearing had been empty the day before. "How can we be sure they don't pick up on our decision to land farther away?"

John took a slug of Scotch from his canteen and offered me some. I declined. "The way I see it, the VC are at spot X. Now, while they're there, they know the Americans can land all around them at any minute. So the VC commander, while at spot X, has some of his men stand guard at all the nearby clearings where he thinks we can land. He can even start a fight to draw us into a trap. It's a good strategy. If we attack him, he gets a chance to ambush us when we're the most vulnerable, in the helicopter."

"Okay," I said. "But, like I said before, if he *knows* where we'll be landing, as they obviously did yesterday, we'll always be landing in hot LZs unless we find the source of their information."

"Spies?"

"Sure," I said. "Did you ever ask one of those smiling interpreters you see running around sometimes to show you his South Vietnamese Good Guy card? I mean, all our plans have to be coordinated with the Vietnamese. That means they have to be translated and passed on to the gooks. So where do you think the leak is? The Pentagon?"

John took another belt of whiskey. "It seems hopeless. If we aren't able, with all our might, to get into landing zones without the VC knowing about it beforehand, what *can* we do? We should be out there marching, taking real estate and keeping it. Fuck taking little landing zones over and over again." He stood up suddenly. "Fuck it!" His anger and disappointment showed on his face.

"It's not that bad, John. Things are looking up. This war could end on our tour." I tried joking to cheer him up. "The press says we're going to win. When the gooks get that last issue, they'll roll over and quit. Nobody fucks with the press."

He smiled, darkly. My best lines were wasted. "Well, Mason, I'm going now." He turned to leave, but stopped. "Listen, if you ever want to sell your derringer, I'll buy it."

Even John started smiling the next day. We flew a lift to Happy Valley without even sniper fire. Charlie was not responding, almost as though he *had* read that article. We decided that we had won in Happy Valley.

As the threat of death seemed to subside, we got cocky. We flew around the division, Route 19, and most of Happy Valley without getting shot at. The VC had been out-classed by our power, seen the light, and would soon be giving up. I was feeling good. I was right-seat qualified, and battle-tested (I thought), and the VC were giving up. I felt my confidence soaring because I was a member of the team and the team was winning.

I was so happy about maybe living through this war that when we had to scramble just before dinner that night, it didn't bother me. In fact, when I got back from the screwed-up mission, I wrote Patience an exuberant letter. I submit it here as a record of my last happy letter from Vietnam.

[October 23]

We had an alert to pick up some troops as soon as pos-sible at about two minutes before evening chow. We all ran out to the aircraft thrashing through the mud screaming, "Where's my aircraft? Where are we going? What's the freqs? Gosh, I'm getting all muddy!" and other confused remarks because somebody screamed fly and didn't say why.

With the thought in mind that the first one airborne is the leader, we hurtled into the air like a swarm of blind bugs and flew off into the sunset.

The leader called for an aircraft to guide him to the area and followed the wrong one. After we landed in the wrong LZ, the leader discovered his mistake and zipped off to find the right place. Since he didn't both-er to say not to on the radio, all the rest of us zipped off with him. It's rather hard to appreciate the sight of seven helicopters trying to fly formation on a leader who thinks he's alone unless you've done it!

Hooray! We found the right place! Naturally since it was an emergency, we sat on the ground for half an hour waiting for the "eager, waiting" troops.

While waiting, the happy, boisterous company pilots all gathered together and sang:

(*The Fuckee's Hymn*)
He stood on the steeple
And pissed on the people
But the people couldn't
Piss on him.
Amen

After this rousing chorus we grabbed our steeds and leaped into the air, pressing onward, ever onward in the true flying horseshit tradition!

We didn't really sing that song while on the mission, but we did when we got back that night. It was the company song from the old days.

The siege of Pleime was still going strong in Ia Drang valley, but in our battalion nothing was happening. You would think that this lack of combat while we just flew ass-and-trash around camp would please us no end. But as the period of relative calm continued, it seemed to last an eternity. It wasn't that we wanted to fight so much; it was that if there was no fighting to do, let's go home.

As the assaults became routine, even the grunts got lax. As we loaded up for one mission, a grunt got on board carrying an M-79 grenade launcher. He slammed the butt of the weapon on my cargo deck and the thing went off. The grenade went up through the roof of my Huey, up through the spinning rotor blades. After several seconds, it fell back down through the blades and landed next to the ship five feet from my door. It didn't go off. When I turned around to yell at the dumb grunt, all I could see was me holding a smoking .45 with the same sick smile on my face. However, Resler was with me, and he yelled at the guy. An armorer later explained to me that the grenade had to travel a few feet before it spun enough to arm itself. Its hitting the roof so soon had stopped the process. Nevertheless, from that moment on I had all M-79s checked for safeties on before I would allow them to board.

We took these troops to Lima for the umpteenth grouping for the umpteenth mission up Happy Valley. They got out, and we got orders to haul ammunition, fuel, and food for our infantry. Many of the loads were rigged as sling loads, so I got some practice. I had sling-loaded stumps once with Connors.

"Okay, they've got the lines on the mule. Let's go," said Leese. (A "mule" was a small, four-wheel-drive vehicle.)

I picked the ship up to a high hover about twenty-five feet above the dry rice paddies. One grunt stood on top of the mule and held a loop attached to four support lines over his head. Another grunt stood fifty feet beyond him to direct me as I approached. I was flying from the left seat. I hovered forward, and the man holding the loop disappeared between my feet as I moved over him. The swirling wind from my rotors whipped the fatigues of interested watchers to a blur. With hand signals he apparently made up as he went along, the guide out front tried to shepherd our whirling beast to squat above the mule.

"Did he touch his nose?" I yelled. "What the fuck does touching his nose mean?" I wanted to show Leese that I knew what I was doing.

"It's all right, Bob. You're lined up fine," said Leese.

"Reacher, lean out and tell me what the fuck's going on. That asshole looks like he's conducting a symphony!" I said.

"Yes, sir." Reacher lay down on his stomach and pushed the top half of his body out over the edge of the deck, holding on to his monkey strap. "About three feet left and five down."

"Look at him. Now he's telling me to cut power!" The idiot guide was drawing his hand across his throat.

"You're far enough down. Just a couple of feet to the left," Reacher instructed. "There. They put it on the hook." Meanwhile, the guide became so interested in the hookup, he simply watched.

I pulled enough collective pitch to take up the slack and let the Huey pull itself to the point of equal tension on the four lines above the load. From there, I increased pitch gently to pull the thousand-pound mule into the air. As the weight transferred to the Huey, the increased pitch of the blades slapped the air loudly. With the load off the ground, the instruments showed that I had enough margin of power for takeoff. The cyclic felt stiff as I corrected for drift.

The fuselage of a helicopter in a hover is like a weight at the bottom of a pendulum, the top being where the mast joins the rotor hub. The addition of a sling load makes it a sort of compound pendulum. Coordinating the movements of the two takes practice. Pushing the cyclic forward, for example, causes the rotor disk to tilt forward, pulling the fuselage along after the rotors like a rock on the end of a string. With the sling load hooked up, the swing of the fuselage is slowed by the inertia of the attached load. The helicopter acts like it doesn't want to move forward. There's a danger at this point that the pilot will apply even more forward cyclic to overcome this resistance. When the momentum of the two pendulums coincides, the ship will be nose low and sinking. Pulling back quickly to correct for this causes the fuselage to swing back first, then the load, each at its own rate. When everything stops tugging weirdly at the ship, it'll be moving too slowly and can stall back to the ground. All this means that when I started to move forward for takeoff, I wanted to keep going.

"Jesus, I'm up here, twenty feet over his head, and he's signaling me to come to a hover!" I was getting ready to land and go choke the guide.

"The load is clear, sir," said Reacher.

I moved slowly forward so as not to antagonize the two pendulums. The guide, however, stood his ground, frantically giving me unrecognizable signs. The heavy load swung toward him, accelerating. I was hoping to hit him, but he dove clear at the last moment.

As we climbed up, Leese said, "Disarm," and reached up to the overhead panel and flipped off the circuit breaker for the electrical hook release. We kept it on when we were close to the ground because the pilot could hit a switch on the cyclic control grip to drop the load in a hurry. Airborne, the hook was disarmed to prevent it from releasing itself accidentally, which it occasionally did. Somebody in our company had dropped a mule from 3000 feet the day before, and the grunts were still pissed about it. The thing looked as though it had been dug out of a King Kong footprint.

I could feel the tugging as the mule fought the wind while I flew back to the Golf Course. For the landing, all I had to remember was to start the deceleration early and keep the ship high. Leese armed the release. I settled into a high hover with the mule ten feet off the ground and slowly approached the ground guide at the maintenance depot. I watched him suspiciously, but he knew what he was doing. As I felt the mule touch, he signaled to release, and I pushed the button on the grip that caused the belly hook to release the lines. The Huey lunged toward the sky when the load released, and I let it go, pulling in even more power to urge it up to a nearly vertical climb, turning to the right.

"Cowboy," said Leese, but when I looked over to him, he was smiling.

The combat lull continued, but I was still getting plenty of flight time. Eight or nine hours a day was typical. I could've stayed out longer because of the unhappiness at tent city. Boredom was breeding widespread depression. With apparently no one to fight, the Cav was just twenty thousand men sitting in the middle of Vietnam in their mildewing tents, wondering why they were here.

It didn't help that the anti-Vietnam-war demonstrators were becoming prominent in the news. With the company in such a black mood, the protesters' remarks were so much salt in our wounds. No one likes being the fool. Especially if he finds himself risking his life to be one.

"I think I'd rather kill one of those fuckheads than a goddamn gook!" yelled Connors. He threw a magazine on the ground inside our tént. "Cocksuckers think they know everything! Did you read that?" He spoke to no one in particular. It was late, and I was up, writing a letter on my cot. "That asshole says that Ho Chi Minh was sold out by the Americans! He says that gook was once our ally and that we let a British colonel turn South Vietnam back to the French!" He stopped. I looked over. He sat on his cot in his shorts with a beer in his hand, staring angrily at the canvas wall behind me. His face calmed when he saw me. "You ever hear that before, Mason?"

"That was the first time," I said.

"Do you think it's true?" he pleaded. To him, I was an educated man, having been to college for two years.

"No," I said.

The siege of Pleime in the Ia Drang valley ended on October 27. For more than a week the North Vietnamese Army (NVA) units had launched one fanatical attack after the other. Six thousand uniformed regulars hit the tiny fort, twenty miles from the Cambodian border, with waves of men and mortars and recoilless rifles. They fought from as close as forty yards away, using trenches they had secretly installed under the advisers' noses weeks before. Inside the triangular compound, hundreds of mercenaries from the Montagnard tribes fought under the leadership of the Special Forces advisers, the Green Berets. From II Corps headquarters, thirty miles north at Pleiku, a relief force of tanks, artillery, and a thousand ARVN infantrymen was sent. Some ships from another assault company in the Cav lifted in 250 South Vietnamese Rangers. Then our air force bombed and strafed. In six hundred sorties, twenty planes were hit and three were shot down. A helicopter was downed, and an American sergeant was killed trying to get to it. When supplies ran low inside, the air force dropped pallets of food and ammunition into the compound. Two men were killed when one pallet landed on them. Another pallet went through the mess-hall roof.

It ended with heavy losses to the enemy and, finally, their retreat. *Time* gave us some of the credit for scaring them away. "As elements of the U.S. First Cavalry swarmed in by low-flying helicopter, the Viet Minh faded reluctantly away from Pleime. 'They're headed west, straight for Cambodia,' groaned one Aircav platoon leader. 'I suppose we'll have to chase the bastards all the way there.' "

He was right.

5.
Ia Drang Valley

You should never believe a Vietnamese. He's not like you. He's an Asiatic. The Vietnamese of today has seen too much dishonesty, too much maneuvering, and he doesn't believe in anything anymore. He automatically thinks he's got to camouflage himself. He doesn't dare tell the truth anymore because too often it brings him unhappiness. What's the point of telling the truth?
—Nguyen Cao Ky, in *Life*, July 23, 1965

November 1965

Action walked in the door with Shaker. The wiry black captain watched intently as we packed for the battalion's move to Pleiku. I saw him suppress a smile as he looked up the aisle at the confusion he'd caused. His half smile faded quickly as several pairs of eyes met his expectantly. Another announcement? He lowered his eyes quickly.

"What the fuck kind of way is this to live?" he suddenly shouted. "Look at this!" He kicked a clod of dirt from the aisle. "You people *like* living on a dirt floor?"

I was about to tell him we hadn't had time to put the floor in yet when Connors said, "Yes, sir."

"What?" Shaker turned to face Connors.

"That's right, sir, it's great like this." Connors beamed.

"And why do you think it's great like this, Mr. Connors?" Shaker asked, smiling reluctantly. He liked Connors.

"Well, sir, I don't know about the other guys, but I'm a heavy smoker, and this place is like living in a giant ashtray. Flick a butt anywhere. It's great!"

Shaker covered his mouth to hide a smile. He recovered quickly when he turned around and saw us staring at him. We were staring at him because he smiled and also because he never came in here unless he had bad news.

"You can put the floor in when we get back from Pleiku. Anyway, that's not why I came here," he announced. "Where's Riker?"

"Right here." Len stepped away from a rice-mat partition hung between his cot and mine.

"What's that for?" Shaker looked at the rice mat.

"Privacy."

"Oh." He started to say something, but didn't. "Riker, you and Mason have got a mission to fly a tactical command ship for the grunts. Around Pleime. You gotta leave now because they're in a big hurry." The rest of the tent resumed packing. "Leave your stuff here and we'll take it with us when we go to Pleiku." He turned to leave. "So get your shit together and come to the operations tent for the details."

"How long are we supposed to stay with the grunts?" asked Riker.

Shaker stopped at the door. "How the fuck should I know?" he said gruffly. Then, quietly, he said, "Just today, I imagine," and left.

I sat in the left seat and watched the road through the chin bubble. I had counted four blown-out bridges so far.

Riker had never been to Pleiku before, so I held up my worn-out map and gave him a guided tour. "Up here at the right side of the Mang Yang pass"—I moved my finger to the spot—"this place is known as the French Graveyard."

Riker nodded. "Big, grassy mountain?"

"Yeah."

"I see it. Couple miles ahead?"

"Yeah, that's it." I let go of the intercom switch and looked over the black ledge of the instrument panel. My hand rested on my knee when I wasn't talking. On the left side there was no floor switch for the intercom, so I had to put my hand on the cyclic to pull in the trigger switch one click to talk to Len. I clicked in. "When we get closer, you can see a whole bunch of places that look like graves all over the side of that mountain."

"I can see them."

"Well, down there beside it, in the pass, the French lost hundreds of men in a big ambush."

"When?"

"I don't know. Ten or twelve years ago?"

"Damn."

"And up ahead there, where the road starts to turn southwest, is where those guys got shot down last month. Fifty-caliber."

Riker nodded and pulled in some pitch. The Huey climbed 500 feet higher.

"That make you nervous?" I asked.

"Naw. You?"

"No," I said, breathing a sigh of relief. "At the pass we're halfway to Pleiku and about twenty miles from the Golf Course."

"On the horizon now, at about ten o'clock?"

"Yeah, that's Pleiku," I said. "Actually, what you see is the big airstrip at New Pleiku. That's where the air force and the II Corps headquarters are. A couple of miles beyond that is the village, and a little bit this side of it is the adviser compound, Camp Holloway."

We cruised quietly for a few minutes in the cool air above the pass. I looked down between my feet and watched the road change. After its steep climb up the other side, it gently descended through the foothills into the rolling elephant grass of the plains beyond.

Camp Holloway was about ten miles from the western border of a long valley extending from Kontum, thirty miles north, to the Chu Pong massif, forty miles southwest. The muddy Ia Drang River, which meanders by the massif on its way to Cambodia, was the valley's namesake.

"It's pretty on this side of the pass," said Riker.

It was pretty. The tall grass flowed over the hills. The soil was red where ravines and road cuts exposed it. With the exception of the two American compounds and the village of Pleiku ahead, it looked uninhabited from the air.

We were close to the adviser compound. "Where we're headed is about five miles due south of that little airstrip at Holloway," I said.

"Where's the company going to set up camp?" asked Riker as he looked out his triangular window.

I checked the map. "See that big field there, between Holloway and New Pleiku?"

"That's it?"

"Yep. It's been named the Turkey Farm."

Riker and I landed at the edge of a sea of tents: the grunts' camp, called the Tea Plantation, adjacent to a real one owned by a Frenchman.

The man we were assigned to support, Grunt Six, was a full colonel, or "bird colonel," as they say. He ran toward us in a crouch, ducking the rotors. Two captains followed, one wearing pilot's wings. They climbed on board and grabbed the radios their assistants handed them. While they set up the radios, the captain with wings leaned forward between our two seats and pointed to a spot on a map where he wanted us to go and motioned thumbs-up for takeoff.

Riker brought the Huey up to a hover and nosed it over to go. As we climbed to the altitude they wanted, I turned around to watch.

Grunt Six and the other captain sat on the bench seat facing forward. Coiled cords ran from their headsets to the pile of radio gear on the deck in front of them. The other captain, assigned to aviation-liaison duty with Grunt Six, sat forward on the floor with his back to us. He was supposed to advise the grunts on how to use the aircraft and the crews assigned to them.

The infantry commander and his assistant studied a plastic-covered map mounted on a square board balanced on the assistant's knees. They talked through their own intercom system, and the assistant made marks on the map with a grease pencil.

Grunt Six switched his radios constantly from one channel to another. I tried to listen in, but I didn't know which frequencies he used. Once in a while, he would come up on the channel I monitored.

"Red Dog One, Grunt Six." The number six in the call sign always meant boss, chief shit. Red Dog One was the radio call sign for one of his subordinates, probably a lieutenant, leading a patrol in the woods below.

"Yes, sir."

"Status."

"No contact yet. Still proceeding on azimuth one-eight-zero."

"Roger, maintain, out." He immediately switched channels to someone else. He was all business. There were thousands of men down there among the bushes and tree clumps, over their heads in elephant grass, trying real hard to make contact with the retreating NVA.

If I hadn't loved flying so much, the job would have been boring. All we had to do was fly compass courses that crisscrossed the south end of the valley. The aviation captain hooked into our intercom and gave us the new headings as Grunt Six dictated.

At the far south end of the valley, about eight miles north of the Chu Pong massif, Grunt Six had established a forward command post on the top of an isolated hill. At about two o'clock the captain gave us the coordinates and told us to take them there. The valley from the hill to the massif was all flat plains covered with elephant grass. It ended where the Ia Drang River changed course and the ground rose sharply to a massive plateau of rough, tree-covered mountains that descended gently on the other side into Cambodia. At the base of the rise was the beginning of a series of sharp, jungle-covered foothills that twisted their way up into the massif. It was in these foothills that the enemy was thought to have a base.

Riker flew to the lone hill covered with tall brown grass and a few small trees. Circling once to see where they wanted us to land, he made the approach. As we came in over the edge of a sharp drop-off covered with tall bushes, a pup tent flew away in our rotor wash. Its owner bounded off through the tall grass trying to catch it. We landed about a hundred feet from the headquarters tent, sinking into the grass up to the cargo deck. The captain with wings jumped out and signed a cut-throat and Riker shut down the Huey.

Grunt Six marched off to the tent. His other assistant said, "We'll be here an hour, so get something to eat."

So far, so good. This command-ship flying was okay. At least we weren't in the assaults going on near Pleime.

While the rotor was spinning down, Reacher pulled

the C-ration case from the aft compartment. I walked past the still-spinning tail rotor to see how the kid who lost his tent was doing. He was peeling his tent from a bush below the steep edge of the hill, up to his armpits in weeds. The tent was snagged on something, but he finally got it loose. Clutching it to his chest, he trudged back toward me.

"Sorry about that," I said. "We didn't see you when we came in."

"Oh, that's okay, sir." He smiled and threw the tent down near a bush. "I didn't want you to see me. I'm building a camouflage position here." He pointed proudly to a pile of brush near his crumpled tent.

"Well, that could be a bad spot for it." I nodded back toward the Huey. "You're downwind, and you'll be on our approach path every time we land."

"I never thought of that." He wiped his forehead with his T-shirt, pulling the stretched-out bottom up to his head. "How come you don't come in like this?" He made his hand stop in midair and drop straight down.

"Vertically," I said.

"Vertically. Can't a helicopter do that?"

"We can in a pinch," I said, "but it's dangerous. We like to keep some forward motion so we'll be able to autorotate in case we lose power. What we can do, now that we know where you are, is to come in a little steeper, which should keep you out of the rotor wash. But another helicopter coming in here will just blow everything away again."

"Well, thanks for explaining that. But I think I'm just going to rebuild it here, stronger." He smiled and started back to work.

"You want beef with noodles or boned chicken?" Riker came up beside me.

"Neither."

"That's all we got."

"Boned chicken." Riker threw me the box and walked back to sit on the edge of the cargo deck.

Riker and I and Reacher and the gunner sat around the Huey and ate lunch. Grunt Six was in the headquarters tent, making plans.

I approached the headquarters tent after lunch. About five of the fifteen or so grunts on the hilltop were outside the tent hanging around. I said hello and sat down on a stack of C-ration cases. Beyond the group of T-shirted enlisted men, I could see the wooden legs of a map tripod through the tent door. The meeting between Grunt Six and his men was still going on.

A Vietnamese soldier walked out from the tent. He was dressed in the camouflaged, tight-fitting, big-pocketed uniforms of the Vietnamese Rangers. He was, however, not a ranger but an interpreter. He was smiling. A smile is a safe thing to hide behind. I waved him toward me, happy to see an interpreter. I saw this as a chance to learn how the people here really felt about the war. The Cav was so isolated from the ARVNs, I had never had a chance before.

"Hello," I said.

"Hello," he said.

"I've been wanting to talk to a Vietnamese who spoke English."

"Yes," he said knowingly.

"Well, how do you think we're doing so far?"

"Yes," he nodded.

"No, I meant *how* do you think we're doing? Are we winning?"

"Yes, that could be so," he assured me. "How are you?"

"Me?" Must have trouble with my accent. "I'm fine. Fine."

"I am fine, thank you." He bowed slightly.

I looked quickly over to the smiling faces of the grunts and realized that they all knew he couldn't speak English worth a shit.

"Great," I said. "I understand that this hill is going to sink into the valley today."

"Yes, that could be so."

What fun. "They've been thinking about moving Saigon up here this weekend so we won't have so far to go for R&R." I heard a little cheer from the watchers.

"Saigon." He nodded with happy recognition.

I was just getting into it when a private stepped out of the tent and yelled, "Hey, Nguyen." The smiling, wide-eyed interpreter nodded abruptly and ran back to the tent. At least he knew his name.

At about three o'clock we loaded up and flew back to the Tea Plantation. Grunt Six had us drop him off near a waiting Jeep. We hovered over to a fuel bladder at one end of the field to refuel. We returned to the hilltop command post by ourselves. I made the landing steeper, and this time the brush blew away, but the tent stood.

At the HQ tent the officer in charge, a captain, showed us what they were up to on the big map on the easel. The gist of the business for the rest of the afternoon was to move men around. They were ganging up the patrols where they had had some action.

We flew all over the south end of the valley all afternoon without incident. Sometimes a single ship was safer than a group. Our explanation for this phenomenon was that the enemy thought a single ship was scouting for them, so they didn't fire and give away their position. Later we found out we had been flying over Charlie all day.

By late afternoon we were looking forward to rejoining our company. They'd be at the Turkey Farm by now, eating inside the adviser compound. In a real mess hall.

Taking real showers. At this point we had logged six hours, and Riker and I were both pretty tired.

"Tonight we want you to fly the old man again," the captain at the command post told us after we landed. "You'll be flying this end of the valley so he can talk to his people here." He pointed to the map. "Shouldn't take more than a couple of hours. When you finish, though, we want you to stay at the Tea Plantation. The Colonel isn't finished with you yet."

The couple of hours became more than four, and we finished at ten o'clock. Grunt Six sped away in his Jeep among the thousand tents that crowded the field. We were left to fend for ourselves. Len had mentioned that our company and our gear were only five miles away, but Grunt Six wanted us to stay here.

"Park your chopper down by that Medevac," he said to Len before he left. His deep voice matched his thick build. "Go find those boys from that helicopter and tell them to give you a place to sleep. Gotta have you boys around here in case I need you quick."

The "fatigue factor" in flying helicopters for long periods is high. The constant vibrations, deafening noise, and total concentration required made the army restrict pilots to four hours of flight time per day. Four hours was a good workout, and still twice as much time as some of our jet-jockey cousins in the air force flew. Naturally, the realities of combat pushed us beyond these limits nearly every day. Six or eight hours was pretty common in the Cav. Len and I had just flown ten hours for Grunt Six, and as we watched him disappear into the darkness, we felt numb. We were both so tired that we didn't want to mess with the C rations. Instead we wanted to find that other helicopter crew and get a place to sleep.

We found them about two hundred feet from their Huey in a four-man tent. "I don't know why he told you to find us. There's no extra tents here," a tall warrant officer told us. "You're welcome to sleep on a couple of our stretchers if you want. They'll keep you off the ground."

"That would be good," said Len. "Our crew chief and gunner can have the Huey to themselves." He nodded toward our distant ship, invisible in the darkness. "No fun trying to sleep all four of us in there."

"Well, you're welcome to set up right here." He pointed to the ground in front of their tent with a flashlight. "We even have a poncho you could string up for shelter."

"Naw, that's okay," said Len. "Looks like it'll be clear tonight. Won't have to fuck with it." I looked up at the starry sky. It was inky black, with bright jewels of stars. The stars looked almost the same here as they did on the other side of the world. Polaris was closer to the horizon. Big Dipper there. Orion. I had spent a lot of time looking at the stars as a kid. I kept hoping that I'd be able to see the Southern Cross.

Len had been calling my name several times. "Bob, you okay?"

"Yeah, just looking for constellations."

"Well, I don't know about you, but I'm tired enough to sleep standing up. I'm going over to get one of those stretchers."

"Me, too."

I went first to our ship to make sure Reacher and the gunner knew where we would be. I picked up a stretcher from the Dust Off ship. "Dust Off" was the radio call sign for the Medevac helicopter. I was developing the habit of calling everything by its call sign. I put the stretcher under my arm and walked off toward the Big Dipper, in the direction of the tent. With the activity of our setting up the stretchers, the Dust Off pilots stayed up to talk awhile.

I was pretty quiet. While Len and the tall warrant officer talked about their recent adventures, I sat on the stretcher looking interested, somehow believing that they could see my face when I couldn't see theirs. I sat that way for a minute and then decided to lie back and look at the stars.

The back of my hand touched something cold and sticky beneath my head. I sat up quickly and said, "What's that?"

The other pilot from the Dust Off crew pointed a flashlight at the stretcher. A small piece of human flesh was spotlighted on the green canvas. "You gotta brush them off pretty good," he said. "Stuff sticks like crazy." He shrugged with professional aplomb and reached over to push it off with the flashlight. The red part stuck tightly. He finally peeled it off with his fingers and tossed the unidentifiable piece of person into a clump of grass.

I was pretty awake now, so I listened.

"One of our ships went into a hot LZ and picked up four wounded," the warrant said. "They were doing okay until they took off. Flew right over the machine guns. Charlie shot the living shit out of them. Killed the whole crew and all the wounded when it crashed."

His buddy with the flashlight continued. "And we got shot down during Pleime," he said as he wiped his hand on his trousers. "We landed too close to some trenches the gooks had dug right next to the Pleime compound. The guys inside didn't know that Charlie was that close. Anyway, we went in to pick up some wounded. They got us on our approach. Killed the gunner. We had to jump out and run for it. We just made it into the compound." He paused while his partner grunted in agreement. "That's why we can't land in hot LZs anymore. Charlie thinks the red cross on the side is a bull's-eye. Fuckers don't respect the Geneva accords at all."

"Geneva accords?" I said.

"Sure, the agreement is that ambulances, even air ambulances, are supposed to be left alone," said the shorter warrant.

"I don't think Charlie ever signed the Geneva accords. I know the United States didn't," I said. I was becoming argumentative, against my will. "The accords don't allow shotguns, either, but I know we have crates of them at our company for perimeter defense." I put this fact on the scales to balance Charlie's transgressions against Dust Off. I had always enjoyed playing devil's advocate, and here I was, behaving true to form, defending our enemy.

"Whose side are you on?" the tall warrant asked.

"It may sound bad," I said, "but if neither side signed the agreement, then one side can hardly accuse the other of breaking the agreement."

"You can if the other side is a bunch of fucking gooks," the tall warrant said angrily.

The opposition made an interesting point. He also outweighed me by forty pounds. "Well," I said, "that's another way of looking at it."

"I think rules for war is a crock of shit," said Riker. I couldn't see his face, but I knew he was smiling.

"I agree," the tall warrant said. "I think that war is war, and we should get this one over with and go home."

"We might do that soon," said Riker. "If we can trap the NVA before they get to Cambodia, we'll knock the shit out of 'em." Riker paused, and our hosts grunted their agreement. "After we knock the shit out of 'em, I think they'll want to quit fighting and make peace. They'll want to give up and go home."

"I'm for that," I said.

It was eleven-thirty. Everyone was tired, and we decided that we would put off winning the war until tomorrow morning. I switched ends on the stretcher to avoid the stain from the piece of meat.

Lying on my back, I watched the stars again. *Stuff* watching stars. My thoughts drifted to the other side of the world, where Patience, at this same moment, would be getting Jack to the table for lunch. When I last saw him, he was fourteen months old and just beginning to toddle around without falling down too much. He liked to play a game of not doing what his mother wanted him to do.

"Time to eat, Jack," she would say. "No." He would laugh and run to the bedroom. "Jack, come to the table." Jack giggled in the bedroom, climbing up on our high bed. Patience came to the doorway and looked in, smiling. "Jack, you come eat right now. It's not time to sleep."

"No." He laughed defiantly.

"Yes. Now, get up," she said firmly.

"Come on, get up." Riker shook my shoulder.

"What?" I opened my eyes, and the stars were still there. "What time is it?" Maybe if I pointed out what time it was, he would change his mind.

"Twelve. We've got to go on another mission, right now."

"Mission?"

"Yeah. Come on. Grunt Six is going to meet us at the chopper in ten minutes."

We got to the ship and woke up Reacher and the gunner. Minutes later, I could see the tent shadows cast by Jeep headlights dancing across the side of the Huey. The Jeep stopped fifty feet away. Figures walked from behind the headlights into their bright cones of light. Silhouette tunnels of darkness arrowed out and wavered in front of them.

Grunt Six approached Riker and me with his two captains in tow.

"Which one of you is the aircraft commander?" Grunt Six asked gruffly. Light gleamed off the sweat on his neck.

"I am," said Riker.

Grunt Six paused a second to look at Riker's name tag and his inked-in warrant insignia in the faint light. "Mr. Riker, I have a captain on my staff who's an aviator."

"Yes, sir," Riker said.

"I want you to let him sit up front to get a little stick time tonight."

"Sir, we have orders not to let anyone outside our company fly our ships."

You tell him, Len.

"Mr. Riker"—Grunt Six grew taller and louder—"you and your helicopter are assigned to me. You are now in *my* unit, and I want you to change the crew for this flight." He moved closer to Len as he spoke. His thick, burly body contrasted with Len's tall lankiness. "I think that Mr."—he glanced at my name tag quickly—"Mr. Mason should stay here."

"I don't think that's right, sir," Riker argued. "Bob was assigned to fly this mission with me."

"Okay, no problem," Grunt Six assented. "Let him sit in the back."

Some compromise! Me sit in the back? An infantry commander can't push us around. Riker will put him straight.

"Okay," said Riker unhappily. "He'll sit in the back with you and your assistants."

"I won't be coming along this time; just my assistant," said Grunt Six. "He'll use your radios."

What the heck, I thought. It's only for one flight. It wasn't until we were already in the air that I realized how bad it really was. I had given my replacement my helmet, and I sat on the bench seat deaf and dumb. Reacher and the gunner sat in the darkness behind me, in the pockets. They had helmets. I'll make Reacher give me his. No, they have to know when to use the guns. I felt like a fish out of water. I was just a passenger on my own ship and not even able to communicate with anybody on board or on the ground. I burned with embarrassment and anger.

So I sat in the blackness feeling stupid while Riker flew. In the dim glow of the instrument lights, I could see that the dumb shit sitting in my seat wasn't flying after all.

We circled the moonless sky. The ground was the darker half of the universe where the stars didn't shine. Somewhere below, a patrol leader talked to the captain. The captain would then call Grunt Six and tell him what the patrol leader was up to. And so on. We circled for about an hour. I stared at elusive, dark shapes below and watched for tracers. The constant whine of the turbine and the rush of wind were my only company.

I felt the ship sink. I looked at the altimeter, but it was too dim to read. Were we going to land? My heart raced. Without the controls at my hands and feet, I felt like a worm on a string.

We continued to descend; the changing air pressure in my ears and the relaxed whine of the turbine told me that. I could make out the very vague shapes of trees in the starlight. Getting close. To what?

The tracers rushed silently up and past us like a string of red UFOs in a hurry. Quiet, relentless, pretty. For pilots, the bullets are always silent until they hit. First a short string of them, then a longer burst leapt up from the dark. The ship lurched and we banked steeply away. "What's going on?" I screamed in the noise of the ship. If anyone had heard me, I wouldn't have heard his reply.

I leaned out the door and looked back. The tracers lagged behind. They couldn't see us, and were aiming at sounds. They stopped. This was too much for me. I had never felt more alone and exposed in my life. I called for reinforcements. That meant I promised God that I would quit smoking and I would never touch a whore, not even get a hand job, and I would even believe in Him if He would only let me live.

The Huey turned back to where the guns were. "You didn't believe me!" I yelled. "Please, God, goddamnit, please believe me." As I groveled in the back, waiting for a sign that He heard, they shot at us again.

Tracers are bright at night. They glow bigger and look closer than during the day. Just being in the same sky with them made me nervous. I was seeing this stream nearly head on, which meant that it was aimed our way. If you saw the line of tracers from the side, then they were going somewhere else. Riker banked the ship hard, turning away from their path. The glowing stream searched vainly in the darkness behind us and stopped. Riker kept turning and headed back to the Tea Plantation.

That was it! No more backseat flying for me!

When we touched down, I bailed out and jerked open the left door where the captain sat. "You're not flying one more second, Captain!" I yelled, surprising myself. I was not open to argument. We were next to a fuel bladder, and the light of a Jeep shone from behind me. The captain had been scared. He looked at me, handed me my helmet, and said, "Don't worry. That was enough for me."

By the time we had refueled and loaded up Grunt Six's other assistant with his radios, it was almost three in the morning. This tactical-command-ship bullshit was lasting longer than either Riker or I had expected. It wasn't over yet. Now they wanted us to fly back to the place where we had been shot at so the captain in the back could direct artillery.

I flew high while the captain talked to a trapped platoon. During my jittery stint as a backseat pilot, we had flushed out the position of a machine gun that was part of a force of NVA keeping the grunts immobilized. There were several skirmishes in the area, and we spent the next three hours, until dawn, acting as a radio-relay ship for Grunt Six and as forward observers for the artillery. The patrol was not overrun.

At dawn, God said, "Let there be light and also let Bob and Len go back and have some coffee." The excitement left with the coming of dawn, and I suddenly felt wrung out. The relentless, insistent sleepiness that comes with that time of day was getting to me. I made a dream-like approach to the Tea Plantation and bounced it in roughly. Riker giggled like a drunk at my efforts. I started laughing, too. Not funny laughter. It was more like sobbing with a smile. As we sat in the cockpit, the captain hauled his radio over to a Jeep. He turned and signaled a "cutthroat" because I still had the Huey running at operating speed. His gesture struck me as immensely funny, and I keyed in the intercom to say so to Riker, but he beat me to it.

"See that, Bob. He wants to kill himself!" Oh, that was rich. We laughed hysterically at this for so long it hurt.

Reacher appeared by Len's door and shrugged. "What's wrong?" he said. I wiped the tears away and shut down the Huey.

Time to find some coffee. Reacher stayed behind to take care of his ship. He had either nerves of steel or brains of custard, because he had fallen asleep during the last flight. Now he was energetically climbing all over his helicopter, inspecting every nut and bolt and fluid level. It inspired me to see him doing that. It was a tedious job at best to keep a Huey running properly, and Reacher did it without complaint.

"You love that helicopter, don't you Reacher?" I said.

"Yes, sir. I also don't like flying around these fucking jungles in a machine that could quit and fall out of the sky."

We sat at a table made of used ammo crates. I was eating some reconstituted scrambled eggs when the captain with wings joined us.

"You guys must be tired." He marveled at what must have been a couple of haggard faces. "I tried to get a ship out here to replace you. No dice." He stopped to light a cigarette. "There's going to be a bunch of troops lifted down there today." He pointed to the south. "Looks like we're stirring up some real trouble. More and more skirmishes. Anyway, your battalion said we were lucky to have you. All the rest of their ships are being used in the lifts."

"No problem," said Riker, rising to the occasion. "After this breakfast and coffee, we'll be ready to go." His freckled face brightened with a smile.

"Good, because we're going to need you all day."

I groaned. I would've groaned louder had I known that Resler had been on the ground with the trapped patrol. He was shot down trying to resupply them and spent the entire night crewing a machine gun with the grunts. But I wouldn't find that out until I got back to the Preachers.

We flew alone in the valley between Pleime and the massif, moving small patrols to new locations. We were so tired that caution, proficiency, and even fear left us while we dropped into virgin LZs without company or cover. I had felt pretty good after breakfast, but by ten o'clock I was pranging the Huey again. So was Len. "Pranging" was an unofficial term we learned in flight school. It was descriptive of both the sound and the deflection of a helicopter's skids during a very hard landing—the kind of landing that would get you a pink slip and a dirty look from your instructor.

I was having lapses in concentration. I would set up an approach to a clearing and then just sit there sort of drooling stupidly until the ground hit the skids. When we hit, it would shake me enough to wake me for a more or less good takeoff. But when the flight lasted more than ten minutes, I would fade. Len and I took half-hour turns. We were both rotten.

Noon marked twenty-four hours since we had left the Golf Course. It seemed like a month. We had been flying nearly twenty of those twenty-four hours. No wonder we both snickered when we pranged our landings. We were delirious with fatigue.

We continued to fly all the rest of the day and into the night. I don't remember refueling. I don't remember the landings. I don't remember who I carried or where I took them. I didn't record the number of sorties or anything else I was supposed to do. We were complimented later about our calmness under fire. I don't even remember the fire.

Grunt Six's man called us and said we could quit. We got back to the Tea Plantation at ten that night.

I fell asleep on the Dust Off stretcher without conversation.

At six the next morning, we were back in the air for our zealous commander, whose entire air force consisted of our Huey and us.

It was a very beautiful morning for flying. I had a canteen cup of coffee with me while Riker took his turn at the controls. The coffee and the cool air cleared my mind. I felt much better after my night on the stretcher.

The day was bright. Deep-blue skies blazed over the shrub-covered hills and valleys of elephant grass. Below, on the side of one shallow hill, eroded ravines had exposed the red earth in a pattern that resembled a drawing of a tall-peaked hut, an aerial signpost set there to show us the way to the Montagnard village nestled in the jungle just a couple of miles beyond.

I sipped some coffee as we passed over the village. The familiar ground plan featured one hut in the middle of the village that was at least four times taller than its neighbors. I think this was the chief's hut. Parallel to this row of huts was another row of small cubical buildings that sat off the ground on four posts. There was one of these directly across from each dwelling. I saw these villages peeking out of the jungles and tangled hillsides all through the highlands. They seemed peacefully removed from the business at hand.

We landed at the hill and were briefed. Same routine as yesterday. The captain on the hill told us, "You gotta move the guys from this list of coordinates to this list of new coordinates." He handed me a piece of paper. "Keep your eyes open. The net is beginning to tighten up on those gooks, and they might get fidgety."

When he said "gook," I saw that dumb interpreter smiling broadly. On the way out of the tent I said, "How are you this morning?"

"Yes." He nodded.

Riker and I were pissed off about having to go out there and fly single-ship again. Where's the rest of our company? Why haven't we been relieved yet? The little sleep we got last night was not enough. We were both "off," and we were bouncing the Huey again. We finished moving the squads around by noon and returned to the hilltop for lunch and to pick up our new mission. On approach, I noticed that the kid had given up and moved his tent somewhere else. I shut down and the rotors were still turning when an aide from the tent ran out with a message.

"You got to get back up. A Jeep was just mined five klicks from here."

Reacher, who had just opened the cowling of the turbine to check something, slammed it shut as the four of us jumped back into the Huey while I lighted the fire. A medic jumped in as we got light on the skids.

The medic briefed us by talking through Reacher's microphone as we cruised over the trees at 120 knots.

"The Jeep was carrying six men from the artillery brigade. The two that were in the front seats are alive. The other four are either hurt or dead. They've got a prickten radio (PRC-10), so they can talk to us."

I saw the smoke ahead at the spot that matched the coordinates scribbled in ball-point on the medic's palm. "There they are," I said.

We landed in front of the Jeep, or what was left of it. It was twisted like a child's discarded toy. The edges of the crumpled and torn metal were smoking. It had been destroyed by a howitzer round buried in the road and triggered remotely. Landing in front of the Jeep was dumb; there could be more mines. It was one of those cases where we trusted the ground guys to pick the spot. A sergeant ran up to my door. He told me through my extended microphone that two of the guys in the back were still alive. "Should we put the dead on board?" His eyes were wide.

We nodded. They started loading up. The two wounded were unconscious, torn and bloody and gray.

One of the dead had had his right leg blown off with his pants. I didn't see the other body yet.

Some journalistic instinct struck me and I took a couple of quick pictures as the wounded were carried toward us. I got one shot of a grunt carrying a severed foot when I realized what I was doing. I stopped. It seemed like the ultimate violation of privacy. I never took another picture of wounded or dead.

I was twisted around in my seat, watching them load, directing Reacher through the intercom. The man that had lost his leg had also lost his balls. He lay naked on his back with the ragged stump of his leg pointing out the side door. A clump of dirt had stuck on the end of the splintered bone. My eyes shifted away from his groin, then back. Only the torn skin from his scrotum remained. Riker looked sick. I don't know what I looked like. I told Reacher to move him back from the door. He could fall out. The scurrying grunts tossed a foot-filled boot onto the cargo deck. Blood seeped through the torn wool sock at the top of the boot. The medic pushed it under the sling seat.

I turned around and saw a confused-looking private walking through the swirling smoke with the head. of someone he knew held by the hair.

"A head? Do we have to carry a head?" I asked Riker.

The kid looked at us, and Riker nodded. He tossed it inside with the other parts. The medic looked away as he pushed the bloody head under the seat. His heel kicked the nose.

"We can't find his body. I don't think we should stay to look for it. Is his head enough?" a grunt yelled.

"Absolutely. Plenty. Let's go," Riker answered.

I flew toward Pleiku as fast as the Huey could go. Reacher called from the pocket that "One-Leg" was sliding toward the edge of the deck. I had him tell the medic, who put his foot on One-Leg's bloody groin. That kept him from sliding out, but the torn skin of the stump flapped in the wind, spraying blood along the outside of the ship and all over Reacher as he sat behind his machine gun.

A grunt was crying. One of the wounded, his friend, had just died. The other was just barely alive. I wanted to fly at a thousand miles an hour.

Riker called ahead so we could land at Camp Holloway without delay. We went by the tower like a flash and landed on the red cross near the newly set-up hospital tent. The stretcher bearers ran out to unload the cargo.

I could see that they had been busy lately. There was a pile of American bodies outside the hospital tent.

The other wounded man died.

We had lost the race.

The stretcher bearers' technique was to cross the cadaver's arms and then, with a twist, flip it off the deck onto the waiting stretcher. I watched as two specialists unloaded One-Leg. They dropped him in a grotesque heap on the canvas. The sun glinted off a gold band on his left hand. The specialists were laughing. About what, I don't know. Maybe they were so accustomed to their job that they thought this was hilarious. Maybe it was nervous laughter. Regardless, their nonchalance was too much for me. I jumped out and made them stop before they got to the tent. I braced them on the spot and yelled and yelled and yelled.

"Okay, a company from the First of the Seventh [1st Battalion, 7th Cavalry, a First Cav unit] is trapped here," Shaker pointed to a spot between the Ia Drang River and the Chu Pong massif on the big map in our briefing tent. "Charlie has them completely pinned down. The grunts say that Charlie can't overrun them, but they have some bad wounded to get out." Shaker paused a moment while he checked his notes. "I'm going to take five ships out tonight. There's no moon, so the darkness will be our cover." He stopped to suck on another cigarette. He smoked even more than me. Chain smoking made him look nervous, but I don't think he was. I think he was so intense because he was the only black platoon leader in our battalion. He took another puff and began reading the names of the crews and their ship numbers. I didn't listen too carefully because I knew that Riker and I were going to sit this one out tonight and get some rest. Then I heard, ". . . and Riker and Mason in eight-seven-nine."

"What?" Riker exclaimed. Shaker seemed not to notice.

Shaker looked at his watch. "It's 1730 now. Eat some chow and be on the flight line ready to crank at 2000 hours." He turned to leave, but stopped. "Those of you not on the mission tonight will stay in the company area on standby." As he left, the crowd broke up, and I heard rumblings of disappointment about having to hang around. Apparently there were some good bars in Pleiku.

Riker looked as unhappy as I felt. It seemed that our earlier debriefing had fallen on deaf ears. We had got back from our marathon mission with Grunt Six just two hours before. Shaker knew we had already put in eight hours of flight time today and twenty hours the day before. What was he trying to do, kill us?

"No, I'm not trying to kill you." I had caught up with Shaker on a sidewalk in the adviser compound. "Mason, you're new to our unit and fresh out of flight school, and I'm responsible for your training. You need all the night flying you can get."

"But—"

"You got some sleep last night, right?"

"Yes."

"So be ready to go at 2000 hours." He left before I could even get started. I wanted to tell him how miserable I felt, how tired I was. But I got angry instead.

Fresh out of flight school, my ass! I said to myself as I walked back to the mess tent. Need night time, hey? Want to see if I can hack it? Well, let's just see if I can hack it! I now had a goal that superseded survival.

The NVA allowed us to land without opposition. They even waited for the crew chiefs and gunners to get out to load the wounded. When they were sure we were on the ground and busy, they opened up. The thing that saved us was the moonless night. As I sat in the cockpit, I remember not being able to see the two Hueys in front of me at all. All our position lights were off. The only light was the faint-red glow of our own instrument panel—until Charlie started shooting. Bright-red tracers streamed in from the dark tree line at the front. They couldn't see us, so they sprayed the whole LZ indiscriminately. The grunts scattered and started firing back.

Shaker yelled, "Yellow flight, take off!" Then he went. He didn't realize that his crew chief was still outside trying to get to another wounded grunt. Stranded, the crew chief was going to be a grunt for a few hours.

We had got four on board before Shaker yelled. The two ships behind us were empty.

We took off single file into the tracers. The NVA were firing at our noise, and they were hitting. From where I sat, it looked pretty bad. I was on the controls and veered quickly left and right as I took off, thinking I could actually dodge the bullets. As I dodged, the world became distant. There was no sound. The burning red globes streamed past me. I banked hard to the left as soon as I saw the dim horizon, and the red death left me and licked up, looking for the others.

The sound came back and I heard the chatter on the radio. Four of the five ships had been hit. We were the exception. Amazingly, no one had been hurt.

There were still eight wounded to get out back at the LZ, along with Shaker's crew chief.

We flew back to Pleiku and dropped off the wounded. En route, Shaker instructed two ships to join him on the return flight. Riker and I were chosen to try our luck again.

Back over the LZ an hour later, Shaker was told by the grunts that the LZ was too hot, so he elected to land about two miles away and wait.

I remember being so keyed up with adrenaline that I wanted to go back in, regardless. I even thought Shaker was chicken.

We stayed strapped in our seats with the Hueys shut down. The clearing was pitch black. This LZ had been taken earlier in the day and was supposed to be secure, but no one believed it. We stayed put.

The adrenaline high I had produced during the action was now wearing off. I sat in my seat watching little white spots drift in front of me. I felt drained of my strength. The undefined world of my dark surroundings mingled with my black thoughts. Somehow this has got to stop, I thought. I can't think straight. If the VC don't get me I will. What's Shaker thinking of sitting here in the middle of nowhere? Riker and I did not talk.

I heard a small observation helicopter (H-13) over the spot where the trapped men waited, a scout from our 1/9 Cav squadron. I imagined the pilot bristling with Western .45s and cowboy boots, having a waxed mustache and a firmly set jaw, glaring down into the darkness, looking for signs of the NVA. Theoretically, he would fly low and slow, so the VC would shoot at him. Then, if he survived, he could locate them for the artillery or gunships. Fourteen of the original twenty pilots of that scout unit would be killed in less than six months.

He circled, invisibly. There was no reaction from the NVA. He grew tired of this passive search, and either he or his crew chief started shooting down into the jungle with a hand-held machine gun. His tracers formed a red tongue of flame arcing down from nowhere. That worked. After a few of these bursts, the NVA opened up on him. Tracers leapt out of the jungle to a spot where they guessed he might be. When they fired, he stopped. They had just given away their position. Minutes later, mortars *whumped* in from somewhere near where we sat. They kept it up for almost five minutes. The whirlybird went back to check it out. He fired into the jungle again and flew even lower than last time, but he could not draw fire. Either the machine gun had been wiped out or the enemy had gotten smart. We would have to find out which.

Shaker sent his gunner back through the blackness along the parked ships to tell us it was going to be one ship at a time: Crank up and wait, and monitor the radios until he got out.

We waited while both Shaker and the next ship got in and out successfully. We were last.

The approach was eerie because I did it without lights. The large landing light and even the small position lights would make excellent targets. The machine gun was apparently out of action, but the grunts were now saying there was some sniper fire from the tree line. I was on the controls, and I decided to keep going. I talked on the radio to a grunt who promised to switch on a flashlight when I got closer. I lined up on the general area and made a gentle descent into the darkness. The grunt on the radio talked me down.

"Okay, now left. You're doing great. No sweat. Keep it coming like you are. Let down a little. I think you should go more right. Okay, you should see the flashlight. Can you see the light?"

"Roger." The dull glow of an army flashlight with a special filter on it popped into existence below me, making the man holding it a target.

A single point of light in pitch blackness doesn't tell you much. You could be upside down for all you know. Without other references to compare it with, the light seemed to drift around in the blackness. I kept my eyes moving, not staring at the light. Disorientation was a common occurrence at moments like this. It was never clear to me just how I did manage, but the ship touched down in front of the flashlight; the skids hit the ground gently before I realized that I was that close. Apparently we got no sniper fire on the way in. Of course, I would know about it only if we got hit or if the grunts told us.

We picked up all the remaining wounded, which amounted to two stretcher cases and one walking. The guy with the flashlight jumped on board, too, just before we took off.

I was very cautious on takeoff and avoided the old machine-gun position by making a sharp turn as we cleared the trees. The Huey was low on fuel and therefore light. I stayed low for a while to accelerate and then pulled the cyclic back hard to swoop up into the night sky. I switched on our position lights so that any other aircraft could see us, and 3000 feet and thirty seconds later we saw fifty-caliber tracers sailing up, glowing as big as baseballs. I switched off the lights, and when we became invisible again, they stopped firing.

During the half-hour flight back to Pleiku, the flashlight bearer never stopped talking.

"Mister Riker," the gunner said, "that guy that got on board back there is acting crazy. He's talking fast, but he won't talk into my mike."

Riker was taking his turn, so I looked back to see the kid sitting on the bench next to the rushing wind. He made wide gestures with his arms, which I could see, but it was too dark to make out much else. His shadow arms were orchestrating a private nightmare. Make that three wounded and one loony on board.

We dropped off the wounded at 4 a.m., but the kid stayed with us. He wasn't wounded, at least not physically. Riker thought we should take him to our operations tent. While we walked there, the kid just followed, talking gibberish.

We turned in our flight records and mission report to Sergeant Bailey at the operations tent while the kid stood off to the side, mumbling and looking wildly around at nobody. We didn't try to stop him. We discovered, through Bailey, that he was not supposed to be with us; he was supposed to be out where we got him. Bailey did not call his unit but used the field phone to call the hospital tent as we left. As Riker and I trudged off to find our tents, his voice faded to silence.

Someone got me up at six and said I had to fly. I remember only that I stumbled into the operations tent and said, "I can't fly now. I have flown too much." A simple statement of fact. I turned and stumbled away. I heard a voice say, "He can't fly. He and Riker just got back two hours ago."

There was a moment of pleasure as I slipped back into my blankets. My air mattress was flat, but I didn't care. I was awake enough to realize that they all had to work, but I was going to sack in.

I was forced to get up again three hours later. Not by the army. God did it. He wanted me to get up. His method was simplicity itself. Just heat up that miserable tent with the sun and bake me out. I felt myself cooking and rolled off my deflated air mattress and pushed my face into the cool earth. My eyelids were swollen shut, and I was drenched with sweat. The cool-earth remedy wasn't working. For one thing, it tasted terrible. Enough! I reached over to my flight bag to find something clean to wear. The bag had been sitting in this dank tent for the last three days and smelled like an old laundry hamper. I pulled out a set of clean fatigues that smelled dirty and dressed while lying on my back. Boots. My hands found them next to the canvas wall. I noticed that the tent had been designed to hold moisture inside; my hand got wet looking for the boots. I tried to open my eyes again, but the sun was so bright through the fabric that I couldn't stand it. With my eyes still shut, I laced the boots automatically, and minutes later I launched myself outside. I staggered around feeling like Frankenstein's monster. I tripped over the tent rope, and during the resulting fall I was forced to open my eyes.

The watery view through my swollen eyelids revealed the general layout of the camp well enough for me to know where the latrine would be. I probably could've just closed my eyes and sniffed it out, but I didn't want to fall in.

The latrines at the Turkey Farm were long frame benches built like ladders with maybe four places to sit placed over a corresponding number of sawed-off oil drums. The neat thing about the Cav's latrines was that they were not enclosed for privacy. I mean, real men can sit out in the middle of a busy camp and shit. No one will watch when you wipe your ass.

I got a cup of coffee at the operations tent and stumbled over to a homemade tent the guys had jury-rigged while Riker and I had been away. They called it the Big Top. It was, basically, a giant tarp stretched over two thick twenty-foot poles. Compared to the tent I just got out of, it was cool and breezy inside.

Recovering from my zombie spell, I recounted the activities of the past few days. Riker and I had flown eleven hours yesterday, ten hours the day before, and twenty hours the day before that! That is a lot of time in a helicopter. No wonder I felt so shitty. A new world's record. No doubt about it. Probably I will be sent home a hero for that, all right.

When my mind cleared, I realized that I had the day off and could go into town.

I went into the operations tent to check out. Neither Captain Owens or Mr. White, the operations officers, was in.

"Owens and White out flying?" I asked Sergeant Bailey facetiously. He was always there because he did almost all the work.

"No, sir, they're in the compound." Bailey had been a colonel once. When he didn't make brigadier, he was "rifted" (for "reduction in force": the army's way of controlling its reserve-officer-corps population). He chose to stay in the army as an NCO. He made it a point to call a warrant "sir."

"They sleep in the compound?" I asked.

"Yes, sir. They had a rough night last night. Up till 0400."

"I didn't see them when we got back."

"They were on alert in their quarters." Bailey didn't believe that any more than I did.

It was my first wake-up at the Turkey Farm. I had nosed into the doings of the Bobbsey Creeps because they pissed me off. I wanted them to be out flying like the rest of us. My fatigue and this added irritant started to push me into a depression.

Riker, clever about sleeping late, had got up before dawn and transferred himself to a cot in the compound vacated by one of our higher-ranking officers who was out on the morning mission. I bumped into him by accident at the compound mess hall. Over another cup of coffee we made plans to go to town.

We got a ride on a truck that bounced along the dusty road to the village.

On the outskirts of Pleiku, the beer-can-metal walls of the huts recently built by refugees lined both sides of the road, just like An Khe. As my tour progressed, I would see these instant slums spring up outside every town and village I passed.

We jumped out of the truck near the center of town, and Len and I could see that we were the only Americans around. We were out of phase with the usual nighttime crowd.

On the unpaved strip of red dirt between the main

street and the sidewalk, men made shoes from discarded tires and women sold produce. Montagnard women squatted patiently among their baskets, waiting for their men to finish shopping.

Riker and I walked along the narrow sidewalk, gawking at the strangeness of it all. We smiled at everyone, and they smiled back. Even with their smiles, the people looked afraid. I imagined that our French and Japanese and God knows what other predecessors found Pleiku to be very much the same as we did. So the smiles were probably those of self-defense. I think ours were, too. There was no detectable difference between the people who milled around us now and the ones who tried to kill us every day. It wasn't paranoid to believe that they were one and the same.

The fearful smiles of the street drove us inside to the more professionally confident smiles of the restaurant owners, shopkeepers, and bar girls. The more convincing their smiles and back-patting, the bigger their bankroll became.

We walked inside to the darkness and coolness of a bar-restaurant and ordered a beer and a steak each. I always asked for a New York strip; it made the water buffalo taste better. We had two thin strips of very well done buffalo, french-fried potatoes, and crisp-crusted bread served with canned butter from Australia. It was a meal fit for a king, or even for two helicopter pilots fresh from three days of nonstop flying. We were the only people eating. Other than the three or four ARVNs who drank at the bar, we were the only men there.

There were, however, several women. We found ourselves surrounded at the table. Ah, to be the center of so much feminine attention again.

They were not the desperately bold women of An Khe. No one grabbed my crotch. They were, as I remember, beautiful. Riker's normally red face got redder when one girl insisted on waiting on him hand and foot. She poured his beer, got him more bread and butter, and other little things. She had, as they say, zeroed in on Riker.

We were talking about the war and the company's shitty camp and flying and the food, but the conversation was getting difficult. Riker's haunting angel kept drifting in and out of his attention. In a matter of minutes I found myself being ignored.

I, of course, had no choice but to strike up a conversation with the girl who sat next to me. Riker and his new friend soon left for the stairs at the back of the bar.

I forgot all about the war and my promises as the dark-eyed lady smiled and talked in a magic way. The magic was that she spoke almost no English, but I understood her anyway. That she truly loved me was not to be doubted. That her pleasure was my pleasure was obvious. That we should walk down those stairs was inevitable. My promises to Patience when I left home, and to God in the back of the Huey, were forgotten.

Riker and I had nothing but good things to say about this bar. It became very popular with the men of our company. Later my buddy Resler would become so enamored of one of the delightful ladies that he stayed past curfew, too late to return. He had to spend the night inside the place, trapped, as it were, downstairs with his true love and twenty other girls. His stories about that night became legend.

The next day was business as usual. I was scheduled to fly with Leese. He was going to teach me one of his valuable lessons.

We had been assigned to fly a single-ship mission to haul a load of high-explosive rockets from Pleiku to a Special Forces camp about thirty miles south. The rockets, 2500 pounds of them, were the type used on our helicopter gunships. We often placed caches of them near the action to cut the wasted time of return flights.

They loaded Reacher's ship while it was shut down. We were parked on the apron next to the PSP runway and across from the latrine at the Turkey Farm. The rockets were packed so tightly that Reacher and the gunner were pushed out of the pockets and barely had room to sit. I doubted that the load could be lifted, but Leese said it would be a cinch.

Leese, as was his practice, let me do all the flying. I liked that.

"Let's go," he ordered.

The starter motor screamed. The turbine whined familiarly and the rotors blurred above the cabin.

When all gauges showed green, I slowly raised the collective to pull the Huey into a hover. No go. I pulled in full power, but the Huey just sat there shuddering. We stirred up a lot of wind, but we didn't get one inch off the ground.

"You'll have to make a running takeoff," Leese said.

If a helicopter can't hover because of an overloaded condition like this, it can be made light on the skids with the collective and then urged forward with the cyclic so that it slides across the ground on its skids. If it can slide along the ground long enough, it will take off like an airplane, even though it can't hover.

It is not graceful. I skidded and scraped along the runway to the takeoff position at the field. The noise of the skid plates scraping against the steel runway chattered and growled through the ship.

I radioed for clearance and ground slowly down the runway. The tugging of the skids against the corrugations of the runway made the ship rock back and forth. We moved about a hundred feet at a slow walk.

The idea is to get going fast enough for the rotors to

start swinging through undisturbed air rather than in their own turbulent downwash. When the whole rotor system is spinning in clean air, it suddenly lifts very strongly—translational lift.

So I was skidding and bumping along the runway, trying to get the beast to translational-lift speed. It felt like the Huey was disintegrating with all the noise and shaking, but Leese smiled confidently from the left seat. "No problem."

With about a third of the runway left, the overloaded and suffering Huey finally got to flight speed and struggled into the air. Reacher cheered his baby from the back.

We wanted to climb to 3000 feet, but during the thirty-mile flight I got no higher than half that altitude. As we lumbered along, I realized we were so heavily loaded that an autorotation would be a lot rougher than anyone would like when carrying more than a ton of high explosives.

The one factor that was actually improving as we labored along was that we were burning a bunch of fuel. The ship would be lighter for the running landing I was prepared to make at our destination.

At the camp we were going to, the commander had left the job of picking the landing spot to a sergeant especially schooled in the workings of the aviation branch. However, this sergeant was not around, so the job of picking the spot had passed to his assistant, who, although he looked as though he knew what he was doing, didn't.

We made a long, very gentle descent toward the camp.

I spotted the assistant. He had his arms held high, indicating the grassy strip near the forward edge of the camp. It looked as though the spot he was pointing to was just outside the stretched-out coil of concertina-wire fence that ran between the perimeter of the camp and the nearby trees. There was enough room to land, so I didn't question his judgment.

As I got closer, lower, and slower, I brought in the power. It would take all we had just to cushion the impact.

I crossed the small wall of trees that ringed the camp, and flared. I was six feet over the grass outside the fence when I heard a panicky voice in my earphones.

"Don't land there!" the voice screamed. "That's a mine field!"

"Minefield!" Even Leese was impressed.

If Leese was impressed, I was petrified. The Huey was mushing inexorably toward the ground. I was too low to extend my landing beyond the fence. I pulled the collective to my armpit and waited for the noise. The Huey, God bless it, came to a shuddering, engine-wrenching hover just inches from the ground. The low-rpm warning siren blared in my ears, and for a few horrible seconds I wondered if it could hold the hover. The engine was bogging down with the strain. I had to reduce the power or lose it, so I reduced the collective a bit to let the ship drift down closer and give the turbine a chance to wind up a little. When the skids almost touched the grass, the siren stopped and the rpm slowly returned. When it finally stabilized, I hauled it slowly back up to about six inches above the minefield.

Reacher's illegal tune-up had just saved us, but we still had a problem. The four-foot fence in front of us was too high to get over, and the trees behind us blocked any retreat.

"Well, at least we can stay off the ground," said Leese.

We were, from my point of view, 2500 pounds of high explosives tearing at the air to stay away from the high explosives under us.

We could just stay there, hanging, until we got lighter,

but there was the problem of getting shot at near the edge of the camp, and neither of us knew how long the Huey—even Reacher's Huey—could grind away like this at full power. And we couldn't dump the cargo.

I pulled in more power, and the Huey climbed another foot, but when it got that much farther out of the ground cushion, the engine strained and the ship settled back down toward the grass. I tried it a few more times and discovered that while it settled back down from the climb, I could milk a few more rpm out of the engine. In this way, I figured I could use the little extra power gained on the way down to pull it a little higher on the next try. I did this over and over, floating a little higher each time.

This technique, and the fact that we were getting lighter by burning fuel, finally allowed me to get the skids fence-high. But when I tried to cross the fence from the top of a bounce, the Huey sank too fast. By moving forward, I had moved out of the ground cushion.

What now? I had Reacher look behind us. He said there was another row of concertina wire about fifty feet behind us. I hadn't even noticed that. My hope was that by backing up a little, I could get some room for a forward run to clear the hurdle. So I backed up as far as Reacher could clear me, and went for it. No good. I was within a foot of making it, but I had to flare to a stop before I tangled up in the wire. I drifted backward to resume my low hover over the mines.

Leese said, "Try a right-pedal turn."

Perfect. That's why Leese had lived to fly through two wars. He understood his machines. The pedals control the anti-torque rotor, the tail rotor. Turning to the right—with the torque—would make more power available to the main rotors.

So I backed up again. Instead of charging straight

ahead, I hovered parallel to the fence for a few feet and then banked hard right toward it. It worked! This was the extra boost I needed to clear the trap.

I kept turning as I crossed the fence and landed sideways on the other side. Drenched with sweat, I felt as though I had just flown the Atlantic with my arms.

"Not bad," said Leese as we landed on the safe side of the concertina wire. "Now, I hope that this has taught you a lesson." His voice was calm.

"Lesson?" I said weakly. "What lesson?"

"Never trust a grunt," he said.

That night at the Turkey Farm we were not allowed to go into the village. Somebody had been stealing from the adviser compound again. There were complaints about a missing refrigerator.

After my first night in that miserable tent, I moved to the Big Top, where I built a kind of bunk—a shelf, really—to sleep on. I used the wood from some old ammo crates. I put my leaky air mattress on top and set it in a corner of the airy tent. Several other guys did the same; it was cooler and drier than the tents we had with us.

Since we couldn't go to town, we sat at a long wooden table in the Big Top, playing chess and listening to the radio. We were listening to Hanoi radio, the best music on the dial. Every night the news was broadcast on this station by Hanoi Hanna. There was more than one woman who announced the news, but we called them all by one name. We wanted to believe she was another Tokyo Rose.

Hanna, for the first time in nearly three months, mentioned our unit by name. She said that it was too bad about us, poor guys, but we were going to get mortared at midnight.

We all looked at each other and laughed. Bullshit. Heh heh heh.

"Hey, I was thinking of digging a hole anyway. Weren't you?"

Minutes after her announcement, digging foxholes became a popular pastime. Dirt flew. The rule that forbade the digging of holes that would ruin the grass was ignored. The men inside the Camp Holloway compound slept behind sandbag walls and had bunkers to duck into if the mortars came. But camped out in their front yard, so to speak, we suddenly felt very exposed.

The red ground at our campsite was so dry and hard that the holes weren't even waist deep by midnight. When the predicted hour came and went without incident, the digging slowed down. I dug mine near the end of my bunk, and it was one of the deepest.

Mortars came, not at the Turkey Farm, but at our refueling depot at the Tea Plantation. Of all the mortars that hit in that attack, one lousy little mortar landed right in the middle of the tent where our refueling crew slept. Seven people, including three privates from our company, were killed. We comforted ourselves by saying that they never knew what hit them.

The next morning at our briefing, we learned that the French owner of the real tea plantation next door had complained.

"To the VC?" Connors asked from the back of our crowd of forty pilots assembled in the Big Top.

"No, not to the VC, to us," said Williams. "He says that our being so close to his farm is going to cause him damage. He wants us to move the refueling depot and the troops."

"Are we?" somebody asked.

"I don't know. The Colonel went to see him this morning."

"Unbelievable!" Connors said. Williams stiffened as Connors continued. "We're donating lives to free this stupid country, and that French asshole is still paying off the VC and doesn't want us to get our scummy army too close to his tea bushes. I think we should accidentally napalm the cocksucker!"

Williams ignored Connors and continued the briefing, but a lot of us agreed with Pat.

As it turned out, we didn't napalm him; nor did we move the depot. The Cav simply agreed to stay away from his plantation. We were instructed to avoid flying over the place, especially at low level.

"The longest week began on a sun-drenched Sunday morning in a small clearing, designated Landing Zone X-Ray, in the Chu Pong foothills. Intelligence had long suspected the Chu Pong massif of harboring a large Communist force fed from the Cambodian side of the border. X-Ray seemed like a likely spot to find the enemy, and so it was." I read this in *Time*, the week after the Tea Plantation incident.

The results of nearly two weeks of searching and probing by the Cav were hundreds of dead NVA soldiers and a very good idea of where to find the main force of three NVA regiments. On November 14 our battalion lifted the 1st Battalion, 7th Cavalry (Custer's old unit) into LZ X-Ray, where they were expected to make contact. Our sister company, the Snakes, made the first assault in the morning and received very little opposition. By early afternoon, though, the two companies of the Seventh Cav they had lifted in had been surrounded, and suffered heavy casualties. Our company was assigned to support the Snakes, to lift in reinforcements.

We picked up the troopers at the Tea Plantation, eight to each Huey. It was easy to tell where we were going. Although we were still fifteen miles away, the smoke was clearly visible from all the artillery, B-52 bombers, and gunship support concentrated around the LZ to keep the grunts from being overrun. As we cruised over the jungles and fields of elephant grass, I had the feeling this was a movie scene: the gentle rise and fall of the Hueys as we cruised, the perspective created by looking along the formation of ships to the smoke on the horizon, the quiet. None of the crews talked on the radios. We all listened to the urgent voices in the static as they called in air strikes and artillery on their own perimeters, then yelled that the rounds were hitting *in* their positions.

LZ X-Ray could accommodate eight Hueys at once, so that was how the ships were grouped in the air. Yellow and White in the first group; Orange and Red in the second. Leese and I were Red Two. As we got closer to X-Ray, the gap between us and the first group got bigger to allow time for them to land, drop off the troopers, and take off.

Five miles away, we dropped to low level. We were flying under the artillery fire going into the LZ.

A mile ahead of us, the first group was going over the approach end of the LZ and disappearing into the smoke. Now the radios came alive with the pilots' calling in where the fire was coming from. The gunners on all the ships could hear this. Normally it was helpful, but this time, with the friendlies on the ground, they could not fire back. Yellow and White were on the ground too long. The artillery still pounded. The massif behind the LZ was completely obscured by the pall of smoke. We contin ued our approach. Leese was on the controls. I double- or triple-checked my sliding armor panel on my door side and cursed the army once again for not giving us chest protectors. I put my hands and feet near the controls and stared at the scene.

"Orange One, abort your landing. Fire in the LZ is too heavy," a pathfinder called from X-Ray. Orange flight turned, and we followed. There was a whole bunch of yelling on the radios. I heard two ships in the LZ call out that they were hit badly. What a mess. Orange flight led us in a wide orbit two miles away, still low level. Now A1-E's from the air force were laying heavy fire at the front of the LZ along with the artillery and our own gunships. What kept everybody from flying into each other I'll never know. Finally we heard Yellow One call to take off, and we saw them emerge from the smoke on the left side of the LZ, shy two ships. They had waited in the heavy fire while the crews of the two downed ships got on the other Hueys. One crew chief stayed, dead. One pilot was wounded.

We continued the orbit for fifteen minutes. I looked back at the grunts who were staring at the scene. They had no idea what was going on, because they had no headsets.

"Orange One, make your approach," the pathfinder called. Apparently a human-wave attack by the NVA on the LZ was stopped. "Orange One, all eight of the ships in your two flights are keyed to pick up wounded." "Keyed" meant that they had groups of wounded positioned to be loaded first.

"Roger. Red One copy?"

"Red One roger."

Orange One rolled out of the orbit and we followed. The A1-E's were gone, but our gunships came back to flank us on the approach. Even with the concentration of friendlies on the ground, the gunships could fire accurately enough with their flex guns and rockets, so the grunts allowed them to. Our own door gunners were not allowed to fire unless they saw an absolutely clear target.

We crossed the forward tree line into the smoke. The two slicks that had been shot down were sitting at the front of the LZ, rotors stopped. That made it a little tight for eight of us to get in, but it was okay. The grunts jumped off even before the skids hit the ground. Almost before our Hueys had settled into the grass, other grunts had dumped wounded men, some on stretchers, into our ships. No fire. At least nothing coming our way. Machine guns and hundreds of rifles crackled into a roar all around us as the grunts threw out withering cover fire. The pathfinder, hidden in the tree line somewhere, told us everybody was loaded and to take off to the left. Orange One rogered and led us out. Fifty yards past the perimeter, some of the ships took hits, and we cleared all our guns to fire. Our ship was untouched.

After we dropped off the wounded, Leese and I were delayed by taking some men to an artillery position, separating us from the rest of the company for a half hour.

We were on our way to rejoin them when we saw a fighter get hit near X-Ray. It was a prop-driven A1-E. This scene, too, was right out of the movies. Orange flames burst from the root of his right wing and billowed back toward the tail, turning into coal-black smoke. The flames flared thicker than the fuselage and in moments hid the multipaned canopy. The pilot was either dead or unconscious, for he did not eject. The plane screamed toward the ground from about 3000 feet, not more than half a mile from Leese and me. Black smoke marked its path as it streaked into the jungle at a steep angle, exploding instantly, spreading wreckage, and bursting bombs, unspent ammo, and fire forward, knocking down trees.

I made the mistake of calling our headquarters to tell them of the crash.

"Roger, Red Two, wait one," was the answer in my phones.

"Ah, Red Two, Grunt Six has relayed instructions that you are to proceed to the site of the crash and inspect same."

I wanted to go flying around where an air-force plane

just got shot down like I wanted to extend my tour. Leese advised flying by very fast and taking a quick look-see. I dumped the Huey from 3000 feet, using the speed of my dive to swoop over the burning swatch in the jungle.

I told headquarters to tell Grunt Six that nobody had jumped out before the plane had hit and that there now remained only some smoldering pieces of airplane and some exploding ammo in the middle of the burnt clearing.

"Ah, roger, Red Two, wait one."

Whenever they asked you to wait, you knew they were up to no good.

"Ah, Red Two, Grunt Six says roger. But the air force wants you to land and do an on-site inspection."

Leese shook his head. "Negative, HQ," I radioed, "this area is hot. We will return to do a slow fly-by and check it again, but we know there's nobody left." Leese nodded.

Now, you would think that that would be good enough. I had just volunteered the four of us in our lone Huey to fly back over a very hot area to double-check the obvious.

It was not good enough. The air-force commander, via a relay through our HQ radio, wanted more.

"Red Two, the air force wants you to land and inspect the crash site for survivors," announced the voice in my flight helmet.

I told them to wait one, that I was in the process of doing another fly-by to check it out.

While our guy at HQ got back to the air-force commander, Leese and I and Reacher and the nervous ex-grunt who was our gunner approached the crash site. I wanted to be sure this time. I slowed to about thirty miles an hour just above the trees surrounding the new clearing. I started to circle the smoke and flames below us when we heard explosions. Leese, who always stayed off the controls, said, "I got it." He took the controls and dumped the nose of the Huey to accelerate. "Probably just some leftover ammunition from the fighter exploding," he said, "but I want to come back around in a fast turn just in case." He glanced out his window. "Somebody shot down this guy, and they're still around here somewhere." Leese began a turn to the left to circle back to the smoke. He picked up speed fast, and when we got to the clearing again, he banked very hard to the left. We all sank into our seats feeling the pressure of at least two Gs as Leese put the Huey into an almost-90-degree bank. I looked across at him in the left seat, through his side window and directly down to the wreckage. I had never experienced such a maneuver in flight school. My first thought was that the Huey would disconnect from the rotors, that the Jesus nut would break.

The view was, however, unique and totally revealing. And we were moving so fast we would be harder to hit.

From this dizzy vantage point we could see a few metal parts that hadn't melted and the flashes of exploding ammo. We hoped that all his bombs had gone off in the crash. We radioed that the pilot was definitely dead.

"Ah, roger, Red Two, wait one." We circled at 2000 feet about a mile away.

"Red Two, this is Preacher Six." Major Williams was now on the horn. "I have just talked to the air force, and I agreed that you would land to do an on-site inspection."

Leese, in his capacity as aircraft commander, answered. "Preacher Six, Red Two. We have already confirmed that no one is at the crash site, alive or dead. We have already risked more tha ꞁ we should have to determine this."

Leese should have known better than to try to be logical.

"Whether you have risked enough is my decision, Red Two. You are ordered to proceed to the crash site and land. You will then have your crew get out and inspect the wreckage firsthand. Over and out."

There was silence. I'm sure Leese considered telling him to stuff it, but he had to play his role.

He played it correctly. "Affirmative."

We were now back at the wreckage, circling once again in a scrotum-stretching Leese special. The left side of the Huey was really straight down. After two of these furious turns, he pulled away to set up his approach. He had decided not to try to land in the wreckage-strewn clearing itself because we wouldn't be able to land far enough away from the fire and the exploding ammo. Just behind the point of impact, there was a natural thin spot in the jungle where a few bare, 75-foot trees stood. It certainly wasn't big enough to put a Huey there, but that's where he was headed. Leese was going to show me another trick.

He settled into a hundred-foot hover directly over the tall trees and moved around searching for the right spot to play lawnmower. He had Reacher and the gunner lean out to watch the very delicate tail rotor. He found what he liked and began to let the helicopter settle down into the trees.

He had picked the spot perfectly. The tail boom with the spinning rotor on the end had a clear slot to follow down to the ground. The main rotor only had to chop a few two-inch-thick branches off some trees, a maneuver not even hinted at in flight school. When they hit the first branches, it sounded like gunfire.

Splintered wood flew everywhere. Treetops towered above us as we chopped our way down. We settled to the ground amid swirling debris, ass end low on a gentle slope covered with dense undergrowth. There was a moment of silence as the twigs and leaves settled around us. Nothing had been broken.

Reacher and the gunner grabbed their rifles and leapt

into the thick tangle of weeds, galloping toward the still-exploding wreckage. The cords from their flight helmets trailed behind them.

Leese and I sat at the bottom of the vertical tunnel he had cut, our heads swiveling on nervous lookout. So far, only the sound of exploding ammo occasionally popped over the sound of the Huey. Reacher and the gunner disappeared through the thicket of trees between us and the wreckage.

We waited.

Whump! Whump, whump! Mortars! From wherever they were hiding, the NVA launched their worst.

We were alone. HQ had not sent a gunship for escort or even another slick to watch over us. Leese and I looked at each other as the mortars got closer. His mouth was thin and his jaw was tight. I wondered if this was as bad as landing gliders. In the dense foliage around us I heard the mortars crashing heavily, shaking the air, searching for us. They sounded like the footfalls of a drunken giant. A big crunch nearby, then one to the side, then another behind us as the invisible giant staggered around trying to stomp us. The NVA were very good with their mortars, but it took time to zero in on a new target like us. Since they couldn't see us from where they were, they had to walk the rounds back and forth until they got us.

Just when my fear was at an all-time high, Reacher and the gunner finally broke through the thicket to release us from the trap. They were both pale with fear as they dove on board. Leese had never let the Huey relax, so to speak. He had been ready to go at any second. As the two men hit the deck, Leese went.

He climbed back up through his tunnel in the trees like an express elevator and nosed the Huey over hard just as the rotor cleared the treetops. A mortar went off below just as our tail cleared the last tree.

Reacher told us that there was not even a little piece of the pilot left, and the air-force commander was finally satisfied. "Not only that," I fantasized he would write to the widow, "but I sent four suckers from the army right back in there to make sure your husband was dead."

Leese and I joined our company for the next lift after a trip to the Turkey Farm for refueling.

X-Ray was quiet this time. We dropped off the troopers and picked up wounded. At the hospital tent next to the runway at Holloway, I couldn't believe how many bodies were piling up outside the tent. Williams radioed that Leese and I and another ship could fly over to our camp and shut down because he wouldn't need us for the last lift in. I looked at the pile of dead, and shivered.

Back at our camp, Sergeant Bailey leaned out of the operations tent and yelled that the company was on its way back to Holloway. Two pilots had been hit.

Leese and I had been laying back for ten minutes at the Big Top, drinking coffee and enjoying every minute away from the gaggle. As Bailey yelled, I noticed the whole battalion on the horizon coming up from the south. Getting closer, the swarm was so noisy it sounded like a war all by itself. It wasn't too hard to imagine how the VC kept track of where we were.

The battalion broke into trail formation a few miles south, and the string of Hueys looped around, landing from the west. Leese and I were downwind from the flight line, and a warm, sweet breeze of burning kerosene from the turbines drifted by us.

The Hueys lined up side by side. Engines were shut down, and the pilots jumped out, carrying their gear. The crew chiefs waited patiently to tie the blades down and postflight their machines. As the pilots got closer, we could hear some whooping and yelling in their midst. It wasn't what we expected to hear after the news of the wounded.

At the Big Top, it was obvious why they were happy. The two wounded pilots, both from the other platoon, were walking with them, grinning and laughing with the rest. The blood from their wounds had dried in their hair and on their faces.

Both men had been hit in the head on the last lift. One had been shot from the front and the other from the side. Both were clutching their helmets, pointing at the holes. One guy had had a bullet hit the visor knob on the forehead portion of his flight helmet. The bullet had crushed his helmet and glanced off. His scalp was bleeding.

The other lucky soul walked around holding his helmet with a finger stuck into the holes on each side of it. Dried blood matted his hair on each side of his head. It was a magician's illusion. The bullet had to have gone through his head, from what we could see. We wanted to know the trick.

"I figured it out on the way back," he said. "I mean, after I stopped feeling for the holes on each side of my head and asking Ernie if I was still alive!" He was still pale, but he laughed. "The bullet hit while we were on short final to X-Ray. Luckily, Ernie was flying. It felt like somebody had hit me on the head with a bat. It blurred my vision. First I thought that a bullet had hit me on the helmet and somehow bounced off. Ernie first noticed the blood. He'd turned to tell me about a round going through the canopy in front of him when he saw it." I could imagine the guy seeing the jagged hole in the side of his friend's flying helmet, blood dripping down his neck. "I reached up to feel my helmet and felt the hole on the right side, but Ernie said the blood was coming from the other side. I put my left hand up and felt *that* hole! I pulled both hands down quickly, and they were both bloody! I felt the helmet again. Two holes all right. Two wounds all right. One on each side of my head. I couldn't believe I was still alive!" He passed the helmet around while he continued his story. "See, it hit here." He pointed in front of his right ear. "The bullet hit this ridge of bone and deflected up between my scalp and the inside of my helmet. Then"—he shook his head in disbelief— "then it circled around inside the top of the helmet and hit this ridge of bone on my left side." He pointed. "It was deflected out here, through the helmet and on through the canopy in front of Ernie!" He beamed. I saw the path the bullet made as it tore its way around through the padding on the inside of the helmet and the two wounds on each side of his head. I shook my head. God again?

As soon as he finished his story, a Jeep drove him and the other pilot across the airstrip to the hospital tent. As I watched them go, I saw the eastern sky fill with a huge formation of helicopters coming from the direction of An Khe. The Cav was sending the 227th to join us. That's about as near to full strength as the Cav got.

I joined Resler and the rest of the pilots going over to the compound for chow. About a hundred of us walked across the runway, spread out, talking to our buddies under the twilight sky. We passed the hospital tent, where the smell of blood was strong and body bags concealing grotesquely contorted corpses waited in the shadows.

The next morning, Leese and I stayed behind when the company left. We left a half hour later, to go on a single-ship mission before joining them later.

We had an easy mission to an artillery unit. We were supposed to drop off some radios, the mail, and the unit's commander, who was dropping by to talk shop with his boys. When he was finished, we were to take him back to Pleiku and then join our company.

The grunts were in the middle of a fire mission. Twenty steel barrels grouped on the north side of the clearing pointed eagerly toward the sky in the south. Concussion rings sprang away from the muzzles in the high humidity. The guns rocked back. They were shooting at targets five miles away.

They cleared us to come in, but kept on firing. The landing spot was in front of the guns.

Landing at artillery positions was a thrill. They were always in the middle of a fire mission, and they would keep firing until the ship was just about in front of the first tube. Naturally the final decision about what was too close for comfort was entirely up to the man pulling the lanyard on the cannon. The timing varied a lot. It depended on the mood of the gunner, which in turn depended on whether or not a helicopter had ever blown his tent away.

This was only my second landing into an artillery position. I set up my approach to the clearing in front of the guns and cautiously crept in, constantly reminding them on the radio that I was coming. As I crossed the trees, they were still firing. I glanced at the blasting muzzles on my left and realized that we were beginning to line up on the barrels. They stopped firing. I looked into the black muzzles and watched smoke drift lazily out as I flew through the still-turbulent air in front of them.

Someone decided to resume firing.

I was so close to the guns, looking right down their barrels when they went off, that I thought they had made a mistake and blown us apart. The sound went through me. My chest vibrated. The shock of the explosion rocked the helicopter. I landed and checked the seat. Clean.

The artillery commander told us he'd be about an hour, so I got out and walked around the place.

Twenty 105mm howitzers were grouped together on

one side of the circular clearing. They took up about one fourth of the available space, the rest being kept clear for helicopters.

Spent brass casings glittered in the grass. They took these, eventually, to a large cargo net laid out near the middle of the clearing to be carried away by a Chinook when it was full.

I walked around behind the guns to watch the crews work. They were in the middle of a big salvo, going toward X-Ray, and the pace was hectic. The explosions were more than loud; they shook my body and my brains. I stuffed toilet paper in my ears and kept my mouth open. This was supposed to keep your eardrums from bursting.

One man near each gun took a chain of four or five powder bags out of the shell casings and tore off one of them. He threw it into a nearby fire, where it flashed brilliantly. The strength of the charge was controlled by discarding packets not needed for the distance they were shooting. After adjusting the charge, the man put the round—the business end of the package containing high explosives or white phosphorus—onto the open end of the brass casing. Ready to fire, the shell was stacked on a pile near the gun crew.

A hundred shirtless men worked, sweating, in practiced synchronization in the hot, stagnant air of the clearing. I watched them fire round after round in a fifteen-minute barrage that finally ended when the command "Cease fire" was shouted down the line.

When the thunder stopped, the quiet was startling. The men in the crews began clearing away spent casings and rearranging some of the litter around them, but they were clearly interested in the outcome of their efforts. I heard calls of "How'd we do?"

The aerial observer several miles away, at their target, radioed the news. "A hit. Body count over 150." A few isolated cheers sprang from among the twenty crews.

Their sweat-covered backs glistened in the sun as they sat down for a smoke break.

Theirs was an odd war. Working feverishly in tree-walled clearings dotted here and there, away from everyone else, their enemy remained unseen, and the measure of their success or failure was a radio call from an aerial observer counting bodies. The work was hard and the noise was oppressive. During the month-long battle of Ia Drang valley, it went on twenty-four hours a day. Could a man ever really sleep in such cacophony? I tried it once and couldn't.

I talked to some guys in the crews, and they liked their job, especially as an alternative to being a trooper or a door gunner on a Huey. Their only real danger, aside from their guns blowing up, was being overrun. So far this hadn't happened in the Cav.

They asked me a lot of questions about what was happening. They could see the big flights of choppers heading south. They were having more fire missions with big body counts. The pace was quickening. They were excited about the idea of trapping the NVA. Maybe, just maybe, the enemy could be surrounded and killed. Maybe after suffering such a defeat, they would give up. We could all go home. It seemed possible. We were winning, weren't we?

The number of wounded we were carrying was growing fast. That week Leese and I flew more than a hundred wounded to the hospital tent. Other slicks carried a similar number.

When there was room and time, we carried the dead. They had low priority because they were no longer in a hurry. Sometimes they were thrown on board in body bags, but usually not. Without the bags, blood drained on the deck and filled the Huey with a sweet smell, a horribly recognizable smell. It was nothing compared to the smell of men not found for several days. We had never carried so many dead before. We were supposed to be winning now. The NVA were trapped and being pulverized, but the pile of dead beside the hospital tent was growing. Fresh recruits for graves registration arrived faster than they could be processed.

Back at our camp, I was feeling jittery after seeing too much death. I heard that two pilots had got caught on the ground.

Nate and Kaiser had gone to rescue them. Nate was almost in tears as he talked to us in the Big Top. "The stupid assholes. They had been relieved to return for fuel. But you know Paster and Richards: typical gunship pilots. Somehow they think their flex guns make them invulnerable. Anyway, on the flight back they were alone and spotted some VC or NVA or somebody on the ground and decided to attack. Nobody knows how long they were flying around there, because they called after they got hit. When Kaiser and I got there about ten minutes later, the Huey was just sitting there in a clearing looking fine. There were two gunships with us, and they circled around first and took no fire. Kaiser and I went behind the grounded ship. When we landed, I saw a red mass of meat hanging off a tree branch. It turned out to be Paster, hanging by his feet with his skin ripped off. There was nobody else around. The guns kept circling around and a Dust Off landed behind us. I got out, Kaiser stayed with the ship. The medic jumped out and ran with me." Nate kept patting his breast pockets, looking for his pipe. He never found it. "Paster's skin hung down in sheets and covered his head. The bastards had even cut off his cock. They must have just started on Richards, because we found him lying half naked about a hundred feet away in the elephant grass. His head was almost off." Nate stopped for a second, looking pale. "I almost threw up. Richards and I went to flight school together. The medics cut Paster down and stuffed him into a body bag." He shook his head, holding back tears. "Remember how Richards always bragged about how he knew he'd survive in the jungle if he got shot down? Shit, he even went to jungle school in Panama. If anybody'd be able to get away, it'd be Richards."

Nate's story hit hard. I remembered Richards and his jungle-school patch. Big deal, jungle expert. You got a hundred feet on your one big chance to evade the enemy. All that training down the drain. The thought of his wasting all that training brought tears to my eyes.

The pace remained hectic. The next day several assaults were made to smaller LZs near X-Ray to broaden our front against the NVA. Farris was assigned the command ship in a company-size flight, a mix of ships from the Snakes and the Preachers. We were going to a small, three-ship LZ. He picked me to be his pilot.

Everyone was tense. Radio conversations were terse. The grunts in the back looked grim. Even Farris looked worried. The NVA were being surrounded, and we knew they had to fight.

Farris and I would be in the first group of three to land. The company, each ship carrying eight grunts, trailed out behind us.

As the flight leader, Farris had the option to fly from any position in his flight. He chose the second ship. A theory from the developmental days of the air-assault concept said that the flight commander supposedly got a better idea about what was happening from the middle or even the end of the formation. Really big commanders flew high above us, for the best view of all.

I think this was my first time as a command-ship pilot, and I was all for survival. I would've been very happy flying the brigade commander up there at 5000 feet, or Westmoreland to his apartment in Saigon. It's amazing how many places I considered being besides there.

In assaults, we usually started drawing fire at 1000 feet, sometimes at 500. This time we didn't.

At 500 feet, on a glide path to the clearing, smoke from the just completed prestrike by our artillery and gunships drifted straight up in the still air. There had to be one time when the prep actually worked and everybody was killed in the LZ. I hoped this might be it.

Fighting my feeling of dread, I went through the automatic routine of checking the smoke drift for wind direction. None. We approached from the east, three ships lined up in a trail, to land in the skinny LZ. But it was too quiet!

At 100 feet above the trees, closing on the near end of the LZ, the door gunners in Yellow One started firing. They shot into the trees at the edge of the clearing, into bushes, anywhere they suspected the enemy was hiding. There was no return fire. The two gunships on each side of our flight opened up with their flex guns. Smoke poured out of them as they crackled. My ears rang with the loud but muffled popping as my door gunners joined in with the rest. I ached to have my own trigger. With so many bullets tearing into the LZ, it was hard to believe anyone on the ground could survive.

The gunships had to stop firing as we flared close to the ground because we could be hit by ricocheting bullets. Still no return fire. Maybe they *were* all dead! Could this be the wrong spot?

My adrenaline was high, and I was keenly aware of every movement of the ship. I waited for the lurch of dismounting troopers as the skids neared the ground. They were growling and yelling behind me, psyched for battle. I could hear them yelling above all the noise. I still can.

My landing was synchronized with the lead ship, and

as our skids hit the ground, so did the boots of the growling troops.

At the same instant, the uniformed regulars from the North decided to spring their trap. From at least three different directions, they opened up on our three ships and the off-loading grunts with machine-gun crossfire. The LZ was suddenly alive with their screaming bullets. I tensed on the controls, involuntarily leaning forward, ready to take off. I had to fight the logical reaction to leave immediately. I was light on the skids, the troops were out. Let's go! Farris yelled on the radio for Yellow One to go. They didn't move.

The grunts weren't even making it to the trees. They had leapt out, screaming murderously, but now they dropped all around us, dying and dead. The lead ship's rotors still turned, but the men inside did not answer. I saw the sand spurt up in front of me as bullets tore into the ground. My stomach tightened to stop them. Our door gunners were firing over the prone grunts at phantoms in the trees.

A strange quietness happened in my head. The scene around me seemed far away. With the noise of the guns, the cries of the gunners about everybody being dead, and Farris calling for Yellow One to go, I thought about bullets coming through the Plexiglas, through my bones and guts and through the ship and never stopping. A voice echoed in the silence. It was Farris yelling "Go! Go! Go!"

I reacted so fast that our Huey snapped off the ground. My adrenaline seemed to power the ship as I nosed over hard to get moving fast. I veered to the right of the deadly quiet lead ship, still sitting there. The door gunners fired continuously out both sides. The tracers coming at me now seemed as thick as raindrops. How could they miss? As a boy I made a game of dodging raindrops in the summer showers. I always got hit eventually. But not this time. I slipped over the treetops and stayed low for cover, accelerating. I veered left and right fast, dodging, confounding, like Leese had taught me, and when I was far enough away, I swooped up and away from the nightmare. My mind came back, and so did the sound.

"What happened to Yellow Three?" a voice said. It was still on the ground.

The radios had gone wild. I finally noticed Farris's voice saying, "Negative, White One. Veer left. Circle back." Farris had White One lead the rest of the company into an orbit a couple of miles away. Yellow One and Yellow Three were still in the LZ.

I looked down at the two ships sitting quietly on the ground. Their rotors were turning lazily as their turbines idled. The machines didn't care, only the delicate protoplasm inside them cared. Bodies littered the clearing, but some of the thirty grunts we had brought in were still alive. They had made it to cover at the edge of the clearing.

Farris had his hands full. He had twelve more ships to get in and unloaded. Then the pilot of Yellow Three called. He was still alive, but he thought his partner was dead. His crew chief and gunner looked dead, too. He could still fly.

Two gunships immediately dove down to escort him out, machine guns blazing. It was a wonderful sight to see from a distance.

Only Yellow One remained on the ground. She sat, radios quiet, still running. There was room behind her to bring in the rest of the assault.

A grunt who found himself still alive got to a radio. He said that he and a few others could keep some cover fire going for the second wave.

Minutes later, the second group of three ships was on its way in, and Farris told me to return to the staging area. I flew back a couple of miles to a big field, where I landed and picked up another load of wild-eyed boys.

They also growled and yelled. This was more than just the result of training. They were motivated. We all thought that this was the big push that might end it all. By the time I made a second landing to the LZ, the enemy machine guns were silent. This load would at least live past the landing.

Somebody finally shut down Yellow One's turbine when we left. Nobody in the crew could. They were all patiently waiting to be put into body bags for the trip home.

Why I didn't get hit I'll never know. I must have read the signs right. Right? They started calling me "Lucky" after that mission.

That afternoon, while the sunset glowed orange behind Pleiku in the distance, Leese and I and some others walked over to the hospital tent.

We came to see the bodies. A small crowd of living stood watching the growing crowd of dead. Organization prevailed. Bodies on this pile. Loose parts here. Presumably the spare arms and legs and heads would be reunited with their owners when they were pushed into the bags. But graves registration had run out of body bags, and the corpses were stacked without them.

New arrivals, wounded as well as dead, were brought over from the helicopters. A medic stood in the doorway of the operating tent diverting some of the stretchers away. Some cases were too far gone. Bellies blown open. Medics injected morphine into them. But morphine couldn't change the facts. I stared at one of the doomed men, fifty feet away. He saw me, and I knew that he knew. His frightened eyes widened, straining to live. He died. After a few minutes somebody came by and closed his eyes.

A new gunner, a black kid who had until recently been a grunt, had come over with me and Leese. We stayed back, but he had gone closer to the pile of bodies just to look. He started wailing and crying and pulling at the corpses and had to be dragged away. He had seen his brother at the bottom of the heap.

Two days later there was a lull in the fighting, at least as far as our company was concerned. We were given the day off. You could hear a collective sigh of relief. Compared to Happy Valley, this was *action*, and living through a year of it seemed unlikely.

What do you do on your first day off after weeks of action when you're feeling tired, depressed, and doomed on a hot, wet day at Camp Holloway, Vietnam? You get in a deuce-and-a-half and go into Pleiku and drink your brains out. That's what you do.

I rode in with Leese and Riker, Kaiser and Nate, Connors and Banjo, and Resler. I remember drinking beer all afternoon—effective because I usually didn't drink—first at one bar and then another. They all blended into one. Though I had started with Resler as my companion, I somehow found myself with Kaiser at a table in the Vietnamese officers' club that night.

"We see Americans as being apelike, big and clumsy with hairy arms," a Vietnamese lieutenant was saying to Kaiser. "Also, you all smell bad, like greasy meat."

Kaiser had got into a conversation with a racist of the opposite race. I watched the two men hate each other while I drank the genuine American bourbon that the Vietnamese lieutenant had so kindly bought us.

"Of course, you won't be offended if I continue?" asked the lieutenant.

"Naw," said Kaiser, squinting. "It's okay. I don't give a fuck what a slope thinks anyway." He belted down another shot.

The two men continued to trade heartfelt insults, the gist of which revealed normally submersed beliefs. Kaiser disclosed the widespread resentment among the Americans that the ARVN units apparently would not or could not fight their own battles. The lieutenant demonstrated that the ARVN resented being rescued by such oafish, unjustifiably wealthy gorillas who were taking over everything in their country, including their women.

After an hour of drinking and insults, Kaiser ended our stay by telling the old "pull the plug" joke to the lieutenant. That was the cynical solution to differentiating between friend and foe in Vietnam and ending the war. The joke had us putting all the "friendlies" on boats in the ocean where they would wait while the remaining people, the enemy, were killed. Then, as the punch line went, we would pull the plug, sink the ships.

Kaiser seemed almost surprised that the lieutenant didn't laugh. Instead the insulted man got up and left. Soon, looks from the other Vietnamese officers told us we weren't welcome. We left to continue our party an another bar.

Somehow we missed the truck back to camp. We went back to the officers' club and borrowed one of their Jeeps. We didn't tell them we were borrowing it; it was made in America, after all. When the Jeep was found the next day, parked in the Camp Holloway motor pool, it caused a stink. No one knew who it was who took it, but Farris looked awfully suspicious when it was reported at the morning briefing. He had noticed that we had come back by ourselves.

"Pretty slick, guys," he said after the briefing.

"Hey, Captain Farris, not us!" Kaiser looked sincere. "It was an inside job."

"Inside job?"

"That's right, sir. Those little guys will do anything to discredit us Americans. You should have heard the stupid things they said about us last night. 'Hairy apes. Greasy meat. Stupid.' No, sir, it doesn't surprise me a bit, knowing how they really feel about us."

"Right." Farris sighed. "Well, Mr. Kaiser, from now on, whenever you get a chance to party it up in town, I'll be keeping you company."

"Captain?" Kaiser looked at Farris, distressed.

"What if you guys had been stopped at the gate? Two warrant officers. You need a captain along to keep you out of trouble. Besides, I don't want to ride around in a deuce-and-a-half when I know you guys can get a Jeep."

Normally, the Cav carried only its own troopers, but we hauled ARVNs one day. I had heard stories about their unwillingness to fight.

"When you land at the LZ, make sure your door gunners cover the departing ARVNs," Williams said at the briefing. "There have been several incidents of so-called ARVNs turning around and firing into the helicopter that just dropped them off. Also, you may have a few on your ship that don't want to get out. If this happens, have *one* gunner force them out. The other gunner should be covering him. If your gunner has to shoot, make sure he knows to stop shooting when he gets the one who made the wrong move. A wrong move is turning around with a rifle pointed at you. We're flying this one lift today as a favor. We won't be doing it again." Williams gave his flock a paternal look. "Keep your eyes open."

I was amazed. This was the first time I had heard the rumors verified. In the months to come, I would hear as much about being wary with the ARVNs as I did about the Cong. If neither was to be trusted, who were our allies? Whose war was this, anyway? The people who had the most at stake wouldn't get out of the choppers to fight?

But we lifted the South Vietnamese without incident this time. We flew them to a big LZ from which they were supposed to patrol the newly liberated Ia Drang valley and maintain the status quo of allied dominance.

Within twenty-four hours they were pinned down by the VC. In two months we would return to retake the valley.

While we waited for a couple of hours to load the ARVNs, I saw a body lying in the field when we landed at the pickup zone next to Holloway. A piece of rope still cinched his neck.

I walked back and asked Resler, "What's the story on that guy?"

"He's a Chinese adviser," Gary said. "The same one we gave to the ARVNs yesterday for questioning." He looked toward the body. "You see him up close yet?"

"No."

"Well, he must have answered one of their questions wrong, because they took a chunk out of the side of his head as big as your fist." He grimaced. "His brains are leaking out. Want to go see him?"

"No. I've seen enough brains to last me."

"Hey, look at those guys." Gary pointed toward the body, about two hundred feet away. Two soldiers from the adviser compound were setting up a pose for a photograph. One man knelt on one knee behind the body while his friend moved around looking for the best angle for a snapshot. He took a few shots, but apparently the pose wasn't lively enough for him. He had his friend grab the dead man by the hair and raise the gory head off the ground, brains dripping. He posed like a man holding a dead gazelle.

With the ARVN in place, the Cav's mission was done. We only killed people; we did not take land. Such was the war of attrition.

By November 26, America had won its first large-scale encounter with the North Vietnamese army. The Cav and the B-52s killed 1800 Communists. The NVA killed more than 300 GIs. The Ia Drang valley campaign was one of the few battles in which I saw clearings filled with NVA bodies. In all, I might have seen a thousand of their corpses sprawled in the sun, rotting. We left them there.

The Cav waited a few days before looking for its missing. That gave the bodies time to get ripe enough for the patrols we lifted out to find them. It was the only way a dead man could be found in the tall elephant grass.

They did not growl now. Stacked on the cargo deck, they still fought, frozen inside their rubber bags, arms and legs stiffly askew. The smell of death seeped out of the zippered pouches and made the living retch. No matter how fast I flew, the smell would not blow away.

"We cut the enemy's throat instead of just jabbing away at his stomach. This is just the beginning," said one of our generals in *Life* magazine.

During the few days we hung around Pleiku before returning to An Khe, I spent most of my time with a couple of kids. I met them on one of my first visits to Pleiku. They were part of the mob who begged for candy and advertised their sisters to the GIs. What stood out about the older of the two brothers was his maturity at the age of nine. When the other kids became very aggressive, I would see Lang off to the side with a disapproving look on his face. He seemed to think that the others were too rowdy, too greedy.

Eventually, when the candy was gone and all the sisters were sold, the others would leave. I would be alone or with Resler, and Lang would come forward, smiling. He liked to hunker down and talk. We squatted in the street and talked of our two worlds in pidgin English and with gestures. He wore a black cotton shirt, tan shorts, and no shoes. He was missing two front teeth, and his hair was cut short in a burr.

Somehow Lang always knew when I would be coming to town. He said he *knew*, and pointed to his head. I think he spent most of his time waiting, if not for me, then for someone. He always ran to greet me as I walked up the street.

One night when Lang introduced me to a dejected-looking child, younger than he, whom he called brother, I couldn't stand it anymore and I took them both to a small store and bought them new shoes and shirts. The people in the shop were impressed. Their faces warmed with expressions of approval.

The next stop was a restaurant where I bought them each a steak dinner. Lang sipped some of my beer and leaned back in his chair, looking proud, as if he owned the place. His brother was very shy, and I never knew him as well.

I spent my last two days with them. By our talks and my asking other people I met, I determined that they were orphans. Where they slept no one knew. With gestures, guesses, and nods we politely discussed how their parents would be back to get them (from where they did not know) and would surely thank me for having befriended and provided for their children. Then we toured the city. As they were always hungry, our first trip was to the restaurant, then a long walk past scores of new shops to the public square, where the loudspeakers blared with news from the government.

The night before my return to An Khe, they knew about it without my saying anything. They knew it was ending, and they cried. My last look at them was from the back of a truck as I pulled away. They stood under a streetlight and waved and cried miserably. The light grew distant as we bounced back to the Turkey Farm. The darkness hid my tears, but no one watched anyway.

Swave and Deboner

A soaking wet Connors pushed open the flap and slogged inside. The rain beat furiously outside. He looked at the mud floor. "I am a swave and deboner army aviator," he said.

"The word is suave," I said.

"Not over here it ain't."

6.
The Holidays

Vietnam is like the Alamo.
                    —Lyndon Johnson, December 3, 1965

December 1965
When we got back from Ia Drang, the rats had torn up
our packages of food and left in their stead little piles of
rat turds artfully lined up along every surface in the mil-
dewed tent. The smell was tangible, but it was home.
And no pilots in our company had been killed, an occasion for thanksgiving.

Our first week back, we installed the floor and bought
chairs, rice mats, and other stuff to shape up the tent. I
even hooked up the lights.

A week later, the Colonel called the battalion officers
to a muddy spot between us and the Snakes. He stood,
bony arms folded against his chest, looking first at the
unruly formation, then at the ground, as if there should
be a box or something for him to stand on.

"I'm wet," said Connors in the drizzle.

"Gentlemen, I have a few things to talk to you about
today. Number one, we've been back for just a week and

233

already we're getting complaints from the MPs about officers crashing the gate at night to get to the village, officers drinking and driving recklessly, officers involved in unnatural sex acts in local bars." The Colonel shook his head, disappointed. "The medics say the VD rate has quadrupled. This behavior is against the code of the American officer, immoral and disgusting. I've decided to do something about it." The Colonel unfolded his arms to step forward for emphasis, but the mud stopped him. "Starting today, no officer is allowed to drive any vehicle: no Jeeps, no trucks, not even a mule. Any officer wishing to go somewhere by ground vehicle must request a driver first. There will be no exceptions. Second, the VD problem. Gentlemen, I know what you're going through. I'm human, too. But what kind of example do you think we're setting for the enlisted men? Those girls downtown are all disease-ridden, a very tenacious version of VD." The Colonel paused, his face a map of concern. "So for the time being, I'm holding every man here duty-bound to exercise discretion and stay totally away from those women."

Murmurs and laughter drifted through the crowd. Did he really think that abstention by the officers would influence the enlisted men? At that very moment, An Khe was filled with hundreds of enlisted men understandably jumping every female in sight. "Men, severe situations require unusual solutions. I know you may think of it as self-abuse, but I, and the commanders above me, think that m-masturbation is now justifiable."

"Is that an order?"

"Who said that!" No one answered. The Colonel glared expectantly at the damp mob, trying to pinpoint the bad apple. The offender did not come forward and throw himself into the mud at the Colonel's feet, begging forgiveness. Disgusted, the Colonel continued. "No, it is not an order; it is a suggestion. And if there are any more cases of the clap among you men, I'm closing the village to all of you. No passes to town for anything."

"Did he just order us to jerk off?" Connors's low voice came from the back of the crowd. Laughter engulfed the formation. The Colonel had not heard the remark.

"I've got a plan that will keep everybody occupied and healthy while we aren't flying. On this very spot, we will build an officers' club."

The brass applauded from the front of the formation.

"Face it, men. We'll be here a long time. Now, having a real club to come back to, a drink after a long day, a refreshing conversation with some nurses, comfortable plush chairs to sit back into, and music—all these things are possible if we start right now."

"Nurses?" Connors again.

"Yes, nurses. There are nurses at the division level. And they will come down here to see us, *if* we have some place for them to come to. You wouldn't want them to visit us in these moldy tents, would you?"

"Yes, I would."

"Who *is* that?" The Colonel peered from side to side trying to locate the heckler. We all turned around, looking at each other, to show that we were innocent. Captain Williams glared toward our group, in the direction of Connors.

"Gentlemen, it's attitudes like that will keep us living like beasts." He shook his head sadly. "So, starting right now, this minute, we will collect the first month's club dues. That money will be used to start buying the necessary materials. Captain Florence will be in charge of the job because he was a contractor in civilian life." Florence beamed and nodded. "Labor will be supplied voluntarily by you men. And each man will be expected to work his share each month until the job is finished."

A few days later, a Japanese newspaper reporter interviewed me. Some guys watched while the photographer snapped pictures. Among them was a tall, lanky captain from Indiana, whom I still think of as the New Guy. He had a healthy, confident aura about him, qualities that had faded from the veterans.

"If they want a new mess hall, let's build it!" he'd said when Williams announced that we'd volunteered to do that, too, along with the club. "I've built a lot of stuff in my day," he said. "I could probably do it myself. And, hell, anything's better than this crummy tent."

Riker had stared at him and growled, "Shit." Connors nodded. "Uh-huh, un-huh." Banjo snickered. That very day, the New Guy started laying out the new mess hall.

"Uh, Bob," said the New Guy. The Japanese photographer was hunched in front of me, dodging for an angle.

"Yeah?"

"Maybe you'd better take down that picture behind you."

I turned around to the pinup I had tacked to the wall of Riker's partition.

"You leave Cathy right where she is," said Connors. "Let the folks back in good old Japan know what we're fighting for."

"But what if his wife sees it?" said the New Guy.

"It?" Connors said. "It? Please, that is Cathy Rottencrotch, queen beaver of this tent. She is not an it, as you can see."

The reporter laughed, and the photographer moved to include Cathy in the shot.

"What is it like to fly into the bullets?" asked the reporter.

Someone wanted my opinion? I had thought about the bullets a lot during Ia Drang. I was always afraid. That was the answer: I was always afraid, every time. I sit before you, a chicken in soldier's clothing, Mr. Reporter. "Well, it's kinda scary at first, but when you get involved in the landings, you get used to it." Shit, yeah, you get used to it. Like to be out there right now doing it again.

"Have you had any close calls?"

Yes, very close. So close it makes me shiver. I could've been in that pile of bodies. "Well, no closer than any of the other guys. A few rounds through the cockpit. Stuff like that."

"Is that what you wear during the assaults?" I was dressed in fatigues, wearing my flak vest and pistol, at the photographer's request.

"Yes."

"Does that—" He pointed.

"Flak vest."

"Does that flak vest stop bullets?"

"No. As a matter of fact, it won't even slow them down."

Everyone laughed.

We flew support for a convoy going to Pleiku and had to laager for two hours at the Turkey Farm.

Foot-tall grass bent over as the wind gusted along the row of twenty or so helicopters. Near noon, as we sorted through the C-ration boxes, somebody at the front of the row knocked over his jet-fuel stove.

"Fire!" someone yelled. Smoke swirled out of the grass next to the first few Hueys. I ran with the rest of the men toward the fire. Orange flames burrowed through the grass. People slapped the rushing flames with their shirts, but it did no good. The breeze carried the flames toward the rear ships. My ship and the two behind it would be right in the path. I ran back.

Reacher stood behind my seat. "Hurry, sir!" I fumbled for my seat belts, but the smoke surrounding us made me realize that there was no time. I cursed myself for not having the ship preset for start up. Too lax. I flipped switches and hit the starter trigger. "Hurry, sir. The fire is almost here!" The blades turned more slowly than ever before. The flames were less than a hundred feet away, moving very fast. The exhaust-gas-temperature gauge read hot. A hot start now? No, it dropped back to green. The rotors blinked, close to operating rpm. When the flames were orange under the chin bubble, I pulled pitch before the turbine was completely up, and the machine groaned into the air. When I pedal-turned the tail away from the flames, my door flew open. Damn. Didn't even have the door latched. The noise of the ship seemed very loud. I could feel the hot breeze, and I realized that I was wearing no helmet. Jerk! I backed away in a hover and set the ship down. The two ships behind me moved out of the fire, too.

Connors hovered to intercept the line of burning grass. He approached from downwind, forcing the flames to pause against the blast from his rotors. I pulled back up to a hover and joined him and another ship in the corraling operation. The fire died against the wall of wind.

While we were at Ia Drang, Christmas packages had been pouring in. Gifts, canned hams, cookies, cards, and loving pictures. We even had a large cardboard box filled with letters from schoolchildren all over America delivered to our mess hall. "Dear American soldier," said one of them. "I am very proud of you. I know you will win. Becky, Grade 5, Mrs. Lake's class." I got a pound cake from Patience mailed in September. After three months en route it was not edible.

Two weeks before Christmas, we launched more assaults into Happy Valley, landing troops on pinnacles instead of down in the valley.

Resler and I began flying together. We were the two most junior warrant officers in the company. It was an honor that we were trusted with our own ship. I usually logged aircraft-commander time.

"Why? We're both equals, you know," Resler said.

"Not quite. I graduated a month ahead of you."

"So?"

"So, I've got seniority on you, Resler. You're the pilot and I'm the aircraft commander."

"We get to trade!"

"Maybe."

We'd both practiced pinnacle landings with the more experienced pilots in the company. It was like approaching a floating island in the sky. Some of the hilltops were easily eight hundred feet above the valleys. The trick was to keep the landing spot below the horizon. If it climbed above it, you were too low, and that put you at the mercy of the buffeting winds on the lee side of the hill. With the heavy loads we carried, the chopper could mush into the hill if we approached through this burble of down-rushing wind. It was difficult to recover because there was no place to dive to get more airspeed. A captain in our other platoon had done it wrong a few days before with the result that he flopped and rolled down the side of the hill, strewing men and matériel out the doors of the Huey all the way down. He climbed out and landed on his hands and knees in a bed of punji stakes. Given that two other people on board had been killed, it wasn't bad. He got to go to Japan to get the shit dug out of the punji holes in his knees.

Resler and I made a good team. We talked ourselves away from trouble.

Resler was on the stick, flaring toward the top of a grassy hill. Our sink rate was high because of the eight grunts we carried. We both knew the landing was going to be hard.

"Power," I said.

"I've got all the power she has."

"Then flare more. You'll hit too hard."

"Look, Mason, I'm flying. I can handle it."

Luckily, it was windy. It was lucky because the wind blew the grass around and I saw part of a large boulder just where we were going to land. Hitting that would trip us, sending us crashing down the other side of the hill.

"Rocks!"

"Huh?" Gary couldn't see them, because he was flying from the right side and had no chin bubble to look through. We were going to hit.

"Rocks!" I grabbed the collective and pulled hard. I hadn't put my feet on the pedals, so the ship yawed to the right. We hesitated crookedly above the boulders, and the rotor wash blew the grass down, and Gary saw them, too. The ship mushed lazily over the boulders. As we cleared the hilltop, Gary dove down the other side to recover the waning rotor speed.

"I have just saved your miserable life," I said.

"Oh, yeah? From what?"

"Those rocks, you blind fuck."

"What rocks?" Gary fumed. "Why did you grab the collective like that? You could've killed us." He shook his head seriously as he started his climb out of the valley. "Lucky for you I was able to save it," he said.

Even though we flew every day, they always found time to give us our shots—plague shots, yellow-fever shots, hepatitis shots—on a regular basis. Naturally, we all hated shot day.

While I waited inside the tent, I watched a soldier having his thumb tended. I watched intently as the surgeon pried up the man's thumbnail. It was smashed and almost black. As the surgeon pulled the nail up, black juice ran out. When the nail finally pulled free, I sank to my knees. I couldn't believe it. This simple little operation brought me to my knees. I almost fainted.

"Shouldn't watch stuff like that," said the medic.

"You're right." I nodded weakly from the floor. "Maybe if it had been regular blood . . ."

Connors was chosen to fly a CBS News film crew around as it followed Gary and me in our ship.

"Hey, you guys, make it look good." Connors stood outside my window at a laager.

"Like how?"

"Like steeper-than-normal turns and lower than low level and flaring steeper than steep. Like that. You know: Make it look good."

So while we swooped all around the valley, dropping off troops—the valley had no war that day—we were being filmed. In a low-level turn, I pulled in close enough to a tree to brush the leaves with the rotors. I flared so steeply at an LZ that the grunts screamed.

"Looking good," said Connors.

Patience said she saw the film clip on television. She knew it was me because there was a square on the door, which she knew marked my company, and "That pilot flew just like you drive."

Nate and Resler and I went to town one morning. There was nothing up that day, so we hung around in the bars and watched the girls. Nate claimed he was immune to Viet clap, so he had most of the fun.

Something did come up, but since we weren't there, the company left without us. We got back early in the afternoon to a ghost camp. Everyone except the Bobbsey Creeps were gone.

"Big battle going on just north of Lima," said Owens. "Where were you guys? The major is pissed. Did you have a pass? It's hot out there. Really, the major is really pissed."

Nate thought the time was right to open the canned

ham he had been saving for Christmas. We had a quiet party. The ham was good.

Just after dawn, Leese busted in through the door flap. "The New Guy was killed."

"What?" said Gary.

"The New Guy. You know, the replacement. He got shot through the head. Hey, you guys, get ready to get out there."

I wondered if I would amount to that much of an utterance someday. "Mason got shot through the head. Hey, you guys, get ready to go out there."

"What's going on?" I said.

"It's hot," said Leese. "Lotta automatic fire. All in the same area where we've been farting around for the last two weeks. Yesterday Charlie decided to fight. It's already hot again this morning. You guys are supposed to crew the next two ships coming back. Mine is fucked. Nate, you and I take the next ship, and Bob and Gary the one after that. Okay?"

There was an hour between Leese and Nate's departure and the arrival of our ship. Resler and I were alone in our corner of the tent. I smoked. Resler cracked his knuckles.

"There's some islands out about twenty miles from Qui Nhon," said Gary.

"I know."

"Twenty miles away. Completely uninhabited, too."

"How do you know that?" I said.

"I've heard."

"Terrific."

"Do you ever think about quitting?" Gary asked.

"Sometimes."

"Me, too. Sometimes. Guess that makes us chickens."

"Maybe. But we do go fly, don't we? That's got to make up for feeling chicken."

"Yeah, I guess it does." He paused. "And when I'm fly-

This is the picture of Patience I carried in Vietnam. She is twenty-two years old, my true love, and the mother of our son, Jack.

Jack is one and a half. He and Patience will wait for me in Naples, Florida.

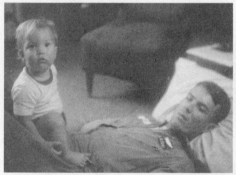

Catching a nap before a night training mission at Fort Benning. We're forming up the First Air Cavalry, the world's first combat airmobile division.

Patience takes a final snapshot of Jack and me. I'm on the way to join my battalion to board a ship for Vietnam.

On the deck of the USN *Croatan*, in the middle of the Pacific Ocean.

Gerald Towler (Resler), brand-new aviator like me, boarding the troop carrier *Darby*.

Officer's club under construction   latrines   Golfcourse (flight line)

2nd Platoon

Operations

The Major & XO

Mess Hall

B Company 229th AHB, An Khe, Vietnam 1965
Call sign: Preachers

In An Khe, Vietnam, we set up a camp for us and our four hundred helicopters. By January 1966, this was the layout of B Company, 229th Assault Helicopter Battalion. I lived in the 2nd Platoon tent with these guys.

Clockwise in this group, Gerald Towler (Resler), Don Reynolds (Kaiser), Bob Kiess (Leese) and Dallas Harper (Banjo); Lee Komich (Connors) and Walt Schramm .

Chuck Nay (Nate) at our posh bathing facilities.

Ken Dicus (Riker), in his cube in the 2nd Platoon tent.

From front to back, my platoon leader, Robert Stinnett (Shaker), Captain Gillette (Gill), and Hugh Farmer practicing his golf swing.

Jack Armstrong and Tom Schaal (T. Shaw), from the 1st Platoon.

Preachers laager in a rice paddy.

Door-gunner Ubinski (Rubinski) during Happy Valley.

Crew chief Bill Weber (Red).

Crew chief Gene Burdick (Reacher) retrieved a Jeep driver's foot, one of five soldiers we tried to rescue.

DON REYNOLDS

Howard Phillips (Morris) and Woody Woodruff (Decker) were always together.

A field briefing where I look for my lighter.

Low-level run up Happy Valley.

Dallas Harper, Neil Parker, and Lee Komich back from a mission.

Gasmasks were a bad idea.

Washing out the blood at the end of a busy day.

Extraction.

Door-gunners started out using bungie straps to hold their M-60 machine guns. Later, they were given mounts.

From inside the cockpit at a sandy LZ in Happy Valley.

Dropping troops off on a hilltop in Bong Son valley.

Kiess, Towler, and Mason in the cockpit.

Looking happy with my new
M-1 carbine.

Towler and I in our hex-tent at Dak To. We
shared these quarters with Stoney Stizzle
(Stoopy Stoddard).

Dawn preflight at Pleiku. I don't think I was
awake without a cigarette.

Lang, the cola girl.

Waiting to crank up
at Dak To.

We spent a lot of time waiting between troop lifts and evacuations.

Towler in custody of the
company's mascot,
Mo'fuck the Mongoose.

Kiess has coffee with
a pilot on a picnic table
made from ruined rotor
blades, Happy Valley.

Towler battles a sandstorm on the beach at Tuy Hoa. That lone figure by the tent in
the background is Stoney Stizzle who is heroically trying to anchor our tent.

Before I made the transition home, I made this swell ammo-box chair.

First day home, I'm at the kitchen table trying to look normal.

My new assignment was the flight school at Fort Wolters, Texas, where I became a flight instructor. The Hiller 23D is idling with the collective tied down while I inspect a practice LZ in the Texas brush.

Our first family Christmas, Mineral Wells, Texas. Home at last.

ing the assaults, I start feeling brave, almost comfortable, in the middle of it all. Like a hawk, maybe."

"I do, too. When I'm in the middle of it. But times like now, I'd quit at the slightest excuse. So what am I? A chicken or a hawk?"

"You're a chickenhawk." Gary smiled.

"Yeah." There was silence. Yes, I thought. We're both scared out of our minds. It felt like we were near the end of our wait on death row.

"How long do you think we could live on a Huey-load of C rations?" asked Gary.

"Shit, probably a couple of years. Two thousand pounds of food."

"Maybe we should take less food and steal a couple of girls to go with us instead."

"Go where?"

"The island."

"You know, you're right. We *could* do it."

"I know we could do it." Resler smiled proudly.

I liked the idea very much. Yes, by God, we could do it! "That's it! You've got the answer. We just keep flying when we go out. We'll have a big load of C's. We can stop in Qui Nhon and get a couple of women, fly out to the island, land, and dump the food and the girls. Then one of us has to take the chopper out away from the island and dump it."

"Why dump it? We can camouflage it, you know." Gary leaned forward eagerly, caught up in the plan.

"Well, we'll see when we get there. Maybe there'll be enough trees and shit to hide a Huey. But if there isn't, we ditch it."

"Okay. If there isn't enough."

"Some booze, too. Can you see it? You and me and two luscious girls lying back under the palm trees. We have to have a radio with us, too, so we can keep track of the war. You know, so we know what we're missing."

Gary looked concerned. "Maybe we could fly to Pleiku first."

"Why?"

"Well, I don't know if I want to live out there with just any girl. Remember that girl, Mary, in Pleiku where I spent the whole night?"

"Yeah."

"Well, she loved me."

"Ah Gary, she . . ." Didn't love you, she wanted your money. She wanted a ticket out of this bullshit country. "She was nice, wasn't she?"

"She loved me." Suddenly we were both quiet. We looked away, into our thoughts. My strength drained away. What a stupid idea. Just hopeful dumb fucking wishing. Face facts. *Face facts.* FACE FACTS!

"Gary, I think we can't go to Pleiku first. I think we could only do it if we flew out of here just like normal and then disappeared. We could probably get away with landing at Qui Nhon. There's a lot of transient traffic there."

"Not without Mary."

"Gary, be reasonable."

"Hey, guys, it's your turn." Wendall ducked into the tent. The palm-tree isle, the bronze nubiles, popped out of existence. "The crew chief is patching some holes, but the ship will be flyable in just a minute." Wendall looked kind of pale. "The old man wants you to join the gaggle at Lima. They've got some more missions to fly today. I hope it's better for you guys."

The crew chief, along with the maintenance officer, had inspected the ship. The holes in the tail boom were a concern because the bullets could have gone through the tail-rotor drive tube or the control cables. They had not. The crew chief covered the holes with green tape that almost matched the olive-drab skin. It was now our ship.

The sky, as if on cue, was overcast. At the An Khe

pass Gary had to drop to within fifty feet of the road to maintain visibility. We landed at Lima.

"What's that all about on the road?" I asked Connors. As we circled Lima on our approach, we had noticed a crowd of men around a big pile of something covered with canvas next to an overturned mule.

"A grunt mule driver lost control and flipped over."

"Was he hurt?"

"No. Killed."

"You and Resler are Red Four," said Leese. He hurried back toward the front of the gaggle. Lima was crawling with activity. Troopers moved around in small groups, looking for their assigned ships. A few Hueys were out over sling loads, hitching up. A Chinook made an approach slinging in a fat black fuel bladder from the Golf Course.

"Shall I put my men on board, sir?" a Cav sergeant asked me.

"Yeah, Sergeant. Let them get on." I looked forward at the other squads moving toward their ships. "We're leaving pretty soon."

He turned. "Move it!" They were in place in about fifteen seconds, I think.

It was a monster gaggle—forty or more ships—the kind I hated the most. And we were flying the four position again. We would have to fly hard to keep up with an outside turn, and flare like hell when the gaggle turned our way. Plus, the ship was a dog. When we took off, she hung down in the turbulence of the choppers in front of us, straining her poor guts out. We caught up to the gaggle at mission altitude and watched the prep going on. Smoke trailed in long streamers drifting off to the west. Air-force jockeys streaked away back to their base, their job done. Our gunships worked the area with their rockets and flex guns. Gary flew, so I just watched the show and smoked a cigarette. Kinda like being at a movie. The grunts behind me were screaming at each other over the cacophony of the ship, smiling, laughing, smoking cigarettes, scared out of their brains. The ships in the gaggle rose and fell on the sea of air. Formations always looked sloppy when you were in them because no two ships were ever at the same altitude. From the ground you got a flat view of the V, and it looked better. One of the noises on the radio was the Colonel.

"Yellow Four. Pull in closer. You call that a formation?" The Colonel was flying above us, being a colonel. There's a reason why they do that, we said. It's from the word itself: colon(el), or asshole. They do exactly what you would expect them to.

"Guns ready?" Gary asked. We were now dropping fast, having crossed the initial point, a meager hut near a tall hedgerow that marked the beginning of the final leg of the assault. The LZ was two miles away.

"Ready."

"Ready."

"Fire at my order only, unless you see something obvious. Don't shoot into the huts."

"Yes, sir."

"Yes, sir."

Can't fire into the huts. If you fired into the huts, you might kill a VC.

As we swooped toward the ground for the low-level run, I put my hand gently on the cyclic; my feet rode the pedals; my left hand touched the collective.

"Flare."

Fifty feet off the ground, Gary was doing well. He flipped the tail past a few trees just when I thought he'd hit them. The gaggle mushed and bounded into the LZ. The troopers leapt out firing.

"Yellow One, it's too hot ahead of you. Recommend you pedal-turn and go back out the way you came." That was one of the Dukes, the gunships making runs at something at the far end of the LZ. The guys up front were yelling that there was a lot of shooting going on, but I couldn't see any back our way.

"Roger. Flight, we're going out the way we came. Wait your turn." The flight leader lifted to a high hover and turned to fly back over us. Each ship in its turn leapt up and flew back over us. By the time it was our turn, the first ships were already calling in hit reports. As we joined up, the ship ahead of us was hit, showering bits of Plexiglas back on us. Next I heard *tick-tick-tick*, and new bullet holes appeared in the Plexiglas over our heads. Gary pulled full power trying to get higher, but the ship was a dog even when empty, so we lagged behind the others. *Tick*. Somewhere in the air frame.

At 1000 feet or so I lit a cigarette and contemplated the new holes. Bad place for 'em. It'll leak if it rains.

We didn't make it back to Lima. We were pulled out with the other three ships in the Red flight for a couple of emergency extractions. Gary and I followed Farris and Kaiser in Red Three to get some wounded out of a hot LZ. The other two ships went somewhere else.

Farris orbited a couple of times to make sure there was no firing going on. We were supposed to wait until the grunts secured the LZ.

"All clear, Red Three." I heard gunshots in the background as the trooper talked on the radio to Farris. Farris did, too.

"You're sure?"

"Affirmative, Red Three. You're clear to land." Of course, he was lying. I would've lied, too, in the same position.

As we made our approach, Farris took the spot I was headed for, so I had to fly a hundred feet past him. I landed in a grassy spot in front of a hedgerow. I saw troopers low-crawling all over the place.

"Secure, my ass," said Gary.

Two bent-over men ran toward us carrying a stretcher. Sand sprayed out of the grass near them, and they went down. The body in the litter shifted like a doll.

"Fire from the front," I radioed to Farris.

The stretcher bearers got back up and made it to the side door, where the crew chief quickly jumped out and grabbed one end of the litter and shoved it across the deck. Another few rounds hit the dirt in front of us. I looked at the radio antenna of the grunt leader swinging around behind the hedgerow. "Fucking liar."

Another litter had been hauled to our other door, and the gunner was out helping. We were locked to the ground. Farris called that he was leaving. "Come on! Come on!" I yelled back between the seats. Two walking wounded rolled on board. The grunt leader stood up for a second and then hit the dirt. All I heard was the whine of our turbine. No shots. Just little puffs of sand in the short grass. At the hedgerow, a man held a thumbs-up. He pointed to a man at his knees and shook his head. For the first time, I noticed the body. Of course it was a body. Strands of intestines had followed the bullets out of his guts and were lying across his abdomen. He could wait a little longer.

I was up. Pedal-turn. Nose down. *Tick*. Go. *Tick*. Climb.

The four wounded lived.

We spent a rainy night back at good old Lima. The new bullet holes leaked.

There was a Christmas truce, but we flew anyway, taking patrols out to check on reported VC violations in our territory. I couldn't get over how bizarre it was. We could decide to stop killing each other for a few days and then start again. I was still young then.

Actually, the reason I was out on Christmas was that I

had fucked up a few days before on a flight with Captain Gillette, our supply officer. He and I were the lead ship in a gaggle of forty-plus ships operating in the hills. On the flight back, I became very aware that there were all these helicopters following me. I had never led a big gaggle before.

All I had to do was bring the gaggle back to the refueling area where the Vietnamese worker had died of snakebite. The lead ship had to fly smoothly—no quick turns, gradual descents. But as I started to slow down for the approach, I was too careful. I kept thinking that they would all ram me. I slowed too late, with the result that I overflew the approach. I missed the whole fucking field! Gillette turned to me in awe. There were rumors around that I was a pretty good pilot, and look—Mason missed the entire field, in a helicopter! I had visions of the whole gaggle laughing behind me as I flew past and set up to return. But it was worse. When I made the turn, I saw that all the others had gone ahead and landed while their leader flew off to La-La Land. I flew back to the field flushed with embarrassment. How would I ever live this down?

So on Christmas Day I found myself flying with Farris. He didn't say as much, but he was checking me out to see why I had fucked up. I was the lead-ship pilot again, but I had spent so much time worrying and thinking about my mistake that I made perfect approaches. I picked the right spots. I allowed enough room for the gaggle to land. My landings, takeoffs, everything, went just fine.

"Gillette said you were having a little trouble with your approaches," Farris said tactfully.

"That one time, I did."

"I can see that. You did just fine today."

"Thanks."

"Merry Christmas."

That evening, after we delivered Christmas dinners to all the patrols, we had our own turkey meal. Later we sang a couple of carols, ate some of the goodies sent by the wives and families, and I, for one, shed a few tears when I went to bed.

"I don't believe it," Gary Resler said, crouching by his bunk. Heavy gunfire sounded outside our GP. "Why?"

I shook my head in the darkness. "Madness." A machine gun blasted just outside the tent. I forced my ass farther under the cot, up against the cross braces. I closed my eyes, trying to make the chaos outside a dream. The blast of the machine gun lost itself in the roll of hundreds of other exploding weapons. I was hiding from the madness.

A shadow ran down the aisle, thumping a loose board under my head. Pistol shots rang out inside the tent; then the shadow was gone.

The firing continued. Riker was inside with Gary and me. The others were outside in the trench—safer, maybe. The cot wasn't going to stop bullets, but I felt safer lying on the floor in the darkness.

"Maybe we should go outside," Gary called from the corner of his area.

"We tried that, remember?" A staccato blast sounded from just beyond the canvas wall. "They won't stop!" I shouted. The madness roared like a storm. I guess I won't forget New Year's Eve, 1965, I thought.

In a lull, Gary said, "I think it's dying down. I'm going outside."

"You'll be back." He didn't hear me. I felt the boards creak as he got up and left. He was back in five minutes.

I felt someone thudding along our aisle again. "Mason, Resler. You guys here?" It was Captain Farris.

"Yeah," I said from down on the floor.

"Well, get out there and stop them. Stop them."

"We tried."

"Well, try again. Let's go." He ducked out through the flap.

"I don't believe this shit," I heard myself say.

"C'mon, let's go," said Gary.

Under the tracer-streaked sky a spec-five held an M-60 machine gun at his hip, blasting away. The light was dim, but that demonic face was clear.

"Stop that!" I shouted. "Put that gun away!"

The spec-five shook his head and smiled ominously. He watched his tracers stream into the sky toward Hong Kong Hill. God, I thought, there are people on top of that hill, lots of them.

It had started with people shooting into the sky for New Year's Eve. Now it was totally out of control, and bullets were going toward the radio-relay team on top of the hill. Suddenly tracers came back from the top. The relay team was firing back down into the division.

The Colonel was a spider scurrying and dodging from sandbag pile to ditch to tent, encountering his men gone mad. Fifty feet away from us, he stopped and screamed at a man firing a machine gun. "Stop! I order you to stop!" The man paused, with an irritated look on his face. His battalion commander was becoming a nuisance. He smiled menacingly and swung the hip-held M-60 toward the Colonel, aiming it carefully at his chest. The Colonel shrank back. He turned momentarily to look at Gary and me.

"Do something," he said, glaring at us.

"What?" We shrugged. He bent over and dodged back toward his tent.

It was quiet at last. At twelve-thirty or so, the battle of Hong Kong Hill stopped. Planes that had had to orbit since the beginning of the melee could now land. The shooting had stopped, and the men had put the guns away. It was still New Year's, but it was now very quiet.

"Some people were killed at the maintenance depot," said Connors.

We all sat quietly on our cots, lights on, as if nothing had happened.

"How many?" somebody asked.

"Seven, I think. There's some wounded, too." He spoke without emphasis and stared at the floor. "Hell of a party, huh?"

They shouldn't allow holidays in a war.

7.
The Rifle Range

The verdict on the First Cavalry concept was in last week. Stepping out of an olive-drab tent at An Khe, after an hour-long briefing on the division, Secretary McNamara was brimming over with praise. The division, he said, was "unique in the history of the American Army. . . . There is no other division in the world like it."
—*Newsweek*, December 13, 1965

January 1966

Not long after Resler and I talked of disappearing with a Huey, a ship from the Snakes, tail number 808, took off on a foggy morning to go out to Lima with C rations and supplies, and never arrived.

The pilots called once before crossing the pass to say that the visibility was almost zero, but they could make it. By 0900 I was involved in the search. By dusk they had not been found, not even a clue.

"Do you think they did it?" Resler asked.

"Nah. It was a stupid idea."

The next day, half a dozen ships from the battalion

combed the jungles for miles around the pass looking for signs. Nothing.

The First Cav—*the* helicopter division—lost one of their own Hueys in their own back yard. It was bad for pilot morale.

Meanwhile, supply sergeants throughout the battalion were keeping their fingers crossed. This was a rare opportunity to balance the property books—once and for all.

Let me explain. In the army, specific amounts of military equipment were allocated to the company supply sections. Once or twice a year, the inspectors general, agents from the brass, came through to check that all property was in the supply depot or properly accounted for. If it wasn't, mountains of paperwork had to be done, including explanations by the commander and the supply officer. Searches were made. That was the formal army system.

The *in*formal army supply system worked around such rules. The supply officers simply traded excesses back and forth to cover their asses, and the IGs never knew. Unless, of course, they had once been supply officers. The informal system made the books look good and protected the supply people, but we still had no jungle boots or chest protectors. Certain things you had to get for yourself. I was able to trade a grunt supply sergeant some whiskey for a pair of jungle boots. The chest protectors, though, were still not available. There were only a handful of them in the battalion.

All supply people dreamed of a way to balance the books—once and for all—without all that trading and shuffling. Flight 808 looked like the answer.

After two more days of searching, a Huey was found. It was the wreckage of a courier ship that had disappeared on its way to Pleiku a year before. The search was abandoned, and flight 808 was declared lost.

Declaring the ship missing started paper gears working

all over the battalion. One of the questions the supply people loved to hear was "Did you have anything aboard the missing helicopter?"

"Well, now that you mention it, I did have six entrenching tools on that ship. Plus some web belts—seven web belts, to be exact—three insulated food containers, four first-aid kits, twenty-four flashlights," and so on.

When all the reports were tallied, I was told by Captain Gillette, it came to a total of five tons of assorted army gear—about five times what we normally carried.

"One hell of a helicopter, don'cha think?" said Gillette.

"Maybe that's why it went down," Gary said. "Slightly overloaded. By eight thousand pounds, I'd say."

"Yep. We'll never see another like that one."

The action in Happy Valley slowed to nothing again. The brass took this to mean that we had won. Won what? A higher body count score, for one thing. And we did dominate the skies. Wendall believed that the Communists had decided to stop fighting temporarily, like they'd often done with the French. Instead of picking up a gun that morning, Charlie went out into the rice paddies and worked. We didn't believe this. We thought the murderous hordes were beaten and whimpering out in the jungles, licking their wounds. But Wendall said they were with the villagers. Because they *were* the villagers.

Back around Christmas, a group of Montagnard mercenaries had revolted and killed more than twenty ARVN officers at the Mang Yang pass. After that the Cav guarded Mang Yang pass and the bridges on Route 19 going to Pleiku. The American patrols had their HQs next to the road. We delivered hot food, clothing, mail, and ammunition to them every day. Four or five ships from our company did the resupplying. Resler and I flew one of those ships, logging six and eight hours daily.

It was difficult to adjust to peaceful times. The deaths, the close calls, and the generally hectic pace of the past few weeks had established a combative mind-set and an expectation of continued action. Just going out to resupply some patrols on a secure road was so bland that we played games to make it interesting. Resler and I took turns flying low level down the road, seeing who could hold the ship in the turns. We also buzzed a convoy. MPs in the convoy thought we were maniacs and radioed our battalion. Farris was waiting for us when we got back that night. He said we had really scared the MPs.

"If I hear of any more cowboy stuff by you guys, I'll—" He had to stop and think for a minute. What could he do? Ground us? Send us home? What could he do that we wouldn't like? "Tomorrow is your day off. You two have just volunteered to work on the club."

Perfect.

Rumor came first, then the news. The 229th was scheduled to go to Bong Son valley. Every recon ship sent to this coastal valley fifty miles north of Qui Nhon had been hit by ground fire. The VC called it their own. A huge joint operation was planned involving the Cav, the marines, the navy, and the ARVNs. The navy would bombard the LZs with heavy guns. The marines would land on the beach north of the valley. The Cav would go into the middle of it and take the place. The ARVNs would mill around somewhere.

One of the recon-ship pilots, a warrant officer from another platoon, walked into the company's HQ tent and turned in his wings, silver wings he had earned before the Second World War. He put them on the table and said, "Enough."

"God! What will they do to him?" said Resler.

"I don't know. Is it legal to just quit?" I asked Connors.

"Got me," said Connors. "Probably they'll shoot him or cut off his balls or maybe even make him work on the club."

The quitter was whisked away. Several weeks later we learned that he was operating an in-country R&R center in Saigon.

It had never occurred to us that we *could* quit. Technically, we were all volunteers, and if anyone couldn't take it, he could resign from flight status. But actually to do it ... just quit. It was definitely an intelligent thing to do, but so dumb. How would he live with himself?

A few days later we flew farewell assaults in good old Ia Drang again, following up reports from the ARVNs that the NVA was gathering strength near the Cambodian border. About twenty-four ships from our battalion, including one with Nate and me, were sent to poke around.

Sherman rarely led a flight. The aging captain—he was in his early forties—needed some combat-command time before he could make major. He was nervous and cocky at our briefing, the dashing leader of a combat mission to the dreaded Ia Drang. His plan had us flying to Plei Djereng Special Forces camp, near the Cambodian border, then breaking up in groups of four to land grunts at strategic points.

Nate flew on the way out and I played with the maps. It wasn't necessary to navigate during a formation flight, but I was always curious about just where the fuck I really was. We crossed the Turkey Farm at 2000 feet, heading west-southwest. A half hour later I saw what I thought was the camp five miles off to our left, but Sherman continued straight ahead.

"Getting close to the border," I said.

"How far?" asked Nate.

"Well, it looks to me like we're almost on top of it right now."

"Really?"

"Yellow One, Yellow Two." Yellow One was Sherman; Yellow Two, Morris and Decker.

"Roger, Yellow Two. Go ahead."

"Yellow One, I think we'd better turn. Real soon," Morris drawled.

There was a moment of silence. I could imagine Sherman unfolding and folding and crumpling maps, trying to figure out just what part of this miserable jungle he *was* over.

"Yellow Two, we're right on course."

"Ah, that's a negative, Yellow One. I've got us past our target."

That was Morris's way of saying that we were over Cambodia.

Another moment of silence.

"Negative, Yellow Two. I've got us on course."

You could hear the static of Morris's mike as he hesitated. "Roger."

Poor Sherman had fucked up and still didn't know it. His very first authentic combat mission as commander. Kiss major good-bye.

Five miles into the jungle marked "Cambodia" on the map, Sherman's ship lurched. He veered left, then right, before he actually made the turn. He made no announcement, simply turned back.

"Man, it's hard to navigate around this fucking jungle, the dumb shit," Nate said.

The radio was silent until our expeditionary gaggle returned to the proper country. From that day on, poor Sherman would get no command more adventurous or prestigious than being put in charge of digging the company's well.

As we crossed the border, the chatter began once again. Sherman called Connors and told him he wanted our flight to stay on the ground as a reserve when we landed. Then he told us all to stretch out in trail formation.

The gaggle strung itself out in single file for the landing at Plei Djereng. As the first ships flared, red dust billowed up and swallowed them completely. The Special Forces people had bulldozed a landing strip, and the dry season had turned it to dust.

"Don't try to hover. Put 'em straight on the ground," Sherman radioed. We couldn't even see the ships that had already landed in the red clouds.

I trailed in behind Connors. When he got within fifty feet of the ground, the dust from the ship in front swallowed him up. He called, "Go around." He pulled up and headed off to the right. I followed. Ships three and four behind us went on in and landed, and then the rest. By circling around, Connors and I put ourselves on the tail of the line. As we set up for the second try, I drifted back farther from Connors to stay away from his dust. Ten feet off the ground, Connors disappeared. Now it was my turn, the last ship in.

Roots and leafless bushes stuck up wildly at the extreme end of the strip. When I flared, the rotor wash stirred up the dust and everything vanished. I felt the ship hit something. I thought it sounded like a stump coming up through the belly, which happened pretty often on the assaults, so I elected to land a few feet farther ahead. Which way was ahead? Which way was up? There were only seconds to figure it out. The compass showed that we were turning to the right. I pushed the left pedal to stop the spin. It didn't work.

This was a tail-rotor failure. The solution was to chop the power quickly to stop the ship from rotating under the main rotors, and then do a hovering autorotation. We had practiced this routine in flight school. Hundreds of times.

I tried to roll off the throttle to stop the spin, but it was locked. Nate, flying right seat, had locked the throttle for cruising. There was no way to release it from my side. There was no time to discuss the problem with Nate. This whole spinning machine was going to go over and beat itself to death, real soon. So I decided to put it down before it spun too fast. The ship hit and twisted on the skids, rocked over toward the left, hesitated precariously, and flopped back level.

We were out long before the dust settled. It didn't *look* too bad. The ship sat crooked on its skids. The tail-rotor gear box was hanging by mechanical tendons. The tail rotor itself was twisted and bent.

Connors came back looking genuinely concerned. "What happened?"

"I'm not sure, but I hit something with my tail rotor."

Nate and I, Connors and Banjo, and the grief-stricken Reacher poked around the ship looking for a stump or a rock or something big that could have done such damage, but there was nothing obvious. Nate finally called us over to where he squatted.

"A root?" I exclaimed.

"Looks that way," said Nate. "See, you chopped it off right here." He pointed to a fresh cut on a scrawny root sticking up through the dust. The cutoff point was two feet off the ground.

"Damn," I said.

"Don't worry about it, Mason. You couldn't have seen it, not in this dust," said Nate. "I didn't see it."

"Yeah, but you weren't flying."

"Couldn't be helped."

I bitched some more about my rotten luck, but Nate and Connors kept saying it wasn't my fault.

Reacher came over and said, "It's okay, Mr. Mason. She'll be flying again in no time." I felt better. Reacher was the one to know. It was his ship, the most powerful ship in the company, the ship Leese had used to haul that impossible load. If Reacher thought it wasn't too bad, then it wasn't too bad.

Nate and I walked to the Special Forces HQ hooch to wait for a ride back. Reacher decided to stay with the Huey until a Chinook was sent out to sling-load it home for repairs.

"You guys want a beer?" asked one of the advisers. He wore a camouflage uniform like the Vietnamese Rangers', covered with red dust. Red dust collected on everybody's skin.

"Sure," said Nate. We weren't going to be flying any more today, so having a beer was okay.

We sat on a cot under a canvas canopy and sipped our beers while the rest of the gaggle gathered their load of grunts, cranked up, and left. A half hour later, the dust finally settled.

"Well, how do you like it?" asked the adviser.

"The beer?"

"No, this place. Plei Djereng. The asshole of the world."

"Dusty."

"Yeah, we keep it that way on purpose. Keeps the shit from stinking."

A lone Huey courier landed at the camp. Nate and I hitched a ride to Pleiku. We had the pilot call our gaggle en route to tell them where we'd be. Sherman said he'd come fetch us near the end of the day. Camp Holloway at Pleiku was familiar territory. We immediately went to their officers' club, drank some more beer, and played their slot machines. I still felt bad about breaking the ship. I couldn't enjoy myself at all. While the rest of the gaggle was out getting shot at, I was acting like a typical adviser, drinking beer, playing slots—jerking off. The whole thing was due to my incompetence; nobody else had hit a root. So I drank more beer than I should have. So did Nate. He suggested that if we had to wait till sunset, we might as well do it downtown. I agreed. We decided that the best way to get there was to walk, and that's what we started to do. We got a mile down the road when the daylight began to fade.

"Hey, Nate, something's wrong with my eyes. Everything's getting dim." I stopped.

"Yeah. Mine, too." The sky turned a pale orange, yet the sun was still high.

"Man, every time I drink too early in the day, I get fucked up. Not like this, though," said Nate.

While we blinked at our dimming world, we saw our gaggle approaching Camp Holloway. The sun got brighter.

"Aha!" I exclaimed. "It's not the booze; that was an eclipse."

"Hey, yeah." Nate grinned. We weren't going to continue to dim out and fade to nothingness after all.

The sun got bright again, and the gaggle thundered and whopped and hissed to a landing. We ran back to Holloway to rejoin our comrades.

The original damage estimate was $10,000, later raised to $100,000. The accident board decided that the cause was extreme, dusty conditions. They had let me off the hook. The usual verdict was pilot error. I mean, if the rotor blades came off in flight, the pilot was posthumously charged with failure to preflight the ship properly. One time, I saw the rotors of a Huey slash through the cockpit and decapitate the two pilots while the ship was on the ground. The pilots were guilty of not checking the ship's log. The ship had been "red X'd" by the crew chief while he worked on the control rods. Pilot error. If you skewered a Huey on a sharp stump during an assault, it was pilot error. If you tumbled down the side of a mountain while trying to land on a pinnacle under fire, it was pilot error. There was usually no other conclusion. So the board was generous indeed when it decided that the accident was due to extreme, dusty conditions. But guess what I thought . . . the pilot was in error.

We'd already taken Happy Valley, but we had to go back out to patch up a few holes in the victory. Somebody forgot to tell Charlie he lost, so he was still out there shooting down helicopters, the dumb fuck.

The news about our victory against the North Vietnamese Regulars at Ia Drang had been so well reported that the Cav was taking on some of the mythical qualities usually afforded the marines. We were the pros.

I knew that the press was doing a selling job when we supported a newly arrived unit from Hawaii. When we landed to pick up the men, they rushed us like kids when they saw we were air crews from the famous Cav. We were celebrities, the vanguard of more units like ours that would squeeze the Communists back up north like so much shit.

In two days we flew twelve assaults into the same areas we had taken several times before. To add insult to injury, the VC fought even harder.

One LZ lay near the thin jungle at the base of the hills. I was flying number-three slot on the left side of the formation. Our squad was the second one to go in. Gunships made their chattering runs beside us, and door gunners killed bushes. Smoke from the prep was billowing skyward, and as we got to within five hundred feet of the ground, red tracers were streaking among us. By now I had learned to concentrate on my job and to suppress my fear. I felt almost brave. This was Happy Valley. I'd been here scores of times before, and it was never as bad as Ia Drang. Besides, I was one of the pros.

The return fire from the invisible Charlies was more intense as we got closer. We continued straight in.

Near the bottom of the approach, maybe a hundred feet off the deck, I saw a steady stream of tracers off to my left. Aiming at somebody else? Who's behind me? Then the stream began to move in toward my ship. He's singled us out as his target. He's got us. Goddamnit, he's got us.

I could not move from my slot, or even dodge around. I was flying tight on number two, and somebody was flying tight on me. Just keep going. I felt Gary get on the controls. The tracers were close, only a second away from raking the cockpit.

I tightened my stomach, like the bullets might bounce off. My arms tightened; my jaw tightened; my hands tightened. The rounds must not go through me. Of all things, my wristwatch stood vividly before me. How could I see my watch? I wasn't even looking at it. It was a gold, square-faced Hamilton that my grandfather had left me. The second hand had its own dial at the bottom of the face. And the hand was not moving. At that moment, I could have unbuckled, opened the door, walked around outside, had a smoke, and watched the flight frozen in the midst of the assault. I would be able to walk between the tracers and use one to light my cigarette. I saw the flight frozen there in midair. I saw myself braced for the impact of that shredding fire. It was almost funny.

An explosive *whoosh* beside the cockpit caused the clock to run again. Smoking rockets followed the tracers to their source. They stopped, just like that. A Duke gunship had nailed that fucker with a rocket right down the stream of fire. I was saved.

There was a lot more fire on the ground when we landed, but it was impotent. It didn't matter: I was saved.

Back at the Golf Course, they told us that our first assault into Bong Son was set for the next morning.

The first assault would be to LZ Dog, to secure a base of operations for the grunts. The navy had blasted Dog, the army had artilleried Dog, the marines were landing on the beach ten miles away, and the Cav was sending a hundred slicks in to take the place.

A flight of a hundred helicopters becomes a train of unconnected parts that bunches up and stretches out like the flow of commuter traffic. One minute you're trying to close a gap between yourself and the flight ahead, and the next second you're practically hovering to keep away.

The villages we saw before we got to LZ Dog were islands in the sea of rice paddies. This was one of the most valuable of all Vietnamese valleys because of its bountiful rice crop. The people who lived here were sympathetic to Uncle Ho, as was 80 percent of the rest of Vietnam. The other 20 percent, in the American-controlled cities, was engaged in maintaining the colonialist system installed by the French and now run by the Americans. I knew this because Wendall had told me. He said, "Just read *Street Without Joy* and you'll see." But there weren't any copies of that book around here, and it wouldn't have made any difference anyway, because I just didn't believe it. I didn't believe it, because Kennedy and McNamara and Johnson and all the rest certainly knew about *Street Without Joy*, and they sent us here anyway. It was obvious to me that Bernard Fall was just another flake, the father of the dreaded Vietniks who were attacking our country like so much cancer. And of course the proof of all this was that Wendall himself was still here doing everything I was doing. And even Wendall wasn't *that* dumb.

"Yellow One, you are off course."

No answer.

"Yellow One, turn left twenty degrees."

Yellow One, the lead ship of this monstrous gaggle, still didn't answer. Instead he slowed down even more and turned farther away from our course. Nate and I (Resler was away on R&R) were way back in the flight, the fortieth ship or so. We were showing an airspeed of 20 knots. The whole gaggle was staggering and bunching up over some villages at an altitude of 100 feet.

"Yellow One, do you read?"

No answer.

"Yellow Two, take the lead. Come left forty degrees."

"Roger."

We had a leader again. Yellow One's radios were shot out, and he had been trying to hand-signal Yellow Two to take over, but Yellow Two just followed him as he tried to break away.

Below us, the villagers were having a picnic, shooting at a lot of helicopters flying low and slow. At one village I saw fifty people just standing around, their hands shielding their eyes from the sun, watching the show. Somebody down there was shooting, because the ships were calling in hits. I couldn't see any guns, just women and children and men watching the helicopter parade.

As the gaggle crossed the next village on our flight path, many ships called in hits. Connors got his fuel bladder raked and had to break away from the flight. Another ship called in that a pilot was killed, and it turned back. Someone in that village was doing a real job, but so far he was invisible. Meanwhile, we still wallowed around, flying low and slow.

One of the ships just ahead of us called in hit. At the same moment, I saw where the gun was. Among all the people, water buffalo, thatched huts, and coconut trees, an innocent-looking group of people stood bunched in a crowd. From the center of the crowd I saw smoke and then the gunner. He had a machine gun.

Before I got into the army, they had asked me a question they asked all prospective grunts: What would you do if you were the driver of a truck loaded with soldiers, traveling very fast down a muddy road, flanked on both sides with steep drop-offs, and a small child suddenly walked into your path? Would you try to avoid her and drive off to certain death, or would you keep going and kill her? Well, everybody knew the right answer: You kill the kid. And it didn't much matter, because the kid and the situation weren't real anyway. So I had said, "I'd stop the truck."

"No, no. You can't stop the truck. It's going too fast."

"Well, then, I wouldn't be going so fast down a very bad road in the first place."

"You don't seem to understand. It's assumed that you have no choice but to kill either the little kid or you and your comrades."

"Since I have no choice, I'll go ahead and kill the kid."

"That's what we like to hear."

Now the question was, How do you kill that gunner, who has just killed some pilots, without killing the screen of innocent people around him?

"I see the gun, sir!" said Rubenski, the door gunner.

"Shoot at the ground first. Scare those people away," I said.

"Yes, sir." Rubenski, one of our most accurate gunners, opened up as we drew closer to the gun position. The spectators were at the edge of their village, directly off our right side, a hundred yards away.

The bullets sent up muddy geysers from the paddy water as they raged toward the group. The VC gunner was concentrating on another ship and didn't see Rubenski's bullets yet. I really expected to see the black pajamas, conical hats, and the small children scatter and expose the gunner. Were they chained in place? When the bullets were smashing fifty feet in front of them, I knew they weren't going to move. They threw up their arms as they were hit, and whirled to the ground. After what seemed a very long time, the gunner, still firing, was exposed. Rubenski kept firing. The VC's gun barrel flopped down on its mount and he slid to the ground. A dozen people lay like tenpins around him. The truck had smashed the kid.

Twenty ships were damaged and five were shot down, killing two pilots and two gunners, while we floundered over the villages on the way to Dog. Dog itself was an ancient Vietnamese graveyard, and we took it without too much trouble. The ships landed in groups, dropped off the grunts, and returned for more. By that night, Dog was an outpost of Americans in a Vietcong wilderness. Nate and I and three other ships were selected to spend the night there with the grunts as emergency ships for the grunt commander. It drizzled all night.

"Why didn't they duck?" I sat in my seat staring into the night.

"The VC forced them to stand there."

"How can you make people stand up to machine-gun bullets?"

"He would have shot them if they had run."

"But if they had all run, he couldn't have shot them, not with us right there shooting at him."

"Obviously they were more afraid of him than they were of us."

"That was it? They were so afraid that they would get killed that they stood there and got killed?"

"Orientals don't think like we do."

Firefights chattered all night, but I didn't lie awake because of that. I kept replaying the scene. The faces were clear. One old woman chewed betel nut and nodded weakly as the bullets boiled in. One child turned to run, chewed up even while he turned. A woman shrieked at the child; then she was hit, too. The gunner kept firing. I saw it over and over, until I knew everybody in that group. And they all knew me and nodded and smiled and turned and whirled and died.

At three in the morning the firefight got suddenly louder at the edge of the graveyard. A grunt ran up and told us to crank. Fifteen minutes later the firing slowed, and the grunt came by and told us to shut down.

The next morning, Nate and I flew fifty miles south to a place called the Rifle Range, where the rest of our battalion and part of the 227th had set up camp. We moved into a GP with Morris, Decker, Shaker, Daisy, Sherman, and Farris. Resler was still gone. My cot was missing, so I built a stretcher out of two poles and a blanket set across two ammo crates.

We were camped on an old ARVN rifle range near the village of Phu Cat, next to Route 1. About a thousand ROKs from the Korean Tiger Division surrounded us as our security. That was nice, because the ROKs (from Republic of Korea) were devout killers. They spent their dawns beating each other up just for fun.

After a quick lunch Nate and I were back in the air in a flight of two squads going back to Dog. At Dog we loaded up with grunts and set out on the mission.

Farris led the flight. A command ship was to meet us en route and show him the LZ.

"Preacher Six, do you have me in sight?"

"Roger," said Farris.

"Just watch me. I'm going in now."

The ship dropped from 1000 feet and set up an approach to one of the clearings below. I thought he was just going to fly over it, but he flared and hovered into the LZ. Rice plants rippled in a circle around him.

"Right here, Preacher flight. It's all clear."

That was the only time I ever saw this technique. It looked pretty good. Here was an LZ that really was quiet. The ship nosed over and took off to the north over a stand of trees.

Farris called, "Man your guns," and we pulled up nice and tight and followed him in.

"Pick your spots," radioed Farris. The LZ was narrow, so I dropped back a little to land behind the number-two ship.

As we flared, spray from the rice paddy swirled around us. I decided not to land completely but to hover with the skids lightly touching the paddy. The grunts jumped out before we touched, not because of the excitement of the assault but out of habit. A routine landing to a cold LZ..

We waited for thirty seconds while Farris made sure everybody had unloaded. Machine guns opened up from three points. They had us pinned with fire from the front, the left flank, and the rear. I could see the muzzle flashes in the tree line fifty yards away, which blocked our take-off path. I pushed pedals furiously and wiggled the ship as we hovered, waiting for Farris. The only gun position I could watch was the one up front, and he was raking us at will. Our door guns couldn't swing that far forward, so the gunners concentrated on the flank attacks. As I oscillated left and right, I heard one *tick*, then Farris took off just to the right of the forward VC gun with the rest of us hot on his tail rotor. As we crossed the trees, another VC gun opened up, showering tracers through our flight. I pulled up higher than the rest of the flight and made small, quick turns left and right. As we climbed out, all the guns below us converged on our eight ships. I just kept floundering around, believing firmly that Leese was right: Anything you can do to make yourself a bad target is to your benefit. Moments later we were out of range. Six of the eight helicopters were damaged, and two gunners had been killed. Our ship had taken the one round that had hit us on the ground.

Later, checking the angle at which the round had hit the ship, I found that it had hit while I was pedal-turning in the low hover. The bullet had come up just beside me, at chest level, and lodged in the base of the tail boom, behind me. I was convinced that my evasive tactics had saved my life.

"If you had not moved at all, the bullet would probably have missed you altogether," said Nate, back at the Rifle Range.

"That particular bullet hit me while I turned right. That means if I hadn't turned, it would have come into the cockpit."

"But you couldn't know that. It was just luck."

"Yeah. *Good* luck."

"But just luck. What if you had turned into a bullet? The same technique could just as easily kill you."

He was right of course, but I was convinced that I had actually dodged the bullet.

"But what about the takeoff? Everybody else got torn to ribbons," I countered.

"Look, Mason, if it's your turn to die, that's it. You can't control the odds. It just wasn't your day to get zapped."

"So you're saying I should just sit there and fly smooth and neat with the rest of the flight? I can't do that. I can imagine myself on the ground trying to shoot down a Huey. If one ship in the flight is going nuts like I do, I wouldn't even try to hit it. I'd go for the others.

Nate nodded and sipped some coffee. "I guess if it makes you feel better, you should do it. But I think you're just pissing into the wind."

We learned that one gunner had taken a direct hit in the chest armor he was lucky enough to be wearing, and it had stopped the bullet cold. It reminded me of my near hit—which would have got me in the chest—so I got pissed off about the lack of chest protectors in our company. After all the fire we'd taken in the last five months, we still had only a few. We just hadn't lost enough pilots yet.

The VC fire in this valley was intense. This was their home, and they were thoroughly dug in. No matter where we flew, we were shot at. In two days we had had forty-five ships seriously damaged in our slick battalions. The Chinooks in the 228th had been hit—which had not happened much at Ia Drang—and had lost ten pilots. We thought the C-130 that crashed and burned at the An Khe pass the day before, killing eighty, had been forced down by ground fire.

That night, Nate and I and Morris and Decker rode to the village down the road. I took some pictures of a group of smiling children. We all bought some candles and soap from the little store. On the way back, in the rear of the truck, we complained about our lack of chest armor. Morris sat with his arms folded as we bumped along.

"I talked to a friend of mine at battalion," he said. "He says we should get a load of chest protectors any day now."

The truck pulled up beside our mess tent, and as we got out, Decker said, "Yeah, any day now. I wonder how fast he'd get them here if *he* was flying in this shit."

The next day, January 31, we launched another mission. This LZ was named Quebec. It was about five miles past Dog.

Dog was now a very large staging area where the bulk of our troopers stayed. If any place was secure in this valley, it was Dog. As the twelve ships on this mission crossed the river for the approach, somebody on the right side of the formation took a hit from the "friendly" village.

We hung around on the ground for about an hour, watching the air-force Phantoms as they hit Quebec with tons of bombs and napalm. I sat on the roof of my Huey and watched the show. At the bottom of their passes, the Phantoms would mush and they'd kick in their afterburners to power out. It was a pretty good show. I could've sat there and watched it all day.

While all this was going on, I idly watched two grunts walk out to/set up a claymore mine a hundred yards in front of us. I had gone through a demolition course in Advanced Infantry Training, so I felt a critical interest. The claymore mine is shaped like a crescent. The convex side is pointed toward the enemy. It's detonated remotely, blasting millions of small wire pieces that shred its victims. As I watched them anchor it in position, it exploded. Both men, one on either side of the mine, were thrown back—torn, lifeless heaps.

What's next in this carnival? I thought.

The Phantoms finished prepping Quebec, and the air show stopped.

"We're up. Let's go," yelled Williams.

Eight grunts jumped on each ship. We cranked, checked in on the radios, and took off. Nate and I followed the number-two ship, Morris and Decker.

The smoke from the air-force bombing drifted lazily at Quebec as we flew past to set up an approach to the south.

"Preacher Six, Antenna Six. Head south now. VC automatic weapons on your route." Antenna Six, the Colonel, flew overhead.

"Preacher Six, roger wilco." Williams started his turn back to the LZ.

"Preacher Six, artillery is still preparing the LZ. Be careful."

"Roger. Preacher Six now on short final." The LZ was a narrow strip of brushy, dry sand next to the foothills on the west side of the valley. Following previous instructions, we moved into a staggered trail formation.

"Preacher Six, receiving small-arms fire from the west!" That was Connors.

"Yellow flight, this is Preacher Six. Pick your spots. The LZ is rough." Williams was just off the ground in his landing flare. Morris and Decker were fifty feet off, and I was behind them maybe a hundred feet.

"Preacher Six, this is Yellow Two. Captain Morris is hit. Captain Morris is hit bad!" Morris's ship suddenly dropped fast from twenty feet and landed hard.

"Yellow Four is receiving fire from the right." There was nothing to see on our right except a long row of dead brush.

"Captain Morris is dead! Captain Morris is dead!"

"Roger, Yellow Two."

"This ship is destroyed. I'm getting out!"

I saw Decker jump out of his Huey as we landed behind him. He leapt to the ground beside the ship, his sawed-off shotgun at the ready. He was faced away from the VC.

Nate called, "Preacher Six, Yellow Three. We'll pick up Decker and his crew."

"Negative, Yellow Three. Clear the LZ for the next flight."

The grunts were off. Some of them scrambled toward Decker, under fire, and pointed him the right way. The troopers stayed low. Sand kicked up under the VC fire.

"Let's go, Yellow flight." Williams took off.

As I made the takeoff run beside Decker's still-running ship, I glanced into the cockpit and saw Morris sitting in the right seat with his head slumped forward on his chest. He seemed to be taking a nap.

Tick. "We're hit." *Tick-tick-tick.*

The gunner that had got Morris was getting us. I pulled in a lot of power and climbed for the sky. I climbed much higher than Williams, and at about 1000 feet, the engine quit. Silence. I bottomed the pitch.

It was my first authentic forced landing, and I was extremely lucky. The spot I was aiming for was the spot I was supposed to land in anyway. It was secure. I skidded ten feet when I hit, and the rotors quietly slowed and stopped.

The crew chief was already inspecting the damage before I got out of the ship. "Four rounds through the fuel lines, sir." We wouldn't be flying that ship anymore today. Nate and I stood around while the flight returned to Quebec. I don't know about him, but I felt cold and clammy while we stood in the blistering heat.

Battalion always had at least one maintenance ship on call for situations like ours. It landed in secure areas to determine whether or not a ship could be fixed on the spot.

I heard the loud *whopping* of the Huey as it crossed Dog, two miles away. How could anyone be taken by surprise by a flight of Hueys? The thudding slap of the main rotors grew quieter when the ship was a quarter of a mile away, replaced by the buzz of the tail rotor and the hissing whine of the turbine. It landed a hundred feet behind us, starting a brief sandstorm before the pitch was bottomed. The turbine shut off and the rotors spun down. Two specialists, mechanics, ran toward our ship. The crew chief showed them the damage under the engine cowling. They all stuck their noses into the Huey's innards. Leaving them to their work, I walked back to the maintenance Huey to see who was flying.

It was Riker.

"Somebody hurt?" said Riker. He did not know about Morris.

I stood next to the skid and tried to word what I was

going to say while Riker finished freeing himself from the straps. As I began to speak, a painful grin possessed my face. "Morris was shot and killed."

Riker's face showed a second of shock and despair, before he too was possessed by the same animal grin. "Really? Morris?"

"Yes. Just a few minutes ago. At Quebec." I spoke jerkily as I fought with the expression on my face. How could I be grinning?

Riker was having the same problem. His mouth curved into a smile, but his face showed pain. He tried to break the spell by speaking of other things.

"How bad is your ship?"

"Not bad. Fuel lines were hit."

"Your ship is okay?" he said vacantly.

"Yep. Okay."

"Where was he hit?" Riker said abruptly. The task of maintaining his composure was beyond him, and his face jerked involuntarily into that horrible grin.

"I don't really know, but I think he got hit in the chest."

"Yeah?"

"I think so."

We were embarrassing each other, so we stopped talking and sat on the sandy grass and smoked a cigarette. The mechanics fiddled with my ship. Nate, who had been watching them curiously, walked over to join us.

"Bob tell you about Morris?" Nate seemed brave and businesslike.

"Yeah. By the way, is Decker all right?" Riker said.

"He's still in the LZ," said Nate.

"Really? Why didn't somebody pick him up?"

"There was too much fire, and Decker jumped out and took cover on the ground. Besides, Williams wouldn't let us wait to get him."

"Why not?"

"Well, he was right. The next flight was right behind us, and we probably would've just got someone else hurt trying to get Decker to the ship."

"It doesn't seem right, just to leave him there."

"He'll be okay," Nate said. "He's got his trusty old shotgun with him."

"Sir, the ship's not flyable," the mechanic called to Riker.

"Okay." We all stood up. "You guys interested in a ride back to the Rifle Range for a new ship?"

"You bet," I said. "Can't wait to get back into the fight."

Nate and Riker smiled at my false bravado. Then Riker said, "You guys remember that model he made of the *Croatan*?"

"Uh-huh."

"I wonder where it is now?"

An hour later, Nate and I were back in the air. We joined a flight taking more grunts into Quebec. Decker had got out on the next flight. Late that afternoon, after we had replaced two second lieutenants who had been killed and hauled reinforcements in and wounded out, the grunts finally took Quebec, both sandy acres of it. Two machine guns and ten rifles had been hidden in a long trench under that innocent-looking pile of brush. At twilight we landed back at the Rifle Range.

Decker was sitting on the end of his cot, elbows on his knees, hands on his cheeks, staring at the dirt.

I was glad to see him back. "Hey, Deck—" Someone stopped me with a shake of the head. I nodded. Instead of walking by him, I went outside and came in through the back flap and sat on my stretcher.

Nate, facing me on his cot, was pouring some Old Grandad into his canteen cup. "Want some?"

"Yeah, I think I will." I poured about two inches in

my cup and stirred in some water with my finger. We sat there silently. Nate reread one of his letters, and I watched Decker. Everyone else in the tent talked quietly, keeping a space around the mourning man.

He was pale. He looked up once, and his face showed that sad child within. He shook his head and made a weak smile. "He autorotated."

We all looked at him, expecting more. But he was silent.

Sherman broke the silence. "Morris?"

"Yeah. As he died, he bottomed the pitch for an autorotation. But we were too close to the ground, and the ship nosed in and sank up to the canopy." Decker squinted in pain and stopped talking.

I was thinking, "Nosed in"? There was nothing wrong with the ship. They'd hit harder than normal, but the ship was just sitting there running when Decker jumped out.

Decker continued solemnly. "The bullet came in through the triangle window and went through his flak vest like it wasn't there and through his heart. The flak vest stopped it on the other side. He pushed the collective down like he was making an autorotation and we crashed before I could stop it." He stopped for a moment. "If I had been a little faster, I could've kept us from crashing."

"You didn't do anything wrong," said Sherman.

"That's what you think. How would you feel if your best friend had just gotten killed and you couldn't even keep the fucking ship from crashing? See, he did the right thing even while he was dying. He set us up for the autorotation, but I just wasn't fast enough to save it."

"But, Decker, Morris was already dead. It doesn't matter about the landing," Sherman said.

Decker stood up suddenly. "He's dead and it's my fault!" He grabbed his shotgun and walked outside.

"Jesus," said Nate.

"I don't see why he's blaming himself," said Sherman. "Morris was already dead. And besides that, the ship didn't crash."

We all looked at Sherman. Of course, he was right. But nobody wanted to be rational. It was so . . . out of place.

The old man said nothing about Morris except that we ought to get some money together for flowers for his wife, but Sherman took it upon himself to give a little speech that night.

"Well, we've been pretty lucky up to now. It was only a matter of time. The other companies have taken a lot more kills than we have, so it's our turn now. It looks like the overall ratio is one in five. One pilot out of five will get killed. We've only lost two guys, which puts us five away from the average. We've just been lucky."

I hated Sherman. Now we were delinquent in our deaths. Running behind in our proper death ratio were we? Well we'll just see about that. C'mon you guys, let's get out there and die!

At dawn the next morning, a Chinook landed, dwarfing our Hueys. A deuce-and-a-half backed up to the door ramp, and men began loading chest protectors onto the truck. Hundreds of chest protectors.

8.
Bong Son Valley

This country cannot escape its destiny as the champion of the free world—there is no running away from it.
—Gen. Maxwell Taylor, in *U.S. News & World Report,* February 14, 1966

February 1966

The beach was slippery red clay. Connors claimed that it was better than the Caribbean. "In the Caribbean you can't slide into the water because of the sand."

True. If you sat on this beach without holding on to a bush, you slipped into the warm red water. Stepping toward the center of the pond, your feet accumulated layers of adhesive clay that made it seem like you were touching bottom when you weren't. When I was chin deep, I stopped to watch the others.

Banjo ducked under and disappeared completely, an act of great courage in this slime, to reappear several feet away.

"Man, how can you stick your head under that shit?" said Kaiser. Kaiser, like me, wouldn't go under for anything, but stood chin deep, soaking in the relative coolness.

Banjo only laughed and ducked under again. An old Vietnamese lady laughed at him while she weeded the fields around the pond. Four or five women and two men watched us skinny-dip in the buffalo watering pond. The women grinned self-consciously. These naked foreigners were clearly making fools of themselves. We interpreted their smiles as friendly approval.

An ROK road patrol guarding a bridge a hundred feet away laughed, too. I found out later that the Koreans were forbidden to undress around the Vietnamese because it was a sign of vulnerability to be thus exposed in front of your enemy.

Nate was sitting on his clothes on the beach, sunning himself, when a Cola girl materialized. When he noticed her, he modestly crossed his legs.

Cola girls were ubiquitous. They arrived at our laagers carrying Cokes in plastic netting.

"Fifty cents, GI. Buy Croakacrola?" They were inevitably young and cute, so I never bought a Coke. I was convinced the soda was poisoned.

"Hey, Nate, I can see your pecker," yelled Connors. Nate glanced at him while he declined the coke and tightened his legs.

"I'm trolling, wise-ass."

"Hey. So that's how it's done. But the bait is so small."
Everyone laughed.

"I don't know where you get off, Connors. You could play a record with your cock."

"So, you're going to do it?" I said.

"Yeah. You oughta think about it, too," said Kaiser.

"Air America. Who are they?"

"Well, they're supposed to be a civilian helicopter service, but it's a CIA front."

"How much do they pay?" I asked.

"That's the good part. They guarantee twenty thousand and the average is thirty-five. Plus you get PX privileges, an airline discount, and ten days of R&R every month."

"Twenty thousand?" I was paid seven.

"Yeah. And you can join them right now, before you get out of the army."

"You doing that?"

"Well, I've only got two months left in service, so I'm going to finish up and move to Saigon as a civilian." Kaiser slapped an envelope against his hand. "Got the letter today. It's all fixed. What do you think, Mason? You want me to give you the address?"

"Naw. I think I'd rather fly crop dusters in Florida than sneak around with the CIA in Vietnam."

"You're going to be a CIA agent?" Nate said to Kaiser.

"Not an agent, a pilot. You know, Air America."

"So, you like this line of work, do you?"

"Shit, they never fly assaults. They mostly do courier work and fly radio teams into Cambodia. Or pick up downed pilots where the army isn't supposed to go. We take a lot more chances than they do, and we do it for peanuts."

"So why do you think they'd let somebody as stupid as you even get close to their operation?"

"Not all of us are morons, Nate. You'll see. In two months I'll be pulling in twenty thou for doing a lot less work and for taking a lot less chances than you."

Nate set a record on top of a box. In one corner of the box there was a fold-out tone arm.

"That's a record player?" I said.

"Yeah. Neat, huh? My wife sent it for Christmas, but it just got here."

Music played. "You're kidding me!" said Kaiser.

" 'Puff the Magic Dragon'? I'm sick!" He got up and left.

"Eat your heart out, Kaiser!" Nate hummed along with the song.

Barber, Wendall's buddy, ducked in through the flap. "Mason, you seen Wendall?"

"No."

"I have. He's over toward the mess tent digging a hole," said Nate.

"Thanks." Barber left.

"What's he digging a hole for?" I asked.

"He keeps saying we're going to get hit. I think he's beginning to take Hanoi Hanna seriously," said Nate.

"Puff the Magic Dragon" was making me uncomfortable. It was the saccharine song that had inspired the naming of the murderous gatling-gun-armed C-47s. I couldn't listen. "I'm going to check out Wendall."

It was twilight, and I could see a small pile of dirt next to the other platoon tent. When I got closer, I saw what looked like a cap sitting on the ground. The cap moved, and Wendall's smile brightened under the brim. "Hi, Mason."

"Hi, Wendall. Nice hole you got there."

"You think I'm crazy, don't you?"

"No. Really."

Wendall tried to hold his chin up at the edge of the five-foot shaft while his shoulders strained low to reach something on the bottom. A large tin can full of sand squeezed up between his chest and the tight walls. He dumped it on the pile around him.

"The VC love mortars, and we have no protection," he said.

"They say we can't dig holes. We're supposed to use that big gully over there."

"That gully's too wide. If a mortar round went off in it, you'd have hamburger. That's why I built this like I did. I'm below ground level and I present the minimum target."

"Pretty smart."

"Not really. It just looks smart compared to what the morons told us to do." He was referring to the Cav's no-digging policy, which was still in effect to keep us from disfiguring the landscape. "Sometimes I think this war is being run by a gardener," he added.

I walked over to the maintenance area and took a time-exposure shot of Reacher and some other guys working on a Huey in the glare of floodlights. Thousands of moths flitted around the lights while Reacher and Rubenski, armed with wrenches and screwdrivers, worked to get the ship flyable for the morning. They did it every night. Our ships were parked in a long row, nose to tail, along with eight or so other Hueys, at the Rifle Range. The rest were invisible in the moonless night.

The music was off when I returned, and Nate was asleep. I stripped to my underwear and crawled under my poncho liner.

I could not sleep. Why couldn't I be more like Kaiser? Get a job with Air America and get out of all this? Imagine twenty thousand dollars a year. Patience had been complaining in her letters about our money problems. We were paying for the new Volvo, a much too expensive bed-and-dresser set, life insurance, and high rent at Cape Coral. Twenty thousand would sure be a whole new world. But it would have to be in this stinking country. Anything was better than that.

A mosquito pierced my arm, but I didn't flinch. A guy I knew in another company was still in Japan living in a hotel while they treated him for malaria.

I was jumpy, worried. My nights were getting harder to bear. I thought of jerking off, but it seemed like too much trouble. You had to be very careful because the slightest noise or creak of the bed might cause some wise-ass to yell, "Hey. I hear somebody fucking his fist!" That would cause a few moments of catcalls, which masturbating men use to cover their last, quick strokes. So far I hadn't been discovered. I knew it was only a matter of time.

Invariably my thoughts turned to a problem I had devised when I first arrived. I was mentally designing a clock to be made of bamboo. I had now determined how many gears I would need, how I would slice the bamboo to make the gears, how I could rig an escapement—almost everything I needed. I reviewed the plan, looking for errors. That put me to sleep.

Whoom! Whump whump wham! I awoke sitting upright but not understanding. Very heavy, ground-shaking explosions came from the direction of the Rifle Range gully.

"Mortars!" someone yelled.

Mortars? Shit! I grabbed my pistol belt and stuffed my feet into my boots. People ran by.

Rounds were exploding beyond the sand berm next to the gully. Men were packed into the bottom of the trench. I didn't go in. Wendall was right: If a mortar went off in there, it would be mass murder. I decided to hide somewhere else.

I had my pistol out in front of me as I ran. The unlaced boots kept sliding off my feet; my cock kept swinging out of my underwear. Our mortar batteries began shooting back. I heard frantic calls for the pilots assigned to evacuate the ships to get going. I wasn't part of that, so I kept looking for a place to hide. Finally, I rolled under a truck and watched the explosions. They were terrifyingly powerful, and random. So far no rounds had hit inside our compound. I was under the truck for a few minutes before I realized that if a mortar did hit it, the truck would explode, shredding me. I rolled out from under and lay in a shallow depression in the sand. Flares cast swinging shadows around the compound. Fifty-caliber tracers seemed to cruise slowly overhead, coming our way, so it must be the VC. I heard the Hueys running for a long time, but they didn't take off. As the flares went off over the ROK positions, I noticed Wendall's helmet moving around in the middle of his pile of sand. Why was he always right?

I heard the sounds of machine guns blasting out of the darkness overhead. Our gunships were on station, shooting streams of tracers into the foothills beyond the ROKs. Still, no mortars had come past the berm next to the gully. Our ships still idled, not taking off.

After fifteen minutes the mortars stopped. Only the familiar sound of outgoing rounds was left. I stood up and tried to dust the sand from my sweating body. My hands shook, and I cursed the Vietcong, the mortars, and the army.

The evacuation pilots were returning from the flight line.

"Listen, asshole, I was assigned Two-two-seven. What the fuck were you doing in my seat?" I heard someone say.

"The major told me I was supposed to fly it, numb nuts!"

The ships hadn't got off the ground, because too many men tried to squeeze on board. The weight of the pilots and crew chiefs stuffed inside the machines kept them grounded while they argued about who was supposed to be flying.

The Koreans had sent out their Tiger teams. They came back with mortar tubes, base plates, and severed VC heads. The Koreans also complained that our gunships had killed some of their men.

We came off as a bunch of amateurs compared to the ROKs.

For the rest of the night I kept snapping awake as though something were happening. But nothing was.

"Preacher Six, there's a machine-gun position on your takeoff path."

The guns swooped back and forth in front of us, chattering.

Williams was up against the tree line in front of us, so he had to pull the guts out of his Huey to make it over. The gunships were in front of us, circling like sharks, firing down into the jungle.

"Preacher Six, turn left. You're heading for the machine gun."

No answer.

"Turn left. Turn left!" The gunship pilot was losing his cool as he watched us take off right over the position he'd warned us about.

It was a single gun. As we crossed above it, it raked us in the belly.

"Sir, one of the grunts just got hit!" said Miller, the crew chief.

The grunt, a black guy, had taken a round in the ass. I heard our gunner, Simmons, yelling incoherently over the noise of the ship.

"Sir, it's Simmons's brother," Miller said.

"Preacher Six," I called, "we have a wounded on board. We're going to the aid station first."

"Roger."

We landed next to a MASH hospital pod that skycranes had lifted in from the Golf Course. The medics ran out and loaded the man onto a stretcher. Simmons ran around from the other side of the ship, crying, and hurried alongside the stretcher into the pod. We waited. He came back a few minutes later, his cheeks wet, but he was smiling.

"The doctors say he'll be okay. He'll be going home," he said to the crew chief.

Ah, the proverbial million-dollar wound. Then I remembered that Simmons had discovered another brother at the bottom of a pile of bodies at Pleiku.

Neither brothers nor fathers and sons were supposed to be in the same combat theater at the same time. I knew of two people in Vietnam who didn't have to be there.

I talked to Simmons after we got back to the Rifle Range.

"Yes, sir, I know," he said.

"So why don't you tell the CO. He'll get you out of here. You've lost one brother, and another was just wounded. Your family has done enough."

He smiled and said, "No. I'm staying."

"Why?"

"Someone has to do it." He really said that. I thought I was in a movie. Maybe he did, too.

The fighting had progressed from the valley floor near the village of Bong Son north to the narrow An Lao valley, surrounded by steep mountains. We landed on the valley floor in the rice paddies.

The grunts jumping out of the Hueys found themselves slogging slowly for cover next to the paddy dikes. The paddies were tricky. If we landed and laagered for a while, the ships sank up to their bellies in the quagmire, anchoring them. Leese had demonstrated the proper technique for takeoff from such places months before in Happy Valley.

"You can't just pull up hard and race out of here," he had said. "First you bring the nose up to start releasing the skids, then level the ship and pull up slowly, very slowly, until the skids slide free. If you don't, one skid will leave first, leaving the other still stuck. Then you'll flip over and go *crash*."

Resler, having just returned from his R&R, was with me. We landed in a paddy in An Lao to await grunts on their way to our position to be extracted.

Once on the ground, each Huey became a kind of island in the rice-paddy lake. The heat was sweltering. The humidity was as thick as the mud under us.

Helicopter pilots, like cats, were finicky about getting their feet wet. That was one of the reasons they were pilots. Grunts got dirty; pilots didn't—so the story went. Anyway, Resler and I crawled over the seats, sat in the shade on the cargo deck, and picked and pawed at the C-ration boxes for snacks.

When the pace of the action was broken by periods like this, we sometimes compensated by indulging in what the army called "grab-ass." That is, we tried to make each other laugh.

"Hey, how're we gonna heat the water for the coffee?" asked Resler.

"Here, gimme that can. I'll make a stove."

"Oh, yeah? How ya gonna get to the fuel drain?"

"You're right. Let's make Miller get the fuel."

"No," said Miller.

"Aw, come on. You want us to be alert, don't you? What if we fall asleep and crash?" Resler coaxed.

"You ain't gonna fall asleep, and I ain't gonna go slog in that shit for the fuel."

I looked at Rubenski in the pocket next to his gun. "Rubenski, grunts are supposed to love mud. Will you go get some JP-4 for me?"

"No. And I ain't a grunt. I was a grunt; now I'm a gunner."

"What's the difference?"

"The difference is that a grunt would go get the fuel for you and I won't."

"Good point." I glanced up and saw a tin-can stove burning on the dike next to the Huey beside us.

"Hey, you guys," I yelled. "Give us some coffee, huh?"

"Get bent," yelled Nate, grinning.

"Hey, have a heart. I'm nothing without my morning coffee."

"You're nothing anyway, Mason."

"Shit, I can't take this whining. I'll go get some fucking fuel." Rubenski jumped out and sank to his knees in the leech-infested bog.

"Now, that's what I like to see—the true determination of an American grunt," I yelled.

"Gunner!" Rubenski yelled back as he slogged heavily toward Nate's ship.

When he was just about there, we heard "Crank 'em!" from up front.

"Goddamnit!" Rubenski turned and slogged back through the morass. "Fuck!"

We cranked and checked in on the radios. The grunts were coming across the paddy, laboring at each step. They were tired and torn, unshaven and grim. Ammo cases clunked wearily on the deck. So did rifles and canteens and helmets. With eight of them in the back, the surface of the deck disappeared under mud and pieces of rice plants.

The flight leader gave us the word to go. One by one the ships wriggled loose from the slime. I rocked the ship back and forth and from side to side as I pulled the pitch. It was especially sticky stuff.

The ship in front of us, an attached ship from the Snakes, had a new pilot, or an old pilot in a hurry. He jerked up through the mud and promptly flipped over. The rotors hit the paddy, exploding into pieces. The mast came off. Parts flew everywhere. When the Huey stopped kicking, men started climbing out the cargo door, now the top of the bent and muddy fuselage. The command ship overhead told us to leave. He would get the men.

While we circled back toward the valley ridge, I saw the command ship and a light gunship land and evacuate the men. I grinned while I imagined what the pilot who had crashed was thinking.

We chased Charlie around his valley for more than two weeks, flying too many hours every day. Observed or reported movements of the enemy were immediately countered with air assaults to the spot. The Cav's Third Brigade fought tirelessly and well in this hectic hopscotch war and was chalking up an impressive kill score. The marines were being misused on the beaches northeast of the war. So far they had not made contact, but a marine had hurt his foot on a beach assault. Things were getting better for pilots because we were shot at less and less in the secured areas. The big question was whether they stopped shooting because they had been defeated or because they just stopped shooting and became civilians.

Colonel Lester, of the Third Brigade, probably wondered about this, too. He decided to find out by putting the VC in a position where they would have no choice but to fight, because there would be no escape. The VC always knew our exact positions by watching the Hueys.

The first stage of his plan was to airlift nearly three battalions of infantry to a crow's-foot of seven intersecting valleys, twelve miles south of Bong Son. Nothing unusual about that, except that once the troops were dropped off, we would not return to support them. Instead, they carried several days' rations themselves and operated independently. For three days they deployed themselves throughout the crow's-foot silently and without any helicopters flying near them, placing themselves in ambush position for the VC who would be coming their way.

Part two called for convincing Charlie that we were

landing huge forces on top of the ridges along the long valley that led to the crow's-foot. We did this by flying empty ships for two days to normally prepared LZs along the ridge tops. We went in with all the hoopla of a standard air assault on every one of the fake LZs. On short final, the door gunners blasted the bushes. We landed and stayed on the ground for thirty seconds or so and then left. Later we'd fly out to "resupply" these units at regular intervals. We were in on the plan. And the fact that there was a plan was a novelty. So, for two days, the VC watched the buildup and decided that things were getting too hot in the valley and began to drift south toward the trap.

After the imaginary forces were placed on the ridges, real troops were landed on the valley floor to act as beaters. The beaters ran into occasional Charlie delay teams that sacrificed their lives so that their comrades could make it to safety. During the next few days we supported these beater troops with hot food and new clothes and the phantoms with counterfeit visits.

Life for the grunts in the valley was grim. In a few days they were reduced to sodden, weary, leech-encrusted men. One company took a break at a particularly scenic spot on the river. A hundred and fifty men stripped themselves of their rotten clothes to bathe in the sandy shoals of the river, leaving a handful of men as security. Charlie was well ahead of them. No one felt the slightest threat of ambush at this delicate moment.

Without warning, Charlie opened up. Naked men scattered in all directions as the bullets churned the water. The sentries couldn't see where the shots were coming from. For long minutes the men were completely exposed. They got to their weapons. The tide of the battle changed abruptly and Charlie was driven off.

I landed next to the riverbank soon after the firefight, and the naked men were still laughing about it. Nobody had been seriously hurt. That was unbelievable, and therefore funny.

We dropped off food and sat on the ground for a while, waiting for the men to eat. I'd spent the night with these guys several times. As usual, several grunts gathered around the machine. Some guys asked all sorts of technical questions. How fast can it fly? How long can you stay up on one fueling? Why don't you make all your takeoffs vertically? Do you get scared? Others would stand back and grin knowingly, as people do around race-car drivers.

Around us, the men were breaking open the boxes of clothes we'd brought. Their old sets, two days old, were literally rotting off their backs.

One man pointed at a bullet hole in my door. "Where'd that round go?" I slid the side armor forward and showed him the crater where the bullet had hit. "Damned if that wasn't lucky."

"Yeah, I'd probably be dead if it hadn't been there," I said.

Somebody poked his head inside and exclaimed, "Do you really use all those dials and switches and stuff?"

"Yeah, but not all at once. We check each one in a pattern."

"What's that one do?"

"That's the artificial horizon, which shows you where the horizon is when you can't see it, like in bad weather."

The soldier nodded and said, "I'd sure like to fly one of these."

"What? You crazy, Daniels?" his friend responded. "You want to be a fucking *target*?"

"It's better than being a grunt, asshole. You stay clean."

"Man, what does that have to do with anything? We get dirty, but we can at least hit the dirt when we're shot at. I mean, haven't you been on enough lifts to get the piss scared out of you yet? Coming into the LZs is the

worst part of this fucking war, because you got no cover.
If it weren't for the shit, I'd kiss the ground every time I
got off one of these birds."

"Yeah, but I bet when you guys get back to base those
nurses really go nuts for you, don't they?" said Daniels.

"Our base?" I started to tell them that our base was
just a pile of sand at Phu Cat and that I hadn't seen one
Caucasian female since I'd been here. "Yeah, it is good
back at base. I mean, we're just regular guys like you.
But, it's true, the nurses do get out of control."

"See, asshole. This is class, in case you can't see it. I
mean, this takes brains. While we're out here eating mud
and fucking fists, these guys are sleeping in soft beds and
scoring all the nooky they can handle."

His friend wasn't impressed. "They can have the
nooky. Look at them bullet holes. They got 'em up there
in the roof, through the doors and the windshields—this
thing is a fucking sieve. I'm staying here on the ground
and nurse my poor aching cock back home to my waiting
mama."

"Ah-fucking-men, brother," someone agreed.

To Daniels I said, "If you'd like to get on one of these
ships, they are always looking for gunners. You can volunteer."

"Yeah, I guess I could." Daniels looked unhappy.
"But I made it this far like I'm doing. Six months and
I'm gone."

"Well, if you change your mind . . ."

"Yeah, if I change my mind."

Rubenski walked up beside the cockpit.

"Just found my friend, Mr. Mason."

"He's in this unit?"

"Yeah, this is my old company. I'm trying to get him
to transfer to the 229th as a door gunner."

"What'd he say?"

"He said yeah. Man, can you see the two of us on the same ship? We would *mow*—I mean *mow*—VC!"

One of the gunners had to be a crew chief, like Miller. I told him this.

"Aw, it don't matter. Just having him in the same company would be enough. Him and me went through a lot together in Chicago. And we have plans for when we get back. You know, sir, with the stuff we're learning here, my friend and I could knock off even a bank."

"Knock off a bank? You're gonna rob a bank?"

"I guess that is kinda wimpy. Maybe even a bigger job than a bank. That's why it's so important to have him with me. We can plan the right job. He's the brains and I'm the muscle."

I was really surprised that Rubenski was considering a life of crime when he got home. More likely it was a day-dream that kept him going. I laughed.

"You think I'm kidding?"

I laughed again.

"Wait, Mr. Mason. You'll see. Rubenski and McElroy. That's the names to look for, sir. The best."

"I'll be watching the papers, Rubenski."

"Great. That's all I ask. Watch the papers. Give us a chance." Rubenski turned around and noticed that the grunts were getting organized. "Be right back." He ran toward a group of soldiers.

The grunts were dressed in their new uniforms, back in business. They loaded the empty food containers on board along with two guys with minor wounds. When they moved away from our ship, I saw Rubenski hugging one of the grunts in farewell. He ran back to our ship as I cranked up.

As the VC were driven southward, they moved toward the crow's-foot in Kim Son valley. In that valley one of the serpentine turns of the river looped back almost upon itself. The piece of land within the loop was the site of a large village.

"This is LZ Bird." Major Williams pointed at the map at our operations tent at the Rifle Range. "North Vietnamese and Vietcong units are holed up here, and in the jungles north of it. Our assault will be to the village itself. The approach path is across this high ground south of Bird, and there doesn't seem to be any ground fire along that route. Antiaircraft emplacements are reported at Bird, but the LZ will be thoroughly prepped before we land. After the initial wave is on the ground, some of you will return to the staging area to pick up more troops and take them to the LZ. Good luck. Let's go."

As we left to walk to the aircraft, Resler said, "Jesus, sometimes I get the feeling I'm in the middle of a war!"

"What did you think? The war'd be over when you got back?"

"I was hoping. God, you should have seen Bangkok. Absolutely precious women, great food, strange sights, and, best of all, no shooting." We approached our ship and threw our chest protectors and helmets up front on the seats. Gary did the preflight walk-around, and I climbed up top to check the rotor hub and mast. "Those girls look so cute and so shy, it's really a shock to find out that they *love* to fuck," he added.

"Give me a break," I said. The rotors were clean, showing no delaminations.

"Really. They practically fell all over me." Then I heard him tell the crew chief, "Missing a rivet here. Course, I don't see how it matters, with that bullet hole next to it."

The dampers were free and there were no cracks forming in the hub, the Jesus-nut safeties were in place, and there were no fractures visible. I climbed back down. "Did you get any sapphires?" I said.

"No. I can't tell a good one when I see it. Got laid, though."

"Gary, I will kill you if you don't stop—"

"They've got the biggest eyes you've ever seen. Small, delicate features; small, firm breasts; and tight little pussies."

"Tight?" I sighed.

"And juicy." Gary cackled and began to walk around to get in.

"God, I need to go to Bangkok," I muttered. "How much?" I called to Gary as he strapped in.

"Free."

"Free?"

"Yep. And all you can handle. If you can walk when you leave, you weren't trying."

"Crank 'em!" someone yelled.

I climbed into my seat and strapped in. "Tonight, Resler, I will strangle you." He laughed so hard he cried.

The fifty-ship gaggle cruised in the cool air on the way to Bird. Gary and I were twentieth or so. We did little talking on the way. It wasn't exactly fear that caused that tickling, queer feeling in my stomach at the beginning of the assaults. At least I wasn't conscious of being afraid. Instead I concentrated on the radio chatter to see how it was going, shrugged now and then to relieve the stiffness in my neck and shoulders that always seemed to be there, and patted my pistol.

As we crossed the ridge, the LZ was visible at the bottom of the bowl. Streams of smoke from the prestrike drifted up to the top of the valley and blew away. The twenty ships in front of us formed a line descending steeply toward Bird, going down a staircase. Up through that line of Hueys, huge tracers from the anticraft guns streaked silently by. The only sounds of battle came through my earphones as pilots talked. I could hear the chatter of their own machine guns.

"Crew chief hit bad! I'm going back," someone ahead of us radioed. Pfc. Miller had taken a direct hit in his chest protector, but the shrapnel from the bullet had ripped off his left arm. He would have bled to death if the pilot hadn't aborted.

"Roger. Get him to the hospital pod." A wounded aircrewman or great structural damage were the only reasons you could abort. If a grunt was wounded, you kept going.

Gary flew. I chanced a few clicks on the camera around my neck while I lightly followed his movements on the controls. I didn't look through the viewfinder; I just hit the shutter a couple of times, shooting blind.

I could never understand how tracers appeared to move so slowly. I knew they were going really fast, but they always seemed to be on a lazy flight. Unerringly straight, but lazy.

The guys up front did all the work, took the chances, and lost two ships. By the time we got closer, the heavy guns were knocked out by the grunts, leaving only one still blasting away.

We landed in somebody's sandy vegetable patch, and the grunts were off, bounding toward the tree line. Gary nosed over and we were off. Gone. Away unscathed. Back to the beautiful sky where small clouds played in the cool air.

"You got it," said Gary.

"I got it."

We had to pick up some more troops and return. Gary flipped on the RDF (radio direction finder) and tuned in the station at Qui Nhon. Nancy Sinatra sang "These Boots Were Made for Walking."

"Pretty good reception, high like this," said Gary.

"FuckyouGIfuckyouGIfuckyouGI!" came over the radio.

"Hey, Charlie's got our frequency," I said.

"Say again, Charlie," Gary broadcast back on the same channel.

"FuckyouGIfuckyouGI . . ."

"Who's calling Charlie?" yelled the command ship.

"FuckyouGIfuckyouGI," said the Oriental voice.

I spun the dial on the FM homer, and when the needle nulled, I had the general direction to the transmitter. "Coming from the south."

Gary called the command ship. "We're monitoring a Charlie broadcast from the south."

"Roger."

"FuckyouGI . . ." The high-pitched voice persisted, and then stopped as a Huey turned off in his direction.

"Little gook's got some balls, don't he?" said Gary.

"Yeah. I bet they're bigger than he is." If all the gooks were killed, I hoped that at least this guy survived. Every time I heard his emphatic staccato rendition of "Fuck you GI" I laughed my ass off. Somebody else pissing into the wind.

While the command ships tried to track down the VC radio broadcast, Gary and I flew back to the staging area and loaded more troops.

The second landing to the LZ was uneventful. We set down off to the right of the village compound in some gardens. We were told to shut down and wait to carry trophies captured in the battle.

Chinooks were slinging in artillery as we walked over to the newly captured/destroyed village. Once-swaying palm trees were now obscene sticks standing awkwardly above the pall that covered the craters and burnt hooches. I saw no living Vietnamese.

VC bodies were piled near a bunker. Some were missing limbs and heads. Others were burnt, facial skin drawn back into fierce, grotesque screams. A VC gunner was lying below his antiaircraft gun with one arm raised, chained to his weapon. American soldiers were policing the dead for weapons and piling what they found in a growing heap. Most were smiling with victory. Woodsmoke from the hooches mixed with the stench of burnt hair and flesh. The sun was hot and the air was muggy.

At the river's edge, some grunts were playing with basket boats: woven boats six feet in diameter. The men kicked and splashed like kids. The villagers had used the boats for fishing. Now, of course, there were no villagers.

Across the river a giant waterwheel still turned. It was about twenty-five feet in diameter, five feet wide, and built entirely of bamboo. Around the edge of the wheel, arranged so that they were always horizontal, long tubes of bamboo, closed at one end, filled with water at the bottom of the wheel and emptied at the top into a trough that carried the water to the fields. The total rise of the water was over twenty feet, and it splashed steadily into the trough, oblivious of the fate of its builders. A grunt in the river grabbed it, trying to stop it. It pulled him out of the water. He let go ten feet up. Immediately, another grunt grabbed the wheel and hung on tight. He was carried slowly up and over the top and back to the river. Two grunts tried it simultaneously, and the wheel slowed, almost stopped, but carried them up and over. When three guys tried it, the wheel pulled them all out of the water before it stopped. They cheered. Victory!

I examined one of the basket boats. The weave was so tight and precise that it stopped water. There was no calking between the flat strands, yet the boat did not leak. Both basket and wheel were built from material found growing around the village. I wondered how our technology was going to help the Vietnamese. Maybe after we had killed off the people—like these villagers, who knew how to live so elegantly in this country—the survivors would *have* to have our technology. That waterwheel was as efficient as any device our engineers could produce.

The knowledge that built it was being systematically destroyed.

We stayed at Bird for an hour. I stared at the wheel and the men playing with it, wondering who the barbarians were.

When we left, I could see where the water was being pumped. No humans walked the field that it irrigated. No crops grew. The water was filling bomb craters.

Instead of going out on the assaults the next day, Gary and I were assigned to fly a special team of radio-intelligence people to track down the VC who were still broadcasting over our frequencies. Intelligence had determined that an NVA general was radioing messages to his men, uninhibited by our presence. The brass was determined to get this general. Special teams of troopers were on standby.

The four men in the team got in the back with their huge tracking antenna. We flew courses up and down the valleys at their direction. One of the men slapped another on the shoulder and called me on the intercom. "Okay, turn to course one-eight-zero. We've got the little fucker."

Troopers were launched, encircling the triangulated location. They found burning campfires, some miscellaneous equipment and food, but no radio, no VC, and no general.

"Okay, come back to course two-seven-zero," said the head of the radio-tracking team. Gary was flying, so I turned back around to watch them.

They looked pissed. "What's up?" I asked.

"That gook general is broadcasting again, and he's laughing."

They swung the cross-shaped antenna back and forth. We changed course a number of times before they once again had the general's location. While we went back for fuel, another team of troopers was sent in.

Back in the air, we learned that once again the site was found empty except for evidence of a hasty departure. The men in the back were shaking their heads. One of them said to me, "That's fucking amazing. That gook is a fox."

After another two hours of crisscrossing the valleys, the general allowed himself to be discovered again. What in hell was he doing it for? Again a team was sent in. Again it discovered a hastily abandoned campsite. The mission was canceled at dusk and rescheduled for the next morning.

The general played this game for two more days until it no longer mattered. A Cav infantry company captured an NVA colonel. He talked, revealing the location of the headquarters the general had been trying to save. The spot, called the Iron Triangle, was in the opposite direction. The general had been leading us away from the nest. He was never heard again. The Iron Triangle was taken after two days of fierce battles. Everyone thought that was it for Charlie in Bong Son valley. But the fighting continued.

Soon afterward, Gary and I heard the familiar singsong message from our old friend: "*FuckyouGIfuckyouGI* . . .*" It was like trying to eradicate crabgrass.

Kaiser stared ahead, his shoulders sagging. He could've been a player on a losing football team, but he was a tired pilot flying a helicopter.

I smoked a Pall Mall and leaned against the door to rest my aching back. We had been flying assaults for more than eight hours, no breaks, and were headed back to the Rifle Range.

"Yellow Two, Preacher Six."

"Roger, Preacher Six. Go ahead."

"Roger. Come up on two-six-niner and do whatever you can for the man."

"Roger," I replied. Kaiser shook his head while I tuned in the grunts.

"Yellow Two, Wolverine One-Six. We're under heavy mortar attack and we've got some serious wounded to get out."

"Roger, we'll be there soon. What're the coordinates?" The lieutenant read off six digits, and I plotted him on my map. He was only two miles away. I pointed to the map, and Kaiser changed course without saying a word. I leaned against the door and flipped my cigarette out the window. Maybe it would clear the jungle.

It was easy to find the guy for all the smoke that filled his clearing. Other than the smoke, I couldn't see any action.

"Yellow Two, we are clear. I repeat, we are clear. The mortars have stopped."

"Roger, we're coming in."

Just like that. Neither of us thought about the fact that the unit was trapped, encircled. The mortars could start again any time. Neither of us cared.

We approached the clearing in the shadows and pall, with the setting sun ahead of us. Even while Kaiser brought us over the tall trees, I felt no adrenaline. I sat up and squared my shoulders, put my hands on the controls, but I felt no anxiety.

Rubenski fired suddenly into the trees to our right.

"Get him?" I asked.

"I don't know for sure."

"That's nice."

Kaiser brought us to the ground with scarcely a bounce. The clearing was a miniature meadow surrounded by tall trees. The grass was short—like it had been mowed. I stared out the canopy. Across the lawn, ten men lay dead in a neat line. One man's abdominal cavity was emptied around him, his remaining arm buried under his own guts. Another man seemed to be sleeping unscathed in the shady meadow. I stared at him while the grunts scurried toward us carrying five men. Ah, I thought, as I noticed the pale gore behind his head. Not sleeping. Brains blown out.

Two torn men were loaded on the back before the mortars returned. As the mortars struck, the grunts hit the dirt, carrying their wounded with them. Aw shit, I thought, another delay.

I noticed that there was a lot of orange light inside the explosions, silhouetting clumps of black dirt at the bottom of the funnel of expanding gases and shrapnel as mortars exploded a hundred feet away.

The grunts must have been as tired as we were. After the first few rounds, they got up and loaded the three other wounded while the mortars continued bursting ahead of us.

I looked back as the last man was lifted onto the deck. He was missing a leg below his knee. A tourniquet kept the blood mostly stanched. Rubenski blasted the tree line on our right flank. How long had he been doing that?

"That's it, Yellow Two. Watch out for a machine gun ahead of you."

Kaiser lifted the collective. I radioed, "Roger."

A mortar exploded at two o'clock, fifty feet away.

Kaiser pulled the ship's guts so hard that the rpm warning siren screamed in our ears. He let off enough pressure to silence the alarm and turned left to avoid a machine gun the grunts had warned us about.

As we crossed the edge of the meadow, I heard Rubenski's gun blasting away, and then *tick-tick-tick*. Ah, must be *another* machine gun. I nodded to myself. Three rounds passed harmlessly through the sheet aluminum and lodged in the hell hole.

It was peaceful again. I lit another cigarette and watched the sunset.

"You guys really impressed that grunt commander," said Nate, back at the Rifle Range. "I heard he's putting you in for a DFC."

"Wrong medal," said Kaiser, already drunk. "It should be the 'I Don't Give a Crap' medal with a V device for valor."

After we dropped off four wounded men at LZ Dog, Banjo and I, Daisy, and Gillette found ourselves returning to the Rifle Range at night. Daisy led the flight and decided to climb to about 2500 feet and have the radar at Dog vector us back to the Rifle Range.

I had used radar vectoring only once or twice during the instrument-training phase of flight school. I wasn't familiar enough with it to want to use it. It wouldn't even have occurred to me to do anything but fly a compass course back. Daisy was nervous about flying into a mountain, but if we stayed away from the ridge to the west, we were well clear of the mountains.

So Banjo flew in formation with Daisy as he climbed up in a spiral above Dog.

"Preacher flight, take up a heading of one-seven-zero degrees," said the radar station. This station was a four-by-four-foot box on the back of a trailer. It was olive drab.

Daisy turned to the heading, and Banjo skillfully turned with him. We found it easier to fly very close, so close that we could see the red cockpit lights of the other ship. At this distance you can hear the buzz of the tail rotor beside you.

"Preacher flight," called the radar guy, "I have lost you."

Lost us? We had been on course for all of two minutes.

At the same moment, we lost sight of Daisy's ship as we flew into the clouds. It really was dark—no up, no down. Which way was Daisy flying? Left? Right? Up?

"Yellow Two, I'm breaking off to the left," called Daisy.

"Roger," Banjo said. He turned to the right. I watched the compass. We were turning right on around to the north, then to the west. West was where the mountains were.

"Hey, Banjo, we don't want to go west," I said.

"I know."

"Okay." I waited for him to change course, but he didn't. Instead he was diving. The airspeed indicator was up past 120 knots. The vertical-speed indicator (VSI) showed we were going down at over 1000 feet a minute.

"Banjo, we're diving."

"I feel fine."

"Look at the airspeed." He did, and the ship slowed back to 90 knots, normal cruise. The VSI was showing a slight climb.

Where was Daisy?

"Yellow Two, Yellow One. We are descending to get out of the clouds. Recommend you do the same."

I could just see it, Daisy wallowing around in the muck, trying to find the bottom of the cloud bank that ends right where a mountain begins. I could see the two of us trying to do this together and colliding before we hit the mountain.

"Banjo, don't do it. Keep climbing. We'll pop out at the top and shoot for Qui Nhon."

"Daisy says to descend."

"Daisy doesn't know shit. Descend into what? Where exactly are we right now? Over the valley? Or are we over the mountains?"

"Okay, we'll climb."

"Do you want me to fly?"

"No, I'm okay."

"Then could you come back to a south heading?"

Banjo began a turn in our featureless world. You can feel changes while flying in the blind, as when Banjo started his turn, but after the bank is established, you can't tell it from straight and level flying. Banjo was staring straight ahead into nothingness, and the ship was diving again.

"Banjo, the VSI."

He said nothing, but he stopped the dive and began a climb again.

I watched my set of instruments, monitoring Banjo. I wished that Gary was flying, or that I was. Banjo had gone through flight school years earlier, when helicopter instrument flying was not taught. Gary and I had completed instrument training at Fort Rucker, in the Huey. Banjo was an old salt with lots of time. In his mind I was still the rookie.

We were diving again.

"Banjo, if you keep diving like this, we'll get into a world of shit." The ship rocked back as he stopped the dive, but he was now turning to the west. "Compass," I said, sounding like my old instrument instructor. "Compass." He stopped the turn but started to dive again. "Airspeed." The airspeed indicator will tell you immediately if you're climbing or diving: If the airspeed increases, you are diving. Obviously Banjo was too proud to say he didn't know what the fuck he was doing, especially to me. I had to talk him through this.

"Ninety knots," I said. That airspeed would keep us in a climb.

Now he was turning again! "Compass." He corrected. It's true, I thought. The FAA had tested experienced pilots in flight simulators to see if they could somehow fly seat of the pants, with no visibility. A hundred percent of them crashed.

God, I would love to see something. What if the cloud goes to twenty thousand feet? Can't go higher than ten or twelve thousand without oxygen. Probably it's clear over the ocean. Yeah, go over the ocean and come back under the stuff. "Banjo, head farther east."

The altimeter read 4000 feet. Jesus, it's got to end soon.

"Mason, what if this shit doesn't end?" said Banjo. "I think we should drop back down like Daisy."

"No."

"What do you mean, no? I'm the aircraft commander."

"No, don't let down; you don't know where you are. Just a few hundred feet to go. I'm sure of it. Airspeed!" We had lost 500 feet while we talked.

Banjo wrestled with the Huey for a minute while I coached. Soon we were back in the climb, passing 4000 feet for the second time.

"I'll take it to five thousand. If it's not clear by then, I'm heading back down."

I said nothing. The idea of letting down blind over mountainous terrain put me into a panic. It *is* correct to climb, I told myself.

"Airspeed!" I shrieked, letting some of the panic come through. "Damnit, Banjo, watch the airspeed. Keep us climbing." Then I calmed myself and said, "Banjo, you sure you don't want me to fly this last little bit?"

"No, I'll fly. You just watch the instruments."

"Okay. I'll watch the instruments."

Five thousand feet and more nothing.

"I'm going back down," he said.

"Wait!" I yelled. "Keep climbing. We're almost there. Besides, we're heading for the sea, and the clouds end there, so we can't lose by climbing, but we can lose by descending. You understand?"

"Goddamnit!" said Banjo. He maintained the climb.

I blinked. Spots before my eyes? Stars? Yes, stars! At nearly 6000 feet, we broke through. The crew chief and gunner cheered. We all cheered, even Banjo. The universe was back, warm and twinkling. We could make out the jewels of light from Qui Nhon.

By the time we landed, we were very angry at Daisy. He was the one who'd got us into that shit. Had we just flown a normal contact path back to the Rifle Range, we would never have been put into instrument flight. Banjo would not have been found lacking. I wouldn't have had to talk him through the weather.

We saw Daisy as we walked in from the flight line. He had a sandwich from the mess tent. Banjo walked up to him.

"You dumb shit!" he yelled. Daisy jumped back. "You almost got us killed."

Captain attacked by chief warrant officer. He backed away.

"Look, Banjo, all you had to do was descend to the valley like I did."

"Brilliant, Daisy. No one ever descends over mountains in weather. You dumb shit."

"I knew where the valley was all the time," said Daisy.
"You liar."

I walked past them into the tent. Farris wanted to know what all the excitement was about.

"Daisy decided to have the radar at Dog vector us back and led us into a cloud bank."

"So what's the problem?"

"The radar lost us in the clouds and Daisy told us to descend."

"So?"

"So, neither of us knew where we were—over a valley or a mountain."

"So what did you do?" asked Farris.

"Banjo and I climbed until we broke through at six thousand."

"So why are you mad?"

"I'm mad because if we had followed Daisy's orders, we could've bought it. It pisses me off to have leaders like him running loose."

"So, you found out that even leaders make mistakes."

"Yeah, I guess that's it—if you classify Daisy as a leader. I'm more inclined to call him a moron that happens to be a captain."

Farris nodded and gave me an understanding smile. "Well, I'm going to finish this letter. See you in the morning."

As I tried to sleep, I kept wondering why I felt so miserable. I kept jerking suddenly awake for no apparent reason. It seemed like I did that all night.

I kept hearing ricochets and ducked every time I did. Farris saw this and smiled. Farris did not duck.

"What the fuck is that?" I said.

"It's nothing. Don't worry."

Nothing doesn't ricochet. I wasn't exactly worried. I was mostly irritated. We were in the middle of another long laager in another ruined garden. Twenty bored helicopter crews sprawled, hunkered, or wandered around the machines, sweating their brains out. When the whining bullets sounded overhead, faces tracked them across the sky.

Adjacent to our laager was a village. From where we were parked you could not see the huts for the trees, over a hundred feet tall. A trail led into the dark-green lushness. I decided to follow it.

In just a few steps I was in another world. Dark and

cool under the canopy of green, the well-worn, clean path led to a kind of courtyard and stopped.

A hundred feet above me a small circle of light broke through the trees. I turned to look behind me for the inevitable bunch of people, the "Hey-GI-you" crowd. No one anywhere. I stepped up on a kind of sidewalk that connected the hooches. I looked in the door of the first hooch. Nobody was home. I leaned in cautiously—somewhere in my brain a voice warned me to watch for booby traps—and saw that the cooking fire at the back of the hooch was glowing. I looked around outside again—nobody.

I walked to the next door, leaned inside, and met a face that had been hiding against the wall next to the door. The face was a woman's. She was smiling, her forehead wrinkled in worry. From behind her black pajama pants peered a small boy.

She bowed slightly and said something to me and then called out to someone. I stepped back outside nervously, wondering why the fuck I was here alone. The woman and boy followed me out, smiling and bowing nervously. Behind me I heard another voice. I turned quickly and saw an ancient lady in black limping across the courtyard.

She smiled, showing black teeth. I didn't remember any words in Vietnamese except numbers. I didn't know what to say except "You Vietcong?"

Suddenly the three of them pointed outside the village. "Vietcong." I wanted to ask them where their men were, but I didn't know the words. Finally, I did the American thing and took their photograph.

I began to feel self-conscious with the three of them huddled fearfully on their sidewalk. I explained to them that I was just looking around and that I was going on along the trail. I waved good-bye.

The trail led to another, identical courtyard. No one

was home here, either. I found some cooking fires still hot, but everybody had obviously beat a hasty retreat. Alone in one of the hooches, I touched the wattle walls and sat in a net hammock. Above me, the exposed bamboo rafters and beams looked well made. The floor was clean, even if it was made of dirt. Not a bad place, actually. Certainly it was a lot better than the tent I slept in. It was not the average American home, but I doubt that the inhabitants paid much of a mortgage.

I walked farther into the village under the trees, passing a suspicious pile of rice stalks that probably hid the entrance to underground bunkers and tunnels. I could've gone over and checked. I could've grabbed my pistol and committed suicide, too. They both would've amounted to the same thing.

The last hooch I examined was the home of a master carpenter. I discovered his box of tools. Inside the box— about the size of a small suitcase—scores of tools rested in neat compartments. Yellow brass gleamed; shiny steel edges glinted. Knurled hardwood knobs held planing blades tight in their handles. All manner of carving tools reposed in their own boxes. The wide selection and the quality of their tools told me that these people, or at least this person, were definitely not savages.

I had never heard of a gook or a slope-head or a slant-eye or a dink who did anything but eat rice and shit and fight unending wars. These tools and that waterwheel convinced me that there was a successful way of life going on around us, but all we saw were savages, backward savages fighting against the Communist hordes from the North. Why were all the men of this beautiful village gone just when the Americans were right outside? Wouldn't people under attack by the Communists welcome the men who were there to save them? Or was I seeing the wrong way? Maybe the only people who wanted us around were the Saigon politicians who were getting rich by having the Americans here. This village was a long way from Saigon. And the people weren't rich; they were just people.

The carpenter had made a bench whose parts fit so well that it didn't need any nails to hold it together. It was so precisely made, and so in tune with the materials that made it, that it held itself together without aid. I saw this as an enlightening symbol of the true nature of the Vietnamese people, so I stole the bench. I carried it on my shoulder back up the trail, past the rice-stalk pile, past the two courtyards, past the still-smiling women, and back out into the sunshine of the sandy garden. I walked over to my helicopter and put the bench in the shade of the rotor, sat down, and said, "Look, no nails." I shifted back and forth to put strain on the bench to show that it did not move. Kaiser came over to see. "See, they put this together so well it doesn't need nails," I said.

"That's because they have to. Dumb gooks don't know how to make nails," said Kaiser.

We had been away from the Golf Course for more than a month when it was hit in a mortar attack. Several people were killed, fifty or so were wounded, and several Hueys were shredded, but that didn't interfere with the scheduled appearance of Ambassador Lodge, who showed up the next day to dedicate our division compound officially as Camp Radcliff. It was too late. The name had become the Golf Course, and we were stuck with it.

"Don't worry about McElroy; he can take care of himself," said Rubenski. McElroy's platoon had been encircled, and we could not get to them. Charlie had set up antiaircraft guns on the hillsides around the platoon, and somebody had already died trying to fly past them. We waited in the dark at Dog for the air force to bomb the emplacements.

"Of course," I said. "But what does being able to take care of yourself have to do with surviving a Vietcong ambush?"

"If you knew McElroy, you'd know he'll do just fine." Rubenski's scarred face brightened in a crooked smile. He once told me that he almost did not get into the army because of all the old fractures in his skull, part of the growing-up process in Chicago. "Listen to this plan," he said. "McElroy's plan."

"Not the bank-job idea."

"No. No measly bank job. That's the point. McElroy has a *mind*."

"So what's the plan?"

"Lake Tahoe."

"Jesus."

"Wait a minute, sir. Give me a chance."

"You want to rob Lake Tahoe?"

"Just listen. Then tell me if you see any bad spots, okay?"

"Go ahead. I'm not going anywhere for a while."

"The target is a casino at Tahoe. Now, McElroy has seen this, but he doesn't know yet exactly how often each week they do it—collect the take from the machines and tables. We'd have to case the place for a while to get the times straight. Anyway, they collect all the loot in garden carts and haul it outside to an armored car. They got guards all around, but for a minute or so millions of dollars is just sittin' there waiting to be scarfed up."

"So all you have to do is walk past a bunch of guards—"

"Wait, sir, let me tell you," Rubenski said eagerly.

"We use gas, like we do here. Three of us wait in ambush and pop the gas when the loot is outside. Then, as we go into the gas to get the carts, you come in with a Huey and land on the road, in the smoke."

"Me? How did I get into this plan?"

"It's gotta be you, Mr. Mason. I've seen you do stuff like this a hundred times. See, that's the genius of McElroy's plan. We take the stuff we learn here and put it to good use back home. You see?"

"Yeah, I see you flying all over the place trying to figure out where to park a Huey-load of money without raising suspicion."

"That's the best part," he continued. "When we drop the CS"—a vomit-inducing agent—"nobody is going to stick around who doesn't have a mask. We also pop a bunch of smoke to cover the loading and the takeoff. We get off with everybody on board and head away low level. We fly for a hundred miles to a lake McElroy knows about. There's a cabin there where we can stash the money and where we can stay for six months while things cool off."

"Nobody's going to notice a Huey parked out on the dock?"

"Oh, yeah. We take the Huey—stolen from the National Guard—out over the lake and ditch it. Then we hang around for six months thinking about how to spend over a million dollars each. Can you imagine?"

"It's a classic plan all right."

"I knew you'd like it."

"I didn't say I liked it; I said it was classic."

The stars were bright enough to see a man running from ship to ship, a shadow. At the next ship we could hear him asking for Rubenski. Rubenski called that he was here, and jumped out to meet the shadow halfway.

Some people had died in the ambush. McElroy was

one. Rubenski came back and sat in the pocket by his gun and cried. Choking sobs filled the Huey.

I stared out into the black night and shed tears for McElroy, too, and I didn't even know him.

"I can't believe anybody'd be dumb enough to walk into a tail rotor."

"I know. And a grunt who'd been on a bunch of assaults, too." We laughed.

It was funny now, on the back of the truck heading toward Qui Nhon. But last night, when we returned from Dog, a grunt had walked right into the spinning tail rotor of the ship in front of me. I almost resigned. It was too much. I could not stand the idea that somebody could get killed by a Huey after the same Huey just saved his life. I was pulling off my helmet as the ship whined down when I saw the guy rush around from the side door of the ship. Before I could even think of saying "Stop," he was driven to the ground. The tail rotor had hit him on the head. Thud. Down.

I didn't resign. There was a trick ending: The guy wasn't dead. His helmet saved his life, leaving him with only a bad concussion and some cuts.

"The dumb fuck is probably on his way home right now," said Kaiser.

"He deserves it," said Connors. "Anybody that is still alive after that should get a medal *and* a plane ticket home."

This truck ride was the first break in a month for the six of us. Other groups of pilots had got into Qui Nhon, and now it was our turn.

Whether by accident or plan, I was with the usual bunch, Connors, Banjo, Kaiser, Nate, and Resler. Farris was also with us—to make sure we came back.

The twenty-mile drive from the Rifle Range at Phu Cat to Qui Nhon took nearly two hours on a bumpy causeway through unending rice paddies. Every so often an island village punctuated the causeway.

"You'd think the fucking army could squeeze one fucking ride in a Huey for a bunch of its ace pilots," said Connors.

"No ships available. Too many down for maintenance," replied Farris, the army spokesman.

We parked the truck where the traffic got thick and hired a kid to watch it for us. Then we wandered down the street, looking to be entertained.

Connors was stopped by an MP. "Sorry, sir. You have to have your sleeves rolled above the elbow," said the MP.

"What?" Connors said.

"Your sleeves, sir. You have to have them rolled up above the elbow."

"You're kidding, right?"

"No, sir."

Connors glared at the MP. We all did. None of us had our sleeves rolled up high enough.

"What if I like my sleeves just like they are?"

"Then I'll be forced to arrest you, sir."

"You would arrest me for not having my sleeves rolled up?"

"Yes, sir. Those are my orders."

"Tell me," Connors said quietly. "Do you know that there's a war going on?"

"Yes, sir. Of course I know there's a war going on."

"Then why the fuck do you care how high my sleeves are!"

The MP flinched. "I don't care, sir. But if I don't enforce the dress codes, I get my ass in a sling."

"Ah. You get your ass in a sling if my sleeves aren't rolled up above my elbow. Now you're making sense." Connors started rolling his sleeves. "See, gentlemen, it's not this specialist's personal perversion that makes him look for sleeve abuse during wartime; it's the personal perversion of his rear-echelon boss." Connors nodded grimly. "Right, Specialist?"

"That's right, sir."

Everybody looked pissed off, but we rolled our sleeves up.

"Damn. I keep forgetting that the army goes on like normal while we're away," Gary said, voicing our thoughts as we strolled down the bustling street.

While we were still in sight of the truck, Farris told us to meet him back there at 1600 hours, to which we reverently agreed.

Kaiser had been here before. "What we need to do first, gang, is to go get a steam bath so we won't repel the lovelies."

"Ah, the lovelies!" Connors swooned.

"You'll need more than a steam bath, Connors," said Banjo.

"I love the lovelies."

"Like, plastic surgery," Banjo continued.

I had always liked the idea of a steam bath, but it wasn't what I expected. It was hot, way too hot to enjoy. I was forced to the floor, to breathe the mythical cooler air there, two minutes after I had closed the door to the steam room. This is fun? After two more minutes, when I was sure I was passing out, I practically crawled outside to the massage table.

A middle-aged Vietnamese man positioned me carefully on the table and began to wreak Oriental vengeance upon my Occidental body.

"Good, no?" he said as he slammed on my back. "You will like . . . *this*." I winced as he pulled my elbows beyond my head. He continued for some minutes. He leaned over quietly and said, "You want blow job?"

"No," I said quickly, embarrassed.

"I can have girl come here give number-one blow job."

I was relieved to know that it was a girl he was talking about, but I wasn't interested. "No. Thanks anyway."

"Yes, you do, Mason." I heard Kaiser's voice beyond the partition. "You owe it to yourself to enjoy the best each place has to offer. The best this place has to offer is Nancy and her magic lips."

The Vietnamese masseur nodded expectantly, but I said no. He shrugged and started beating me up again.

We wandered around, shopping and drinking, more or less as a group, for a couple of hours. I began to lose track of my position. I was somewhere in the heart of Qui Nhon on a sunny street, off a sunny street. Four of us were sitting around a table at a wonderful little bar on the lovely, sunny street talking to beautiful little girls who wanted to fuck us blind. Kaiser belted back more booze while he tried to get a laughing girl to pay him for his services. Gary blushed and talked to an image of a sweetheart. Nate became a sober intellectual as he discussed world affairs with a nodding woman. I drank and watched everything that happened in this sunny, wonderful bar. I never knew just how good bourbon could be.

"Secret?" I said, alerted by the words and face of a girl who had become my confidante. "Where?"

She pulled me to her to whisper the secret. Laughter broke out when Kaiser's girl compromised and announced she would fuck him for free, just like he had said she would. Ah, it's so wonderful here with all these lovely people.

"But if it's a secret, why are you taking off your clothes?" Aha, be witty and she'll love you. The girl grimaced as her pants caught her foot. Haste clouded her face with worry. Magically, my clothes were gone, too. She flinched once when I entered her, but maintained an admirable state of concentration while she waited for me to finish floundering out my months of pent-up lust. She didn't have to wait long. Soon I was being led back to the bar, where I raved about how wonderful it was to get laid by these wonderful, sunny people.

"Ain't it the truth?" slurred Kaiser. "Ain't these little honeys the best little honeys there are? Huh?"

"It's the truth!" said Nate, hitting his forehead on the table for emphasis.

From this point, the events grow faint. We spent the rest of the afternoon wandering the streets and drinking. By the time we remembered Farris and found our way back to the Jeep, we were an hour late.

"We got lost," Kaiser explained.

"Right. Let's go," Farris said brusquely.

Unfortunately, after the two-hour drive back to the Rifle Range, I was stone sober. We bounced along the causeway watching village after village go by until, finally, a sandy, greenish tent city appeared. Ah, I thought, home at last.

9.
Tension

Army infantrymen, Marines and helicopter crews suffer highest losses in Vietnam.
—*U.S. News & World Report*, March 21, 1966

March 1966

I stood with thirty enlisted men on an apron at the airport at An Khe. Sweat dripped down my sides, staining my khakis.

We watched airplanes move around the airport, trying to determine which one was going to take us to Saigon. A silver C-123 transport had taxied out to the center of the field and then shut its engines off. An army Caribou taxiing toward us locked one brake and swung around, bathing us in a hot breeze that evaporated the sweat. This was our plane.

The rear end of the silver C-123 opened. Four men got out and walked toward us. The rear end of the Caribou opened. The crew chief walked down the ramp eyeing us, the eager groundlings, suspiciously. Up through the fuselage I could see the pilots in the cockpit. One of them noticed my wings and nodded hello.

The men from the silver plane got close enough for us to see they were brass—one army, three navy. The crew chief started to tell us to get on board. The pilot waved to him. He carried his clipboard up front to confer.

The brass were closing fast. The one up front was very tall, very big, wore stars, and had his arm in a sling. I racked my brain. Who is very big, wears stars, rides around in silver airplanes, and has his arm in a sling?

"Isn't that Westmoreland?" a private behind me asked.

Right! Westmoreland, the ruler of Vietnam, was only a hundred feet away, heading for us. I turned around, looking for a lieutenant or a captain to take charge of this mob and call attention and all the stuff you're supposed to do when the fucking general shows up. My search revealed that I was the ranking person there. *"A-tent hut!"* I yelled. AWOL (overnight) bags and laundry sacks hit the dirt as the mob dropped everything to come to attention for the general.

He liked that. When I turned around, Westmoreland was nearly on top of us, still marching, smiling, probing for eye contact with the skinny warrant officer who just then flipped a perfect salute. I held the salute until he stopped and returned it. The general and his admiral friends stood facing me and thirty grunts.

"At ease, Mr. Mason," the voice boomed. He stood close enough to read my name tag, so close that he seemed much taller than he already was. What other rank could they make a guy like this? He *had* to be a general.

"Mr. Mason," he began in a conversational tone, "my friends and I are on important business, and my airplane just broke down."

His airplane? All the airplanes were his airplanes. Also all the helicopters. And all the ships. Westmoreland owned everything, even the cannon fodder he was talking to. "I'm sorry to hear that, sir."

"Thank you. Well, Mr. Mason, if it's okay with you, I'd like to take this airplane of yours so I can get these important gentlemen back to their ships on time." The admirals smiled at the joke—"if it's okay with you"—as he said it.

"Yes, sir." Of course, absolutely, my plane is your plane. . . .

"Thank you, Mr. Mason." He smiled a straight smile in a square jaw while a knowing glint flashed in his eyes. "Now, if you could move these men out of the way, we really have to get going."

"Yes, sir." I turned around and gave the command. "Move out of the way!" There was some confusion as the men grabbed their stuff and backed away.

The admirals walked up inside the plane and sat in three of the thirty-five seats. Westmoreland turned back to say, "Thanks again, Mr. Mason. And I hope this doesn't make you too late for . . . where was it you were going?"

"R&R, sir."

"Ah, R&R. There'll be another plane very soon."

Time's recent Man of the Year walked inside to join the admirals. The four men sat in the cavernous interior of the Caribou. The crew chief, looking like he had just been given a couple of grades of rank, pushed the button that raised the ramp and sealed the ship. The prop wash hit us, and the airplane moved away, got smaller, and leapt into the sky. Behind me the dusty mob spoke.

"Gee, I hope they ain't crowded in there."

"You can't mix enlisted and brass too close, you know."

"Why the fuck not?"

"The vapors from the enlisted men make 'em tarnish."

I considered myself very fortunate indeed to be on an airliner cruising smoothly toward Taiwan. My sweat had dried in the air-conditioned plane, and I nursed a drink served by a stewardess. As I stared out the window at the sea, I knew that Resler and the rest of the gang were at this very moment trying to get rid of the rat turds and mildew in our GP. I had to smile.

We had returned from Bong Son just two days before. The VC had suddenly given up or disappeared. After forty-one consecutive days in Bong Son valley, high body counts were announced. Victory was ours. Let's go home.

We couldn't just fly back casually after forty-one days away; we had to do something dramatic. We were, after all, the First Team.

The hundred Hueys moved into trail formation at the An Khe pass and snaked around the sky, trying to spiral to a landing at the Golf Course. The guys on the ground said we looked really impressive. They couldn't hear the chatter, everybody yelling about how fucked up the formation was, how we were bunched up—fussily worrying about how we looked to the rest of the Cav. The hundred ships landed, causing a storm at the Golf Course. The crews walked to their tents.

Once again the rats had prevailed. Their turds were lined up in comfortable disarray, which bespoke rats truly at home. Mildew coated everything. Black shapes with shining eyes darted for cover as we reoccupied the tent.

"We've got to kill these fucking rats!" yelled Connors.

I was smiling stupidly when the stewardess asked, "Care for another drink, sir?"

"Huh? Oh. Yeah."

Connors's exasperation always delighted me. Once, when he came back from a night out, he drunkenly explained that the tent flaps should be down, not up. He sat in the dark on his cot and loudly enumerated the faults in leaving the flaps up. Then he pulled the rope near him that released the flap. It had filled with water. When it unrolled, gallons of water poured over Connors and drenched his bed. He launched into a series of curses, filled with rage and fury. He also lent me a hundred dollars for my R&R. Just before our assault the day before, Connors said, "Mason, be real, real careful, okay?"

"I always am."

"Yeah, but you've never been worth a hundred dollars to me before."

By the time we landed in Taipei, I was feeling very good. Uncle Sam, in his great wisdom, provided all necessities for his warriors—just follow the line. In Saigon we had lined up for various cities: Taipei, Bangkok, Sydney, others. The attraction of each city was the same—drinking and fucking. Or fucking and drinking, depending on your morals.

As we deplaned, a smiling government employee directed us to a bus. The bus cruised the streets while a man gave us a rundown of various hotels, indicating prices and location. I elected to stay at the King's.

When the government dropped us off at the hotel, the Chinese-civilian half of the team swung into action. A kindly, knowledgeable Chinese man-about-town latched on to us as we stepped off the bus.

"Okay, boys. You have come to the right place." He smiled warmly. "Come right this way, I'll help you get your rooms, but we must hurry. There is so much to do in Taipei."

I tossed my bag into the room. A man named Chuck had the room across from mine. Chuck was in his midforties and was a captain back at work. In the hallway he wore a tourist costume much like mine—chinos, checked shirt, and loafers. We had just introduced ourselves when Danny, the guide, came rushing toward us.

"Come, come, gentlemen, we must hurry. There is much to do in Taipei."

Danny hurried us down the hall to the elevator. "Remember, gentlemen, you are here to enjoy yourselves, and I am here to help you. First, we must go across the street to a fine, high-class bar and have a drink to discuss our plans. You must tell me what you want to do and I will be your guide." Danny walked a little ahead of us, almost walking backward as he talked to us. He was so excited that you might have assumed that he, too, just got in from Vietnam.

Danny showed us through the door of the bar. I noticed thirty or forty women sitting along one wall, side by side. He herded Chuck and me toward the beginning of the line.

"Martha! So good to see you tonight," he said to the first girl. She nodded warmly to Danny and then to us.

"Hi," I said. "I'm Bob Mason." Martha looked very pleased to meet me.

We moved up the long line of girls, saying hello to almost everyone. At the end of the line we went up to the second floor and settled around a table where drinks were already being served by some of Danny's friends.

"So, gentlemen, which one do you want?"

"You mean, which one of those girls?" I asked.

"Of course. Tell me which one you prefer and she will be with you like that." He snapped his fingers.

"Well, I did see one girl I kinda liked, but I didn't get her name," I said.

"Where was she sitting?"

"I think she was about the tenth girl. She's wearing a violet dress."

"Ah, Sharon. You have very high-class taste, Bob."

"Thanks."

Chuck described the girl he remembered, and Danny got up and excused himself. "I will be right back, soon. Drink up!"

Immediately after Danny disappeared down the stairs,

the girl in violet, Sharon, appeared and was escorted to a table at the other end of the room. She sat down across from her escort, facing me. How could I feel deceived by someone I didn't know? Of all the girls I had met in the lineup, she was the one whose eyes had locked on mine. As I sat there watching her, I realized that I absolutely loved her. There was something familiar about her. She was smiling gently as she met her escort, but her expression changed slightly when she looked up. She did not look away, and I knew she loved me, too.

Danny came back up behind two women. They were both dressed very nicely and carried evening bags. They sat down across from Chuck and me while Danny introduced them. "Linda, this is Bob. Vicki, this is Chuck." He stood back for a moment, grinning at the happy couples. "I must go see about your drinks." Before he left, though, he leaned over to me and whispered, "Sharon was already—" I nodded quickly.

Linda leaned across the table and whispered, "It is so sad that you could not get the one you loved. Do you wish me to leave?"

Yes, I did. That girl, Sharon, seemed to be an Oriental version of Patience. Patience looked at me the same way when we first met. But there wasn't enough whiskey in me to cause me to become callous. The fact that Linda was willing to leave, to be rejected, stirred what remained of my sensibilities, and I said, "No, of course not."

"She is more beautiful than I am," said Linda, fishing for compliments. In fact, Sharon was more beautiful than Linda, but I reminded myself that neither of them would be near me if I wasn't going to pay. In four days it would be over.

"Don't be foolish; you are more beautiful."

"Thank you for saying so." She smiled.

Sharon still looked at me occasionally. I wondered why.

I have dim memories of the insides of many different clubs, singing in the streets, and bright lights and taxis. I even woke up in a different hotel. My companion, for ten dollars a day, was Linda. She showed me the sights on the island in between servicing my desperate horniness. We ate at different clubs and restaurants every night, never visiting the same place twice. Occasionally, as we toured, I would see Sharon watching me familiarly.

In moments, the four days were spent.

Surprisingly, girls crowded outside the bus as we arrived at the airport. As we got off, reunions were formed by the departing soldiers and their Chinese girlfriends. The girls were actually crying. Why in the world? Perfect strangers five days ago were now sobbing tearful farewells. I climbed down out of the bus, but there was no Linda. I moved past the hugging couples, to follow a roped path to the terminal. Five steps away from the door, I heard my name called. I looked up and saw Sharon. She was smiling broadly, but tears flowed on her cheeks. She held her arms out and I instinctively hugged her. I could not understand why she was doing this.

"Please be careful," she said.

A nearly hysterical feeling of fear hit me as I stepped off the plane at An Khe. The fear welled within me, changing to a prickly, cold terror in the moist heat. I shivered slightly and forced the demons to the background while I looked for a field phone. I shivered in the dark tent while I waited to be connected to my company.

"Welcome back, Mr. Mason," said Sergeant Bailey. I calmed immediately at Bailey's voice. "We'll send a Jeep over right away."

It was gray outside, overcast, humid, incredibly hot. I fired up another Pall Mall and waited.

In a few days I succeeded in almost totally suppressing my fear. We were not taking many hits out in the mountains where the Cav was currently fishing. The closest thing to real action was when one of our gunships shot down a slick.

Major Astor, the replacement for Captain Morris, was a tall, sturdily built man with short blond hair, more like the stereotypical marine than an army pilot. He joined us right after Bong Son valley. He saw only our pleasantly boring missions in the local boonies, which led him to erroneous conclusions.

"They let us go pretty much where we want to go," Major Astor said to John Hall. "How much longer can the VC last if we've got control of the air like we do?"

"We don't have control; they do," said John.

"Yeah. I've seen how tough they are. Actually, though, what could you expect them to do against our helicopters?" Astor grinned.

"You've got it wrong, Major. The little people have just decided to take a small break for a while." John was drinking whiskey; the major beer; and I was listening. We were at the bar of our soon-to-be-opened-built-by-our-own-hands officers' club. There was no bartender yet; people just brought their own bottles.

"You call them 'little people'?"

"Sometimes."

"Makes them sound like elves."

"Well, sometimes you'd think the little bastards were carrying around some fairy dust or something, the way they can be exactly where you don't want them to be."

Connors and Banjo walked in. Connors's shirt was stuck to his sweaty body, and sweat ran down his face. Banjo looked dry in comparison.

"Bartender!" Connors yelled. "Beer! Give me beer!"

"There is no bartender," Banjo said.

"I know that; I'm just practicing." Connors looked around and nodded to the new major. "Good evening, sir."

"Good evening, Mr. Connors. I just found out that you're the company's IP."

"Yes, that is true. I am an ace with a helicopter."

"Just don't get near him when he tries to tie one down," said Banjo.

"Fuck off, Banjo."

"Ever teach at flight school?" Astor said to Connors.

"Not yet. That's probably where they'll send me after this bullshit, though. Why? Are you an IP?"

"No," said Astor. "I just graduated. I was impressed by the training program at Rucker."

"Army helicopter training is the best there is. When you leave, you're almost safe."

"Almost safe?" Astor laughed.

"That's right. Any new pilot is still dangerous. They know just enough to get themselves in trouble. After another five hundred hours of practical flying, learning how to use the aircraft, I'd say they were pretty safe. If you're still alive at a thousand hours, you must have it down pretty good. That's stateside time. Over here you pick things up quicker 'cause of the pressure of being shot at." Connors grabbed the beer that Banjo put in front of him.

"Well, I thought it was a damn good program," said Astor. "And after flying over here awhile, I'm even more impressed at how good the training is."

"Yeah, it is good. But don't judge the action here by what you've been seeing since you've been here. When you start making your approaches to that tight LZ, in formation, with the VC shooting at your ass, then it starts to get tough."

"Even so, if you fly like they taught you, and don't panic, you ought to do okay," said Astor.

"What can I tell you? You got the big picture for sure." Connors turned to me and Hall and rolled his eyes.

"Here's to army aviation." Astor raised his beer.

"Huh?" said Connors..

I left the club to write my daily letter home, mentally totaling my flight time. By Connors's definition I was a little better than pretty safe, with seven hundred hours. Connors himself had nearly three thousand hours, almost all in Hueys. All of this proved to me that I was becoming a professional—a helicopter pilot. When I got back home, I could start my own helicopter company. All I had to do was get back home.

Later that night, I heard the shrill screaming of a man gone crazy. I ran outside, goose flesh rising on my skin.

"God damn them! God damn them!" the voice shrieked.

Near the club, I saw four men carrying one of our pilots, a screaming, twisting, fighting Captain Fontaine. Fontaine hated Owens and White.

"I'll kill them! I'll kill them!"

"Calm down . . ."

"I will kill *themmmm!*" Fontaine's voice trailed into a high-pitched scream. He was a struggling pig going to slaughter, but the four men, one of whom was Connors, held him tightly and carried the writhing man up the short stairs to his hooch. And Fontaine was such a calm guy, too.

"He went fucking nuts," said Connors.

"I can see. But why?" I asked back in our tent, watching Banjo heat some coffee water next to his cot.

"Fucking Owens and White." Connors sat on his cot. "Fontaine says he found out that those two have been faking their flight records. They've been logging a lot of combat time when everybody knows they don't fly at all. Anyway, he got into it with Owens. Owens told him he was just jealous! That cocksucker! He thinks everybody is as much an asshole as he is."

"Why do they want the time?"

"Well, you figure a guy like Owens, coming up soon

for major. He needs the combat time on his records. He might even try to get some medals with it."

"Coffee time. Sorry guys, there's only enough for me." Banjo laughed.

"So why say anything?"

"I'm not sure. I think it makes me feel better when I think I'm living better than you." Banjo laughed. "How 'bout a cookie?"

"You're so generous, Mr. Bates."

"Not at all, Mr. Connors." Banjo bowed, smiling. "Mason?"

"No thanks," I said. "I'm going to bed."

When you put your mosquito netting down around you, you felt isolated, even in the crowded tent. You were still in plain view of everyone, but the feeling was that you now were private, separated. I settled into my poncho liner to sleep.

Blackness surrounded me and something formless pursued me. A presence dove into my mind and flooded my heart with overwhelming fear. I snapped awake, raised on my elbows. Through the gauze of the netting, I saw Connors looking over from the other side of the tent. I tried to remember what scared me, but I could not. Nothing was happening in the camp. I eased myself back down, feeling tired, and watched the top of my mosquito netting.

The next day, Gary and I flew attached to Major Astor's platoon on his first mission as leader. Most of the day was spent flying C rations out to resupply the various patrols beating the bushes for Charlie. So far, no Charlie. Occasional sniper hits were reported. Old campsites. New campsites. Even a few captives. But for all practical purposes, the jungle and bush we scoured was uninhabited.

Astor did pretty well at the beginning of the mission. He had the eight ships assigned to him split up, each one resupplying an area of its own. This made the work go faster. Resupply was considered tedious by most pilots, but Gary and I took these delightfully boring occasions to play with the machine while we did the job. Nothing malicious, like buzzing MPs, but the kind of play that challenged our skills.

It could be something like ticking a tree limb with the rotor in an LZ just to see if you could pull it that close. That would be considered foolish back in the States. Here, that kind of judgment could save your life.

I experimented with the Huey tuck that day. If the Huey was nosed over too far on takeoff, the wind resistance on top of the flat roof would force the nose even lower. The ship would then try to dive into the ground as it accelerated. If this happened over level ground, you were trapped in a vicious circle. Pulling the cyclic back would not overcome the wind pressure on the roof. Pulling up on the collective to stay away from the ground only added power to the system, causing you to crash at a higher speed. If you didn't do anything but curse, you hit the ground at a lower speed. Either way, you lost.

I almost got caught in a Huey tuck once, and I wanted to know just how far over was too far. I found out by simulating a level takeoff from a pinnacle.

I nosed over very hard and pulled enough pitch to keep the ship flying horizontal to the ground. I tested the cyclic, and the ship would not respond. I could feel it happening. Adding power only made it worse. When I could feel the trap and feel how I got into it, I knew I could never get into it by accident. I was experimenting with this over a valley, so all I had to do to recover was dive.

Near the end of the day, Charlie decided to try to wipe out a platoon or two before dark.

We were at a field command post where our ships were being loaded when the grunt commander called Astor over to his command tent.

There were six Hueys in the laager. When Astor came out minutes later, he signaled for a crank-up, then walked over to Gary and me.

"There's a platoon coming under attack just a few klicks from here. We only need five ships to get them out." Astor zipped up his flak vest. "I want you to stay here and monitor our frequency in case we need you." He trotted to his ship, which was already running.

"Pretty tough assignment," said Gary. We both climbed into the cockpit. Gary started up so that we could monitor the radios without draining the battery. Having to get a jump start in the middle of nowhere was something neither of us wanted to experiment with.

I tuned the radios.

"Charlie One-Six, Preacher Yellow One," Astor called. No answer.

"Roger, Charlie One-Six. We are inbound. Throw smoke."

No answer. On the ground we could hear only Astor's side of the radio conversation. He sounded just like he knew what he was doing.

"Yellow One, they are on the other side of the tree line." That was John Hall's voice.

"Negative, Yellow Four. I see the smoke," said Astor.

I started to fasten my straps. If they were that close to pickup, we would be in the air in minutes.

"Negative, Yellow One. The target is upwind of that smoke," said Hall.

"Yellow Four, I am in charge here," said Astor.

"Roger."

"Do you think we should get into the air?" asked Gary.

"Naw, not yet. Wait for Astor to give us the word."

"Yellow Four is taking heavy fire from the tree line!" yelled Hall.

Astor, possibly already on the ground, did not answer.

"Yellow One, we are aborting. My crew chief has been hit." We could hear the machine guns on Hall's ship chatter while he talked.

"We'd better go," I said.

"Right." Gary brought the Huey up to rpm and made a quick takeoff.

"Yellow One, Charlie One-Six. I have you in sight. You're about five hundred meters downwind of us."

It was clear to Gary and me that Astor had really blown it. He had landed downwind of the grunts' secure position, following the drifting smoke, even though Hall had seen the correct position. I saw the flight and called Astor to say we were joining up. He radioed a curt "Roger." We joined up and made the landing to the grunts' clearing without incident.

As the crews mingled after the mission, back at the Golf Course, Astor separated himself and walked away quickly.

"That guy is an accident looking for a place to happen," I said.

"Yeah, he's a disaster all right. . . . Hey. Major Disaster!" said Gary. Everybody laughed. He was christened.

Hall met us at the tent. His crew chief, Collins, was dead. The ship had taken more than twenty rounds. Hall was shaking with anger. He had been right. Disaster had ignored his warnings.

"I'm going to kill him," said Hall.

"I know how you feel," I said.

"No, I mean that I will actually kill him. You know, dead." Hall unsnapped his revolver holster and walked off toward Disaster's hooch. I thought he was just acting tough, but when I got to the mess line fifteen minutes later, I heard Disaster calling for help from inside his hooch.

Hall stood tall and silent, his pistol at the ready, a can of beer in his left hand. He had taken a position midway between Disaster's hooch and the mess tent. About thirty men, getting their evening chow, looked on with interest.

"Hall, if you don't put that gun away immediately, I'll have you court-martialed." The voice came from behind the hooch door.

"You'll have to come out sometime, Major."

"You're crazy! You can't pull a gun on a superior officer and hold him captive in his own quarters. You're going to be in serious trouble if you don't put that gun away. Right now!"

"You killed Collins, Major. Now it's your turn." Hall raised his pistol to aim.

"Help!" Disaster screamed when he saw Williams come near the mess tent. Williams looked up and saw Hall in the darkening twilight. Disaster peered hopefully out, then yelled again, "Help! Major Williams, get this madman away from me!" Williams nodded and rinsed his mess kit before he walked into the mess tent.

Nobody came to Disaster's aid. Once in a while we heard him yell. No one paid the slightest attention. Later that night Hall gave up the vigil. I heard him singing drunkenly on the path outside my tent. The next morning he was still so drunk that he could not be allowed to fly.

That incident seemed to precipitate a series of conflicts among us as tension took its toll. Hall beat up Daisy one night, splitting his lip. He continued to harass Disaster by throwing Montagnard spears at him as he walked around the camp. Soon after Captain Fontaine was carried screaming back to his hooch; Riker told Shaker, very plainly, to shove it, when Shaker told him to go work on the club. Connors and Nate pushed each other around over where the laundry should be hung. Nate and Kaiser scuffled over a territorial dispute.

The farewell party for Williams was very quiet. The major, an excellent air leader, was being transferred to brigade staff in Saigon—a move up. The party was restrained because Williams had never been close to us, like Fields had been.

The next day, after an award ceremony to pass out air medals among us, our new CO, Major Crane, made his introduction speech.

"I think that everything around here is just fine except for personal neatness," said Crane. "This company has an impressive list of accomplishments in the Cav. I'm sure you've been so busy that you just let things slide." He wore crisp fatigues and spit-shined boots. Even Williams, Mr. Hardass himself, didn't worry about that kind of bullshit. Williams concentrated on our missions. Crane was already talking about the busywork.

"You may not think that wearing a shirt in the company area is very important—and, by the way, the shirt must be tucked in—but I do. Sure, it's tough here. This is combat. But if we let just one aspect of our professional demeanor fall to the wayside, our overall performance will suffer." He paused, smiled. Just a regular guy doing his job. "So from now on, we will conform to standard army dress codes at all times. That means tucked-in shirts outside the tents, bloused boots, and clean uniforms."

It's our own fault, I thought. We spent so much time making this place look civilized that this guy thinks he's back at Fort Benning.

"While I'm talking about keeping yourselves clean, I may as well announce a bit of good news." He smiled. "Starting tomorrow, we will be digging our own company well so we can have our own showers." He waited. I think he expected some cheers here. We were silent. "Captain Sherman will be the project leader, and I want you all to give him your fullest cooperation. Dismissed."

"My aching fucking back," said Connors back at the tent. "I was kind of getting used to cleaning up the way I do."

"Shit. How do you think you clean up?" asked Banjo.

"Well, just like everybody else. I keep my uniform on until it becomes a second skin. Then, when I peel it off, it takes all the crud with it."

"I would like to have a shower around here," said Gary.

"Yeah, I would, too. I wonder how deep we have to dig?" I said.

"Maybe all the way to Cincinnati!" Gary said.

Farris walked in. "I have another announcement for you guys." He waited until we gathered around him. "We need volunteers to transfer to other aviation units to make room for the replacements."

"Transfer out of the Cav?" Gary asked.

"That's right."

"When?" somebody asked.

"Sometime between now and the end of next month."

This was my chance. Maybe I could get a cushy job at Qui Nhon, flying advisers or something. I raised my hand.

For the next few days I flew local routine missions or dug the new well. While I filled buckets and watched them being hauled up on a rope, I daydreamed about my new assignment. A friend of mine from flight school had written saying that he was assigned to a navy carrier with his own Huey. I knew there were better jobs than the Cav. Maybe a 9-to-5 courier pilot in Saigon. Imagine, no more mud, tents, or boonies.

At twenty-five feet we struck rock. Sherman called in some guys from the engineers who said we'd have to blast.

Gary and I flew over the Bob Hope show on our way to Happy Valley. While we flew ass-and-trash that afternoon, we listened to the most bizarre radio conversation I had ever heard.

"Raven Six, Delta One. We have a target in sight." Delta One was a gunship.

"Roger, Delta One. Do you see anything on their backs?"

"Negative."

"Well, there's just no way to be sure. Go ahead and get them."

"Roger."

"What the heck are they talking about?" asked Gary. We had just picked up some empty food containers and were sailing down the side of a mountain.

"Got me," I said.

"Raven Six, our guns just won't stop them."

"You tried to get them in the head?"

"Roger."

"Use the rockets."

"Roger." Silence. Gary was setting up for an approach to the road patrol on our resupply route.

"Raven Six, Delta One. That did it. We got both of 'em."

"Glad to hear it, Delta One. I was beginning to wonder if anything we had could stop an elephant." Elephant? We're killing fucking elephants?

"Roger. Anything else?"

"Of course, Delta One. Go down and get the tusks."

"I'm sick," said Gary. "Killing elephants is like blasting your grandmother."

Back at the company, there was general outrage at the

news that the ivory was delivered to division HQ. It was okay to kill people in a war, but don't touch innocent by-standers like elephants.

"Any man who'd do that would come into your house and shoot your dog," Decker said.

"Get your camera, Mason!" Sherman yelled.

"What's up?"

"We're going to blast the well. Get your camera."

I stood back along the trail to the well and pointed my camera.

"Everybody clear?" Sherman yelled.

"Clear."

Bonk. A small cloud of dust rose five feet above the site. I snapped the picture.

"Shit. I thought it woulda made more noise than that," yelled Sherman.

"Yeah. Did it go off?"

"Is there water?" Everybody went over to the well.

"Hoo-fucking-ray," said Connors. "We got more dirt under them rocks."

"We'll just keep digging," announced Sherman.

Somebody had painted a five-by-ten-foot mural of LZ X-Ray on the wall of our new club. I had a bourbon and water in my hand as I walked around. The furniture, shipped in from the States, looked foreign. The chairs were stained bamboo with tropical-print cushions. The tables had bamboo legs and Formica tops.

The place was packed for the official opening. We all knew that the Colonel was going to bring nurses to the affair. The Colonel wasn't around yet. The hundred or so guys passed the time drinking twenty-five-cent drinks in rapid succession.

Nearly everybody from our company was there. Nate

and Kaiser talked seriously at the bar while Nate's hand kept time with a song played on the new stereo system. Connors and Banjo laughed from a table nearby. Farris nursed a Seven-Up but smiled anyway. Hall sat in a corner staring at the mural. Disaster shadowed Crane and talked business. Wendall and Barber watched the tape recorder work. Resler grinned like a child on his second beer. Riker's red face was bright as he drank more than he usually did. I stood by the bar wondering whether I got the clap in Vietnam or in Taipei.

"You're not . . . sick," I had said, pointing to her groin, "are you?"

"Me?" Her face showed pain. "Me? Don't be silly. I no sick."

"If there's one thing I can't do, that's catch the clap," I said.

"Well," she huffed, "I'm almost a virgin."

Just as I noticed the silence, Resler shoved me. "Bob," he whispered, "the nurses are here."

The Colonel had come unannounced, through the club's back door, escorting his promised nurses. They, I'm sure, did not know that they were the inspiration that had built this club. They did have a look of extreme self-consciousness about them. The entire club stared intently and silently as four elderly, high-ranking females from the medical corps took seats at the Colonel's table, cause enough for their nervousness.

The music played on. Two very plump lieutenants followed. I kept looking at the door to see the rest. That was it. After a long minute, that was clear to everyone. Talk began again.

"There must be some real nurses in this fucking division," snarled Connors. Banjo was laughing so hard that he was in tears.

"Those are nurses," said Resler.

"You know what I mean," said Connors. "You know,

nurses. Like with tits that come up here"—he gestured—
"not down here. Shit, my grandmother is more appealing."

The Colonel kept looking around while his aides talked
to the nurses.

"Ladies." A drunken warrant officer walked over and
bowed politely to the nurses. 'Gen'lmen . . ." He nodded
to the aides. "Sir . . ." He bowed again.

The Colonel glared at him. The nurses laughed. When
he turned to leave, the Colonel relaxed. At a moment
when the club was silent, and while every eye was glued
to the scene, the drunk released a fart that stopped
hearts.

The Colonel, his men, and the nurses flinched at the
report. The Colonel grew red in the face and started to
get out of his chair, perhaps to kill the drunk. Noise returned abruptly to the club and he hesitated. Everyone
was laughing. It was as though everyone had delivered
that fart, and the Colonel knew it. He sagged back in his
chair helplessly. The nurses explained that they had to
get back, right away.

Farris said, "I think you men should stop drinking and
go home. We have a big mission tomorrow."

It wasn't a very big mission, just lengthy. Since I'd been
back from R&R, the daily missions were in the mountains forty and fifty miles north of An Khe. We started
each day at 0500, picked up grunts at the Golf Course or
the refueling area, flew them out to the mountains,
placed them at various LZs, and picked up wounded and
dead from the patrols already out there.

This area wasn't too bad for the pilots. We weren't getting killed. The grunts, though not beaten, were suffering
losses from constant sniper fire and devious booby traps.

After a week of our carrying wounded and dead people, the deck and bulkheads of the cargo area got very
rank. Dried blood caked under the seats, and miscella-

neous pieces of flesh stuck to the metal. When it became absolutely necessary to wash out the gore and smell, the pilot would make an approach toward the bridge going to An Khe and land in the river.

Washing out the Hueys spawned a new support industry among the Vietnamese around An Khe. As we came across the bridge, boys would scramble toward the shallow area near the sandbars where we usually landed, ready to work.

The only thing we had to worry about was not getting the electronics wet. Everything else, up to deck level, was unaffected by water. I hovered around in the shallows with the skids underwater until I found a spot that was the right depth. It was safe as long as you kept an eye on the tail rotor. As soon as the engine shut down, the boys would grab buckets and brushes and begin scrubbing the ship. The crew chief usually took out the seats for the scrub-down.

I took off my boots and socks, stashed them on top of the console, rolled up my pants, and made it to the shore. While I stood on a sandbar and watched, the crew chief supervised the project and the boys did most of the work. They even climbed up on the roof and poured water down the hell hole, which was industrious of them but completely unnecessary.

Other forms of business prospered on the sandbars. One was the Coca-Cola business. The other was mermaids. The Cola girls had exclusive territories. The girl in the area I usually landed was named Long. Because I flew to the sandbars a lot, she knew me pretty well.

Long was about ten years old, with waist-length black hair. Her eyes were black, and her skin was darker than that of most Vietnamese. She was a gorgeous and radiant little girl.

"Do you have a wife?" she asked when we first met. I said yes.

"Is she tall like you?"

"No, she comes up to my chin."

"Ah, very tall. Does she have hair on her arms like you?"

"Not like me, like you." I brushed the peach fuzz on her arm.

"Oh, that is good." She laughed. She had never seen Caucasian women.

We became friends over a period of months. Long usually sat beside me on the sandbar while the Huey was washed and talked about how nice it would be when the war was over. She believed that it would be over very soon. There was talk of peace overtures going around. She could not imagine how the VC could beat soldiers that marched through the sky.

When a ship was rinsed out, the crew chief would normally want to let it dry a little. Then he would get undressed to go for a "short swim." The inspiration for this healthy and athletic act came from the older girls, who pretended to be mermaids and beckoned sweetly from downstream islands.

The mermaids showed up at the river the day after the general placed An Khe off limits as a result of the high rate of social disease. For months, while an American-regulated village of ill repute was being constructed just outside town, the mermaid business flourished. I never drifted down the river myself, but from what I could see, it looked very sweet indeed.

Eventually the ship would dry and the crew chief would come back smiling. Long would get up to say good-bye. Standing, she was only a couple of inches taller than I was sitting.

"Good-bye, Bob. Be well." She smiled and wandered off to sell her wares as other Hueys landed among the sandbars.

When I flew a ship to the sandbars, I usually tried to teach the crew chief some basic flying so that he could take the ship in case a pilot got hit, and get it to the ground in one piece. The results of this training were disappointing, because there was never enough time to pursue it. Consequently I never saw a crew chief who was able to fly even a rudimentary approach.

What seemed to me the most basic of human skills—hovering a helicopter—somehow eluded even the most intelligent crew chief. But among the men I tried to train, Reacher was notable. I had flown with him so much that he was almost able to hover, and I believe that in an emergency he might have got a ship down on the ground in one or two pieces.

Rumor was it was getting hot again in the Ia Drang. While the First of the Ninth was over there snooping around, we continued our ass-and-trash missions around the home base. The pilots were tired of this kind of flying, and the ships suffered the mechanical equivalent of lassitude and dishevelment. The flyable rate was less than 50 percent. On the same day that a Chinook was shot down, our company broke four Hueys from just sloppy flying. At the news of the four accidents, the general reaction was "four less Hueys to fly." Malaise had set in.

A brand-new replacement, Captain Hertz, was assigned to fly with me one afternoon. Nate flew with another replacement, and the two of us were going to fly to Qui Nhon and back to check these new guys out.

When the sky was a dull orange behind us, we crossed the An Khe pass heading east. Hertz had been flying since we left the ground. He was doing okay, flying on Nate. We talked a little in the air. He told me he had a lot of flight time in the States.

A formation accident in the Cav had killed ten people.

We heard reports about other wrecks around the country. Night-formation skills were critical. One guy, fucking up just a little bit, could wipe out a bunch of people if those rotors connected.

As it got dark, Hertz began to drop behind Nate. I encouraged him to close up, because dropping back too far caused you to lose perspective relative to the lead ship.

"Move it right up close, just like a daylight formation."

Hertz moved to about two rotor disks' distance of Nate. Unfortunately, he also started to oscillate, swinging too far away, then too close. As he tried to adjust for the swing, he overcorrected. I said nothing. On one swing toward Nate, he scared himself and dropped farther back.

"You gotta keep it closer," I said. "If we were in a regular formation, we'd be screwing up everybody. If Nate decided to make a left turn right now, we wouldn't know it until we were right on top of him."

"I was just dropping back for safety."

"I know. But, believe me, it's safer closer."

"Okay."

As he pulled back up into the slot, he once again began the oscillations. He was on a pendulum that swung out away from Nate and then back toward him. He either knew a real slick trick, or we were going to blend rotor blades with Nate. At the last possible moment, when I realized he had no slick trick in mind, I grabbed the controls.

"I got it." I flared back abruptly and pulled back into position.

"Why?"

"Because you were going to hit Nate."

"I wasn't even close," said Hertz.

"You were close enough that I had to get on the controls."

"Well, I don't think so."

"Well, we're up here tonight for your benefit, not mine. Try it again."

He set up again, and again began to swing in and out. His trouble, I believe, was his fear of collision, which was rational but which wrongly affected his judgment. He overcorrected, compounding the error until it grew out of control. On a wild swing away, I asked, "Are you okay?"

"Roger," said Hertz. Then he swung in toward Nate, and once again I took the controls. "I got it."

This pissed him off. "No one has ever taken the controls away from me, especially not a warrant officer." Ah, what we had here was a dyed-in-the-wool snob who hated warrants.

"Well, as far as I'm concerned, Captain, you should be thanking me for saving your life. I need night training like I need an extra asshole."

"When we get back, I'm reporting you for insubordination."

"Right. Well, it's turnaround time. Nate is going to fly on us on the flight back. You take the controls and just aim this thing back to the west. You got it."

Hertz took the controls. We said nothing more on the flight back to the Golf Course. I did consider the possibility of a steep bank, flip off his belts, open the door, and assholes away. But that was impossible.

Hertz made the approach to our area nicely. In fact, the only thing he had done wrong was the oscillating in the formation. I could've helped him on that if he had just relaxed. On the ground, he opened the door and stomped off. I logged the book, entering myself as the aircraft commander, Hertz as pilot.

"How'd it go?" Gary asked as I dumped my gear on my bunk.

"Shitty. That new guy Hertz tried to kill me and Nate, and when I had to grab the controls, he got pissed off."

"Yeah. I heard him yelling at Farris a little while ago.'

"What'd he say?"

"I couldn't tell, but I heard your name a couple of times."

Nate walked in grinning. "Mason, you really pissed off that new captain."

"I know. He said he was going to turn me in for insubordination. Maybe they'll send me home early."

"No such luck." Nate sat down on my bench. "Farris ended up chewing his ass."

"Really? What'd he say?"

"He said that regardless of rank, you were the aircraft commander. And he said, 'If Mason said you were too close, then you were too close.'"

"Really?"

"Yep." Nate fiddled with a plastic chess piece on the board I'd left set up. "Hertz has to apologize to you, too." Now I felt very good.

"Wanna play a short game?" Nate held up two pawns.

"Anytime," I said.

Short-Timer's Blues

10.
Grounded

And still the little men keep coming, with their awkward, sauntering gait, the mark of a lifetime of transporting heavy loads on carrying poles.

—Bernard B. Fall, in *The New York Times Magazine*, March 6, 1966

April 1966

When a First of the Ninth platoon landed near Chu Pong, they captured NVAs who said that there were at least a thousand more men in the area. Moments later the platoon was under fire and trapped. While trying to get them out, two slick ships were shot down, and fifteen men were killed.

This was bad news to many of us. The strategy of attrition was an endless cycle of our taking and retaking the same areas.

"Why the fuck don't they keep some troops out there?" said Connors. "This is like trying to plug fifty leaks with one finger!"

Week after week, the magazines reported kill scores that we knew were inflated with villagers. There were quotes from generals who reported we had them on the run, and quotes from the leader of the posse, LBJ, that victory was just around the corner.

The perimeter of the Golf Course was now mined, searchlighted, patrolled, and guarded. In seven months the VC had been able to get only a few mortars over it and a handful of men through it.

When the Eastern mind encounters such a hard obstacle, it is inclined to use a kind of mental judo to bridge it. The VC asked themselves how they could get the Americans to give them rides in their helicopters so that they could inspect our defenses.

"Mason, you and Resler go over to the bridge and bring back some prisoners," said Farris.

Gary and I lifted from row three and flew to a small field near the southeast corner of the perimeter. Here a second lieutenant ran over with his M-16 held by the sights.

"Got two suspects for you," he said. He pointed behind him to two kids, maybe twelve years old. They were smiling as the grunts gave them chocolates. One of them smoked a cigarette awkwardly.

"Those two?" I asked.

"Right. We caught them wandering too close to the perimeter."

"Maybe they don't know they're not supposed to be here."

"No, they know all right. Our orders are to arrest anyone who gets too close. You're to take them to the cage."

"Where's that?" I asked.

"You know where finance is?"

"Yeah."

"Well, there's a barbed-wire pen in a field near there. You'll be able to find it easy."

"Okay."

The lieutenant motioned the prisoners toward our ship. The two boys grinned with childish expectation and ran over.

"Do they get blindfolded or something?" Gary asked.

"Naw," said the lieutenant. "They're just kids."

One of the boys sat in the web seat and the other sat on the floor with his legs dangling out—like the grunts did—and Gary and I strapped back in.

Coming back into the Golf Course, we went out of the pattern and circled around the division to reenter traffic on the downwind leg. The boys were all eyes. The one on the floor punched the other and pointed at something. They both laughed.

Gary told the tower we were going to the pen, and they cleared us to fly down row three and beyond. We crossed the northern perimeter, the troopers' garrison, the tube emplacements, the antimortar radar installation, the sky-crane pad, and the long rows of Hueys. Beyond the heliport we flew over the tent cities to a field.

Two clerks on guard duty came over to corral the prisoners. The boys jumped off smiling and went where they were pointed. Five or six prisoners crab-walked around under the three-foot-high barbed-wire ceiling of the cage. One of them waved to the boys. They called a greeting. It did not look like a good place to spend time, but as we were told, no one stayed there very long anyway.

"After we question them, we either send them back home or turn them over to the ARVNs. These two little fucks will probably be sent back home," said the sergeant in charge.

Back in the air, I had the feeling that we had just been tricked. They had just done an aerial survey of the entire First Cav compound, and they didn't even have an airplane.

The perimeter of tangled concertina, land mines, antiper-
sonnel mines, trip wires, and observation towers was constantly infiltrated by the haphazard return of nature; that
is, weeds. With the mines in place, no one could go out to
trim the weeds. Weeds were not only messy; they could
conceal the approach of the enemy. The solution was to
have men spray defoliant chemicals out the doors of a
hovering Huey. There was no way to get out of the minefield if the engine failed. To someone as nervous around
explosives as myself, the chance that just the air pressure
under our hovering ship might trigger a mine seemed
possible. And what about the sticks and stuff that blew
around in our rotor wash? The imagined dangers were
endless. I never thought for one moment about the defoliant itself.

For two or three days, Resler and I drew the job. As
with most noncombat chores with the Huey, it became a
game.

"Whatever you do, don't catch the concertina with the
skids," said Resler.

"What do you think? I bought my license at Sears?"

We flew slowly along the rows of concertina just missing the short iron posts that anchored it. A man used a
long nozzle to spray a mist of chemicals that swirled into
the wire and around the ship. At the end of a three-
hundred-yard pass, we rose slightly, turned, and went
back, paralleling the same route ten feet farther over. One
of the men in the back of the chopper waved to the man
in the observation tower. He waved back, and with his
finger traced a circular path beside his head for good
measure. Guard duty is shit, but at least I'm not stupid.

For three hours Gary and I painstakingly covered every square inch of our assigned section of the perimeter
with weed killer. The stuff swirled into the cockpit, but
was odorless and tasteless. The men of the spray crew

were protected only by buttoned-up collars and pulled-down baseball caps in their never-ending job.

One morning we drew the assignment of flying to Ia Drang as a courier ship. We carried the courier, who carried a pouch containing important messages being sent to various field commanders. It was the kind of job I loved best. No formations, no hot LZs, no screaming grunts, and no red tracers.

After crossing the Mang Yang pass, we flew to a small LZ somewhere south of Pleiku. The courier hopped out and asked us to shut down. We did, then wandered over to a group of brass who were interrogating an NVA. The man's arms were bound behind him. He shook his head quickly when the interpreter shouted sharp questions. A heavy-set colonel reacted angrily and asked again. A major stood behind the prisoner with a .45 drawn but held by his side.

"Tell him to talk or we will kill him," the colonel said. The ARVN translator grinned. "Tell him!" The interpreter switched his face to stern severity and wheeled around and yelled piercing Vietnamese accented with gestures. The prisoner flinched at the words but resolutely shook his head.

"Did you tell him we'd kill him?"

"Yes. I say you talk now. If no talk now we kill now. Boom." He smashed his fist into his hand.

"Good. Tell him again."

He did, but the prisoner stubbornly refused to talk.

"Goddamn it!" the colonel shouted. "Major, put your automatic to the back of his head," he said quietly, so as to not tip his hand. "When Nguyen here asks him again, push the barrel against his head."

"Yes, sir." The major raised the weapon.

The interpreter pounced upon the man, unleashing a torrent of threats, and the major prodded the back of his skull with the muzzle of the gun. The man flinched at the gun stabs and closed his eyes, waiting for the explosion. When the interpreter stopped screaming, he shook his head. No.

The colonel brushed the interpreter aside and put his face in front of the prisoner's. "Listen, you slimy little gook. You talk. Now." He glared. "I'll blow your slimy brains all over this goddamn jungle." He moved his face closer to the prisoner's. "Cock that gun, Major!"

"Huh?"

"Cock the goddamn gun and let him hear it. I don't think he believes we'll kill his ass."

"But we can't, sir."

The colonel wheeled to the major. "I know that and you know that, but he doesn't. Cock it."

"Yes, sir."

The major sheepishly pulled the slide back and let it snap. The loud *click-clack* made the prisoner flinch. He seemed to brace himself for death. He lowered his head. The major kept the gun at the base of his skull. Before the interpreter even asked the question, he began to shake his head slowly. No.

"Okay, okay. Let's take a break," said the colonel. "God *damn* gooks!" He looked around to see the courier and Gary and me. "What do you want?"

"Dispatches from division, sir." The courier handed the colonel a fat envelope and saluted.

"Right." The colonel nodded. "The fucking paperwork can find you no matter where you are."

"Yes, sir," said the courier.

The colonel looked up from the papers. "Well?"

"I have to get a signature on the cover sheet, sir."

"You'll get it. You'll get it." While he patted his fatigues for a pen, he noticed the prisoner staring at him. "Major, I want you to blindfold that slope. And I want you to tell him that I've decided to execute him."

"Sir?"

"That's right. Tell him. Tell him." The colonel shook his head wearily. "Jesus, Major, this is basic stuff. I'm going away for a while, and I want the interpreter to talk nice and friendly to the gook and tell him that maybe he can save his miserable skin. Like if he decides to talk. Get it?"

"Yes, sir."

"Here's your cover sheet." The colonel handed the paper to the courier. "Nice day for flying." The colonel looked at me.

"Yes, sir, it is," I said.

He nodded over and over as if agreeing to several things, then stopped suddenly and looked at me sternly. "Well?"

"Yes, sir," I said quickly, "we're going."

I spit out blood. I had quit smoking and was taking it out on the inside of my cheeks. I sat behind a table in the mess tent trying to figure out how to make sense of a tall pile of papers that made up an accident report. My job, since I had caught a bad cold, was to be the scribe on the accident board. The company was out working the local area, but the word was in that we were going to go to the Turkey Farm in a few days.

I had mixed feelings. The job kept me behind in the safety of the camp, but being left behind for any reason was hard to bear. What a stupid emotion! I'd rather do a mountain of paperwork than be out flying. So why did I feel so rotten? What am I? A lemming? Relax and take it easy while you've got the chance.

"Aircraft commander says he did not realize that the LZ was filled with hidden stumps," the report read. "Aircraft was pinned to a large sharpened stump, causing the aircraft to be abandoned." Who cares? Why do we have to document every accident in this goddamn war? How can a pilot be expected to know everything? What do they expect, X-ray vision?

"Can I sit here, sir?" Sergeant Riles sauntered to my table.

"Sure."

He pushed a file folder aside and put his canteen cup on the spot. "Got to take a break from the fuckin' supply tent," announced Riles.

"Yeah. Gets tough in there." I hated myself for being cynical with one of the stay-behinds. And this one was the company's genuine loser. Riles kept himself drunk by stealing whiskey from the crews' stashes while they were out. He had been a master sergeant once, but because of his drinking he was now a pfc. We called him "Sergeant" because he grew very depressed with the word "Private."

"Well, not that tough." He laughed.

If Riles is a stay-behind and a loser, what does that make me? A feeling of revulsion came over me.

"Like to talk, Sergeant, but I got all this shit to do."

"Right. Don't mind me. Gotta get back anyway. Got this order today that we got to get ready for an IG inspection."

"Uh-huh." I barely glanced over a form.

"Hate that shit. Ever do an IG?"

"Never. Never will, either."

Riles stood up and waited for me to say something. The silence spoke and he finally slumped off. I wanted to call him back and apologize for my thoughts. But I didn't.

While the convoy crawled along Route 19, I thought about the British marching resolutely into American ambushes. The cook had lent me his M-16, which now lay across my lap as I sat in the Jeep. I thought of my rank insignia as the equivalent to the British Redcoat, and turned my collar under. By virtue of my being grounded, I was the officer in charge of our first road convoy to Pleiku.

"Group Mobile 100 ran from An Khe to Pleiku once," said Wendall.

"Who's that?" I asked.

"They were French equivalent to the First Cav," said Wendall. "They ran around these same roads in long caravans trying to beat the Vietminh. Group 100 was wiped out near the Mang Yang pass."

"Thanks, Wendall. Great news."

"Well, it's history. You can learn from history, you know."

"How's that supposed to help me now?"

"Well, if I were you, I wouldn't go to sleep on the trip. Have fun."

The big difference, of course, was that we had patrols along the entire route. Knowing this did not suppress my fears. I had become very skeptical of *secure* LZs, roads, bridges, and camps. During the entire fifty-mile drive I watched the elephant grass along the road, braced for explosions at every narrow pass, and sat lightly on the seat when we crossed each bridge. When we drove into the Turkey Farm, I immediately found the flight surgeon and asked to get back on flight status.

"Sorry, you're totally blocked up. If I let you fly, it'll only get worse. Check back in a couple of days."

In a damp mist a hundred men pulled the bulky GPs from the trucks and began setting them up while the ships were out on a mission. In less than an hour, the flat, grassy field outside Camp Holloway was transformed into a tent city. Water bags, called "lister bags," were set up on tripods; the mess tent was put together; and while the men stacked C-ration boxes around the sides, the cooks started the evening meal.

While all this was going on, I wandered around and

made sure that the baggage for our company got put in the appropriate tents. Then I had nothing to do but deal with my thoughts. I sat on my cot alone in the dank GP and drank coffee and smoked cigarettes. I was tortured by conflicting feelings. The Bobbsey Creeps were the only other pilots on the ground, reinforcing my misery.

At the first sound of the returning ships, I went outside and watched. The Hueys snaked out of the mist and with increasing noise gathered on the field west of the camp. Huey after Huey hovered to a landing. The field became a complicated dance of whirling rotor blades, swinging fuselages, and swirling mist. The roaring rush of the turbines died, and the rotors swung lazily as the ships shut down. The crew wandered up to the camp. They all had come back.

I felt like an abandoned child seeing his family again. Soon the tent was filled with the usual sounds.

"Hey, Nate, the next time you cut me out like that, I'll—"

"Fuck you, Connors. If you'd been watching what you were doing, you'd have kept your distance.

"Jesus Christ! I don't know who's worse, you or the Cong."

It was nice to hear.

My ten days on the ground seemed interminable. Our battalion spent two more days at the Turkey Farm before packing up to go north to Kontum. Again I rode in the convoy.

We found an old French barracks that the Vietnamese had been using as stables and chicken coops. After a lot of cleaning up, this became our Kontum camp. I saw the flight surgeon each morning, and each morning he continued my treatment of drugs and no flying.

Finally, after two days at Kontum, I was put back on

flight status. Riker and I were assigned to fly together. As I walked out to the flight line, I felt weightless with joy. My work had become my home, and I was glad to be back.

The ships were shadows in the early-morning mist. We took off singly to join up out of the fog. Climbing over vague trees, we saw the earth disappear. Riker, who knew where we were going, told me to turn left. Just as I did we saw the phantom of a Huey cross immediately in front of us. I lurched back on the controls, but that was not what saved us from a midair collision. Luck had been with us.

The mission was to resupply the searching patrols. We followed three other ships thirty miles up to Dak To, separated, and flew west to one of our patrols.

We shut down while the grunts dragged out insulated cases of hot food. A sergeant came over and invited us to join them for breakfast. We did. Hot reconstituted scrambled eggs, bacon, white toast, and coffee. We sat on the Huey's deck and ate silently. The mist was beginning to burn off, and the dark shadows around us grew taller, revealing themselves as mountains.

The platoon leader, a skinny second lieutenant, came over and shot the shit for a while.

"Find anything?" Riker asked.

"Just some old campsites." The lieutenant patted his blouse for cigarettes. I offered him a Pall Mall. "Thanks."

"We hear that the VC don't want to fight the Cav."

"Can't blame them, can you?" said the lieutenant. "Every time they do, we clobber the shit out of them."

Yeah, as long as we have helicopters, Phantoms, and B-52 bombers, I thought. I said, "Maybe the war is almost over."

"Maybe. They keep talking about peace negotiations

all the time. Johnson's got 'em in a bind up north, and we're putting the squeeze on 'em down here. They might just see that it's impossible to win."

"Yeah," said Riker. "I don't see how the little fucks can go on much longer. McNamara says we're due out of here in less than a year. Some people say that we might not even serve a complete tour, could end that quick."

"Might be," said the lieutenant. "At least we know we own Dak To."

"We have a guy in our company, named Wendall, says that that's what they did with the French," I said.

"Did what?" said the lieutenant.

"Made them think they're winning, let them set up camps and stuff, and then bam!"

"Totally different war now." The lieutenant flipped his cigarette out to the dew-covered ground. "The French couldn't get around like we can." He patted the Huey's deck. "Machines like this make all the difference. How'd you like to be a guerrilla trying to fight an army that can be anywhere, anytime?"

"You got a point there, all right," I said. "Wendall's a flake anyway."

"Sounds like it," the lieutenant said.

"Yep," said Riker, "I can see it now. Get home early, get laid, and then put the baggage down."

"Well, I'm back to work. Take it easy." The lieutenant smiled and walked back over to his men. "Phillips. Get some men to load those food boxes on the Huey."

"What's next?" I asked Riker.

"We're supposed to go back and drop this shit off and then we fly some refugees somewhere."

Black pajamas, conical hats, pigs trussed in baskets, chickens that watched with upright heads on upside-down bodies, wide-eyed kids, crying babies, rolled-up rice mats, staffs, bundled firewood, and warped metal-clad boxes that stayed together by faith alone were packed into the Huey.

"What a menagerie," grumbled Riker. A pig squealed as the turbine whined. I turned around and saw a young mother with a baby's face pressed to her breast as she watched us with saucer eyes. I nodded to her and smiled. She nodded quickly and smiled back. God, they are scared, I thought. How would I feel if foreigners made me and my family get on a strange contraption to fly me from my home to who knows where?

"Winning their hearts and minds," I said.

"Ain't that a crock," said Riker.

We flew north, past Dak To and the border junction of Cambodia, Laos, and Vietnam. The mountains were the tallest I had ever seen. Misty clouds blanketed this wet, green world.

We were in our slot, one of ten ships, as the flight followed valleys to stay out of the clouds. Past a dark peak that lost its top in the whiteness, a red, freshly cut airstrip appeared in the valley below. New huts with tin roofs were clustered defensively within a sandbagged, wire-topped compound wall. Welcome home, I thought. Eyes in the back watched intently as the flight drifted out of the misty sky to land on the red earth.

Little ARVN soldiers with slung rifles urged them out of the ship. A frightened mother looked back inside to two small kids. A soldier grabbed a pig and tossed it to a pile of rope-trussed belongings. It screamed noiselessly in our hissing, and squirmed like a living sausage. One of the kids screamed tearfully. His frantic mom snatched him quickly off the deck to sit on her hip. He grabbed her blouse tightly as she ducked our rotors and stumbled to her things.

I watched her as we left. She grew smaller as we climbed. Soon she was only a memory, confused and frightened, alone and far away from her family's ancient home. At that moment I hated Communists and was ashamed to be an American. But then I had often been accused of being too sensitive.

We continued relocating refugees all the next day. We were supposed to finish our sweep at this end of the Ia Drang valley and then go home to the Golf Course. By dusk, though, we were landing the last load of people at one of the new villages. The old man decided to stay out and head back in the morning.

Twenty ships landed on a grassy ridge in the gathering dark. The ridge was the site of a temporary ARVN camp. Two large tents were set up for us.

Riker and I carried our sleeping gear over to the tents. We blew up air mattresses in the light of army flashlights.

Dinner was C's eaten down by the ships. Riker and Resler sat on the deck eating from cans while I twisted the opener around a tin of chicken. I was pulling the ragged lid away from the chicken meat when the silence was shattered. *Whomp!* and then ringing. The ringing came from my ears. Nobody announced the obvious: mortars. Cans clanked on the deck and shadows scattered. I dropped my can and ran toward a shallow hole I had seen when we landed. It was only twenty feet away. *Whoomm!* I saw the bright flash of the round as it exploded a hundred yards away. Dropping to the grass, I low-crawled the rest of the way to the hole. *Whoomm!* It was occupied by two crew members from the ship in front of us. *Whoom-whoom!* Goddamn! Where am I supposed to go? *Whoom!* Damn! Real close! I got up and ran back to the ship. The ship was my security. It always got me out of trouble. *Whoommm!* My shadow flashed against the black U.S. ARMY on the tail boom. I dropped and rolled under the deck. My shoulder caught on the fuel drain spigot and I tore it loose. My mind had long since left, and I was blindly scrambling toward the front of the ship away from the fuel bladder. *Whoom!* I reached the cross tube up front and stopped. "Goddamn it!" I screamed "Mother *fuckers!*" Then I realized that the Huey was just thin aluminum and magnesium and Plexiglas and jet fuel, and that if a round hit, I would go up in smoke with it. "Get away from the ship, you stupid shit!" I yelled to myself. I crawled in the foot-deep grass, pressing my nose in the dampness, my nose the runner, my head the sled. Ten feet away I stopped. *Whoom!* Off to the right. No hard hat. No weapon. I cursed my stupidity and swallowed sobs. Silence! A bug crawled on my cheek. I heard a muffled *whoompf* and a *pop*. A flare dazzled and swung in the sky. *Whoompf, pop, whoompf, pop.* Huey shadows intersected and swayed wildly across the grass. A flare dimmed, then disappeared as it dropped below the ridge. Gray smoke made lazy trails in the light of the flares above. Silence. They stopped? After ten more minutes of lying in the grass, I heard voices. "All over." "Jesus H. Christ! How lucky can you get!" I got up. My shoulder hurt where I had hit the drain valve. I believe in God. Really. I walked back to my ship, dropped to my knees, and searched the grass for an already opened can of boned chicken.

The mist was so thick I could barely see the Huey from the tent. The distant mountains from the day before had disappeared. Resler had got up before me, and I could see a friendly orange flicker from his tin-can stove next to our ship. I shivered. It had been a cold and sleepless night.

Nobody had been hurt during the attack. No one could understand why the VC or the NVA or whoever they were had stopped when they did. Certainly it had not been because of any counterattack on our part. They probably just ran out of ammunition. Thank God for VC shortages. We had been sitting ducks.

"Wanna use the stove?" Resler smiled from his hunker. He stirred in sugar from a paper packet. The coffee smelled like life.

"Yeah, thanks." I leaned in against the edge of the deck and dragged the C-ration case over.

"Let me guess. Scrambled eggs and bacon?"

"Of course. It's breakfast time, isn't it?"

"I think you're the only one in the company who eats that shit."

"All the more for me." I got a can from the box and a coffee packet. I poured some water into Resler's cookie can and set it on his stove. While the flame seared the wetness on the outside of the can, I opened the eggs. Inside was the familiar yellow-green egg loaf with small bits of brownish bacon. I spooned it out cold. Resler made an expression of revulsion as I munched. I spooned another chunk out and held it toward him. "Want some?"

"I don't eat puke." He grimaced.

We went through this routine often. It was our morning ritual.

"I've never seen fog this thick before."

"I know." He checked his watch. "It's already seven and it looks like five."

I nodded. The Huey in front of us was a pale shadow, and the one I knew existed in front of it was totally obscured.

"ITO?"

"Probably. When was the last time you did an instrument takeoff?"

"Flight school."

"Me, too."

Farris came swirling out of the fog carrying a steaming cup of coffee. "Just talked to an air-force pilot. Says our valley is filled up with this fog, but it's clear at the peaks." We nodded. "We'll wait an hour to see if it burns off." He continued walking and disappeared behind us.

"Where'd you go last night?" I asked.

"Over there." Resler pointed toward the GP.

"The tent?"

"No. See that kind of ditch up there?"

"Oh, yeah. Man, if they had kept it up—"

"I know. One of these days, they won't stop."

An hour later Farris told us to put our gear inside the ships. He and Riker were going to take off with some other ships, and he wanted us to listen in on the radio. He'd tell us how high up the fog went.

As I followed Resler down the slope, carrying my flight bag, I veered off to the left—nothing very unusual, except that I was trying to walk straight. When I leaned to the right to change course, I kept going to the left. I didn't feel dizzy, just strange. I stopped for a minute and tried it again. I felt myself being tugged off track again but was able to ignore it. When I reached the ship, the feeling had gone. I shook my head. I'm coming apart.

I strapped in while Resler tuned the channel Farris would be on. We listened while Farris called the ships going with him. He asked if we were on the net.

"Roger," Gary answered. Six more ships waiting with us rogered in turn.

"There's no hurry," Farris radioed. "We're going back to Kontum to pick up some troops. You guys can meet us anywhere along that valley we followed yesterday. We should be back through in an hour." We rogered down the line.

While Farris talked, I noticed something in the corner of my eye. Ten feet to the right of our ship, a gray mortar round stuck out of the grass. I punched Gary. He followed my finger and nodded. His eyes rose in surprise. "I'll be damned!"

"It's not as bad as it looks," said Farris. "The fog ends about five or six hundred feet up. Just make sure you take off due west when you leave. Remember, there's mountains on both sides of you."

"Roger," Gary answered. "Yellow One, there's a mortar round stuck in the ground next to us."

"Huh?"

"There's a mortar round from last night stuck in the ground right next to us."

"Roger. Call the ARVNs. They might have a demolition squad here."

I lit a cigarette and stared at the round. It was just about where I had been lying last night.

Gary raised the liaison officer, an American who stayed with the ARVNs. "Roger, we'll take care of it. Don't try to move it yourself."

We both burst out laughing. "Lucky he told us," I said. "I was almost out the door to defuse it."

As courage gathered in each of the seven ships, one would announce he was leaving, and we'd hear him flutter up into the mist. Gary and I decided that the round wasn't going to explode, since it hadn't, so we waited. Neither of us felt entirely confident about the ITO. If we had the time, why not wait to see if the fog burned off? The last ship left. They radioed back that the fog was still about five or six hundred feet deep.

"Guess it's not going to burn off for a while."

"Guess not," I said.

"Wanna go for it?"

"Yeah." I looked at the mortar round. "Let's get the fuck out of here."

I stared at the round as Gary cranked up. Would it be sensitive to the rotors when they started to thud? I guessed I'd never know if it was. "Top-notch demolition crew them ARVNs have. . . ."

"You see 'em coming?"

"No."

"Oh. Yeah. Top-notch."

Gary set the artificial horizon low for the takeoff. "Okay, Bob, you double-check me on the way out."

"Right."

"Everybody on board?"

"Roger," answered the crew chief. "Sir, you sure we shouldn't wait a little longer?"

"Relax, Sergeant. We got this thing under control."

"Roger." He didn't sound convinced. Gary looked over at me and smiled. I nodded.

When he pulled in the power, I glanced at the round. The grass around it was pressing down in the rotor wash. Did it just move? The ship drifted off the ground. The round disappeared along with everything else.

There was no sensation of movement. The artificial horizon was right where it was supposed to be, and the airspeed was picking up. Gary let it accelerate to about 40 knots and held it there. Turn and bank was fine. "Needle, ball, airspeed" was the slogan we learned in flight school. I checked the instruments in that order. Gary was right on the money. White nothingness extended in all directions. The ship hummed, the instruments said we were moving, but the senses said we were parked in some strange void.

"So far, you've got a double-A ride," I said, referring to the grading on the check-ride sheets our instructors used to carry with them. "Don't fuck it up."

"No sweat," said Gary.

The whiteness grew brighter. It blazed. But still you could see nothing. Without reference to the inside of the cockpit, you would swear you were blind. The bright white grew bluish, and we saw a dark-green peak off to our right. "Yea," I said, cheering.

"Great flying, sir!" The crew chief was now a believer.

I looked back. The misty sea beneath us hid the valley where midnight mortars lurked. The mountaintops were bright islands at the surface. I felt a shudder of relief and smiled to myself. It had been a bad night, but the sky was bright ahead.

11.
Transfer

I don't think the elections will result in a Communist or neutralist government, but if they do, we will fight. I don't care if they are elected or not, we'll fight.
　　　　　　　—Nguyen Cao Ky, in *Time*, May 13, 1966

May 1966
Riker and I sat together in the sling seat of the C-123 as it droned to Saigon. My feet rested on the flight bag that contained everything I owned. I was not coming back. Riker was on his way to an R&R flight to Hong Kong. Since I volunteered to transfer out, I wondered why I already felt homesick for the Cav.

"You see Resler break Eight-eighty-one?" Riker said.

"He didn't break it; the new guy did."

"Yeah, but it was Resler's ship."

I'd said good-bye to Gary as he walked out to the flight line with the new guy, Swain, in tow. Gary was checking him out, to see how well he flew.

"Probably won't see you again," said Gary.

"Probably not. At least not if I see you first."

He laughed. "Yeah. Well, it was fun, even if we did argue a lot."

"No problem. I always won anyway."

He grinned and extended his hand. "Gotta go check this new guy out. I've got your home address. I'll write you after our tours are up." We shook hands.

"Yeah, do that. Let's keep in touch." I nodded and let go of his hand.

"See you." He smiled and turned toward the ships.

"See you." I watched him walk away.

I decided to watch him take off, so I sat on some sandbags in front of the operations tent.

"Where they sending you, Mason?" Captain Owens came out and pushed his cap back.

"A place called Phan Rang, Forty-ninth Aviation Company."

Owens nodded. "Never heard of 'em."

"Neither have I, but they're not the Cav." Gary and Swain climbed into their ship, 881, the oldest Huey in the company.

"Ha. 'Not the Cav' is right." Owens grinned. "Nobody's the Cav."

Gary's ship was running now, so I got up to leave.

"Well, good luck in your new company," said Owens.

"Thanks."

They were in a hover, backing out of the slot, when everything came unglued. The ship vaulted backward over its own tail. The rotors hit the ground, and the transmission and drive shaft came off. The fuselage slammed into the ground. Pieces flew everywhere.

"Jesus!" I yelled and ran down the path. The fuselage was crumpled, lying on its back. I saw the crew chief scrambling out of the wreckage, pale and wide-eyed. I humped to get there, visualizing Resler as crumpled as his ship. Then I saw him squirming out through some twisted metal. He was scared but smiling.

"You all right?" I yelled.

Gary brushed himself off and began laughing. Swain was out walking around in circles. The crew chief was on his knees, trying to pull the gunner out of the pocket. Jet fuel dripped in puddles near him. "Come on!" the crew chief yelled, pulling.

Freed, the gunner, was bleeding from a gash on his temple. Gary was wandering dumbly toward the operations tent. Then he stopped and came back to the wreckage.

"You okay?" I ran over to him.

"Sure." He laughed. "Sure, I'm okay. Why'd you ask?"

"Why'd I ask? Look at the ship!"

He laughed again, a giggle from a pale and confused face. "Bad landing!"

Some people walked the gunner up to the med tent. He was the only injury. I relaxed. "It's only a bad landing if you don't walk away from it."

"What happened?" Gary's question was broken by spasms of laughter.

"You don't know?"

"Shit, the last thing I knew I was locking my belts, then *wham!*"

"Swain was flying?"

"Yeah. I didn't think he could fuck it up getting out of the slot, you know."

"Hey, Mason, the Jeep's waiting to take us to the airfield," Riker yelled from the tent.

"Shit. Hey, I gotta go. Again. You're okay?"

"Sure. Why'd you ask?"

Riker dug around in his bag looking for something. The vibrations from the cargo ship were putting my ass to sleep.

"You know, Riker, every time I go to Saigon, you're with me."

"That's right, you lucky fuck. I've got to get a room tonight 'cause my R&R plane's not leaving until tomorrow. Want to share a room?"

"Why not? I've got two days to get to my new assignment," I said. Riker nodded in the loud droning. I looked across the deck, through a window, and saw the plane was banking. Probably getting close. Then we hit some bumpy air. It reminded me of the fly-by for the general.

We had practiced for two days, and the weather couldn't have been smoother. A line of Hueys, Chinooks, Caribous, and Mohawks, even some little H-13s stretched for two miles, looped to the An Khe pass and back toward the Golf Course. "Keep 'em tight," said the Colonel. We did. Resler sat copilot and I flew because our position put my side closest to the ship we were flying on.

"You don't have to go that close, you know," Resler said.

"These guys know what they're doing," I said, referring to Connors and Banjo in the ship we followed. "I'd feel okay overlapping blades with them."

"Fucking daredevil."

I grinned, liking the label, and moved closer. "I knew I should've kept my mouth shut," said Gary.

I moved the rotor tips so that there was no more than three feet between us and the other ship. I held a vertical clearance of three feet to allow for any rough air and the surges it would cause.

"Ever overlapped blades before?"

"Never. Never will, either."

I kept the three-foot vertical space and moved gently in. My left hand on the collective jerked up and down, keeping our blades above Connors and Banjo's. Banjo was watching. He grinned from only a few feet away and raised his fist, thumbs up. Then he waved me closer. The smirk on his face said it was a dare.

"Okay, flight, looking good. Remember to keep the

turns very, very wide. I don't want to see any bunching up," said the Colonel.

"Not in the turn, Mason."

I nodded. I saw only the vertical space between our rotors. The rest of the world did not exist. When their ship bounced up in an air pocket, my hand flicked us up at the same time. I saw I could hold the space, so overlapping would be easy. I moved slowly in as we began the turn.

"Okay. Okay. You did it. Now get back," said Gary.

Connors knew what I was doing and flew as smooth as silk. We made the whole turn with our rotors overlapped by two or three feet. As we came out of the bank, I slid away, and breathed again. "I can't believe you like to do shit like that," Gary said, disgusted.

"What's so funny?" Riker said, inside the C-123.

"Nothing. Just thinking about the fly-by."

"Fucking waste of time, that was."

"Yeah," I said. But I was already thinking about the assault we did in Bong Son. When we got back from our sweep around Dak To, our company was sent over to Bong Son to help the 227th. The VC were retaking the valley we had won two months before. During the briefing at the Rifle Range, the officer in charge said, "So make sure your gas masks are working okay. We'll be using CS and tear gas on this assault."

There were murmurs in our crowd. Gas masks? What gas masks?

Outside, the CO had a quick inventory done and found that we had enough masks for exactly half the men. One pilot in each ship and one of the gunners would have to go without.

"Why don't we just go back and get some more?" somebody asked.

"Not enough time," said the CO.

Resler and I and our two crew members stood next to the ship looking at the two masks. Resler produced a coin. The crew chief and gunner flipped. The crew chief won.

"Heads or tails?" Resler grinned confidently. He never lost.

"Heads."

He flipped.

"Heads."

As it turned out, the gas was diffuse where we landed, and we took only one round as we left. But I remember Resler sitting on his side of the cockpit grimacing, tears flowing, yelling on the intercom, "Shit! Goddamn!"

The plane banked hard. Out the window I could see the outskirts of the big city. "About time," said Riker. "You really enjoyed this flight. You've been grinning the whole way down."

"Yeah. I guess I have. It's just that I'm so happy to be leaving the Cav."

"Yeah. Course, you don't know what kind of unit your new one is yet."

The hotel we got to was a place Riker had heard of. I don't remember its name or where it was. That's partly because we had had a good meal and several drinks that night and got to the hotel after dark.

The hallway was narrow, and the ceilings were twelve feet high. The place was dark and dingy and the clerk uninterested when we checked in. The Vietnamese were getting used to us, it seemed, and they didn't like what they saw. The clerk gave us a key and pointed down the dark hallway.

"Some joint, Riker."

"Guy I know says it's a great place. Big rooms, low prices."

The windowless room had two beds and a dresser and a small wooden table. The tall doorway, which occupied one corner, had a glass transom above it. I flopped on my bed with a copy of *Time*. Riker stripped to his shorts and wrote at the table.

An article mentioned the transfer of General Kinnard, for whom we had the fly-by.

"Hey," I announced, "they've written up Kinnard's transfer in *Time* and there's not one word about mine."

After the fly-by, I had had to take a ship over to the river to wash it out. Long sat with me on the sandbar as usual and talked.

"I am sorry to see you go," she said. Her English was improving every time I saw her. She was a self-taught genius.

"I'll miss you, too."

"Will you give your wife a present from me?"

"Sure, but you don't have to give me any presents."

"Not for you!" She giggled. "For your wife." She removed her gold-wire earrings and held them out to me.

"No." I shook my head. "You can't afford to be giving me gold earrings, Long. I'm the rich guy here; I'll pay you for them." I reached into my pocket. She suddenly looked hurt, genuinely hurt. She was really just being nice.

"Okay, okay. No money. I'll give them to Patience."

She smiled brightly and handed them to me. I wrapped them in a piece of paper from my notepad and put them in my shirt pocket. "Thank you for the present. I'm sure Patience will love them."

She grinned.

I patted my shirt pocket. Still there. Better mail them as soon as I get to the new unit. I wasn't reading the words I looked at, so I put the magazine down. In the meantime, Riker had got in bed. My grandfather's Hamilton said it was eleven o'clock. Someone knocked at the door.

"Yeah?" I called out.

No answer. Then another knock.

"Who the fuck could that be?" I sat up.

"Probably the maid."

I walked over to the door. "Probably." If it was the maid, why was I afraid to open the door? I'm really coming apart, I thought.

When I turned the knob, the door shot inward, slammed into my boot, and stopped. I reflexively pushed back, and as I did, I came face to face with a frowning Oriental only a few inches shorter than I.

"Hey!" I pushed hard, trying to close the door. My boot slipped back as the door opened wider. I struggled harder. Altogether I could see four or five men pushing. Silently. Grimly determined.

"Hey, Riker! Get over here. There's a bunch of gooks trying to bust in here!"

Riker paused for a second until he saw I wasn't kidding.

"What the—?" He got up and ran over.

My boot slid back farther. The opening was almost wide enough to squeeze through. "C'mon, goddamn it! Push this fucking door shut!" I yelled. My boot jammed under the door was the only thing that was keeping them out of the room. Riker pushed, stretching his long legs to the foot of my bed and his back to the door. When the door closed a fraction, I moved my boot ahead to lock it there. Then they pushed with a surge and the pressure on my toes grew until I thought they would crack. Hands came around the edge of the door and grasped air, trying to reach us. The only sounds were grunts and heavy breathing. Riker and I dripped sweat. As the heavy door groaned and thudded, the space was slowly getting smaller. Unbelievably, we were gaining on them. A hand grabbed the edge of the door as it got close to shutting. I smashed it with my fist. It held. I smashed it over and over until it let go and struggled back through the narrow crack of the door. As the fingers slipped out, the door slammed shut. Fumbling, shaking, wet fingers latched the lock and the extra safety bolt. Riker and I looked at each other in amazement. We were sharing a nightmare. Then we heard the thud of a body slamming against the door, and the door seemed to bend inward. The thudding repeated itself rhythmically, like a heavy heartbeat.

"Call the fucking desk!" said Riker.

I ran over to the night table and picked up the phone. Riker dragged the dresser across the room. It made a splintering sound as the veneer split against the tile floor. The desk phone rang.

"Are you calling them?!" Riker yelled as he struggled to get the dresser against the thudding door.

"Yeah. No answer." I wiped sweat from my eyes. "They don't fucking answer!"

After fifty rings I knew they would never answer. We sat across from each other on the two beds and watched the door moving with each animal thud. "Your derringer! Get out your derringer." Riker brightened at the prospect.

"I sold it to Hall."

"You sold it to Hall! I thought that was your fucking last-ditch weapon. Don't you think this looks like an emergency?"

I nodded and shrugged. The gun was still sold to John Hall for twenty-five bucks.

"If that ain't the dumbest thing I ever heard of . . ."

I nodded sorrowfully.

Crack! We both jumped at the new sound. They were throwing something metallic against the glass transom. *Crack!* Then chips of glass fell inside. The transom window had wire mesh embedded in it. At the center of the window a section the size of a fist was now bare of glass.

"Try the phone again," said Riker.

I listened to a mechanical switch click and cycle a

burst of ringing noise, then click, recycle, then noise. Riker took his bed apart. Under the mattress were hardwood bed slats. He smashed one down on my bed. It made a formidable club. I shook my head when he looked at the phone. Then I hung up. "Bastards!" Riker yelled.

At 2 A.M. the thudding stopped. Riker was asleep, proving that you can get used to anything. I sat up against my pillow with one of his bed slats on my lap. When the thudding stopped, I tried the phone again.

There was another small window near the ceiling at the other end of the room. While the phone rang, I looked up to see glass spraying in from it. Riker jumped up at the new sound.

"What the hell is going on here?" Riker pleaded.

I didn't know. I'd been sitting on my bed for two hours, listening to the door being smashed, asking myself the same question. They are trying to kill us, aren't they? Why didn't they just blow up the fucking door? Or use an ax? Or fire? Or some fucking thing besides bodies? Maybe we should let them in and smash their brains in with our clubs. A quick *no* sounded in my head. I felt pretty brave at the controls of a helicopter while people tried to kill me, but trying to smash five darting Orientals with bed slats was just not me. I waited to see what developed. Soon the fuck-up at the desk would return from someplace and hear the ruckus and call the police There were police in Saigon, weren't there? Or the people next door. They would get somebody. But the thudding went on and on. I wanted to scream at the utter unreality of the situation. But I could not scream, because I was a soldier. That thought made me laugh out loud. "GI Joe would've never let a bunch of dirty Nips get away with this," I said. Then I visualized the myriad ways in which GI Joe would murder this mob. Of course, they were all centered around the fact that he always had a weapon stashed somewhere. I clutched my bed slat and waited. What I needed was a flamethrower.

The windowless room showed no light at dawn. My watch said it was six. The thudding had stopped. I woke Riker. We pulled the glass-covered dresser away and cautiously opened the door. There was some debris outside, but no people. Quickly we grabbed our gear and entered the hallway. All clear. As we walked toward the desk, we almost had cardiac seizures when we saw the clerk staring at us.

"Where the fuck were you last night?" we both yelled.

"Sir, I do not work at night. A man named Thieu does."

"Well, where was he?" I said.

"He was here all night, sir. He certainly was this morning when I came to work."

"Bullshit!" I yelled.

The clerk flinched a little but said, "Was there something wrong with your room?"

"Some people tried to break into our room all night long, you fuck!" said Riker.

"Really? That's strange," said the clerk. "Did you call the desk?"

"Yes. Over and over," I said.

"Well, possibly the phone is broken."

"Even if the phone *is* broken," I explained, "our room is at the most fifty feet from here. Nobody could have not heard that commotion last night."

"I will inform the manager of this," said the clerk. He looked at us quietly. His eyes told us he knew exactly what had happened last night and we could yell and scream and complain until doomsday. He was never going to admit it. We hoisted our bags and left.

Phan Rang is near the coast, about 160 miles south of Qui Nhon and 160 miles northeast of Saigon, but that's not where I went first. First I signed in at the 12th Aviation Battalion's camp near Nha Trang. Then I waited in a bar in a sweltering sea-level village and talked to a depressing, sallow, and lumpy engineer who worked for one of the many American companies in Vietnam.

"I hate it over here," he said.

"Why don't you go home?"

"Money's just too damn good." He swilled the last of his beer. "Besides, there's no poontang at home like the stuff that lives over here. I got a bitch waiting for me back home."

It all fit. Anyone who lived with Mr. Darkness had to be a bitch, and the only place in the world he'd get the poontang he wanted was where he was transformed into the Rich American Engineer. I nodded, but said nothing. He told me more about his job, his hooch, his lady, his stereo, his growing bank account. I almost fainted from boredom. At a lull in the drone I announced, "Gotta go." The engineer nodded hazily and turned his snout back toward the barkeep. He tapped the mug on the bar and pointed sternly to it. "More," he said.

The Huey landed on the sandy patch where I waited. The crew chief ran past me carrying a sack of mail to battalion HQ. I threw my gear on board and fished out my flight helmet.

"You're Mason?" said the pilot. I nodded.

"Good. We'll be leaving as soon as he gets back." He pointed to the retreating crew chief.

I climbed into the idling Huey and smoked. It felt good to be back in a helicopter after wallowing around in airforce transports.

The crew chief returned, and the pilot lifted off through the swirling sand. As we moved forward, the wind felt cool against my skin.

Cam Ranh bay was the halfway point on the flight to the company. As we flew by, I saw scores of navy PBYs (seaplanes) anchored in the harbor. For the rest of the flight I had daydreams about owning a PBY and flying cargo in the Bahamas, or running a cross-Canada, lake-to-lake touring business.

When I saw the concrete buildings at the Phan Rang air-force base, I felt a moment of happiness. I was finally going to get to live like a human. But the Huey flew by the barracks and landed on a grassy field, a mile across the runway. I saw a familiar collection of dirt-covered, sagging GPs that I immediately realized was my new home.

The sun was red in the west and the ground was soggy. We squished across the field and left our chest protectors in a tent. The two pilots, named Deacon and Red, escorted me to the club.

"Well, well!" The major grinned endearingly. "Our second Cav pilot in two days." Tall, dark-haired, and smooth-faced, he came over to me and shook my hand. "Welcome to the Prospectors. I'm the CO, and as you'll find out, when I'm not around the boys call me Ring-knocker." The boys, about fifteen of them, sat around some tables in the bamboo-paneled, tin-roofed bar, their company's club, and laughed. I nodded nervously, never having met a CO who was friendly.

"Pleased to meet you," I said.

"You looked me right in the eye when you said that." He grinned. "That's good. Shows you're not afraid." He turned around to the boys. "That's good," he said. They nodded. I wasn't afraid, but I was suspicious. What did he want from me?

"First things first," said Ringknocker. "Hey, Red, take Mason over to your tent. He gets the empty bunk there." I started out the door with Red. "When you get your gear organized, come on back. Chow'll be served in about a half hour, and then we can talk."

"Yes, sir."

He beamed.

The tent floor was rolling red dust, but there was a plywood platform next to my cot. I sat on the cot, which was already made, and looked around. Red was smiling at me from his cot. God, they don't even have a floor, I thought. "Why do they call him Ringknocker?" I said.

"He's a West Pointer, wears a class ring."

"Ah." I had never met one before. Now his aggressive, cordial manner seemed appropriate. "Seems like a nice guy."

"Yeah, he is. Lot better than our last CO. Nobody liked that prick. That's why he woke up one night with a knife sticking out of his chest." Red announced this as though that was the typical way in which incompetent commanders were dealt with.

"You're kidding."

"No. He was black *and* an asshole. We still don't know who stuck him."

"He was killed?"

"No. We got him to Cam Ranh just in time." Red grinned. "It all turned out to the good, though. The replacement CO was Ringknocker, and he's a natural leader. You know what I mean?"

Though I had never met one, I thought I knew what he meant.

The club I had been in was one half of the tin-roofed building. The other side was their mess hall. Dinner was served by Vietnamese waitresses to groups of four sitting at cloth-topped tables set with clean napkins and bronzeware. During the meal, Red told me that everything was paid for out of club dues and the meal tickets. "But don't get used to it; we're never here anyway."

Before we finished, I heard guitar music coming from the club on the other side of the bamboo partition. The building shook as a Phantom F-4C hit its afterburner on takeoff. This *was* an air-force base. The runway was a quarter mile from the Prospectors' camp. The Prospectors were a little band of gypsies camped in a vacant corner of the walled city.

A voice wailed from the club as Red and I walked in.

> Army Aviators sing this song,
> It won't be long for the Vietcong.
> The sky troopers sail through the air,
> To set our traps like catchin' bears.

"Man, that's horrible," said Ringknocker.

"We can change it, but it's a start," said the singer, a captain named Daring.

"Haw, you can take that ditty and flush it, Daring, you asshole!" a pink-faced cherub of a man yelled from the bar. He was Captain King, otherwise known as Sky King.

"Okay, okay, goddamnit." Daring glared at Sky King. "Let's hear what you got."

"What I got goes squish, squish between Nancy's legs. Right, Nancy?" Nancy, a Vietnamese girl of twenty, had special permission to work at the bar until eight o'clock. All other Vietnamese workers had to leave at dusk.

"Nooo! You bad man!" She blushed. To my knowledge Nancy never cooperated with any of Sky King's vulgar requests, or anyone else's, either. She was beautiful, neat, efficient, and an excellent barmaid. To all advances she announced that she was married.

"Hey, Mason." Ringknocker leaned back from his table when he saw me. "Do you recognize your comrade, here?" He pointed to a heavy-set man sitting beside him.

"No, sir, I don't," I said. Ringknocker waved me over.

"This is Mr. Cannon, from . . ." He looked at Cannon.

"Delta Company, 227th," announced Cannon.

"From right around the corner," I said. "Nice meeting you."

Cannon just nodded, looking worried.

"Yep. Cannon flew guns in the Cav," said Ringknocker. "But in our company, we assign pilots to the guns by their weight. You now how weak those B models are, especially loaded up with ammo. So all our gunship pilots are skinny fucks, like you."

A shock hit my body. That's why Cannon looked so worried. Ringknocker was making him fly slicks. And he was going to make me fly guns.

"What's the matter?" Ringknocker said, reading my face.

"I fly slicks."

"Yeah, and I fly guns," Cannon interjected.

Ringknocker lowered his eyebrows to a more official level. "Well, my policy is skinny guys in the guns, fat guys in the slicks. Besides, I don't know what you're worried about, Mason. Guns are a lot safer than slicks. Most of our hits are taken by the slicks. In the guns you at least have something to shoot back with."

A Phantom roared on takeoff.

Daring changed a line: "Sky troopers *sailing* through the air . . ."

"I've flown six hundred hours of combat time as a slick pilot. All my experience is in slicks. And I'm still alive. I don't want to change anything I'm doing at this stage of the game."

"That goes for me, too," said Cannon. "I'm still alive, and I don't want to change nothing."

"Six hundred hours?" Ringknocker looked impressed.

"That's right."

"Shit," he said, "the most anybody, even Deacon, has in our company is three hundred." Ringknocker tapped his ring on the table. "Flew your ass off, hey?"

"Yeah, and I understand slick flying."

"And I understand guns," said Cannon.

"Shit!" Ringknocker looked dismayed. "I have my policies, you know." Cannon sat back in his chair, looking pissed off. I was thinking, *Another fucking book man.* "Okay, okay, all right, fuck it," said Ringknocker. "Fuck my policy. Cannon, you fly guns. Mason, you fly slicks." Ringknocker grinned. "And that's an order."

"Yes, sir," I said.

"It's a deal," said Cannon.

"Settin' our traps to catch them bears ..." droned Daring.

"No, no, no." Ringknocker suddenly leaned into the circle of songwriters. "Horrible, horrible, horrible."

Sky King dropped to his knees, holding his hands on his ears. "I'm sick!" he yelled. He humped over and retched loudly.

"Look. We get a decent song, we get invited to Saigon for two days in the sing-off," Ringknocker announced. "You wanna have two days to fuck off in Saigon, don-'cha?"

I sat there dumbfounded as Ringknocker explained. A *sing-off?* Song contest? Cannon, arms folded across his chest, looked at me and shook his head. *These guys are strange.*

The songwriters argued; then Daring strummed once more. This time three other guys, out of the twenty in the club, sang along. While they sang I noticed something moving on the wall. A human skull mounted above the bar moved its jaw, clacking along with the song. Sky King was pulling the string that led from the skull to the end of the bar. "Sing it, Charlie!" he yelled.

"Charlie?" I said to Red.

"Yeah, Doc made him from a VC head we brought in."

I nodded. What *else* would you call a VC head?

The song ended.

"Puke," said Deacon.

"You really think so?" Ringknocker asked with a worried look. Deacon was one of the two platoon leaders in the Prospectors. He was also the company's IP and part-time sage. He wore a graying flattop over a smooth and sincere face. Ringknocker trusted him implicitly.

"Yes," said Deacon.

"Well," Ringknocker shook his head, "we'll just have to keep trying."

The Prospectors left at dawn. I stayed behind with another warrant named Staglioni. We were to bring out a slick that was being repaired.

Staglioni told me that four or five ships in the company were already out in the field at Nhon Co. "That's what we usually do. We have some guys go ahead and set up camp while the rest of us come back here to take a break." Staglioni was tall and soft and dark. His accent was New York to me.

"Flatbush. That's in Brooklyn," he said.

"So, we just wait until the ship is ready and then fly out?"

"That's it. Maintenance told me it should be ready tomorrow morning."

We watched a flight of four Phantoms take off. When they hit their afterburners on the climb-out, it was like thunder. "Looks like fun." I said.

"It is," said Staglioni. "I tried it once."

"You flew a Phantom?"

"Yeah. You could, too, if you wanted. They come over here all the time. They like to trade flight time."

"They want to fly Hueys?"

"Yeah. They're all the time betting that they can hover a chopper first time up."

"I bet they can't."

"You're right. None of them have so far. One of their pilots even flew a mission with us one day. He hated it. He felt like we were too close to everything, you know, right down in it. They really don't see much on their strikes. They aim at puffs of smoke in the jungle, drop their shit, and *bam,* they're back home. Their total time in the air from takeoff to landing is one hour and twenty minutes. It's a quickie. Then they hop in an air-conditioned van and cruise back to the club. And that's it for the day. A hundred missions and they go home." He paused for a minute while a Phantom came in for a landing. "Can you imagine? A hundred missions? Shit, I'd be back home twice already."

"You guys log missions?"

"No, not officially. I keep my own log. The last time I told one of the air-force guys how many missions I'd flown, he said, 'What do you expect? The smart pilots are in the air force.' That fucker."

I watched another Phantom take off. If I had stayed in college, I lamented, I would be flying those and living on the other side of the runway.

"It's true," I said.

"What is?"

"The smart pilots *are* in the air force."

The camp was a dirty-fabric ghost town. The trail that led from the club past the row of ten GPs was completely deserted. Staglioni went to his tent and I went to mine.

I wrote Patience a letter to bring her up to date and give her my new address.

A Vietnamese woman dressed in black pajamas ducked in through the tent flaps. She nodded as she walked by. She walked to the other end of the tent and began to sweep the dirt floor with a bamboo whisk broom, drawing neat parallel lines in the dust. When she got to me she bowed slightly and then waited expectantly for me to raise my feet off the plywood platform. I raised my feet and she swept under them. Then she began making up the beds. There were four in the GP. When she got to me again, she bowed. Her smile was black from betel nut, and she waited for me to get up. I jumped up.

"Oh," I said.

"Ah," she said. She stripped the whole cot, remade it, and carefully rearranged my gear. Folded flak vest here, .45 and its holster on top there, just so. She stood back and shared with me her artistic arrangement and nodded that I could place my ass back on the blanket.

"Thank you," I said.

She grinned betel black and ducked outside.

So, even if the army had drawn the dreary side of the field and the dreary domiciles, Ringknocker had gone to some lengths, allowing some luxuries to brighten the dreariness. I hadn't seen anything yet.

I walked back and forth in the tent for a while. I ducked outside to watch a Phantom take off and nodded to a passing hooch maid. I wanted to go talk to Staglioni, but he had said he was in the middle of a good book. I remembered mine. I was in the middle of the second volume of the *Lord of the Rings* trilogy. Gollum was slithering down cliffs head first as he followed Bilbo. I identified with Gollum and loved his voice. "Yesss," he said. I tried talking that way back in the Cav: "Yesss, we likes to go on missionssss." But people thought I was developing a lisp. No one knew who Gollum was. The most popular books were James Bond adventures.

While I read, something went wrong with my brain. Something had to be wrong, because instead of lying back with the book on my lap, the book was on the dirt floor and I was reaching for my .45 and saying, "What?"

"What?" I roamed the tent, looking in corners. I looked outside.

"What?" Something was very wrong. I was tense. I was ready. I waited.

A dark head pushed through the flaps. That? As I drew my pistol, I saw it was Staglioni. "Chow," he said, and ducked back outside. He had not seen my gun. Abruptly the feeling of impending doom passed. A danger was past. What the danger had been I didn't know, but it was gone. I holstered the .45 and walked to the mess hall.

I sat at a table with Staglioni and two air-force pilots from across the base. All during the meal I kept worrying about what I had just done. There wasn't anything wrong. It's me. I'm going crazy.

"Wanna try it?" The air-force lieutenant asked.

"Try what?"

"Fly a Phantom."

"I fly slicks."

"I know. You wanna trade a ride?" He looked at me quizzically.

"No."

The Huey was not ready the next day. Or the next. Each day I waited, the routine was much the same. Breakfast, read, lunch, read, dinner, read, sleep. The routine was punctuated by moments of nonspecific terror. I spent my nights hopping up out of bed looking for the source of my fears. One afternoon, while I read at a table in the club, I blacked out. One moment I was reading normally; the next thing I knew my face was resting on the pages. That scared me into taking my tortured soul over to the flight surgeon on the air-force side of the base.

"I have these dizzy spells, I keep waking up at night thinking that I'm dying, and yesterday my face fell into my book," I shamefully admitted.

"Take off your clothes," said the doctor, with sympathetic fascination.

"What does that have to do with anything?"

"I'm going to give you a neurological examination."

And he did. He poked me with pins, scraped my soles, tapped my elbows and knees. He had me follow fingers and lights with my eyes, stand on one foot, and touch my fingertips with my eyes closed. And when he finally looked into my eyes with his ophthalmoscope, he said, "Hmmm."

"Find something?" I asked.

"Nope. Nothing at all. All your circuits check out fine."

"So why am I having these blank spells and dizziness?"

"I don't know."

I sagged with disappointment.

"It could be a couple of things," he added hastily. "You might have a rare form of epilepsy, which I doubt. Or you're suffering from stress. I would think that with the kind of job you have, it's stress. But I suggest you check with your own flight surgeon when you get to see him. If you keep having the symptoms, they'll probably ground you."

Four days after I had arrived, a week after leaving the Cav, I joined my new unit in the field at Nhon Co.

The Prospectors' ships were parked in a narrow airstrip cut into the jungle by the French. The camp was up on a hill next to the strip. I carried my gear up and found Deacon, and he showed me to one of the twenty six-sided tents scattered around the sandy, weedy dunes at the top of the hill. My tentmates were two warrants, Monk and Stoopy Stoddard.

"Hey, a new guy," said Monk. He looked up from filing magazine clippings in a shoebox. He had square jaws and a compact, sturdy body. "But"—he squinted in the glare of the light behind me—"I'd say you're not new to Nam." He was looking at my belt buckle. The green tape that covered it was filthy and almost black, the mark of the veteran.

"That's right. I'm a transfer from the Cav."

"Really?" said Stoddard. "The Cav? That's a tough

outfit." Stoopy was an overweight child of a man who said irritating things like "Gosh" and "Wow!" and even "Neat."

I nodded and said, "Can I put my gear over here?" I pointed to the back of the tent.

"Sure," said Stoddard. I threw my bag against the cloth wall and sat on it. Monk resumed filing his clippings. Ragged copies of *Stars and Stripes, Newsweek, Time,* and other magazines lay strewn in the dirt around his bedroll. He carefully cut each item with a Swiss army scissors, then flipped through alphabetized index cards to find its proper place.

"Are you a writer?" I asked.

"Monk, a writer?" Stoopy giggled. His belly and fat cheeks shook. I noticed chocolate stains on his lips and then saw the chocolate bar grasped in a grubby hand. "He thinks you're a writer, Monk." He laughed brightly. Monk shot him a glance that killed the laughter immediately. Stoopy blinked hard and sat quietly and respectfully.

"No, not yet," said Monk. "I'm just collecting my material. Someday . . ." he trailed off, apparently avoiding a touchy subject.

"That's an impressive amount of stuff you got there." I nodded at the shoebox.

"Thanks, I've got more." He pointed to four more rubber-banded boxes resting against the tent wall. "Someday . . . You'd be surprised to know what they're saying about this war." He nodded slowly and knowingly. I signaled agreement.

"Well, well, well. Look who's here," said a voice from the flap.

"Wolfe!"

"Wow, Mason, what a memory!" We both laughed. Wolfe was a former classmate.

"I didn't know you were with the Prospectors," I said.

"I was one of the shmucks that set up this camp. I was out here when you arrived."

"Well, you picked a nice place."

"Thanks."

Monk seemed irritated by Wolfe's intrusion. He rolled a rubber band off his wrist around the shoebox and stashed it carefully with the others. Then he stood up and squeezed past Wolfe without saying a word. Wolfe ignored him as he left. Apparently they were not friendly.

Wolfe and I talked awhile. He had arrived in-country a month before. He was very impressed that I was a short-timer with only two months to go in my tour. I told him I had been in the Cav and that I had recently talked to some classmates of ours up near Kontum. We shared rumors concerning the whereabouts of the rest of the class and agreed that probably most of them were somewhere in Nam. Somebody called that it was chow time, and Stoopy, whom we had completely ignored, leapt outside. As we emerged from the tent, we saw Monk balanced on his hands, walking up a small sand dune.

"That's pretty good," I said as we walked away.

"The guy's a jerk," said Wolfe sourly.

That evening I delivered a letter from the air-force doctor to Doc Da Vinci, our flight surgeon. He agreed that it was probably just a stress reaction and gave me some tranquilizers to take. He warned me to use them only at night. I couldn't fly with them. I slept well that night.

The next morning I was back in the saddle in a Huey. The aircraft commander was my platoon leader, Deacon. We flew three missions of local ass-and-trash, single-ship stuff. Deacon let me do all the flying. In four hours that morning, I landed in a clearing so small I had to hover vertically down, also landed on a tight pinnacle, carried two loads that were so heavy I had to make running take-offs, and finally joined up with three other ships in a formation flight back to the airstrip. I had been thoroughly checked out.

"Damn good flying," Deacon said from the left seat as I landed behind another Huey back at the airstrip.

"Thanks," I replied. Coming from an IP, that was a real compliment.

"If you fly that good again tomorrow, I'll sign you off as an aircraft commander."

The next day was also the Prospectors' last day at Nhon Co. So at the end of another day of local ass-and-trash, we flew directly back to Phan Rang. Other ships brought the tents and gear back. I did fly well, and, true to his word, Deacon signed me off as a qualified aircraft commander. On the walk to the company area, Deacon told me that Ringknocker was arranging another big party.

"We seldom get a break like this; we'll be here four days. Ringknocker likes to see the men enjoy themselves. I'd roll my bedroll up if I were you," Deacon said.

"Roll up my bedroll?"

"Yeah. Just roll your mattress up and tie it."

"Why?"

"You'll see."

It was nine o'clock and the party was in full swing. Doc DaVinci sat next to me at the bar and explained how he had prepared the skull that now sang on the wall. He was drunk. The members of the songwriting team sat facing each other in a circle of chairs in a far corner, producing sounds that clashed with a Joan Baez tape. They were drunk. Sky King and Red Blakely Indian-wrestled in the middle of the floor. Sky King held a brimming mug of beer, claiming that he would not spill a drop while he dispatched Red.

"I boiled it," said DaVinci.

"In the kitchen?" I asked, interested.

"No, no. They wouldn't let me do it in the kitchen. I built a fire out back and boiled it there. Boiled it a whole day."

I glanced at the skull, clacking with Baez's words, admiring the clean gleaming white of it. "It's so . . . white."

"Not naturally. I bleached it after I pulled off the meat."

I drank some bourbon and nodded. "Of course." I put my drink down. "Bleach."

"It's a fact," DaVinci said. "Clorox will give your skull a whiter, brighter look."

"They're coming!" Sky King yelled. Everyone stopped talking. I could hear a siren wailing in the distance.

"You rolled your bed up?" Deacon had walked up to me.

"Yeah . . ."

"Smart boy," he said.

"Who's coming?" I asked Doc.

"The ladies, of course."

The siren got louder, then stopped. Somebody outside said, "Back 'er up." In the light that shone through the windows I could see the rear end of an army ambulance moving toward the open door. It stopped and someone opened the back. Packed inside were at least a dozen smiling Vietnamese women. All the Prospectors were standing, applauding, whistling, while the ladies were helped out of the ambulance.

It's hard to say what happened next except that once the women were all inside the club, they began to disappear. Men grabbed giggling girls and ran out the doors into the night. It all happened in minutes. I sat there on the bar stool, open-mouthed. I had just seen an ambulance back up, unload a bunch of whores, and they were carried away?

"There must be some kind of rule against that," I said.

"Hey, it's our ambulance," Doc said.

"If that happened in the Cav, everyone here would be up for a court-martial." I shook my head in disbelief.

"It works great," said Doc. "The security guards never stop an ambulance. Best damn thing we ever traded for."

"You traded for an ambulance?"

"Yeah. Ringknocker got an ambulance, a deuce-and-a-half, and a Jeep for one Huey."

"A Huey?" I shook my head.

"Yeah, a Huey. It was one of ours that got shot to shit. It was declared a total loss, and its number was taken off the registers. It was just wreckage when Ringknocker made the trade. Part of the deal was that our maintenance guys would piece it back together. It looks like shit, but it flies."

"That's incredible."

"I know. Ringknocker has got a creative mind."

It had been only fifteen minutes since the girls were carried off when one of them walked back into the club escorted by her partner. "Next," he called out.

Doc slapped my shoulder and nodded toward the girl. "It'll change your luck." He grinned.

"No thanks. I'm still fighting a case of clap," I said. Inside, I was awed by their style—these Prospectors were out of a dream. "You go ahead."

"Not me. Every time I try to examine them, they get pissed off." He blew a kiss to the girl.

"No you!" she said, shaking her finger. Doc laughed loudly.

She left with someone and two more came inside.

> Silver wings upon their chests,
> Flying above America's best.
> We will stop the Vietcong,
> And you can bet it won't take long.

I had forgotten about the songwriters. They were still in their corner rehearsing their latest lyrics, apparently undisturbed by the intrusion of the lovelies.

I left the party at one o'clock. The girls had been sent back out through the gates in the blaring ambulance, but the Prospectors partied on.

"Okay. We're taking two ships. Deacon, you pick a crew. I'll fly the other with Daring." Ringknocker held a briefing at a table in the mess hall the next morning. Deacon and Daring nodded. I watched from the next table while I ate fresh scrambled eggs. "The target is the Repair and Utility compound, here." Ringknocker pointed to his frayed map. The R&U compound was a fenced-in field at another air-force base, heavily guarded, surrounded by all sorts of security, where the civilian contractors stored their mountains of building supplies. Such things as tin roofing, lumber, air conditioners, refrigerators, sinks, toilets—everything needed to build a truly American base. "Now I'm trying for an ice maker, but anything will do," Ringknocker explained. "Deacon, I want you to fly cover while I go down. Keep me posted when the guards start moving our way." Deacon nodded. "Okay, let's go." The group of men got up and left, dressed for a mission.

Ringknocker's Huey came back an hour later carrying a huge wooden crate on a sling. He landed it on the back of his deuce-and-a-half, which drove it immediately to the maintenance area. When they opened the crate, they discovered that it contained another refrigerator, just like the one they already had. Ringknocker was happy anyway, and by late the next day he had arranged to trade the refrigerator to an air-force unit on the other side of the base for a brand-new ice-making machine. For the next two months, wherever we went in the field, someone got the job of moving the five-hundred-pound ice machine as part of our field gear.

On the afternoon of the fourth day of the break, Deacon told me to take a ship up to our headquarters and pick up two new pilots.

I flew with Sky King, who chattered during the entire thirty-minute flight. He was a happy man and very likable. His total disregard for army formalities made me forget that he was a captain.

We landed at the sandy pad at headquarters, shut down, and walked to the tent with the mail courier. From a hundred yards away I thought I recognized one of two men carrying flight bags on their shoulders.

"Those must be the two pilots," said Sky King.

I nodded, staring at the distant, frail figure who sagged under the weight of a giant flight bag. I knew that walk.

"Shit!" I said with a wide grin on my face. "How far do I have to go to get away from you?" The two men were twenty feet away.

"Damn! They told me there wasn't a chance you'd be in this unit," Resler replied. I helped him carry his bag back to the ship.

12.
La Guerrilla Bonita

Neither conscience nor sanity suggests that the United States is, should or could be a global gendarme. The U.S. has no mandate from on high to police the world and no inclination to do so.
—Robert S. McNamara, in *Time,* May 27, 1966

June 1966

It struck me as ironic that the Prospectors, located two hundred miles south of the Cav, were assigned to Dak To, the Cav's last hunting ground. Within a month of my transfer, I found myself once again scouring for VC in an area in which the Cav had drawn a blank. This time, I flew with a different unit in support of the famous 101st Airborne in Operation Hawthorne. The VC had chosen not to fight the Cav, but apparently they thought they'd try their luck against the 101st.

Our camp was west of the village of Dak To, in a grassy plain south of some low foothills. Our tents were set up in three straight lines, paralleling the red-dirt airstrip. A mile from our camp, the 101st bivouacked and maintained security for themselves and for the Prospectors.

We spent a day filling sandbags to build low walls around our tents. On the morning of the second day, it was announced that we would fly a little mission for some ARVNs before we started direct support of the 101st.

"The best thing that could happen to you is to get a minor bone wound," said Wolfe. He stood in the awning of the tent I shared with Resler and Stoddard.

"A *bone* wound? I feel weak just thinking about it," I said.

"I'm saying that if you had to get wounded, that's the one to get. A bone wound will get you out of this fucking country."

Deacon walked down the row between the tents. "Let's go," he yelled.

"How about no wounds?" I said. "Maybe they'll just call the whole thing off." I reached for my helmet. My .45 was already strapped on over my flak vest. I was ready.

"Fat fucking chance," said Wolfe.

"Good luck." Gary ducked out of the tent to go to his ship. He and I couldn't fly together in the Prospectors, because they didn't let junior warrants do that. We felt safer together. Especially since the pilot who replaced me back in the Cav, Ron Fox, had been killed sitting in the cockpit with Gary. He had taken a round up through his chin. Gary said that his brains poured out when they removed his helmet. Fox's death was one of the reasons they had sent Gary on a R&R on the way to the Prospectors. We'd both been working on Deacon to let us fly together—told him what a great team we'd made in the Cav—but so far, no dice.

"Good luck," I said. I left the tent walking a little way

with Wolfe. "What do you get for a scratch?" I said.

"A free cup of coffee. What do you think? You got to get something that takes time to heal but won't be a permanent handicap."

"Yeah, I see. I'll work on it." I saw Sky King waiting for me by the Operations tent. "See you after the mission. Good luck."

"Right." Wolfe gave me a salute.

Sky King smiled. "Hey, this is my lucky day. I get to fly with a veteran. I feel so . . . secure."

"Yeah, yeah. Spare me, please."

"No, really. Just being in the same ship with you makes me feel like everything's going to be okay." We walked toward our ship, one pair of pilots in a long, straggling line of helicopter crews walking over the red dirt to their ships.

"You know, you can be a pain in the ass, sir."

"Haw!" Sky King yelped. "Got you." We walked up to our ship. "You know, Mason, I like you. And to prove it, I'm going to let you in on a little business deal. I'll tell you all about it when we get back."

"Thanks."

"No, really. You'll love it. You'll see."

One thing different about the Prospectors, aside from such informal relations between officers and warrants, was that they had chest protectors up to their eyeballs. They had so many, in fact, that they kept the extras up in the chin bubbles. Seeing one of them at my feet made me feel guilty. For the lack of one of these, Morris had died. Maybe there was another pilot somewhere in Vietnam, right now, who was wondering why the fuck he didn't have one. Maybe one was dying right now.

"How did you get so many of these things?" I pointed to the armor.

"We've always had them," said Sky King. He looked at me like I had asked a dumb question. "Why?"

"Just wondered."

The weather was great, puffy white clouds in a brilliant blue sky, a nice day for flying. Since I had been here once before, I knew that there were no VC around. I felt that I had retired from heavy action after leaving the Cav. My only concern was the ARVNs. I kept hearing such bad stories about them. A Prospector told me that an ARVN had turned and fired at his ship when he dropped them at an LZ. I'd heard that before.

We picked up eight ARVN Rangers wearing tight-tailored camouflage uniforms. They stared nervously, smoked cigarettes, and got aboard reluctantly. They did not bolster my sagging opinion of our ally.

The twelve slicks in the mission were to fly the ARVNs a few miles up the valley from Dak To. There we would cut across the eastern ridge and land two at a time on an eight-foot-wide ridge running to a small concrete fortress. While the flight stretched to get the necessary spacing, we heard on the radio that the VC were there, too. From a couple miles away I could see a daisy chain of Phantoms hitting the hill directly across the small valley from the fortress. Sky King and I were to be one of the second pair of ships to land. As the first two ships landed, they called hits.

From several VC machine-gun emplacements on the facing hill, tracers flicked out at the Phantoms. The fighters swooped, releasing monstrous bursts of cannon during their blindingly swift passes. The tracers converged on them.

I had the controls on the right side of the ship. Our buddy ship was taking a spot just in front of the fortress, leaving us the stark ridge nearest to VC guns. I set up the approach. The two ships in front of us took off after what seemed to be an awfully long time on the ground. With a hundred yards to go, our right-door gunner opened up on some muzzle flashes. At the same time, a Phantom began billowing black smoke in the middle of his strike. He climbed up sharply in an almost vertical climb—and we saw one man eject. As we landed, I saw grazing rounds kick through the dirt on the ridge in front of us. The emplacement was just a little higher than we were. The right door gunner blazed away, and I waited for the ARVNs to get the fuck out. When the crew chief hadn't called that they were off for what seemed to be an hour, I looked back and saw him trying to force an ARVN off the ship from his awkward position in the pocket. The other ARVNs kept ducking their heads in the gunfire, waiting with wide-eyed anticipation for me to leave. I shook my head and started screaming, "Get off! Get off!" and pointed at the door. They sat there. I heard a round go through the air frame. The old, familiar *tick*. The crew chief pulled his .45 and pointed it at the soldiers, waving it toward the door with murder in his eyes. When they saw I wasn't going to go anywhere and that the crew chief might indeed kill them, they began to get off. I looked at the fortress to see if we were getting any cover fire. No one in sight. No guns were in action; everyone was on the dirt behind the walls. The black, billowing trail of the Phantom disappeared in the jungle. A pearl-white chute blossomed in the blue sky.

Our buddy ship took off. "They're out!" yelled the chief. I glanced across the deck through the door to the ARVNs hiding on the low side of the ridge. I took off. As we crossed in front of the fortress, we saw the defenders lying low. Not one gun was in position.

A half mile away, it was over for us. That was it—one load to the ridge. I cruised the five miles back to the camp, steaming.

"I've never seen anything like that. How the fuck are they going to win this stupid war if they fight like that!"

Sky King nodded gravely and said nothing. He'd worked with ARVNs before.

When we landed, I thanked the crew chief, Blakely, for using his brains and getting the ARVNs off.

"Any time, sir. Next time I'll do it sooner." He grinned. We all went around the ship to count hits. There was one. It was hard to believe that they had shot down a Phantom and missed us as we parked on the ridge, but that was the way it was.

"Lucky, lucky, lucky," said Sky King.

"Astounding," I said.

We walked back to the Ops tent and waited for the rest of the gaggle to return.

"Wolfe just got hit," said Maj. Richard Ramon, the operations officer, as we walked inside. "Friend of yours, isn't he?" He looked at me.

"Yes, sir. A classmate."

"Well, he got his arm messed up. He'll be here in a minute." He shook his head. "Hell of a way to start the day."

I kept seeing ARVN asses glued to the deck of my ship.

"Daring's boys are out there now trying to get that gun position," said Ramon. "And we had a slick and a gun out looking for the air-force pilot."

"One?" I asked.

"Yeah, your friend Resler picked him up, the other guy never got out. Poor bastard."

Two more Hueys cruised in fast, low level, down the airstrip. When they landed, Wolfe staggered out, helped by the crew chief. He held his arm across his chest, dripping blood down his pants. Doc DaVinci met them halfway and walked them to the tent. Wolfe was pale, as if all his blood had drained out of his arm. He smiled blankly at me as Doc used scissors to cut his sleeve away.

"Fuckers shot my smokes!" exclaimed Wolfe. With his arm down, we could see that his chest-protector pocket was blown away, revealing the ceramic strata beneath the green cloth. The round had torn through his right fore-arm and blasted into his chest protector.

"Do you see that? The fuckers blew away my smokes!"

I nodded and handed him a lit cigarette.

"Can you move your fingers?" asked Doc.

"Sure." Wolfe puffed the smoke.

"Well, move them."

"I am."

Doc looked at Wolfe. "I think you're going to get home on this one."

"I told you, Mason! A bone wound will do it every time."

I raised a weak smile. "You got it right."

Doc wrapped Wolfe's arm in a bunch of bandages while Sky King and I went back out to the flight line to get the ship ready. We were going to fly him to Pleiku.

During the flight, Wolfe chain-smoked cigarettes handed him by the crew chief. When I dropped him at the hospital at Pleiku, his color was better and he was smiling like a man who just won a lottery. He had landed right after me in the same spot on the ridge. I almost wished it had been the other way around.

Later that day, Sky King and I flew out to lift a load of grunts from the 101st—to rescue the ARVNs—and back. We had experienced fairly heavy fire the second time out, but no hits. Meanwhile, Daring's gun platoon was swooping all around the hill, trying to get at the emplacement. It seemed impossible that the gooks could last through the Phantom strike and a whole gunship platoon, but they had. When the sun dropped behind the ridge, the guns came back one by one. They had taken many hits. Two pilots had been wounded and were taken immediately to Pleiku.

"Where the fuck is Seven-oh-two?" Major Ramon asked no one in particular. A group of us sat around in the operations tent listening to the radios: 702 was the last of the gunships out there. He had called five minutes before that he had been hit, but then there was silence.

"Let's get somebody back out there." Ringknocker spoke from the tent door. "Maybe he forgot how to get back here." He frowned at his own joke.

Then we all heard the familiar whopping of rotors, and in the dusky light we saw the ship skid across the dirt fast and slide to a stop on the strip.

"Fancy landing," somebody said.

With a collective sigh of relief, the crowd began to break up. I stopped outside with some others because something odd was happening with 702. Nobody was getting out. The ship just stood there hissing. Its rotors swung lazily. Somebody ran over to the ship and started waving frantically, calling for Doc. All four people on board were unconscious from wounds.

While they loaded the crew of 702 on a slick going to Pleiku, I walked back to the tent. Stoddard was showing Resler a six-foot section of a Huey tail-rotor drive-shaft tube. As I got closer, I could see a bullet hole in the tube.

"My first hit," said Stoddard proudly.

Resler nodded agreeably but cautiously. Stoopy had taken the hit early in the day and had had the crew chief give him the ungainly trophy.

"Going to take this thing back home," said Stoopy.

I was feeling kind of guilty for thinking that Stoopy was a jerk. He was ... just a little too exuberant, or something.

"You're a moron," said Resler. I laughed for a long while.

"So, this is the deal." Sky King talked as we sat in the mess tent. "Ice."

"What are you talking about?"

"Ice, man." Sky King's eyes gleamed in the light of the

mess tent's bare bulb. Our generator grumbled and popped in a hole fifty feet away.

"This is the business deal you were talking about?"

"That's it, kimo sabe. Ringknocker's agreed. We start taking a ship down to Kontum every day and load it up with ice. You know, big blocks of ice. We bring it back here and sell it to our own mess, the company's beer tent, and the rest we unload to the grunts at the 101st. We'll charge the grunts enough to pay for our ice. Nice deal, eh? The Prospectors get free ice."

"We have an ice machine."

"We do, but it only makes chipped ice. And just barely enough for drinks. We're talking about big twenty-five-kilo blocks of ice to cool the beer. Besides, there'll be a profit, and we can use the money for the club. What do you think?"

"What do you want me to do?" I said.

"Just volunteer to fly down with me every day."

"Sure. Why not?"

"Exactly. Partner."

We couldn't land a Huey in downtown Kontum to get ice. Sky King had arranged for a truck from a nearby Special Forces camp. The deal was that we could use their truck and driver if we let them use our Huey and a pilot.

On the first day of the ice business, Sky King took the truck into town while I flew the Special Forces CO—a lieutenant named Bricklin—on his jungle patrol. We covered his normal route through the scrub and jungle at low level in twenty minutes. The same trip via ankle express took him and his Chinese mercenaries a full day to complete. Naturally, he couldn't see much from a speeding helicopter, nothing like what he could've seen had he walked, but he could honestly report that he had covered the entire route. This made him and his men very happy.

Only fifteen or twenty of the two hundred men at this camp were Americans. The rest were Chinese mercenaries from Saigon. When we landed back at the compound, Bricklin pointed out the arrangement, indicating that that side was for the Chinese, this for the Americans.

Bricklin was a tall and lean Montanan. He—like most of the Special Forces—was of the old school concerning the proper way to handle the war. Charlie was treated somewhat like a band of mischievous outlaws whose chances of actually taking over the country were nonexistent. Bricklin believed that with the Americans dominating the Kontum area, the people would eventually come to trust the Americans and their ways, especially if the Americans educated their children and supplied medical care and other material goodies that even backward peasants come to crave when they are exposed to them.

Bricklin had begun to point out the advantages of the patient method of converting the Vietnamese versus the so-called war of attrition when he saw the Cav's horse patch on my right shoulder.

"The only trouble with those guys," said Bricklin, "is they kill a lotta people that just happened to get in the way. Every time a villager or his water buffalo gets killed, the VC boys talk it up real big. 'See how much the Americans love you?' they say. 'Killed old Mrs. Koa yesterday and she was seventy-five and never hurt a bug.' Course, old Charlie had come through the same village and executed the honchos, but who trusts politicians anyway? These wide-screen raids the Cav and other units are doing are wrecking everything these people have. Sure, they beat the NVA units and the VC units, but they're ignoring the stomping they're doing to the people we're trying to help. And this relocation thing is about equal to dying as far as the villagers are concerned. These people are born, grow up, and die all in the same village—the village of their ancestors. That village is everything to them. So what do we do? We come marching through, burn it down—to keep the VC from occupying it—and move the people out to God knows where and turn them overnight into refugees and welfare cases and honest-to-God American-haters. The VC are winning because we're losing." Bricklin had said all that before he popped a beer inside the small metal building they called their club. "Just show 'em by example. Show the VC how good the American way is, and they'll come around. These people'll go the way that works."

Bricklin and I sat at a folding table in the small bar. I drank a cup of coffee while he drank beer. I had to fly.

Everything about the place was easygoing. Even the slot machine was easy. The machine's covers were off; you could see the gears and wheels and the money box. You could reclaim your losses by reaching into the back. Bricklin's philosophy got me into a political mood.

"Do you think we ought to be here in the first place?" I asked.

"Well, that's another question altogether, isn't it? Fact is, we *are* here."

"To me it's *the* question."

"You may be right, but things like this are real hard to stop once they get going. I think we're going to be here a real long time."

"Do you think we'll win?"

"Not if we keep bustin' up the villages and killing the people we're trying to save, we won't."

"A lot of people say that if we had allowed the Vietnamese to have their elections, they would've voted for Ho Chi Minh and there wouldn't be any war."

Bricklin nodded. "Yeah, I've read that, too. And it's probably true. But like I say, we're here now."

"So why can't we just pull out?"

"Do you think LBJ would ever walk out on this gunfight?"

"No."

"You're right," Bricklin said, and smiled.

The ice truck rolled through the gate and stopped by the bar. Sky King got out and pushed through the screen door. "Man, the prices around here." He sat down beside me. "Fuckers charge two-fifty for a fifty-pound block. The same thing costs seventy-five cents at Phan Rang."

"Well, we had the Cav come through here a month ago," said Bricklin. "Those guys paid whatever the people asked for—ruined them for bargaining. They just don't understand the locals." He winked at me.

Sky King had a beer and talked to Bricklin. He told him that the deal was working fine, and if it was okay by him, we'd be coming down every day.

"Just make yourselves at home," said Bricklin, "and bring your Huey."

We walked out to the ship as the last of the blocks were put on board. There was a total of twenty blocks—a thousand pounds of ice—packed wetly on the deck. I cranked up. Because of the extra weight, I couldn't hover up over the flagpole, so I turned the ship around and took off the way we came in.

As we headed up the valley on the thirty-mile flight back to Dak To, Sky King smoked cigarettes, chattered about the business, and nervously watched the cargo melting in the warm, hundred-mile-an-hour wind.

"Shit, we'll be lucky to get back with half the ice we bought," he said. "How 'bout we close the doors?" he asked the crew chief.

"If we do that, sir, we can't get to our guns," said the chief.

"Oh, yeah." He turned to me. "Next trip we got to bring a tarp to put over that stuff."

He turned around, watching the cargo. "Shit, look at it go! Each one of those drops is a fucking dime!"

"We're almost there," I said.

"Thank God. Can you imagine getting back to the company with a fifty-dollar puddle? Ringknocker'd kill me." He laughed.

I landed on the strip at a spot near the mess hall. A truck pulled out, and the crew began unloading the ice as I shut down. From there it was trucked to one of our tents, where it entered a complicated distribution system that delivered ice to our company, the nearby engineers, and the 101st before dark.

Being in the ice business gave me the trading material I needed to build a bunker. Both Gary and I were nervous about being mortared. The Prospectors thought we were overreacting. They had never been mortared. We enlisted Stoddard's help. He was an energetic excavator. Within a day, with Stoopy doing most of the digging, we had a four-by-four hole, six feet deep. While Gary and Stoopy filled sandbags to wall the bunker, I took a Jeep over to the engineers and struck a deal with a captain there. He gave me three sheets of PSP for one block of ice. I took the steel planks, on account, and brought them back. We layered three levels of sandbags on top of them. It was a snug little bunker. And though we knew it probably could not withstand a direct hit, it might, and that gave us great comfort.

Meanwhile, the Prospectors laughed. But Gary and I knew better.

That evening Gary and I sat on our bunker, quietly talking about going home. We were now short-timers with less than seventy days to go.

"They say they're going to use short-timers only on noncombat missions during their last month." Gary sipped his daily Budweiser.

"I heard. I think a great plan would be to take a leave ten days before that; when you come back, you're finished fighting. Just fly rice and stuff around back at Phan Rang."

"You going to?"

"Yeah, why not? We could both get a leave together. I found some great places in Taipei."

"I heard *it's* better in Hong Kong."

"*It* is, eh? Okay, Hong Kong. I've never been there. You wanna take a leave there?"

"Yeah."

By the end of the first week, we had lifted companies of grunts from the 101st into positions at the north end of the valley. They were getting into firefights, but nothing big. We also established an artillery position in the foothills, placed so that it controlled the semicircle in which the 101st fanned out. Intelligence had reported that there was at least a battalion-sized NVA unit out there, and the 101st was eager to make contact.

My schedule was always blank in the afternoons, and I continued flying the ice runs. After a few days, Sky King and I had worked out a procedure in which the one of us who stayed with Bricklin could drink, while the one who went for the ice stayed dry—so that there would be at least one sober pilot to fly back. This made the daily flights more enjoyable. I was beginning to like being a Prospector. They might be eccentric, but they got the job done, and had a good time doing it. And except for the six casualties we experienced on that first day, no one had been hurt. It was, almost, pleasant.

Things seemed to be going well with the Prospectors. Joviality reigned among them while the action lulled. But something was different about us when compared to the outside world, as we demonstrated the next day.

Most people were in camp when a Chinook landed from Saigon. Ringknocker went out to greet four Red Cross girls as they stepped out of the back of the ship.

Deacon joined Ringknocker, and the two of them escorted the girls back toward the camp. I was sitting on my cot, watching the party coming our way. Looking down the tent row, I noticed that everybody had disappeared. The place had suddenly become a ghost town. Gary peered out at the women and announced, "Doughnut Dollies," but stayed inside. As Ringknocker walked the girls down the company street, obviously looking for someone to introduce them to, he could find no one. The girls began to look nervous as they peered into the dark tents, occasionally seeing a shadowed face peering silently back. They walked down the line of tents and back. Ringknocker and Deacon escorted them back to the Chinook. Meanwhile, the crew of the Chinook had deposited a pile of cardboard boxes on the airstrip. We watched Ringknocker nodding as someone explained them. The worried girls shook Ringknocker's hand, looked quizzically around the deserted camp, and boarded their ship. Minutes later they were gone. When the ship was safely away, the Prospectors reappeared as if nothing had happened.

"Why did they do that?" I asked Gary.

"Why did *you* do that?"

"I don't know. I just couldn't go out and meet them. We all must be nuttier than we think. I mean, round-eyes. Everybody talks about seeing round-eyes again, and here they were five minutes ago, and we all hid?"

"Gratuitous issue." Deacon pointed to the boxes.

"What's that?" asked Gary.

"Free stuff from the Red Cross."

We walked over and drew gifts of soap, combs, toothpaste, and cartons of cigarettes. And everyone looked guilty. They came bearing gifts and we shunned them. Sky King ran out to the airstrip and cupped his hands to his mouth. "Come back!" he yelled. "Come back!"

———

I watched the sagging top of my mosquito bar from inside. Resler kept a light on and wrote letters. Lying on my back, I noticed that I would have to find another place to put my electric shaver and assorted junk that I kept on top of the mosquito netting. It sagged too much.

Stoopy was buried under his blankets, asleep. One nice thing about the highlands, it was cool at night. Gary turned off his flashlight and for a while I heard him wrestling with his cot and blankets as he tucked in the mosquito netting. Then it was quiet. From far away, I could hear the occasional noises of battle. The 101st was getting more action every day.

I could not sleep. I stared into the darkness and thought about how it would feel to be out of the combat assaults. Gary and I had requested leave to start in two weeks. If all went as planned, we would both be into our last thirty days when we got back. A barrage of artillery sounded in the distance. I felt tense. After nearly a year of unconscious listening I could instantly tell incoming rounds from outgoing, even if I was sleeping next to the artillery or mortar positions. There was something ominous about the noise from the north end of the valley.

The electric razor above me sparked. My throat tightened in fear. *The* booby trap? The sparks grew to a white blaze. From the intensity of a Fourth of July sparkler, it suddenly blazed to a blinding white flame. I rolled out of the cot onto the ground and stood up. Flickering shadows were cast by the intense blaze. The inside of the tent was brighter than daylight. "Gary! Fire!" I shouted as I backed into a tent rope. The dazzling light flickered green through the canvas of the tent. When Gary said, "What's the matter?" the light flicked off. I stood out in the cool night, in my underwear, sweating and shivering. Gary was beside me.

"What's the matter?" His voice was calm.

"You didn't see a fire?"

"What fire?"

"In the tent. My razor blew up. You didn't see it?"

"I didn't see anything."

"Come on, I'll show you." I walked cautiously back into the tent. Stoddard was still asleep. I used Gary's flashlight and shined it on the top of the mosquito bar. My razor gleamed in the light—intact. I touched it cautiously, then picked it up. It was cold.

"How can that be? It *was* burning, as bright as a magnesium flare. I saw it!"

"Bob, nothing burned."

"Look, I've got spots from looking at it in my eyes right now."

"No one can see another person's spots."

"They're the proof. That razor burned." I stopped when I understood the words that I spoke. I had never seen anything more clearly in my life, but here I stood with Gary, in the tent, holding the razor. The razor had not burned and blazed and blinded me, at least not so that anybody else could see.

I walked over to DaVinci, who stood by our bunker. I told him exactly what I had seen, in detail. He nodded as I explained.

"Here." He handed me a small pill.

"What's this?"

"It'll help you sleep. I'll give you another one tomorrow night, too. Try to relax."

"I am relaxed—or I was."

"Try harder."

The next night we watched the sky over the north end of the valley fill with tracer tongues of fire from Puff. The NVA were overrunning the artillery position. Four ships from Daring's gun platoon were in the middle of it, flying back and forth in front of the artillery piece under attack. Of the four cannon there, that one was now separated from the others as the NVA concentrated on it. Puff, the DC-3 with the Gattlings, blasted unbroken tongues of fire from the black sky. Flares popped white, dazzling and swinging over the battle. The NVA kept closing in. The tube was depressed for point-blank fire. One of the gunship pilots told us that when the NVA swarmed into the gun position the men were so mixed that they had to stop firing. The gun was taken.

We were on alert all night. By three in the morning, when we still hadn't been called to do a night assault, I went to bed. Another little magic pill and I slept.

By dawn the next morning, the tube had been recaptured by the 101st, with the considerable help of our gunships.

Capt. John Niven came by early and said that he and I were going out. We were going to try to get some ammo to a trapped company.

Niven said in a friendly way that I was a better pilot than he. As the aircraft commander, he chose to handle the radios and let me do the flying. Our first stop was the trapped company's HQ area at the 101st's camp. We landed there to get the exact coordinates and to wait. The company was under fire, too heavy for us to get in. We shut down next to a small rifle range, inside the wire-strewn, mined perimeter, and waited.

At noon, we were still waiting. We could hear the company commander, Delta Six, calling on the radio in a nearby tent. He had seven fighting men left; thirty-eight more were either dead or wounded. He sounded bad, kept telling his HQ the names of the people he knew were dead, and also kept saying, "It's still too hot for that ship. We may have to wait till dark."

As I listened to this and waited, I wandered into the

tent and got a case of .45-caliber ammunition from a sergeant. I took the five hundred rounds back out to the rifle
range and proceeded to kill the rest of the afternoon by
firing hundreds of rounds at beer cans. By three o'clock,
even I was impressed by my accuracy. I was regularly
hitting beer cans at a hundred yards. By four o'clock,
some grunts had joined me, and I borrowed an M-16 and
shot a few clips with it. Another grunt let me try my luck
with an M-79 grenade launcher. As I shot, I became
calmer. I realized how much I needed to shoot. Shoot
something, anything.

Niven came out of the tent as I blasted a beer can
again. "We're going to try for it," he said. I slid the hot
.45 into my shoulder holster and went to the ship.

"I think I'll make a takeoff," said Niven. "I could use
the practice."

"Sure, help yourself."

Two grunts climbed inside with us after loading the
ship full of ammo cases.

Niven cranked up, did a power check at a hover, which
revealed that we were just able to hover. He nosed over, a
little too much, and took off over the concertina wire.
Unfortunately, the ship was too heavy for the amount of
angle he had set for the takeoff, so the ship stayed low.
We felt something tugging as we crossed the minefield. I
looked out my window and saw barbed wire caught on
the skid, trailing back, dragging in the other wire.

"We're caught in some wire!" I yelled. He realized
what was up as soon as I yelled, and reared back to level.
What he did next caught me completely by surprise. Instead of staying at a hover over the minefield and backing
out, he set the ship down. I lifted myself off the seat,
against the straps, bracing myself for the explosion.

Niven forgot the mined perimeter. He remembered as
soon as we were down. I looked at him as the ship idled.

The sun shone through the Plexiglas. Sweat dripped over his face. He looked as scared as I felt. There was no explosion.

The grunts told us to stay put. Men who knew the layout of the mines came daintily stepping out to us with wire cutters and cut us free.

Niven was so shaken he had me fly.

As we drew near the trapped company, we saw gunships working the facing hill. Their efforts were frustrated by the exceedingly deep and dense foliage. In fact, the company itself was under a seventy-five-foot canopy of trees.

"Too hot, Prospector. Wait till dark," said Delta Six.

"Roger," replied Niven.

We turned back, frustrated. The tension was building to a high peak. I had looked the spot over, and I could not see a safe approach. The company was trapped on a low, tree-covered knoll surrounded by higher ground. If the NVA were still there when we came back, we'd be sitting ducks.

I landed back at the company's HQ and shut down. It was two hours till dark. We had chow and waited.

There was no moon when we took off, and the sky was very dark. After a ten-minute flight up the valley, I switched off the position lights and began to descend. As we sank, the tops of the mountains, blacker than the sky, rose above us. I used the contours of the valley and the hills that I had come to know in two weeks of flying over and around them. It's possible to see ground contour from low level even on the darkest night. Even if there's no moon. Even if there is an overcast. There are always enough clues to construct an image. I had learned not to stare at what I wanted to see, but to see it with my peripheral vision.

So, as I moved slowly toward the knoll, I knew its treetops were lighter than the back hill behind them. Delta Six radioed that we sounded like we were on course. I had picked the right shadow.

"You're close," said Delta Six. "Keep coming, slowly."

As the ship dropped out of flight and into hover, the load became evident. The dim instrument lights showed that I was using maximum power in the hover. We drifted forward, six feet above the trees, at Delta Six's beckoning.

Delta Six said, "We hear some shooting." I saw muzzle flashes from the hill facing us.

"I think that's about right . . . wait . . . I can hear you right over us, but I can't see you. We have wounded lying all around here, and I don't want them hit by the ammo crates."

I hovered, not looking at anything in particular, just noticing the different shades of black. Muzzle flashes began to twinkle from the hillside.

The low-rpm warning siren blared. I glanced at the dial and saw the needle dropping fast. The ship was sinking into the trees. If we didn't drop that ammo we'd go down.

"We've got to drop that ammo," said Niven.

"No! You're right over the wounded." Delta Six's broadcast was filled with the crackling noise of rifle fire.

Were we or weren't we going to drop the fucking ammo? I moved a little farther to the right. The crew chief and the grunts had the boxes poised at the edge of the deck, but it was still wrong. A treetop rose up, brushing the nose. That was it. If we didn't go now, we'd be joining the men below us as pieces.

The shuddering Huey resisted as I tried to move forward. The warning siren blared. It was on the verge of quitting; moving forward was real effort. I heard a loud slap as the rotor hit a treetop. I couldn't climb. If anything, I had to descend, to get the rotor speed back to normal. I turned to the right, getting a little power bonus that way, and dragged the skids across the treetops. Within a few feet I was able to drop down the side of the knoll into a black ravine.

"Now what?" asked Niven.

"I'm going down to the end of the ravine, circle back, and try it again."

"We're too heavily loaded."

"Yeah, but I think I know where he wants it now."

Niven called Delta Six.

"Thank you," said the grateful voice.

As I cruised slowly toward the knoll, the muzzle flashes began. Then a tongue of tracers flitted off to our left. Apparently we were hard to see, because we hadn't been hit yet. From the conversation during the first attempt, I had a feeling where Delta Six was and where he wanted us to drop the ammo.

"That's it!" he yelled. "Hold it right there."

I stopped the ship. As she sank toward the trees, Delta Six called, "Okay, dump 'em."

With much scraping and bumping, the boxes were shoved from the ship. They dropped seventy-five feet through the branches and leaves. The ship gained power as it lightened.

"Great job!" yelled Delta Six. "Nobody was hit. Great job. Thank you, Prospector."

I hit one more treetop on the way out, bounced toward the ravine, and accelerated. Ten minutes later we were back at HQ being credited with saving their lives. Delta Six and his men had fired the last of their ammo to cover us.

The next morning, Delta Six had managed to push back the NVA—or the latter pulled back—and a Chinook hovered over the spot and hoisted out the wounded. Another Chinook pulled out the last of the living along with the dead.

———————

The 101st was getting the action they had craved. Unfortunately, the territory was the enemy's home field. In some of the LZs the grunts had cut on hilltops, the stumps were so close together that it was difficult to get the skids to fit between them. The American patrols hacked through the brush, struggling toward objectives, only to become hopelessly lost. Commanders constantly reported men missing in action who were in fact lost— you couldn't see a man ten feet away. While they fought the jungle, the NVA harrassed them, attacked them, and sometimes overran them. When platoons and companies came under heavy attack, rescue units sent out to help them became lost, scattered, and surrounded. For days, the 101st had lost units looking for lost units looking for lost units. It was total confusion. In that confusion, many men died.

In these conditions our helicopters were the least effective in helping the grunts. We were constantly out trying to find men who cried for help on the radio but who were totally hidden in the jungle. One company we tried to save was completely wiped out as we flew above the canopy trying to find them. Their radio went dead, and they were gone.

Another company—led by a West Point football player, Bud Carpenter—became famous because Carpenter called in an airstrike on his position as he was being overrun.

Sky King and I were in the air, orbiting Carpenter's position. Carpenter was trying to get to an old LZ to be extracted. We listened on the radio and watched the LZ, waiting for him to show up.

"We can't make it to the LZ," radioed Carpenter. "They're all around us."

"What's your position?" implored Gunfighter Six, Carpenter's CO.

"I'm one hundred meters east of the LZ," said Carpenter calmly. Gunfire crackled with his voice. "I see only six men around me," he lamented. "They're moving closer. I want an airstrike here, now."

"On your own position?" asked Gunfighter Six.

"Yes. Hurry."

Two A1-E's were already on station. They got their instructions in seconds and began to hit the coordinates. They dropped napalm, bombs, and then strafed. Carpenter's position was covered in smoke. A long silence followed.

"That did it," said Carpenter's tired voice. "They stopped."

Gunfighter Six said, "If things don't work out to the good, I want you to know that I'm putting you in for the Medal of Honor."

No reply.

"Also, I'm sure that when we get to you, we'll find a lot of dead VC."

"All I can see are my own people . . ." said the quiet voice.

"We're sending help," said Gunfighter Six.

Moments later, Gunfighter Six called us. He wanted us to land at his position, near the artillery emplacement.

"I can't understand it," he said. He sat on the deck of our Huey holding a plastic-covered map board. He looked gaunt and sad. He pointed to a circled spot on the green paper. "I don't understand it. They've got to be here." He was talking about a platoon he was trying to send to Carpenter's position. But the platoon wasn't there, because when the men fought in the direction he directed, they found nothing and became pinned down. Gunfighter Six was depressed. He had it all worked out on his game board, and the labels were all in the right place, but the men weren't.

"I want you to fly out and find this unit." He pointed

to the map. "Find them and give them an azimuth to here." He moved his finger across the board to Carpenter's position.

A major and a captain got in the back of our ship with a big radio. We took off.

I flew slowly across the treetops, listening to the grunts' radio instructions. They could hear our ship. Using our sound, they directed us right over them. During the crisscross search pattern, the enemy did not shoot. But when I found and circled a unit, they opened up from the high ground around us. I heard one *tick*. I flew past the unit, turned, and came back over them in the exact direction they were to go. "Go this way," radioed the major from behind us.

The unit rogered its orders. The major had us look for another lost patrol. Again, while we cruised back and forth over the jungle, right in front of the enemy's hillside, they did not shoot. But as soon as I circled, they opened up. The hillside was peppered with muzzle flashes. We were so close to one NVA barrage we could hear the crackling rifle fire. I felt a thump in the air frame and turned around and saw the major hitting the deck—not shot, but following his instinct to hit the deck under fire. It was kind of funny that he thought the deck was any protection—bullets went through it like tinfoil—but I didn't laugh.

I turned and came back over the invisible men on the heading they were to follow. As we crossed them, Sky King radioed, "Two-six-zero degrees." The lieutenant below rogered.

And we did it again. And again. In a couple of hours, we had redirected all the lost units. The ones who still talked, anyway. They were converging on one spot to join up. Gunfighter Six was not only going to secure Carpenter's position; he was also getting his men together to pull out. He had had enough of this shit. It was time to call in the Cavalry.

We landed back at Gunfighter Six's position and watched while he told his aides what he had in mind. The plan amounted to this: He was going to have the First Cav send out a battalion or so of troopers and position them north of the fighting, to wait on some ridge tops. He believed that if the air force bombed this area, and then the 101st went back in, they would beat the NVA up to the Cav. The crazy thing was that he believed that the NVA would travel along the ridge tops, not in the valleys. Looking at the map, I could see a thousand ways the NVA could get away, but then I wasn't an infantry commander. I'm glad I wasn't.

The briefing was interesting, but we were called out in the middle of it to rescue wounded men.

Sky King told me later that he didn't believe we were going to make it. The clearing was a tight circle cut out of a stand of saplings, and the grunts had put too many wounded on board for us to hover. To top it off, we were under continuous fire.

What I did was considered reckless. The solution was automatic. The ship lost rpm at a one-foot hover, I could not leave anyone behind—because men were dying—and we were surrounded by fifteen-foot bushes and saplings. But we were on a hill. My instincts told me that if I could get through the barrier, the ship could dive down the side of the hill and we could fly. So, while Sky King advised me that we would have to drop at least one man, I shook my head and headed for the thinnest section of the vegetable wall. Luckily, the rotors are so high above the ground that they had to cut only the thinner tops of the saplings. Our nose forced through the branches and leaves, the skids tugged on clinging things, and the rotors exploded into the stuff. It sounded like we were crashing.

Men screamed in the back of the ship. But even as we struggled through the trees and leaves and bushes, the ground dropped beneath us. The rotors cleared the tops, and we dragged the fuselage through the last of the foliage. We burst out of the thicket in a swirl of debris—a turbine-powered brush cutter. I sailed down the side of the hill, picked up some airspeed, and then climbed out. Sky King said, "I don't fucking believe it!"

I laughed. I was surprised myself.

By that evening, the scattered patrols, platoons, and companies consolidated themselves. It turned out that Carpenter had lost fewer men than he had thought. Only half his company were among the dead or wounded. The others had been separated in the tight brush. The jungle was the enemy's ally, and as long as he forced us to fight in its strangling hold, we would lose. Carpenter's heroic, suicidal solution left him miraculously unscathed—and had stopped the rout. But we lost the battle.

The grunts were pulled back past the artillery position to wait for the Cav and the air force. The air force was sending B-52-loads of one-thousand-pound bombs from Guam.

The bombs were supposed to kill a lot of NVA; the survivors were to race up the ridges, pursued by the 101st; and the Cav—way up north—would smash them. The scope was too big. The delay caused by waiting for the air force was too long.

Early the next day, Gary and I and the rest of the Prospectors stopped in our tracks in the company area. A monstrous storm thundered up the valley from the south. The noise grew so loud you couldn't hear the voices around you. The storm was the monster gaggle sent by the Cav.

The Cav raced up the valley, at least eighty ships, at

low level, and fast. The gaggle flew over us and continued north to their assigned objective. Minutes la†er, the last of their formation disappeared, and the roar silenced.

"Damn! I don't think I've ever seen so many Hueys flying all at once," someone said. I admit that I felt a sense of pride on seeing my old unit. They were—in this part of the world—the big time.

The Cav's image lost some of its gloss that same afternoon.

The 101st fought scattered firefights among a hundred branching valleys. A Cav gunship company was borrowed to help out. It was to support a ground commander who had radioed that he wanted the Cav to pulverize a spot where he would throw smoke. Yellow smoke.

Near where the 101st wanted the Cav to strike, a radio operator walked along with his patrol. He carried several smoke grenades on his belt. One of them, of course, was yellow.

At the moment the grunt commander, a mile away from the radio operater, announced that he had thrown yellow smoke, a branch pulled the yellow-smoke grenade from the radio operator's belt, popping the pin. The radio operator and his platoon were immediately swallowed up in the chalky yellow smoke. The Cav gunships happened to be only a few hundred meters away, looking for the yellow smoke that marked their target.

The gunship rogered that they saw the smoke, and attacked. They even saw people running around under the smoke and thought they were getting old Charlie.

When the commander noticed that his yellow smoke was not being hit—that someone else's yellow smoke was being attacked—he screamed at the gunships to stop.

It was lucky he did. In just a few seconds they had already killed the radio operator's platoon leader and wounded twenty-one others, including the radio operator himself.

It was a freak accident, but the Cav was labeled clumsy. And after such a dramatic entrance, too. It ruined their image. The Prospectors and the 101st felt safer, knowing that the Cav would be way up north, somewhere, as the anvil. We were the hammer.

The following day, all the 101st units were pulled back in preparation for the bombing.

The NVA were not dummies. They knew that something was up. They faded into the jungle. According to the hundreds of grease-pencil marks on the maps, the NVA were surrounded, about to be driven along the ridge, north, into the hands of the clumsy but mighty Cav. The next morning, the air force was due for its part of the squeeze.

Sky King and I were assigned to carry a television film crew up and down a dirt road that marked the western boundary of the bombing zone. Pictures of bombs, especially gigantic bombs, going off have great PR value, everyone knows.

The clouds sank into the valley, hiding the mountaintops. Sky King and I cruised nervously, at 500 feet above the road. We had been assured that the air force did not miss, that it was practically impossible to be hit by a stray bomb. Our feeling was, "Bullshit." The air force misses, a lot.

At the exact moment the bombs were supposed to hit, they did. I had just turned back, heading up the road, when we saw the hillsides a quarter mile away begin to erupt. Intersecting concussion spheres, visible in the close air, suddenly expanded away from the ground. Circles in the heavily wooded hills became instantly nude. The thousand-pound bombs fell in rapid succession, systematically and devastatingly, traveling along the ridges, in the ravines, against the hillsides, a visual staccato of overlapping blasts, tearing the earth asunder. We heard oohs and aahs from the film crew. The pattern of destruction had started across the valley from us and moved closer. Somewhere, 30,000 feet above the cloud cover, some very good bomber crews were keeping the bombs within the designated area. Charlie must be turning into hamburger.

After a half hour of this, the bombs had reached the road. The concussion rings were not only visible; they were tangible. The ship rocked in the explosions. They were going off right *on* the road, so I moved off the track. One bomb exploded in front of us, past the road, and for a minute I thought we might be seeing just how well a Huey holds up to thousand-pound bombs, when the bombing stopped.

Silence. The valley swirled in stringy smoke. Leafless trees stood at bizarre angles. The ground was gray and charred between monstrous craters. No one could have survived that apocalypse.

The end of the bomb run was the cue, and scores of Hueys flew in, dropping grunts all over the torn valley floor. It was the end of our mission, so I lingered only a little while before turning back to the airstrip.

I was impressed. The film crew was impressed. The grunts were impressed. But the gooks were not impressed. They were gone. They did leave behind a few men, and these were captured, dazed but intact—something like twenty NVA.

So now it was up to the Cav.

The Cav searched the ridges and the valleys for two days. And then they closed back to the bombed valley. When the net was closed, no fish were found. The dumb little barbarians had got away, showing not the least respect for superior technology. They had used judo, and bent with the force.

But a bombing was a bombing, and fighting is fighting, and many men had been heroic indeed. The battle, though lost, had been impressive.

General Westmoreland himself flew up from Saigon to

pin on medals. Captain Carpenter was given a silver star and was put on Westmoreland's staff.

Near the end of June, I got very twitchy. Being a short-timer made life difficult. It would almost be better not to know when you were due to return. As the day drew closer—only fifty days to go—the possibility of dying seemed more imminent, like I had already used up my breaks and would be getting it any day now. Somewhere between now and the day I left was *the* mission, probably a typical little mission—light fire—and just one little stray bullet would go through my forehead.

Nights were hell. Even with the tranquilizers Doc DaVinci gave me, I kept snapping awake at unseen dangers. Daytime was fine when I flew. The ice business also kept me busy. But when I wasn't flying—a few hours between missions, or a day off—I grew morose. Nothing that I saw convinced me that we were doing the right thing in Vietnam. I even harbored a sympathy for the enemy, which made me feel guilty.

The local war, the one I was in, went on every day. I was part of it. In the air, I did my job the best I knew how. I flew, as did all the pilots, into hot LZs, because in the middle of the confusion the hazy principles over which the war was fought disappeared. Everything else was excluded. Even I was excluded.

When Deacon finally let Gary and me fly together, our first mission was to resupply a small patrol in the jungle. We used off-course navigation to find them, a method that wasn't taught in flight school. Monk had told me about it.

In standard dead-reckoning you corrected a plotted course for wind drift, but you never knew which way to look when you'd flown long enough to be at your target.

The wind-drift correction was a calculation. The actual track you'd made was off to one side or the other. But which side?

In off-course navigation you don't correct for wind drift. You fly the magnetic course you plotted on the map for the length of time you calculated, and then you *know* where to look—upwind.

We found our resupply target without incident.

After lunch a firefight broke out close to the airstrip, near where we had left the ARVNs that first day. There were casualties, and the men needed ammo. Gary and I made it into a tiny clearing cut on a ledge. There was just enough room to squeeze the rotors in, leaving the tail hanging over space. The grunts threw some of their wounded on board, gunfire began crackling, and the grunts waved vigorously for us to leave. Takeoff from such a nook is backwards. As the nose and the rotors clear the obstruction, you push the right pedal and the whole machine pivots as it's flying so that the nose and tail trade places, putting you back to the normal posture. That's what we did.

At the hospital pod, the medics had the wounded off in seconds. Gary and I took off to go back for a second load.

"Damn. They said this whole damn area was secure weeks ago," Gary complained.

"They must not have told Charlie," I said.

"That's the truth."

The unit told us to wait. There was a small firefight going on.

I circled high over the valley, out of small-arms range. From the orbit, we could see some smoke up in the north where we had worked that morning. To the west was more smoke from some 101st units who were moving in that direction. The Americans were working a very large section of territory, but from up high it seemed very small. The sea of jungle stretched for hundreds of miles in every direction. And you could go anywhere you wanted under that canopy.

"Okay, Prospector, we're secure."

"Roger, we're on our way," called Gary.

From the orbit, I dropped toward the peak of the hill, dropped below it, and settled into a descent along a ravine that led to the nook. We had picked up a load of ammo on the way and could barely hover at this altitude. I had to time the approach so that I lost translational lift as the ship moved onto the ledge. When we were moving at maybe 30 miles an hour, with 100 yards to go, our right-door gun exploded. The gunner saw muzzle flashes. With 50 feet to go, the most critical part of the approach, the ground guide started waving me away.

This was no place to stop.

I kept coming. Then two more men jumped up and waved me away. At the same time, a voice on the radio yelled, "Don't land. We're under heavy fire!"

This was a new one for me. Normally, I could just fly over the LZ if we had to abort. But this one was on the side of a hill. Enclosed on both sides by the ravine, I couldn't turn away either. But there was space behind and below us. I flared the ship to stop the approach Since it couldn't hover, it began to sink. Nose high, the ship slid tail-down into the ravine. As we fell, I used the right pedal to bring the nose around, but I let it continue to fall, to get airspeed. I accelerated into the ravine. The airspeed came up to about 70. Then we were a flying machine again, and I swooped up between some trees on the ridge beside the ravine. The grunts had seen us tumbling into the ravine. We disappeared as the ravine turned, and they thought we crashed. But lo! the Huey jumped out of the jungle, to their amazement.

We finally got back to the nook, dropped the ammo, and picked up the rest of the wounded. As usual with the last trip, some dead men also rode back with us.

That afternoon, I took Gary with me to pick up the ice.

13.
Tell Me You're Afraid

I am sure we are going to win.
> —Nguyen Cao Ky, in *U.S. News & World Report*,
> August 1, 1966

A Communist military takeover in South Vietnam is no
longer just improbable . . . it is impossible.
> —Lyndon Johnson, August 14, 1966 (after conferring
> with General Westmoreland at the LBJ Ranch)

July–August 1966
Sleep no longer gave me peace. I had escaped Vietnam
with an R&R to Hong Kong, but I had not escaped my
memories.

Twenty-one men lay trussed in a row, ropes at their
ankles, hands bound under their backs—North Vietnamese prisoners. A sergeant stood at the first prisoner's feet,
his face twisted with anger. The North Vietnamese prisoner stared back, unblinking. The sergeant pointed a .45
at the man. He kicked the prisoner's feet suddenly. The
shock of the impact jostled the prisoner inches across the
earth. The sergeant fired the .45 into the prisoner's face.
The prisoner's head bounced off the ground like a ball

434

slapped from above, then flopped back into the gore that had been his brains. The sergeant turned to the next prisoner in the line.

"He tried to get away," said a voice at my side.

"He can't get away; he's tied!"

"He moved. He was trying to get away."

The next prisoner said a few hurried words in Vietnamese as the sergeant stood over him. When the sergeant kicked his feet, the prisoner closed his eyes. A bullet shook his head.

"It's murder!" I hissed to the man at my side.

"They cut off Sergeant Rocci's cock and stuck it in his mouth. And five of his men," said the voice. "After they spent the night slowly shoving knives into their guts. If you had been here to hear the screams . . . . They screamed all night. This morning they were all dead, all gagged with their cocks. This isn't murder; it's justice."

Another head bounced off the ground. The shock wave hit my body.

"They sent us to pick up twenty-one *prisoners,*" I pleaded.

"You'll get 'em; you'll get 'em. They'll just be dead, is all."

The sergeant moved down the line stopping prisoners who tried to escape. The line of men grew longer than it had been, and the sergeant grew distant. His face glowed red and the heads bounced. And then he looked up at me.

Forgotten events dogged my sleep.

A wounded VC lay on a stretcher, one end rested on my ship's deck, the other end held by a medic.

"I don't think he appreciates this. I think he'd rather die," said the medic.

The VC stared at me. His black eyes accused me. He lay in a black pajama top—the bottoms were gone. He had a swollen, stinking thigh wound from days before. He'd been hiding in the jungle.

"He's going to lose that leg," said the medic.

The man stared at me. The stretcher grated against the deck as the medic shoved. The crew chief reached across from the other side and pulled. They slid the stretcher up against the cockpit seats. While they shoved and jostled the stretcher, he kept his eyes on mine.

"That fucker either has the clap or he's turned on by us." The crew chief grinned. He pointed to the man's groin. What looked like semen dripped from his penis and glistened on his thigh. I looked away, feeling his hate. I felt his exposure. I looked back to his eyes and they stared, black and hot. The scene stopped. I thought I was waking up. But then it was the human shield I'd seen during LZ Dog.

The eyes blinked and wrinkles formed at their edges. The old woman with black teeth said something to me, then screamed. There was no sound. Her wrinkled hand held a child's smooth arm. The child hung lifeless and dragged the old woman down. She moved slowly, like she was falling through water. The crowd around her gasped silently and flinched and fell. The machine gun stuttered from a distant place. The woman fell slowly to the ground, bounced, dying and dead. The old woman had been saying something. When I saw her lips moving, I knew that she had been saying "It's okay. . . ."

The scene changed again. I sat in my Huey waiting for the grunts to finish inspecting a napalmed village.

"It's okay." A man looked in my cockpit window.

"She's dead!"

"They're all dead. It's okay."

The crowd was gone. I sat in my cockpit while the man talked to me from outside. The place had been a village. The wet ground smoked. Scorched poles and mud-daubed walls and thatch smoldered. Charred people lay twenty feet away. The smell of burnt hair and smoldering charcoal sank into my lungs and brain.

Why was there barbed wire in the village? Was it a pen? A defense perimeter? I couldn't see the scene beyond where the child stuck to the wire.

"This is wrong," I said to the man.

"It's okay. It's the way it is. They had their warning. Everybody else left the village. They're VC."

"She's VC?"

The man looked down. "No. She's unfortunate."

She was burned to the barbed wire. The wire was growing from the charred flesh of her tiny chest. She was bent over the wire, a toddler who had run away from the hell from the sky. The lower half of her two-year-old body was pink from intense heat; her tiny vulva looked almost alive.

"This is not war. It's—"

"It's okay. There's always going to be some innocent victims."

The man talked on, but his voice became silent. The little girl's stark body, half charred death, half pink life, leaned against the wire, almost free. Suddenly I heard ringing.

I awoke hearing my voice echoing off the far wall. The phone was ringing on the night table.

"Hel—" I gulped. "Hello?"

"Your call to the United States will be coming through in fifteen minutes," said the voice.

The call! Of course. The call to Patience. "Thank you."

"We wanted to make sure you would be here for the call, Mr. Mason."

"Yes. Yes, thank you. I'm here."

The phone clicked off and I held the buzzing receiver in my hand for a minute before setting it back on its cradle. I shivered as an air-conditioned breeze chilled me. The sheets were wet and twisted.

I lit a cigarette with shaking hands and sat up to wait

for the call. I was having these dreams almost every night. I began to feel better. I was awake, after all, away from the dreams.

After four miserable nights, I decided to cut my leave short and return to Vietnam. The leave had been a disaster. Gary had come to Hong Kong with me, but he left the second day for Taipei. I had bragged about the women there too convincingly, and the call girls in Hong Kong were too experienced, too professional, and too expensive. Resler packed up and left. I was going to follow, but when I tried to get a ticket to Taipei, I was refused because I was a serviceman on leave to Hong Kong, and that's where I'd have to stay. I don't know how Gary slipped through the red tape, but I was alone.

I had not the slightest desire to hire a call girl; I really just wanted to talk.

"I love you. Over," I said.

"I love you too. Are you okay? Over," said Patience. Her voice struggled weakly through the hiss and whistles of the radiophone connection.

"I'm fine. They say I won't have to fly any more combat assaults when I get back. Over."

"No?"

"That's what—"

"The party has not said 'over,' sir."

"Oh," said Patience. "Over."

"That's what the doc said when I left. He said that the Prospectors were going to put their last-month short-timers on ass-and-trash missions. Over."

"Oh, I hope they keep their word. Over."

"They will. These guys are not the Cav. Over."

I listened to the howl and echoes of interfering electronics, sorting out the words. Patience, my son, Jack, and my family had become phantoms. They were dreams, too. When we finally stopped talking, when her voice melted into the static, the tenuous link to my home fantasies broke. "Over," I said.

And there I sat, on the edge of the bed, just like after every other dream.

It was very similar to my hometown, Delray Beach. There was a beach; it ran north and south. There were palm trees, sandy roads, salt smells, girls playing in bikinis, and quietly rolling surf. It was late afternoon, almost dusk, and the sun glinted off parts of the heavy wire screen that surrounded the terrace. My table stood near the front of the terrace, allowing me the best view.

Voices chattered quietly behind me. Vietnamese sounds lovely even if you can't understand it.

It did feel like home.

Golden dolls, wearing bikinis so brief they were ribbons of modesty, strolled with pale GIs. As it got darker, the beach crowd broke up, drifting into the town.

"*Manh gioi khoung?* How are you?" said the smiling waitress. I noticed her Vietnamese glance of nerves and felt comforted by familiar behavior. "What would you like?" she asked.

I would like to jump you like a rabbit. "I'll have another beer, please," I said. The girl prompted immediate lust. Perhaps I could find solace in solace. My conscience immediately began to pummel me with shots of raw guilt, delivered at high voltage. "Monster!" it railed. "Married. Short-timer. And not only that, but you're just getting over the clap!" It was mercilessly rational. I succumbed to its barbs.

The waitress bowed and left to get the beer. I smiled as I watched my phantom flit naked from me to the girl, to hump her happily while she leaned over the bar.

She returned, beaming, friendlier, and served my beer. Her arm brushed mine and I felt warm electricity flicker between us. My mind savored salty-sweet smells and orgasmic contractions, hearing her voice as an echo. "Would you like . . ."

Her voice was obliterated by the sudden ripping, zipping howl of a stylus skidding across a record. She dropped to the floor and rolled under a table.

At the sound of crashing chairs and breaking glassware, I turned and saw the Vietnamese taking cover. Five men crouched low behind the bar. I sat alone on the porch and took a sip of beer. The girl knocked over a chair as she crawled toward the back of the porch.

All because of a stylus skidding across a record? Damn, they were even jumpier than I was. I looked around the bar. Nothing was happening. There was no fight. People peered from behind the bar and tables, looking up front. It had just been the sound that spooked them. They had absolutely no confidence that their city was secure. They knew the facts. The VC were everywhere.

Cowards, I thought. Anger flushed through me. I felt betrayed, revolted. They're really afraid.

For five minutes I had complete quiet as I watched the surf foam glow in the gathering dusk. At the end of that time, the bar, the customers, the porch, came back to life.

I paid my tab and walked to the room I had rented.

I sat against the wall on the bed, thinking about the panic at the bar. The old question "Why don't the Vietnamese fight the VC like the VC fight the Vietnamese?" seemed very valid. Without the support of the people, we were going to lose. And if they didn't care, why were we continuing to fight? Surely the people who were running this fiasco could see this, too. The signs were obvious. Plans leaked to the VC, reluctant combatants, mutinies in the ARVN, political corruption, Vietnamese marines fighting Vietnamese marines at Da Nang, and the ubiquitous Vietnamese idea that Ho would eventually win.

I stabbed a cigarette into an ashtray. Without American financial support and military support, the South Vietnamese government would have failed long ago, as a natural result of its lack of popular support.

The whole problem settled on my shoulders. In a few hours, I was going to voluntarily go back into battle and risk my scrawny neck for people who didn't care.

I stayed up and smoked cigarettes all night. I tried to sleep, only to jerk awake, sitting in bed, listening.

I was back at Dak To, home, the next day. Here, the war was simple. We did our job well, beat the VC almost every time, and kept them on the run. Here, I was a member of the honorable side. The reluctant, cowardly Vietnamese were not visible to remind me that they didn't care. I could go on believing that simply by killing more and more Communists we would win. When I crawled into my cot my first night back, I fell instantly asleep.

The next day, Gary and I sat on the deck of our Huey waiting for the grunts to finish eating. Their platoon was one of several that were pushing toward the west, scouting for the VC. We joked in familiar surroundings.

"You shoulda come, you know," said Gary.

"I tried, asshole. They wouldn't let me. How did you get a ticket?"

"I just went to the ticket counter and bought it."

"Well, you must have looked like a civilian, because they wouldn't sell me anything."

"It's really a shame. You missed Grass Mountain."

"What's that?"

"Grass Mountain is packed with geisha houses. Wanna know what it's like to go to a geisha house?"

"No."

"They start off with a bath. Just you and two naked girls. They wash you first, then soak you, then massage you."

"Didn't you hear me?"

"I heard you," Gary said. "The two of them massage you so well you think you're going to crack. Then, at the perfect moment, one of the girls sits on you and puts you out of your misery."

I nodded my head with closed eyes, kicking myself for not getting laid when I had the chance.

"And that's just the beginning."

"Just the beginning!"

"That's right. It takes hours to get out of this place. They give you more baths, and tea and food and massages, to keep you going, and then they pass you down the line to teams of two or three girls who work you over in different ways." Gary's face brightened at his memories.

"I never even heard of Grass Mountain when I was there," I lamented.

"Never heard of it? Where the hell were you?"

The next day I was flying with Sky King. In the middle of a laager, a grunt lieutenant came to our ship. "We just had a newsman wounded. Will you guys pick him up?"

"Sure," I said.

"The squad leader with the guy said it was a sniper. They say they've got the place secured."

"No problem. Where are they?"

The lieutenant showed me on his map. They were only a mile away. When I turned to get into the ship, Sky King and the crew chief were all ready to go. I strapped in as Sky King cranked up.

Sky King flew at fifty knots heading for the place.

"Over there," I pointed to four or five soldiers standing around a prone man in a thicket of leafless trees. "You see them?"

"Got 'em."

As we flew by, the men hit the dirt, leaving one man standing. He was aiming a movie camera at us.

"Great place for a landing," said Sky King.

The base of the clearing was wide enough for our ship, but the scrawny branches twenty feet off the ground crowded over the circle, making it too tight to get in.

"Axle One-Six," I radioed. "Can you move to a better clearing?" Sky King circled, looking for a way to get through the trees.

"Negative, Prospector. We're still getting sniper fire, and this guy is wounded pretty bad."

Sky King set up an approach and closed in. As he got to the treetops, it became obvious that he was going to hit branches with the main rotor, so he aborted.

When the squad saw us heading across the LZ, they radioed, "Can you make it, Prospector?"

Sky King shook his head. "I can't get in there. You want to try it?"

I nodded and took the controls. While Sky King had approached, I thought I saw a way. "We'll get in, Axle One-Six. Just hang on."

The plan was simple. I would come in ninety degrees to Sky King's last try and then turn sharp. I thought that in a bank the rotors could slip through the narrow slot that Sky King had shot for. I lined up on a tangent to the clearing and let down.

I hit the turn fast, banked hard over, and as we slipped toward the ground, I saw that I was going to hit some stuff anyway. The main rotor smashed some dead branches, sounding like machine-gun fire. I flared for the landing and we were down.

"Great. Now how are you going to get out?" said Sky King.

I didn't answer, because I didn't know how I was going to get out. The grunts grabbed the wounded man. He was unconscious, his fatigue blouse sopping with his blood. At that point I noticed the cameraman standing back filming the whole thing. The grunts were prone beside him, laying out cover fire toward the jungle. When I saw him aim the camera toward the cockpit, I sat a little straighter, and thought cool thoughts, in case those, too, might somehow be recorded. The crew chief called that we were ready, and the cameraman jumped on board.

In fact, there was no acceptable way to get out. There was not enough room to accelerate and bank back out through the slot. Some of the high branches hung over our rotor disk. By the book, we were trapped.

But I had seen rotor blades stand up to incredible stress before, so I decided to take the brute-force option. I picked up to the hover, turned the tail until it matched a slot in the overhanging branches, and then pulled the pitch. We climbed straight up twenty feet before the rotors smashed into cane-thick branches at nearly every point of their circle. It sounded like the rotors were being smashed to pieces. Seconds later we cleared the treetops and I nosed over, accelerating toward the airstrip five miles away.

"Someday you're going to hit a branch that's just a little too big," Sky King said after a long quiet.

"What then?" I asked.

"Then your ship's going to come apart, and you're going to kill yourself and everybody around you."

"Now *that's* frightening," I said. "I think maybe I oughta quit this job and go home."

"This guy's still alive, sir." The crew chief's voice buzzed in my headphones. "The cameraman says he's the *president* of CBS News. Imagine that."

"Ain't that a kick," Sky King said. "I guess he got bored with his nice safe desk job, the dumb shit."

When we landed at the hospital tent at the 101st, the cameraman jumped out and filmed his boss being unloaded. He filmed Gary and me in the cockpit, then put the camera down and gave us a salute.

I nodded, brought the rotors up to operating, and leapt

off the pad. As I flew back to retrieve the empty thermos containers we left with the grunts, I recalled the cameraman's salute and felt slightly heroic.

When we shut down that night, Sky King showed me the creases and nicks in the rotors and scolded me. "Look at this. You've ruined them."

"Naw. They're fine. Just creased is all. No holes. Look at the bright side. The guy's alive."

"Yeah, but look at those rotors."

During the second week of July, Operation Hawthorne began winding up. The patrols and reconnaissance companies were getting very little opposition in the battle zone. The NVA had slipped away.

"If they're gone, and we killed two thousand of them, we won," said Gary.

"What did we win? We don't have any more real estate, no new villages are under American control, and it took everything we had to stop them," I said.

"We won the battle. More of them got killed than us. It's that simple."

"Doesn't it bother you that it takes so much equipment and men to beat the NVA? If we were equally equipped, we'd lose."

"Yeah, but we aren't equally equipped, and they lose. Besides that, I have a month to go and I don't give a shit."

"Unless they make you fly assaults during your last month."

"If they do that, then I'll give a shit."

While the First Cav slipped unceremoniously back to An Khe, the 101st decided to end the operation with a parade. There would be no spectators except for the news reporters—unless you want to count the men in the parade as spectators, and of course they were.

Hundreds of bone-weary soldiers gathered at the artillery emplacements and began the five-mile march back to the airstrip. They marched, in parade step, along the dusty road. Insects buzzed in the saturated air. No virgins threw flowers. No old ladies cried. No strong men wept. They marched to their own muffled footsteps.

"I bet they're pissed off," said Gary, leaning against his door window, staring down at the column. "Especially when they look up and see all these empty helicopters flying around."

We flew up and down the column in four V's at 500 feet during the entire march. Supposedly we were generating excitement, or underscoring a memorable event. But according to a grunt, "We wanted to know why you fuckers wouldn't come down and give us a fucking ride."

When the head of the column finally reached the 101st section of the airstrip, the band played, the Hueys whooshed overhead, and the general beamed.

With all the troopers back in camp, noses were counted. Nearly twenty people were unaccounted for. It was presumed that these men were all dead. There would be a search operation to find their bodies in a few days.

The next day, while the missing moldered, the 101st had a party for the survivors. Their camp was within walking distance, but our aviator egos demanded that we fly. After seeing too much death and injury, the survivors celebrated life. We had a boisterously good time to emphasize that we were still alive.

Business was so slow during the next few days that Gary and I decided to follow up a rumor. Other than the daily ice flight, and an occasional ass-and-trash, air operations in support of the 101st had stopped while loose ends were tied up.

The rumor was that our old First Cav company, the Preachers, was camped at Cheo Reo, a hundred miles south of us. So we went to Ringknocker and said, "Major, can we use a Huey to go visit some old friends of ours?" The question sounded stupid as I asked it. I wouldn't have even thought about asking Farris or Shaker for a ship in the Cav. Helicopters were never, never used for personal business, unless maybe you were bringing in a load of ivory and you outranked everybody else.

"Visit friends?" Ringknocker stood in front of his tent dressed in shorts, on the way to the shower we had built. "What kind of friends do you have in Vietnam?"

"Our old company is camped down by Cheo Reo," said Gary.

"Oh, those old friends." Ringknocker seemed relieved. "Sure. Go ahead. But"—he smiled warmly—"be home before dark."

And that was that. I didn't even have to get the ice. Sky King agreed to take the trip for me. We had at our disposal a half-a-million-dollar helicopter, two hundred gallons of fuel, a full crew, and nothing to do but drive south to visit some friends. It was like getting the family car.

After lunch, we climbed up into the cumulus sky. Crossing Pleiku at 3000 feet, we changed course to 140 degrees for the flight to Cheo Reo.

"We'll get some storms outta those clouds this afternoon," said Gary.

I nodded. I was flying at the base of the clouds, changing course now and then to thread between the gaps. Below, the clouds cast dark shadows on the jungle. The river beneath us changed from gleaming sparkle to dull black, in patches.

"There she is." I jutted my chin forward. After nearly an hour of flying, we saw our objective.

"Ah, good old Cheo Reo. . . . I remember it well." Gary smiled. We'd camped here once with the Prospectors.

I let down and circled a field where I saw a bunch of Hueys parked.

"That's them." Gary keyed the mike to broadcast. "Preacher Control, this is Prospector Oh-four-two."

No answer. Gary repeated the transmission. "Of course they don't answer," he said. "They wouldn't be using the old frequency anymore."

Meanwhile, I saw a group of men shielding their eyes with their hands, staring up at us. "It's them all right. I can see Connors," I said.

I rolled out of the orbit and let down. We landed next to one of the Preacher ships, killed the turbine, and stepped out.

"In-fucking-credible!" said Connors. "Don't tell me. You were on your way to Saigon and you got lost, right?"

"Wrong. We're on our way to Paris and we stopped for fuel," I said. I saw some more men walking our way. One of them was Farris.

"Mason and Resler!" Farris said. "I don't believe it. What the heck are you two doing down here all by yourselves?"

"Just visiting, Captain," said Gary.

"Really? Just visiting?" Farris was trying to figure just how such frivolity was possible. His First Cav logic could not fathom it. "They let you . . . just *visit* people?"

"That's the way they do it on the outside, Captain," I said.

Farris shook his head in wonderment. "Well, come on over and join us. The cook just made up a new batch of brew."

All the way to the mess tent, Gary and I had our backs patted and hands shaken by friends we hadn't seen for two months. At the mess tent, we also saw a whole bunch of new faces. As a matter of fact, almost all the faces we saw were new people. They were breaking up that old gang of mine. I saw Major Astor walking out to the flight line. His nemesis, John Hall, was no longer in the company. Banjo was still there. And so was Riker. Kaiser had gone to work for Air America. And that was it. A few old faces, some rumors, were all that was left of the original Preachers. The second shift was taking over. They were moving into An Khe, never realizing all the work that the original guys had done to make it the way it was. It was funny how the hardships that I hated the most became the core around which I built memories of camaraderie.

We sat around drinking coffee and telling war stories.

The Preachers had been overrun on an overnight laager. Four new pilots had been wounded. And a month before, a new pilot was killed in an assault.

We told them about the gunship that had landed with everybody unconscious (it had become the Phantom Gunship), about hauling the reluctant ARVNs to the fort, and how the NVA overran the 101st artillery position. But most of all we bragged about how much better we lived under the reasonable leadership of Ringknocker. Ice runs, beer parties, Vietnamese labor to build bunkers, and ambulances loaded with party girls: just a way of life with us, all right. As we listed these things, calculated to shock their Spartan sensibilities, Farris began to look uncomfortable.

"That guy would be hung in the Cav," he said with a knowing nod.

"He gets the job done," I said.

Farris nodded, but I could tell he didn't believe me. If the Cav wasn't doing it, it wasn't getting done.

We had chow and stayed longer than we should have. The sun was low in the sky, leaving us an hour or so to get back. We said good-bye for the last time.

"Hang in there, short-timers," said Connors.

"Yeah, it's not long now," I said.

"Don't forget, we'll have a party when all this is over," Connors called as we walked away.

I called back, "Call us when you get to town."

The last missions we flew at Dak To were to recover bodies. We dropped teams at various spots around the bombing zone, and waited for them literally to sniff out the bodies, which had become very ripe during the few days we had been packing up the camp.

We just had a party not too long ago, I said silently to a lumpy body bag. Someone tried to push down a knee that jutted awkwardly. The knee moved down but sprang back up when let go. The smell grew so strong that I gagged. You should have been there, I thought.

On July 17 we were back at our permanent camp at Phan Rang for a four-day rest. Next stop would be Tuy Hoa.

Gary and I had passed our thirty-day-to-go mark on the twelfth. Four replacement pilots had come to the company. We really believed that we would be staying back at the camp to fly admin flights for the battalion or the ARVNs.

"I'm sorry, but it just didn't work out that way," said Deacon. "Ringknocker had been to some pre-mission briefings and says we're going to be very busy at Tuy Hoa. We have to support two units, one being Korean. We're just going to need every pilot we have."

I looked at Gary. Gary looked at me. We both looked at Deacon.

"So why has everybody been saying we'd be doing admin flights during our last month?" I said.

"We thought that that's the way it would be." Deacon looked unhappy. It was ruining his expectations, too. The "last month" program was fading to the dream that it probably had been all along. "I know that both of you are getting pretty jittery. Just keep doing what you've been doing and hang on. You'll be home before you know it. If it helps, just remember the rest of us have more than six months to go."

"Well, Deacon, I hope that when you get short, they give you some kind of a break. I'm telling you now that you'll need one. I do," I said.

"I know. I'm sorry." Deacon left the tent.

Now I had to reset my clock. Every sunset had put me one day closer to getting out of here. My mental calendar had ticked off the moments until it believed that it had reached zero. Adding twenty-five more sunsets to the calendar was a real strain.

"Look," I said to Doc DaVinci, "I'm tired. I can't sleep at night. I have to take tranquilizers to function. I need a break. Can't you do something?"

"I'd like to help you, Bob. But physically you're fine."

I glared at him. "Look at me. I weigh less than a hundred and twenty pounds. I look like shit!"

"Another three weeks of being skinny won't hurt you."

"It's not that I'm skinny; it's *why* I am skinny. I'm worn out. I'm frayed. I want to fly admin flights like hundreds of other pilots do every day."

"Well, if you tell me you're afraid to fly, I can ground you."

"If I tell you I'm afraid to fly, you'll ground me?"

"Yes."

Why is he setting me up like this? I thought. Why does he want me to say that I'm afraid? Why can't he just use his professional authority and put a medical restriction on me?

"I can't say that. I'm not afraid to fly, I just don't think I or Gary or any short-timer should have to fly combat assaults anymore. We have each flown more than a thousand missions already. Isn't that enough? Why couldn't they bring up a couple of Saigon warriors to take our place? They could use the experience, and Gary and I could finish off our tours flying VIPs around or something."

"I told you what I have to do."

"I can't do that."

"Well, just don't take the tranquilizers during the day," said Da Vinci. That was the end of the conversation.

Gary and I sat at a table watching the Prospectors whoop it up at the party that night. Neither of us could join in. The laughing skull was no longer funny.

We had camped on the beach at Tuy Hoa for one day when a storm struck. Seventy-mile-an-hour winds blew clouds of sand in horizontal sheets. Tents began to collapse. Hueys approaching along the beach had to fly sideways. The only direction their noses could point in was into the wind.

Gary, Stoopy, and I had pitched our tent a quarter of a mile nearer the ocean than the headquarters tent. We got back from a mission in time to see Stoopy wrestling with the flapping canvas. Blankets, mosquito netting, and clothes were rolling across the dunes like tumbleweed.

"Jesus Christ, Stoopy. Why did you let the tent collapse?" yelled Gary.

"This is just like a desert storm you see in the movies." Stoopy grinned, shoveling sand into what he believed would be a protective berm.

"Shit," I said, "let's get this fucker nailed down."

"The wind keeps pulling the tent pegs out," said Stoopy.

"So we make dead men," I shouted in the wind.

"What the hell are you talking about?" yelled Gary. He had wrapped a towel around his neck and head to keep the sand out.

"A dead man is something you tie a rope to and bury,"

I said, blinking. "We can tie the ropes to sandbags and then bury them."

"All right, let's do it." Stoopy's shout barely rose above the wind.

Stoopy filled sandbags while Gary and I went around the tent tying them to the ropes and burying them. When we finished, the tent was concave on the windward side; it shook, but it held. We ducked inside to try to get the sand off our gear. The salty sand stuck to everything. My carbine gritted when I worked the bolt. I watched Gary slapping his cot with a towel, trying to dust about ten pounds of sand away. Stoopy lay on his cot, on a mixed pile of clothes, blankets, and sand, eating another candy bar.

"Stoopy, why don't you get that fucking sand off your stuff?" I said.

"It'll just get sandy again."

I shook my head in disgust.

"It will. I'll clean it up before I go to sleep tonight."

"You're a slob, Stoopy," said Gary.

"So?" said Stoopy. "Somebody has to do it."

Gary and I laughed. Stoopy's grin showed the chocolate stains on his teeth.

With two weeks to go, I had very little tolerance for a person like Stoopy. But I realized that his intentions were good. He was friendly; he really wanted to be a good pilot; he wanted the Americans to win the war; and he flew into the assaults without showing fear.

The problem was that he was a terrible pilot ("professional copilot," we called them); he was overweight; he was a slob; he was juvenile; and he was downright dangerous.

At Dak To, he had unloaded a parked flare ship by throwing the flares out the door. Unfortunately, the flare canisters were still attached by lines from their fuses to the deck. Normally this allowed them to ignite automatically as they were pushed out at 2000 or 3000 feet. But since Stoopy was unloading the ship on the ground, he was soon surrounded by a giant cloud of white smoke and blinding magnesium flames. Strangely, he was not hurt. He was also famous among us for not being able to keep himself in his formation slot. In just the few months he'd been with the Prospectors, he'd become known as the "smiling menace."

Naturally, when battalion requested that Ringknocker send his best pilot to Saigon to work for the VIPs, Ringknocker sent Stoopy. All the pilots had to vote for the best pilot, and he would be sent to Saigon. At the meeting Ringknocker told us the rules: Vote for Stoopy. "We have a terrible shortage of pilots already, so battalion gets what I can afford," said Ringknocker. "Stoopy Stoddard is what I can afford. You gentlemen will vote for Stoopy and then we can get back to work."

When I had first dealt with the Koreans at Bong Son valley, I was impressed by their zeal. When we drove by the Korean bridge guards, they jumped to attention with a shout. When we were mortared, the Koreans were the ones who came back to the camp carrying VC heads and the mortar tube. From the first time I saw them, I thought we'd be better off just giving the Koreans the country, if they could take it. They probably would've.

At Tuy Hoa, we flew missions for the Koreans. At the pickup point, Gary and I watched five or six Korean rangers load our ship with food and ammo in less than a minute. Very few Koreans spoke English, so when the ship was loaded, a young soldier ran out to us and gave us a slip of paper with a list of coordinates written on it. The soldier saluted and left. We were to fly to these places, and they would know what to do.

At the first stop, the ship was barely on the ground when a whole team of Koreans unloaded their portion of the load in seconds. No words were spoken. At the next stop, the same thing happened. And the next. By eleven o'clock in the morning, we had finished a resupply mission that would have taken us all day had we been resupplying Americans.

All the Korean ROKs were hand-picked, highly trained volunteers. They were dedicated professionals who took the job seriously, and because they were performing under the watchful eyes of their original teachers, they were out to prove their abilities. They did.

We flew almost every day. The missions were numerous, but I don't recall them very well. I was preoccupied. Gary had received his orders to leave Vietnam, but I hadn't. I sent letters to Patience to contact the Pentagon. I checked daily with our admin section. I believed that it was possible for the army to forget that I was even there.

On a rare day off, I dragged a parachute canopy (that Gary and I had scrounged from a treetop) to the shore. I spread it out so that it made a circle of soft nylon fifty feet across. Carrying a towel, I walked to the center of the chute and lay down to sunbathe. I wanted to look tropical for Patience. I was trying to be healthy. I had even stopped smoking again, on the chance that God would be moved to spare me.

I heard someone clumping along the boards that led back up to the tent areas. My eyes were closed while the sun baked me.

"Hey, Mason, what are you doing?"

I looked up. "Sunbathing, sir."

Ringknocker grinned and began to step on my giant beach blanket. "I had something—"

"Don't walk on this," I quickly interrupted as Ringknocker put his foot on the parachute.

"What?" Ringknocker stopped and stepped back.

"Don't walk on this. This is my beach blanket. People

don't walk on other people's beach blankets," I said seriously.

Ringknocker first showed a smile. But that faded to concern as he saw that I wasn't kidding.

"You're serious?"

"Yes."

Ringknocker nodded sadly and walked back up the board path.

Behind him I saw the maintenance ship take off carrying a damaged rotor blade attached to the sling hook. Maj. Steve Richards, the maintenance officer, had been hitching the rotor blade to his ship's cargo hook to carry it out to sea and drop it. He did nothing more dangerous in this war than to check out freshly repaired helicopters. When the blade had been attached to the hook, Richards asked if anyone wanted to go for a little ride. Five men, mostly mechanics, jumped on board.

As the ship took off, it became obvious to the men on the ground that carrying a rotor blade dangling vertically beneath the ship was not going to work. It swung wildly under the ship as Richards gained speed. The maintenance sergeant ran after the ship, yelling, "Major Richards! Stop! Stop! The blade is swinging!"

I saw the blade whipping around under the ship at 300 feet. Apparently Richards could not tell that the blade was gyrating under him. Before he reached the water, the blade slashed up behind the ship, knocking off a section of the tail rotors. Richards flared back, trying to slow the ship, but it was no use. As he flared, the blade knifed forward under the ship and swept up and hit his main rotor. The damaged main rotor flew off. Time seemed to stop, and I saw the ship nose down, invert, and then disappear behind some tents and smash onto the beach. It fell like an anvil. There was a brief moment of quiet after the crash and then a *whoosh*. The flattened Huey burst into flames. Orange flames first, as the fuel burned, then bright-white flames as the metal ignited. Helicopters contain a lot of magnesium.

People ran toward the ship, only to be driven back by the fire.

Major Richards, his crew chief, his gunner, and three mechanics were incinerated. I was still alone on my precious beach blanket. I cried.

That evening, on the beach, six flight helmets were placed on stakes in a line. The chaplain conducted the service.

My one comfort in the hell of waiting was that I had a companion. Gary and I flew together always. Then, with five days to go on our tours, Gary left for Phan Rang.

"Don't worry, Bob. They'll get your orders."

"I know."

"Really, it's just a minor fuck-up. Ringknocker's going to tell you tomorrow or the next day that you can leave. Really."

"I know. I'm okay."

"So, I'll see you back in Phan Rang in a day or two. Okay?"

"Of course. A day or two. See you soon."

"Good-bye."

" 'Bye."

Gary ran out to the ship going back to our main base. After a few days of out-processing, he'd be in Saigon, getting on a big bird for the States.

Ops assigned me to fly with a new pilot, Lieutenant Fisher, the next day.

Fisher and I flew to a place in the jungles west of Tuy Hoa to pick up a reconnaissance squad. When we flew to the coordinates given us, it was an almost circular funnel of a valley. The squad was at the bottom of the giant funnel. They told us on the radio that they were getting occasional sniper fire and that we should be careful in the approach. I took the opportunity to show Fisher how to get down to the bottom of this place without getting shot.

I flew toward the funnel at 80 or 90 knots, heading on a tangent to the rim of the funnel.

"I'm gonna keep us low level all the way to the bottom," I said.

Fisher nodded from the right side of the cockpit. This was his first mission in-country. For a second I saw myself there, wide-eyed, riding with Leese on that low-level run in Happy Valley. I had been overwhelmed by the speed at which things happened, and I'm sure that Fisher was experiencing the same feeling.

As I crossed the rim, I banked hard, putting the ship level with the incline. "If we stay close to the treetops and keep moving fast, they won't get us."

We spiraled down the funnel. The squad called and said that they heard many shots. "Don't worry," I said to Fisher. "They're shooting blind."

There was a stand of trees at the bottom that would force me either to pull away from the tree cover or to go through the trees. Since the whole point of this approach was to maintain cover, I chose to go through the trees. Near the end of the spiraling ride, I leveled the ship and rushed for the stand of trees. The squad was behind them. As I leveled, I had also dropped below the trees out of sight of the squad. Because we didn't come over the top or to the side, the squad assumed that we had crashed. When they called us, I was busting through the trees. I had swerved off to one side of the stand and then swung back in fast. This allowed me to bank very sharply so that the Huey and its big rotor disk squeezed between two tall trees thirty feet apart. After hurdling through the trees, I flared the ship quickly to make the landing. The radio operator who had been asking where we were said, "Oh." We landed right in front of the squad.

As the team quickly loaded, I noticed muzzle flashes ahead of us. The team leader pointed all around, at places he had seen shots fired. We were right on time. The squad was surrounded, and the VC were moving down the funnel to get them. Altogether there were eight grunts, not a giant load at sea level but enough that climbing out of this place was going to be slow. "I'm going to accelerate across this field as fast as I can, and then we'll do a cyclic climb up the side of that hill." I hovered for a second, then nosed over hard, lumbering off across the field. I kept the ship at 4 or 5 feet until we reached 90 knots. Then I pulled the cyclic back and the ship swooped up. The climb was very fast at first because we were using the accumulated energy from the acceleration run. As we neared the top of the funnel, however, we slowed to a grinding crawl. I knew that this was when they would be shooting in front of us, taking a lead, as a hunter does with a duck. So when the ship was straining hard, with very little forward velocity, I did an abrupt pedal turn at the top of the climb and headed back in the opposite direction. That took everybody by surprise, and I heard shouts from the back. Fisher involuntarily reached for the controls, but stopped himself. A few seconds later we were beyond the ridge, heading back to the beach.

"Beautiful!" said Fisher. He was grinning.

"Just remember, keep yourself low when there are trees, keep moving as fast as you can, and never use the same route twice." I grinned as I said that Leese had told me the same thing a year ago.

When I was flying, my life was in my own hands. When I was back at the camp, the army was in control of my destiny. And the army still hadn't found my orders

"This is a hot one," said the operations officer, Major

Ramon. Every pilot in the Prospectors was at the briefing. The major droned on with battle plans, frequencies, ship numbers, crew assignments, and suspected enemy locations. It was so much noise to me. My hand was writing information down on my pad, but my mind was in shock. Two days to go, said my mind. Two fucking days to go and I'm going on a hot one. "We will make a total of three lifts this morning," said the major. Three chances. Step right up. Three, count them, three Huey rides in a combat assault absolutely free. Win yourself a body bag. Become a hometown hero. Become a memory early in your life. "Okay, you've got everything you'll need. Let's go."

I walked across the quarter mile of sand with Fisher. I kept checking my gear, like a novice. Pistol, flak vest, maps, chest protector. Oh, yeah, the chest protector is in the ship. Helmet. Courage. Where is my courage? Oh, yeah, my courage is in the ship.

"Lose something?" asked Fisher. He had been watching me check myself, patting my pockets and gear.

"No, I've got everything."

"This is really exciting," said Fisher.

"Yes. It's very exciting." You dumb shit. I hated Fisher when he said that. Exciting? Is that like excitement at the old football game? It's exciting to get killed? Fool. Wait a few months and then tell me it's exciting.

Fisher climbed up to the rotor head, and I checked the air frame. As I opened the radio hatch at the nose, an orderly ran up to me and said, "They want you back at ops, sir."

"For what?"

"I don't know, sir. Major Ramon told me to tell you they have something for you at ops."

"Right." I looked up at Fisher. "I'll be right back." Fisher nodded.

I pushed the flap aside and walked into the ops tent.

Ramon wasn't there. "Where's Major Ramon?" I asked the sergeant.

"I don't know, sir."

"Well, what did they want me for?"

"Who wanted you, sir?"

"Ramon, I thought. I was just told that somebody had something for me here, and I'm here. Is this some kind of joke?"

"I don't know, sir. I don't know anything about it."

I heard the turbines winding up to shrills behind me. The Prospectors were cranking up. I turned and left. If I didn't hurry, I'd hold up the mission. I ran across the sand. A hundred yards away the lead ship took off. What the fuck. I waved. "Hey, wait. There's only one pilot in my ship!" I ran faster. Then the whole flight took off. I stood in the sand, watching the flight cruise west, completely confused. A Jeep I hadn't noticed before drove back from the flight line. The driver stopped next to me. "Want a ride, sir?" The driver was the orderly that had come with the message. All my flight gear was in the Jeep. I got in.

"What the fuck is going on? Where's Major Ramon?"

"Major Ramon is flying your ship, sir."

I wasn't the only one who thought I needed a break.

The next day, August 10, I was called into the operations tent and handed orders. I was to proceed to Saigon to catch an eleven o'clock morning flight on the fourteenth. I was exhilarated.

That afternoon, I was flying a Huey back to Phan Rang. The ship was due for a major overhaul, and so was I. I flew along the coast and went through a notch in a tall hill next to the ocean. As we crossed the ridge, the crew chief, a new guy, called me. "Sir, we're being shot at from that hill. Shall we engage?"

Shall we engage? I couldn't believe what I heard. Shall we engage?

"Not today, Sergeant." I turned to Staglioni, the co-pilot, and grinned. "Not today." I laughed so hard that I cried.

Sitting in the soft airline seat, I savored the air-conditioned crispness of the air and breathed in the scents of the passing stewardesses. I had a grin on my face that wouldn't quit. I was the Cheshire cat. The man who sat next to me was Ken Klayman, a guy I had met on the *Croatan*. We were both aboard a chartered Pan American 707 going to the land of the big PX. We were no longer in-country.

"I suppose now we could say we're out-country?"

"Yes. Definitely out-country," said Klayman.

"It seems like a dream."

"Yeah. It is nice to wake up from a bad one. And just when you thought they had you."

Since I had left Phan Rang, every time I checked the time I remembered that the maid had stolen my watch. The maid who neatly arranged my gear for me, who'd never steal a thing—until the day you left. I had considered the watch a charm.

It had been lifted once before—the first night I tried out the new shower we'd built in the Preachers. I hung it on a nail, took the shower, and it was gone.

"I'll get it for you," Rubenski had said.

"You know who took it?"

"Not yet. But don't worry. I'll find the fuck. Stole your grandfather's watch. What slime."

An hour later Rubenski walked into my tent carrying the watch. "Here ya go, sir. And don't worry; it won't happen again," Rubenski said.

"Hey. Thanks a lot. You're amazing."

"It was nothing," he said. "Just remember, Lake Tahoe . . ."

Klayman and I reverted to early adolescence during

the flight back. Neither of us could sleep during the twenty-hour trip. Instead we cracked jokes and pretended we were flying the plane. The pilots we played didn't know much. "Compass? What's that?" "Holding pattern? Are you crazy?" "I can't put the gear down. We're too close to the rooftops."

We landed at the Philippines and then headed for Hawaii. At Honolulu, we were invited to get off the plane to stretch our legs, buy gifts, and such. Klayman told me to pick up a small chess set so we could play on the long nonstop flight to Fort Dix, New Jersey.

I found a small traveling set at one of the airport gift shops. I also grabbed a *Newsweek* and went to the counter to pay. The clerk, a young woman, took my money and asked if I was returning from Vietnam. I said yes, proudly. She suddenly glared at me and said, "Murderer." I stared at her for a long minute, feeling confused. Then I smiled. I realized that she was talking about someone else.

Epilogue: And Then What Happened?

Ground war here in Vietnam is taking on a new cast—with more and more direct conflict between U.S. and North Vietnamese troops. At this point, no one is sure how far this dangerous confrontation will go.
—*U.S. News & World Report*, August 15, 1966

"I made it." I smiled as Patience ran toward me. She was crying. Jack toddled across the parking lot at the bus station, holding my sister's hand. He looked bewildered; I had been away half his life.

"I thought you'd never get here," said Patience.

We spent our first week in an apartment my father had rented for us near the beach. We spent the days at the beach, which I enjoyed. My nights were troubled. I kept waking up three feet in the air above the bed, frightening Patience. The dreams continued relentlessly, though the dreams were not what woke me.

Back at Fort Wolters, Texas, I began training to become an instructor pilot. During this training phase, my sister asked me to come to her wedding. She wanted me to wear my uniform.

"I don't think people would like to see me in uniform, Susan."

"You look so good in your dress blues. And I'm proud of you."

"Okay."

I flew to Fort Myers for the wedding. I wore the uniform, the silver wings, and a bunch of ribbons. Looking good. During the reception, I heard some laughter when I walked in the door. A man I did not know asked loudly, "Hey, where's your flag?" I flushed with anger. The place was quiet for a minute, people looking at me. Susan looked horrified. A fight at her wedding? No, no fight. The only fight going on was the one inside my head. I should have gone over and decked him. Alas, there are no time machines. I cooled myself by thinking, If he knew me, he wouldn't have said that.

I took the instructor-pilot job very seriously. It gave me the chance to cull out potential Stoopy Stoddards. During the two-month cycle each group of four students spent with me, I taught them stuff not covered in the school syllabus. The school was interested in getting numbers out the door. I was interested in their survival. For example, the school no longer allowed simulated forced landings to the ground. Instead the instructor had to take control of the ship and abort the landing before the ship hit the ground. I thought that actually skidding across the ground, finishing the autorotation, was a key experience, so I let each student do it.

Instructor pilots flew half days. The flights alternated weekly, so that you flew mornings one week, afternoons the next. I spent my free time learning photography. I taught myself how to print photographs and enlarged some of the pictures I took in Vietnam. (I won an army photo contest with one.) Invariably, I tore my displays off the wall. I wanted to say how I felt about the war, but my pictures weren't doing it. I took pictures around central Texas, mostly of abandoned farmhouses, and my technical skill grew with the practice.

A few of us who flew the H-23 Hiller were picked to cross-train in the new army trainer, the Hughes TH-55A. When I became rated in both trainers, I became a substitute instructor pilot in addition to my normal load. The demand for new pilots was growing monthly.

The new trainer was falling out of the sky, killing veteran pilots and their students. The ships were always found the same way—nose down in the ground, mush inside the cockpit. One or two pilots and their students were killed each week. After two months of this, an IP called in as he crashed. He said that the ship had tucked n a simulated forced landing and the controls had no effect on the dive. Then he died. They found out that if the cyclic was moved forward when the power was cut, the ship would immediately nose over and dive. Once in this position, pulling back on the cyclic was useless.

Hughes test pilots discovered that the ship could be saved if the pilot pushed forward on the cyclic (not back, as he would instinctively do), and if he had 1000 feet of air to wait for the recovery. We flew at 500 feet in the training areas.

We were told to demonstrate the tuck and its hairy recovery to all our students. I had it shown to me a couple of times, but I felt that students were not going to be able to appreciate the subtlety of the maneuver, especially since they were still trying to get the trainers into the sky and back to the ground in one piece. I found that a vivid explanation of the tuck effect and an immovable hand in front of the cyclic were adequate.

Four students stayed with me for a two-month cycle,

and then four more would take their place. They were overjoyed to be in flight school. So was I. I flew all the time. I began to know each of the hundreds of confined areas the army had rented from the local farmers. Even though we had so many places to train, the fact that there were fifteen hundred helicopters milling around the sky each training day made flying dangerous. Midair collisions, especially between two solo students, became commonplace.

One afternoon, I cut the power on a student, near a grassy clearing used to demonstrate forced landings. The student reacted quickly, bottomed the pitch, maintained airspeed, and maneuvered the ship toward the clearing. He was doing just fine. Unknown to us, however, another ship was autorotating to the same field at the same moment. I noticed a shadow above us while we sank toward the clearing. He was descending faster than we were. As his skids closed on our rotors, I knew there was no way out. If I moved the disk, the rotors would swing up into his skids. We were already descending as fast as the ship could go. At the last second, the other ship saw us and jerked violently away. By my reckoning, he missed us by an inch. But close calls in training were not what was bothering me during the night.

"Every morning the truck comes. I have to open the back door; I know what's out there, but I still go to the door," I said. "It's always the same. The driver backs the truck to the door and says, 'How many do you want?' He points to a truck of babies. Dead babies. I always gag at the sight. They all look dead, but then I see an eyelid blink in the pile, then another." I stopped.

"Then what happens?" Doc Ryan flicked an ash on his desk.

"Then I always answer, 'Two hundred pounds, Jake.' I laugh when I say it. Jake picks up a pitchfork and stabs it into the pile and drops a couple of corpses on a big scale. 'Nearly ten pounds a head,' he says. Inside my head, I'm yelling for him to stop, that the babies aren't dead, but Jake just keeps loading the scale. Each time he stabs a kid, it squirms on the fork, but Jake doesn't notice a thing."

"Then what?"

"Then it ends."

"What do you think it means?"

"I was hoping you'd tell me."

"I'm more interested in what you think it means."

"I don't know."

"Well, time's up, anyway. Think about it. Same time next week?"

"Okay."

Dr. Ryan, Captain Ryan, led me to the door.

"The tranqs helping?"

"They help me sleep, but I can't fly with them."

"A little more time," he said. "You'll be back up."

I was grounded. Seeing Doc Ryan each week was part of my new schedule. This was the second time I had been grounded at Wolters.

The first time, I was with one of my best students, landing at the main heliport. At the end of the training sessions, the heliport was normally crowded with hundreds of returning trainers. Usually the instructor flew the ship in this congestion, especially on the flight line, where the competing rotor wash made hovering tricky. As I hovered toward the parking slot, I felt the ship rear back. I pushed the cyclic forward, then realized that the ship wasn't falling backward. I was. I squeezed the intercom trigger. "You got it." The student grabbed the controls instantly, thinking I was just giving him one more surprise test. He maneuvered into the slot, landed, and shut down. While he did that, I fought the dizzy feeling. Back at the debriefing, I complimented him on his landing and gave him a double-A grade for the ride. Then I went directly to the flight surgeon. He could find nothing physically wrong, but he grounded me for a month.

Being a grounded pilot in the midst of flying pilots is torture. I worked in the tower, kept records, and drove trucks out to the stage fields. I was performing a job normally held by a pfc.

During the month, the nightmares continued and my wake-ups became worse. I lived long nights alone in my own home. After Patience and Jack were asleep, I paced, read, built model airplanes, anything to become sleepy. Generally I would get to bed at four or five in the morning.

I reasoned that things would only get worse if I didn't fly. The trauma of being grounded was inflaming the problem. When I saw the flight surgeon again, I told him everything was just fine. I felt great. Sleeping like a log. When can I fly? He said that if I went another week doing as well, he would put me back up. And he did.

I taught flying again. I showed students how to get into and out of confined areas, how to take off when you couldn't hover, how to fly formations, and I even demonstrated night autorotations. Leese would've been proud.

At the end of the cycle, the students, whom we had put through hell, were so happy that they usually gave their instructors gifts. The traditional gift was a bottle of whiskey. I did not drink at the time, so my gifts accumulated in a cupboard at home.

My days were good; my nights were hell. I had been back from Vietnam for over a year. The dreams still oppressed me, and the unseen fear kept me bouncing out of bed. On one of my late-night wanderings around the house, I decided to have a drink. Three drinks later, I climbed into bed and fell asleep. I tried it again the next night. It worked, though I had to drink a bit more to do the job.

After I'd taught two more cycles, the dizziness returned. I was flying cross-country with a student when I felt the ship rear back.

I was grounded again. This time it would be permanent. That was when I started seeing Doc Ryan.

While the school was trying to find a job for a nonflying pilot, I spent two weeks taking psychological tests. For one set of tests I had to go to Fort Sam Houston for a consultation.

In the parking lot at Fort Sam, I met Niven, the Prospector who had caught the wire in the minefield. He was now a major.

"Well, how do you feel about your DFC?" asked Niven.

"What DFC?"

"For the night we dropped that ammo, remember? You tried it once, started to fall through, and went around and did it again."

"Yeah, I remember that."

"Well, the grunt commander on the ground that night put us in for DFCs. I've got mine."

"I never heard a thing about it."

"I can't understand." Niven frowned. "It couldn't have been because I was logged as the aircraft commander?"

"That sounds typical."

"Well, you should check it out, anyway. It can help your career."

"It doesn't matter. I'm leaving the army."

"Why?"

"I'm grounded. Without flying, the army gets old quick."

"Why'd they ground you?"

"I'm nuts."

I walked through a hallway at the Hospital. Fort Sam Houston is the burn center for the military. I saw eighteen-year-old boys with their faces burned away, bright-pink skin grafts stretched over strange, stunted noses. Had someone photographed the men there, twisted and deformed with featureless faces, by the hundreds, the war might have ended sooner. But probably not.

With the results from my various tests, the army gave me a new medical profile. A sentence in the profile reads, "Aviator may not be assigned to duty in a combat zone." At a time when the army was shipping pilots back to Vietnam after only a few months in the States, this no-combat restriction was known as the million-dollar ticket.

People who knew me knew that I wrote stories. The head of the faculty-development branch found out and interviewed me. He asked if I'd like to try writing lessons for ground school and be a platform instructor. And that is what I did during my last six months in the army.

As a platform instructor I taught incoming pilots from Vietnam how to train students effectively. I stood on the stage, a has-been, and gave expert advice on how to do it. If you can't do it, teach it. I was witty. I was popular. I was a closet basket case.

I was drinking half a bottle a night to get to sleep. Even though I could never go back to combat, the war enraged me. I watched television. The war was going stronger than ever before. The scores were always ten to one, proving that we were winning. Only a few people seemed to realize that the war was wrong. To the rest of the people, the war news droned on every newscast and had become an annoyance. People didn't want to stop it; they wanted it to go away.

Meanwhile, pilots were being sent back for their second tours.

At the officers' club one night, a pilot I knew came through to say hello. He was visiting his wife on a leave from Nam. A week after that, we read his obituary in the *Army Times*. The pilots read the obits and calculated their odds of surviving the second time around. The joke about going on the second tour was "If they try to send me back, they'll have to have a door on that plane big enough for me and my telephone pole." That was so much bravado, for almost all went. It was either that or end your career.

For a year and a half, Patience and I had been going to the mandatory monthly cocktail party at the club. Patience hated army etiquette. We went through a receiving line each time, shaking hands with the post VIPs. One night she told a colonel that his sunglasses made him look cool. He took them off, glaring. Luckily I was leaving the army anyway.

After one of these receptions, I wandered around the club looking for old friends. Some of the instructors at Wolters were former classmates or guys I had flown with in Nam. I heard a familiar voice.

"Mason, I'll be damned."

I thought I recognized the voice.

"It's me. Hawkins," he said.

"Lady Killer Hawkins?"

"That's it."

Some people moved behind me, allowing more light to shine on Hawkins. Something was wrong. That was definitely his voice, but his face . . .

"Just got here," said Hawkins.

"How come? I've been here a year and a half." The first thing I noticed was that Hawkins had no eyebrows. Or ears. His hair was patchy from implantations. His nose was shiny and deformed. Hawkins? The handsomest guy in our class?

"I've been in a hospital. For a long while."

"Jesus. It is you. What the hell happened?"

"Crashed and burned," said Hawkins. "I got knocked out in the crash. I was unconscious in the fire for quite a while."

"You're lucky to be alive."

"That's what they tell me. . . ." Then his voice trailed off. "I don't feel so lucky."

"They'll get you back in shape. Don't worry about that. The army has the best—"

"They've already done their best."

Patience and I went to New Orleans for the weekend with another couple. It should have been fun. Instead, I collapsed while touring a catacomb. I sank to my knees, feeling death. I felt like I was going to roll over and die on the grass. The tombs seemed to beckon me.

Later, when we got to a bar, I anesthetized myself. That helped. If I stayed drunk, I could cope. When I was sober, life was unending anxiety with no focus.

I did so well as a platform instructor that when I told the head of the department I was leaving the army, he offered to get me a direct commission as a captain if I would stay. But I would be a captain who walked. I could wear my wings and walk to the flight line and watch the ships fly away. So, when I left the army in 1968, it was as an ex-pilot and, in my mind, a failure.

A lot has happened since then. I have followed a pattern of behavior that is typical of many Vietnam veterans. The funny thing is, I wasn't aware of the pattern until I wrote it down. It has taken a very long time for me to see it.

I returned to the University of Florida to complete the

education I had begun in 1960. I saw student demonstrations that accused veterans of being fools for going to Vietnam. I felt like a double loser; some internal flaw had caused me to lose my flight status, and now I learned how dumb I had been for having gone to Vietnam.

I studied art, mostly photography. I tried to learn a new career and rejoin society. I could not sleep without having nightmares. I arrived at my eight o'clock morning classes only after at least two stiff drinks. If I drank all day, I could sleep at night. I could not face a campus filled with young, smiling faces while guys still leapt screaming out of helicopters, killing and dying for a cause unworthy of their bravery. They deserved to be heroes, but they were fools.

I kept jumping out of my skin at night, so I asked the Veterans Administration for help. They declared me a 50 percent disabled veteran by reason of nervousness, now called Post-Traumatic Stress Disorder, Chronic (DSM III, 309.81), and issued me tranquilizers. I still drank, but now with the tranquilizers, and also smoked pot (introduced to me by students—I never saw the stuff in Vietnam). After nine months of school I dropped out and moved my family to a small village in Spain. While we were there, America put the first man on the moon. After seven months, there was no improvement in my outlook or attitude, so we returned to the States.

I worked as a technician in an electronics company. To the drinking, tranquilizers, and pot, I added a new vice: a girlfriend. When Patience said she was going back to school, with me or without me, I also returned.

During the two years it took to finish my degree in fine arts, Patience and I broke up for a month. I was up to almost a bottle of whiskey a day, and four or five Valiums, yet I was still as tense as a snake. I was seeing shrinks weekly at the VA, but the nightly wake-ups continued.

When I graduated, in December 1971, I started a commercial photography business. In less than a year it failed. I tried to get a job with the government as an aircraft dispatcher, deciding what ships were flyable and what ships needed maintenance. I wanted to be around helicopters. I was turned down because of my disability. Even Congressman Don Fuqua could not get the government to hire this disabled vet, though he tried hard. The turn-down notice sent me was in an envelope stamped with the slogan "Don't forget, hire the vet."

The war was still going on in Vietnam, and inside my head.

My father risked some money to start an import company with me. I wanted to buy pocketknives in Spain and market them through the mail. I had a car wreck in Portugal, broke my hip, and we ended up selling thirty knives. So much for importing.

Finally, through an intricate series of business deals over a three-year period, I became vice-president of a mirror-manufacturing company in Brooklyn. There I had the money I wanted, I had fifty employees under me, and I quit using alcohol and tranquilizers. Still, I was painfully dissatisfied. And I continued to jump awake at night.

By now I had been back from Vietnam for ten years. I would not allow myself to believe that my unhappiness could be a reaction to my experience there. Instead I drew the conclusion that I was somehow basically inferior or mentally disturbed.

Two and a half years after I started at the mirror company, I resigned my position. We moved back to Florida, to ten acres of land next to the Santa Fe River. I built a cabin. Encouraged by my wife and friends, I decided to write about Vietnam.

Things went badly. I had arranged a separation settlement from the mirror company that allowed us to survive while I built the cabin and wrote. When the money ran out, Patience got a paper route to make ends meet. I looked for work too, and finally decided also to run a paper route because of the free time it would give me for writing.

The car broke down and the bills began to pile up. For the time I had spent writing, I got four rejections.

What did the desperate man do? I can tell you that I was arrested in January 1981, charged with smuggling marijuana into the country. In August 1981, I was found guilty of possession and sentenced to five years at a minimum security prison. I am currently free as of February 1983, appealing the conviction.

No one is more shocked than I.

Afterword

I recently visited the Night Stalkers, the 160th Special Operation Aviation Regiment (Airborne). These army aviators perform rescues, medical evacuations, and combat assaults wherever in the world they are needed. (Their mottos: "Night Stalkers Never Quit." When they want to be more specific, they use: "Death Lurks in the Dark.") They lost two Blackhawk helicopters and several pilots and crewmembers in Somalia which was depicted in the book and film *Black Hawk Down.*

The Night Stalkers had invited me and Bill Reeder (Col. USA Ret) to talk about jungle flying. Bill tells people that if they want to know what it was like to fly helicopters in combat in Vietnam, read *Chickenhawk*. Which is a stretch considering that I was a WO-1 Slick pilot, a landing-craft-of-the-air driver who got out of the army the moment his commitment was up. Reeder is a two-tour combat pilot, shot down on both tours in Vietnam. He was shot down first in a Mohawk surveillance airplane in 1969. He and his copilot were recovered by the air force after a firefight with the encroaching enemy. In 1972, he was shot down in a Cobra gunship while defending the

Special Forces camp at Ben Het, which was being overrun by the NVA. Bill, his ankle wounded, his back broken in the crash (his front-seater died soon after impact), was able to evade the enemy in the jungle for three days before being captured. He spent almost a year as a POW, first in a cage in the jungle and then, after a 400-mile walk, at the Hanoi Hilton, from which he was released in 1973.

Colonel Andy Miliani, Regimental Commander of the 160th, told us that because the Night Stalkers were flying in the deserts and mountains of Afghanistan and Iraq, they were not as knowledgable about jungle operations as he thought they ought to be. Considering the present state of the world, Colonel Miliani thought it would be good for his men to hear from us what it was like to fly helicopters in jungle missions.

More than a hundred Night Stalker pilots showed up for the presentation, which consisted of Bill and me talking about our experiences thirty years ago and taking questions. Almost all of them were younger than my own son, Jack. And almost all of them were veterans of Afghanistan or Iraq, or both. They flew CH-47 Chinooks, UH-60 Blackhawks, and OH-6 Little Birds, which, except for the Blackhawk, were flown when I was in the army; at least there were aircraft then with those same names. They looked about the same to me, until they showed us one of the Chinooks that the Night Stalkers use in Afghanistan. While they had suffered mechanical problems and were grounded several times early in the war, the new Chinook is reliable and amazingly powerful, able to lift more cargo than our heavy lifting Sky Crane could in 1965. All their helicopters are now highly advanced fighting machines. Computers, electronic cockpit instrumentation, night vision goggles, contact radar, and incredibly tough training allowed the Night Stalkers to do things with helicopters that Bill and I had never dreamed possible. Using contact radar, these guys routinely fly Chinooks at zero visibility, low level in mountain ravines, at night, in fog or rain or snow, following the moving needles on the dials of their instrument panels. Sweat pours off aviators focused this intensely. The slightest deviation could kill everyone on board. These pilots were the best ever. What the hell could they learn from us?

Well, some things never change. They still have to land and take-off from tight LZs, overloaded with troops. They still have to dodge bullets. They still get shot down.

Safety tips when flying combat missions in the jungle? My advice: don't go! Which they thought was pretty funny. As it turns out, these pilots have the same questions about the decisions that move them into the hottest places on earth as we did about being in Vietnam. The bottom line now, as then, is that it's not their call. They are doing their jobs, unknown to most Americans, better than any group of aviators in the world.

At the beginning of the talk, Bill asked the pilots who had read *Chickenhawk*. Almost all of them raised their hands. It turns out that *Chickenhawk*—over twenty years in print—has become a sort of handbook for helicopter pilots all over the world. Since it was published in 1983, I've gotten a letter, a phone call, or an e-mail from a reader every day. The North Sea oil pilots read *Chickenhawk;* I've heard from air force, army, navy, and marine pilots. Military pilots in Great Britain and Australia read *Chickenhawk*. It's published in English, Dutch, Hebrew, Polish, and Chinese, with a Czech version on the way. Now that I have a Web site (robertcmason.com), I get messages almost every day from *Chickenhawk* readers all over the world.

When I wrote the book, I had no idea where any of the guys I was talking about had ended up. A few months before publication, though, I located Jerry Towler through the Department of the Army. When the book got to the stores, accompanied by television interviews, great reviews, and news stories of my subsequent time in prison, I started hearing from my friends. They all approved of the book. And they wanted to know why I hadn't used their real names.

The answer was that my original editor at Viking thought that in our litigious society, we would get sued. I took his advice, and changed the names of my friends to protect their privacy and our butts. However, none of that was necessary. You have to lie about someone to get convicted of slander. I don't lie in my memoir. Errors, yes.

Because of this new edition of *Chickenhawk,* I have the chance to mention real names and make some corrections. I served in two aviation units during my year in Vietnam. The Preachers really existed—B Company, 229th Assault Helicopter Battalion. I made up the name for the Prospectors. The Prospectors lived and performed their duties much differently than did my compatriots in the humongous First Air Cav. My descriptions of ambulance loads of Vietnamese call girls showing up at the club, the Prospectors stealing ice-making machines from the R&U compound, or the fact that maintenance was trading Hueys, reconstituted from wreckage, for trucks, among other incidents, really made my editor nervous. The real name of the Forty-Niners was the 48th Aviation Company, call sign Blue Stars. This independent aviation company operated all over Vietnam from 1966, when I joined them, right up until 1973 when they were stood down. In 1972, the Blue Stars were part of the infamous Lam Son 719 invasion of Cambodia, and paid dearly for it with lost pilots and crew. By the time of the Lam Son invasion, the North Vietnamese Army was not only using Soviet-built tanks as they invaded South Vietnam, they also had acquired heavy antiaircraft guns, which they used against our choppers, a fact that gives me sweaty palms just thinking about it. By 1970, pilots in my old units, the Blue Stars and Preachers, were figuring out how to avoid heat-seeking missiles! I consider myself lucky to have been a pioneer combat assault pilot with the Air Cav, in the good old days of spears and man-traps, rattling assault rifles, thudding 50-caliber machine-guns, whumping mortars and artillery.

I arrived at the Blue Stars just a week before Gerald Towler (Resler, because he'd been a wrestler in college). Jerry and I flew together in the Cav and the Blue Stars. A former crew chief, Tommy Dorsey (PFC Miller), told us recently that in the Preachers, we were known as The Kids. We were both fresh out of flight school and twenty-two years old in 1965. Most of the other Preacher pilots were career soldiers. By the time we got to the Blue Stars, we were old salts in the business of flying helicopters in combat, having logged three or four times as many combat hours as anyone in the unit. They had only arrived in-country in 1966.

This edition contains a photographic section showing some of the pilots I knew in the Cav, mostly the people from the 2nd Platoon.

Our trusty platoon commander, Captain Robert Stinnett (Shaker) was an avid chess player. There's a photo of him playing a game with Captain Gillette (Gill) while Captain Hugh Farmer (Marston), calm as ever, practices his golf swing in the background.

Jerry Towler (Resler) and I flew together as WO-1's both in the Cav and when we were infused to the 48th Aviation Company.

Lee Komich (Connors) and Dallas Harper (Banjo Bates) were a team, flying together often. Lee was also the company IP, and he helped me learn formation flying and the value of careful preflights, among many things.

I think Don Reynolds (Kaiser), the best gambler I ever knew, won enough at poker to buy a new car when he got home. Don became an airline captain for Eastern. He died of his second heart attack two years ago.

Woody Woodruff (Decker) and Howard Phillips (Morris), both from Arkansas, were like brothers. You can see it in their eyes in the photograph. Phillips, a skillful woodcarver, as well as combat assault pilot, is on the Wall in D.C.

Captain Duane Denton (Farris) was our section leader. He made Jerry and me line the walkways with rocks, and yet we still liked him. He died in an airplane crash, a training accident, not long after he got home.

Chuck Nay (Nate) is captured for eternity modeling a towel in our bath area in one of the photos. I guess Chuck can go ahead and sue me.

I don't have any good photographs of Bob Sweazey (Wendell) or Ken Faba (Barber), another team that usually flew together in the Preachers. Sweazey was the amateur photographer and Vietnam historian, the one who kept reminding us that the French had been there, done that, and lost.

Captain Sherman was really Bruce Thomas. He's a lot nicer than he was during the times I ended up talking about him in the book.

I say that Ron Fox, the pilot who had replaced me in the Cav, was killed. It was WO-1 Allan L. Cox, killed by a sniper bullet in the forehead on August 1, 1966. That same day, at the 48th, Ringknocker was walking the board trail across the beach at Tuy Hoa. A minute later, I'm watching our maintenance officer, Major Frank Gundaker (Major Steve Richards), trying to use a Huey to haul a junk rotor blade over the ocean and dump it. The blade is whipping around under him as Gundaker hovers forward. People on the ground are yelling, waving. The three maintenance guys along for the ride, PFC Ronald Russell, SP5 Ernest Shuman, and SP4 Donald Wallace, are waving back. The blade whipped up into the Huey's main rotors. Gundaker's ship tumbled out of the sky and burst into flames on the beach. Everyone on board was killed.

Crew chiefs and gunners made the whole combat assault thing work. They worked in the field, at night, all the time, keeping the choppers flying. There's a photo of my door gunner, PFC Ubinski, in the back of our Huey. I called him Rubinski in the book. He was one of my best friends over there. I can't find him these days.

Gene Burdick (Reacher) is shown running with the boot during the extraction of wounded when a remotely triggered road mine blew up their Jeep.

PFC Tommy Dorsey was hit by 50-caliber antiaircraft fire during the assault at LZ Bird in 1966. A single bullet was deflected by his chest protector, and the shards tore into his shoulder, tearing off his arm. I saw him bleeding in the back of his Huey, his arm hanging by a tendon. Tommy's pilot called, said he was turning back to the aid station. The next time I saw Tommy was at an Ia Drang reunion. He has the arm. They sewed it back on. But he said it doesn't work too well.

The crew chief I call Collins was actually Keith Maynard, who was a big help when we needed parts, from wherever, to keep 'em flying.

We were in Orlando at the VHPA twentieth annual reunion in July 2003, and there were Ringknocker and Sky King sitting at a table in the Blue Stars room. I pointed them out to my wife, Patience, and we walked over. Sky King, my old partner in the ice business at Dak To, looked up. His impish grin shone through the age gathering on his face. Then Ringknocker, who's been a retired general for twenty years, looked up, smiling. "Mason, it's great to see you!" he said. "What a book! I had no idea you had such an imagination."

"Sir? It was my memoir."

"Memoir?" Roper is grinning. "Where did you get all this stuff about stealing supplies from the R&U compound?"

"Or that myth about us trading Hueys we salvaged for trucks?" I ask.

"Yup. That one, too."

Patience laughs. She says, "The ambulance load of whores?"

He shakes his head. "Not a chance."

"Or you letting me and Towler borrow a Huey like the family car to go visit our friends."

"Definitely wouldn't have allowed that." Ringknocker is still in form, having fun. He holds up his drink. "Here's to *Chickenhawk,* fiction though it may be." He laughs as Jack Horne, Jerry, and I raise our drinks. Harry Roper, graduate of West Point, retired brigadier general, has been racing his sailboat single-handedly back and forth across the Pacific. And at seventy-two, he's winning races.

Turns out that Jack Horne, my partner from the ice cartel at Dak To, is a partner in a law firm in Atlanta that specializes in intellectual property, patents, contracts, and he wants to help me get my VTOL (Vertical Takeoff and Landing project) going. You know, gratis, until I make enough money to be interesting.

During the two and a half years I spent writing *Chickenhawk,* I was not able to do formal research about the war. I relied on my memories and I made mistakes. I confused Stoney Stitzle (Stoopy Stoddard in the book) who shared a tent with Jerry and me at Dak To with someone else. When Ringknocker was told he had to transfer his best pilot to headquarters aviation unit in Saigon, I thought that Ringknocker chose Stoopy because he was not that good. Commanders wanted to keep the best pilots. But I was completely wrong, and I apologize. Ringknocker sent someone else. Stoney Stitzle became one of the Blue Stars' most accomplished assault pilots after Jerry and I shipped home.

Captain Daisy and I are friends these days although he doesn't want me to use his real name. He says my description of the way he flew during combat assaults is incomplete since a pilot can fly a helicopter into combat while scrunched up behind his chest protector. We still have this difference of opinion, but I respect Daisy for having gone to Vietnam, flying in combat, and doing the best that he could.

As depicted in the movie *We Were Soldiers Once . . . and Young,* Colonel Harold Moore (Grunt Six) was the first man on the ground at LZ Xray during the Ia Drang battle. Around Veterans' Day every year, at the annual Ia Drang Valley reunion banquet, Moore has everyone stand up at their table and sound off, "like you got a pair!" with their name and what they did at Ia Drang. At two of the tables some of the aviators who were in the battle, including me, sit with our wives: Jerry Towler, Lee Komich, Daisy, Dallas Harper, Walt Schramm, Ken Dicus, Bill Weber, Neal Parker. We all sound off. Don Reynolds used to stand up and shout, "Don Reynolds, helicopter pilot, LZ Xray and LZ Albany!"

Dicus and I, Jerry and Reynolds, Kiess and Harper are mentioned in *We Were Soldiers* for making the midnight extraction at LZ Albany. We've even met some of the men we hauled out that night at the reunions. They like to shake our hands and thank us for the ride out of hell.

At dawn the next day, we gather with General Moore by the Wall at the Vietnam Veterans Memorial in D.C. where he and Joe Galloway perform a roll call of the dead. It's obvious to me that General Moore really cares a great deal about the men who did not return.

There are a lot of real people I haven't mentioned so far. Ray Ward, my friend throughout basic training, advanced infantry training, and flight school, is Ray Welch, now a building contractor in New Hampshire. Ken Klayman, who I traveled with over and back, and who I've never seen again is Aaron Varon. WO-1 Tom Wolf is a classmate of mine, Jim Nunn. We called Dick Armstrong Jack Armstrong, and he still owes me a camera and photos that were in my ammo box in the back of his Huey.

The names of the people I don't know, or whose privacy I want to continue to respect, will remain unacknowledged here.

In 1993, the sequel to *Chickenhawk* was published. My friend, Mike Costello (author of *A Long Time from Home*), described it as, "a litany of fuck-ups that makes you glad you're not Mason!"

Back in the World was intended to flesh out the sketchy last chapter of *Chickenhawk,* which ends, "No one is more shocked than I." Referring to big trouble with the law. Now that I'm a graduate of the federal prison rehabilitation process, my criminal tendencies are mostly in check, although I still speed. In *Back in the World,* I described my life after Vietnam, jobs I tried, businesses I started, marital problems. I also told about my sailboat pot run to Columbia, my arrest, conviction, and imprisonment. My life's an open book, but this one didn't sell well and went out of print. You have to buy that chapter used.

Inspired by two young television producers, Chris Fetner and Jeremy Wood, I decided to produce a documentary about the Army helicopter pilots of Vietnam. I flew out to Bell Helicopters in Fort Worth to talk to John Wright, the head of sales for North America. While I was there, bending John's ear about giving me money to produce the show, he had their senior test pilot take me for a demo ride in their latest Bell 407 helicopter. John said that it was same as Harrison Ford's. "Even Patricia Cornwell owns one," said John. "You're a writer, too. When you going to get one?"

"How much you say they run?"

"Full tank of gas and everything you see here, one point four would do it."

"I'd buy it, John, but it's just the wrong color."

We flew the gorgeous red-with-white-swoops high-tech Bell 407 from Fort Worth out to Mineral Wells. Fort Wolters, former home of the U.S Army Primary Helicopter School, has become a rundown industrial park. We flew over countryside full of sagebrush and willow, out to Stage Field 3, one of the practice fields where we used to train thousands of beginning pilots how to fly. The six lanes at Stage Field 3 were covered with tall grass growing through the spidery network of cracks in the concrete. The control shack leaned, the window was broken, a shutter banged. We came to a hover on lane two. We hovered a minute, watched the grass blowing in the rotor wash. Then we took off, heading for the Brazos River.

I used to come play on the river with a Hiller H-23D I'd borrow from the flight line on Saturdays. I would sit on a ledge, high over the river, then just leap off backward, spin around, dive, and skim down to the sandbars. We didn't do that that day with the 407, just took a little ride down the river. We swooped out of the riverbed and back to the Bell factory heliport.

When I was thinking about who should be the narrator in my documentary, I recalled that John Wright said Harrison Ford owns a 407. So I called John, asked if he could ask Mr. Ford if he'd be willing to help me out.

John had me send a book to Mr. Ford's business manager. Two weeks later, the phone rang. Patience answered. Her eyes widened. "The *real* Harrison Ford?" She squeaked and handed the phone over to me. "Here! Talk to him!"

"Robert Mason?"

"Yes, hello."

"Robert, I read your book. I think you and I have a lot in common. Consider me a fan."

"Well, I'm a big fan of yours, too, Mr. Ford.'

"Call me Harrison."

"Okay, Harrison."

And he agreed to introduce my documentary on screen, and to record additional narration. Free!

Just before we started filming the host introduction scene in September 2000, Harrison invited me to come up to New York and go for a ride in his chopper. His Gulfstream G-4 was coming down to National, in D.C. I could ride back on it. I flew up, the only passenger in this beautiful jet, spent the night at a motel near the airport. Harrison picked me up the next morning, took me to his hangar at Teterboro. We sat in the office and talked about a script for his narration for a while, then we went into the hangar to get his chopper. As we walked under the G-4, he said he didn't fly it, just the small planes and the chopper. He waved around the hangar. Five airplanes and a Bell 407 were parked around the G-4. I noticed a Beech Bonanza and a DeHaviland Beaver. The Beaver was restored, perfect down to the rivets. He said it was in better shape than the one he flew in *Six Days, Seven Nights*. We walked over to his 407. It was equipped with emergency floats, skinny tubes above the skids that can be inflated to full size in a second if needed. Harrison grabbed a powered tug, steered it over to his 407. He slipped the tug under the fuselage between the skids, then pushed a button. Jacks whirred up to the skid supports then lifted the machine an inch or two off the floor. Harrison steered the tug outside, set the helicopter down, and removed the tug. We climbed up the side of the 407 and checked out the rotor head and pitch-change links and stuff. We climbed down and talked while he finished his walk-around inspection. We were both impressed with the size of the turbine under the cowl. This helicopter can carry seven people at 150 miles an hour, yet either of us could've lifted the engine barehanded (well, Harrison could have). We got inside the cockpit where I watched him go through his checklist. He flipped a switch. The chopper whined, whirred, did its own instrument and power check, green light blinked on. We both wore headsets with voice-activated mikes. I heard Harrison call the tower for takeoff. He lifted off, steady as a rock, hovered out to the active runway. He nosed over, we were off, heading for Manhattan. This was in September 2000. We flew from Teterboro down the Hudson at about 400 feet. When we flew past the World Trade Center, Harrison said, "Can you believe they let us fly this close?"

Harrison let me take the controls for a few minutes as we flew past the ventilator shafts for the Holland Tunnel. I held altitude and airspeed okay. I was working on feeling the aircraft, but I was pushing too much right rudder and the ship was out of trim. "Left rudder. Left rudder," Harrison said.

"Yeah, I'm a little rusty, eh?"

"Yeah," said Han Solo, Decker, and Indiana Jones, disappointed.

Later, after we pulled his chopper inside the hangar with the tug, I asked Harrison why he had read my book. "Everywhere I go, if it has anything to do with helicopters, people tell me I have to read *Chickenhawk*. So I did. And I agree."

When he sat down at his desk to fill in his logbook, I noticed he had about five hundred hours in helicopters. He's quite good for that amount of time.

Three months ago I had the chance to go visit my cockpit buddy, Jerry Towler. He lives close to Detroit, near one of our Vietnam pilot friends, Bob Baden. Bob had just restored a 1973 Bell-47G2 (the *M*A*S*H* helicopter, known as an H-13 in the Army). He'd let me rent it at cost, to see if I could still fly.

I rummaged around, found my army flight records, and checked the date of my last official flight. June 6, 1967! When I took the controls of Bob's 47, I had not flown a chopper for almost thirty-seven years. What I wanted to do was attempt to get it up to a hover and not crash, unaided. Bob, who's been flying all those thirty-seven years, agreed.

I'd never flown an H-13, the army's designation of the Bell 47, when I was in the army. I knew it was a good machine.

I gradually got the machine light on the skids, feeling it beginning to shift a little, twitch like it was alive. Instincts took over. We lifted off the tarmac, the little Bell sounding far louder than the much larger Huey. Turbine engines are beautifully quiet in comparison to the 400 HP, six-cylinder, fuel-injected, snarling beast behind the cockpit seats.

It was thrilling to be drifting around just three feet off the ground. I wasn't locked over a spot like I would've been thirty-seven years before, but I wasn't dangerous, either. The chopper was noisy, it vibrated, and the throttle was sloppy—something Bob, who had worked as a helicopter mechanic and pilot for thirty years, advised me to notice. I was able to turn around, hover forward over the grass next to the runway. Mercifully, Bob operated the radios. I had my hands full keeping the machine within the confines of the taxiway. We were cleared with the local traffic for takeoff. I nosed the Bell forward, holding her close to the ground while she accelerated. We hit translational lift, surged up, free of gravity. You can call it translational lift, but that hardly describes how much fun it is.

Bob points beyond the plastic canopy. Don't fly over those warehouses; avoid this neighborhood; break right here; give the highway plenty of clearance.

I'm looking for a place to land in case the engine suddenly takes a nap.

I was taught to fly as though the engine, brand-new or not, was preparing itself to enter motor oblivion precisely when you needed it alive and chugging. But there was nowhere to land below us except little tiny postage-stamp yards, wire-draped suburban streets, and a few swimming pools.

"Forced landings?"

"Anywhere you can fit it. Except roofs," he said, nodding toward a vast complex of flat-roofed factory buildings.

"Why not?"

"Chances are you'd fall through the roof when you hit, probably kill some people working inside."

"The highway?"

"Yeah, if you've got no other choice."

I listened to the Lycoming grumbling. "She sounds great, though."

Bob nodded, smiled.

I kept the airspeed somewhere between fifty and seventy, altitude around 500 feet as we fly toward the main airport. I was still grinning about how much pure fun this is! So what was nagging me? We flew across a crowded parking lot. Then I realized I've never flown over houses full of people before. That's what was making me nervous? Houses? I flew combat assaults in jungles. Never neighborhoods. Flying over a perfectly normal American neighborhood, apparently with nobody shooting, made me wary.

Patience and I stayed with Jerry and Martie Towler while I went out to the airport every other day for flight instruction. And after a hiatus of thirty-seven years, everything I did was fresh and exhilarating. I still felt the thrill of practicing to control a machine that has been built to hover off the ground and not kill you. I was happy in the world of foot pedals, collective, throttle, cyclic. By my third hour with Bob, it was beginning to come back. We did autorotations: hovering, straight-ins, one-eighties, to make sure I'd at least be competent enough to survive a forced landing. If I had been grading me, I'd have given me a C ride. I could do the maneuvers, but not with the smoothness of a practiced hand. But it was still fun. I would only get better each time I flew. Unfortunately, even at the reduced rate my friend Bob was letting me pay for the Bell, it's obvious why it's only military pilots and people like Harrison Ford who can fly helicopters around for the fun of it.

There's got to be a way to make a more affordable hovering aircraft.

Patience is a publisher, writer, and editor. Her book *Recovering from the War* is still in print. She gives talks to veterans all over the country about post-traumatic stress disorder.

My son, Jack, is in school learning digital graphics. I have a grandson, also named Jack, who visits me on weekends, and who is the best grandson in the world.

My plans keep me busy. That frustrated engineer inside me is getting out more often. I'm writing, too. Upcoming is a book about the invention of vertical flight, a screenplay about Bill Reeder's survival as a POW in Vietnam, a third Solo novel, and a movie I want to write and produce myself.

Where do I file for a life extension?

Robert Mason
High Springs, Florida
October 10, 2004